Ecomedievalism

Studies in Medievalism XXVI

2017

Studies in Medievalism

Founded by Leslie J. Workman

Recently published volumes are listed at the back of this book

Ecomedievalism

Edited by
Karl Fugelso

Studies in Medievalism XXVI 2017

Cambridge
D. S. Brewer

First published 2017
D. S. Brewer, Cambridge

ISBN 978–1–84384–465–5

ISSN 0738–7164

D. S. Brewer is an imprint of Boydell & Brewer Ltd
PO Box 9, Woodbridge, Suffolk IP12 3DF, UK
and of Boydell & Brewer Inc,
668 Mt Hope Avenue, Rochester, NY 14620–2731, USA
website: www.boydellandbrewer.com

A CIP catalogue record for this book is available
from the British Library

The publisher has no responsibility for the continued existence or
accuracy of URLs for external or third-party internet websites referred to
in this book, and does not guarantee that any content on such websites is,
or will remain, accurate or appropriate

This publication is printed on acid-free paper

Typeset by www.thewordservice.com

Printed and bound in Great Britain by
TJ International Ltd, Padstow, Cornwall

Studies in Medievalism

Founding Editor Leslie J. Workman
Editor Karl Fugelso

Advisory Board Martin Arnold (Hull)
Geraldine Barnes (Sydney)
Rolf H. Bremmer, Jr. (Leiden)
William Calin (Florida)
A. E. Christa Canitz (New Brunswick, Canada)
Philip Cardew (Leeds Beckett)
Elizabeth Emery (Montclair State)
David Matthews (Manchester)
Gwendolyn Morgan (Montana State)
Nils Holger Petersen (Copenhagen)
Tom Shippey (Saint Louis)
Clare A. Simmons (Ohio State)
Paul Szarmach (Western Michigan)
Toshiyuki Takamiya (Keio)
Jane Toswell (Western Ontario)
Richard Utz (Georgia Institute of Technology)
Kathleen Verduin (Hope College, Michigan)
Andrew Wawn (Leeds)

Studies in Medievalism provides an interdisciplinary medium of exchange for scholars in all fields, including the visual and other arts, concerned with any aspect of the post-medieval idea and study of the Middle Ages and the influence, both scholarly and popular, of this study on Western society after 1500.

Studies in Medievalism is published by Boydell & Brewer, Ltd., P.O. Box 9, Woodbridge, Suffolk IP12 3DF, UK; Boydell & Brewer, Inc., 668 Mt. Hope Avenue, Rochester, NY 14620–2731, USA. Orders and inquiries about back issues should be addressed to Boydell & Brewer at the appropriate office.

For a copy of the style sheet and for inquiries about **Studies in Medievalism**, please contact the editor, Karl Fugelso, at the Dept. of Art+Design, Art History, and Art Education, Towson University, 3103 Center for the Arts, 8000 York Rd, Towson, MD 21252–0001, USA, tel. 410–704–2805, fax 410–704–2810 ATTN: Fugelso, e-mail <kfugelso@towson.edu>. All submissions should be sent to him as e-mail attachments in Word.

Acknowledgments

The device on the title page comes from the title page of *Des Knaben Wunderhorn: Alte deutsche Lieder*, edited by L. Achim von Arnim and Clemens Brentano (Heidelberg and Frankfurt, 1806).

The epigraph is from an unpublished paper by Lord Acton, written about 1859 and printed in Herbert Butterfield, *Man on His Past* (Cambridge: Cambridge University Press, 1955), 212.

Studies in Medievalism

I: Ecomedievalism: Some Perspective(s)

II: Interpretations

Illustrations

The editor, contributors, and publishers are grateful to all the institutions
and persons listed for permission to reproduce the materials in which
they hold copyright. Every effort has been made to trace the copyright
holders; apologies are offered for any omission, and the publishers will be
pleased to add any necessary acknowledgement in subsequent editions.

Volume XXV 2016

Two great principles divide the world, and contend for the master, antiquity and the middle ages. These are the two civilizations that have preceded us, the two elements of which ours is composed. All political as well as religious questions reduce themselves practically to this. This is the great dualism that runs through our society.

Lord Acton

Editorial Note

From the frozen highlands of George R. R. Martin's *A Song of Ice and Fire* to the balmy seas of Hal Foster's *Prince Valiant*, from the lush forests of J. R. R. Tolkien's *Lord of the Rings* to the desolate steppes of John Fusco's *Marco Polo*, medievalism is unusually fertile territory for ecotheory. In part, this stems from the undeniably agrarian nature of the Middle Ages. But it also springs from post-medieval exaggeration of that proximity to the land. Many films, novels, and podcasts leave one wondering what medieval rulers did besides hunt, fish, and frolic in the royal gardens; some portray everyone beneath the monarchs – and occasionally even them – as so close to the earth that they are literally covered in dirt; and more than one suggest that even the end of the Middle Ages witnessed vast bands of nomads roaming the countryside and living off whatever they could scrounge with their crude implements and even cruder intellects.

Which is not to say that the medievalists are entirely to blame for such caricatures. From Isidore of Seville to William Langland, medieval writers (and artists) sometimes address nature in sensitive, insightful ways that suggest they perceived it as a provider that must be sustained and coordinated with human needs and desires. Yet they are far more likely to ignore it, dismiss it, or treat it in such broad terms that we cannot be sure precisely how they saw it. Moreover, even when they do clearly and specifically acknowledge it, they are often so far apart from each other in time and/or space that their remarks cannot easily be applied beyond the individual who made them. Thus, while medievalists have a great many leads on this issue, they also often have tremendous leeway in interpreting them.

This flexibility invites medievalists to record their perceptions of not only the medieval state of nature and medieval responses to it, but also environmental conditions during the medievalist's own time. Indeed, medievalists constitute a particularly revealing index of post-medieval perspectives on the environment (as on so many other issues), and that is why I issued the following call for papers in November 2015:

> *Studies in Medievalism*, a peer-reviewed print and on-line publication, seeks 3,000-word essays on the application of ecotheory to medievalism and neomedievalism. To what degree do ecocriticism and ecomaterialism inform these fields? How are constructed environments deployed in response to the Middle Ages? How, if at all, are these settings legitimized? How are they applied to postmedieval circum-

stances and concerns? How is human agency defined in relationship to them? What, if anything, do they tell us about the larger scope of medievalism and neomedievalism, particularly the relationship between those fields? Potential contributors are welcome to discuss particular examples of pertinent neo/medievalism, but they should do so in the course of directly addressing one or more of these questions.

To facilitate representation of contemporary ecological concerns, I deliberately kept my guidelines as flexible and far apart as I could while simultaneously focusing the authors on what I perceive to be the core issues in ecomedievalism and on broad applications of their work. And the responses were indeed instructive. Their small number relative to those for my cfps in previous years suggests that ecotheory is only now gaining traction among students of medievalism and that many scholars may not yet be comfortable with it. And that newness would seem to be confirmed by the wide range of the contributors' historical examples, of their interpretations of ecotheory, of their methods in applying it, and of their conclusions about the actual or potential impact of ecomedievalism. Yet one point on which all of the authors concur – and by which they reveal much about their collective moment – is that the idealization of nature, particularly as it supposedly existed during the Middle Ages, grows in proportion with the medievalist's exposure to industrialization, urbanization, consumerism, and other ills associated with modernism.

In "'A Sense of Life in Things Inert': The Animistic Figurations in Nineteenth- and Twentieth-Century Medievalist Texts," Scott Riley allows that such a backlash may be behind the great degree to which he sees contemporary ecocriticism as somewhat parallel to, and foreshadowed by, animism in medievalism of the last two centuries. Citing texts that range from James Fenimore Cooper's *The Last of the Mohicans* to J. K. Rowling's *Harry Potter* series, he finds three forms of ascribing sentience to nature: nationalistic recognition of countries as "supra-human constellations of being"; antimodernist treatment of the lines between natural and artificial object as "arbitrary and, therefore, mutable"; and ecocritical attempts to offer a window into "the ontologies of nonhuman beings." As specifically suggested by his rubric "antimodernist", all three forms of animistic figuration may be seen as representations of a pre-humanistic worldview, yet they also look forward to a post-humanist worldview in which nonhuman beings are conscious, intelligent, and willful. Even as these figurations may be guilty of anthropomorphism, they orient audiences toward the ontology of another, nonhuman being and foreground an important goal of contemporary ecocritical discourse: recognition of the limitations of human imagination and communication.

Progressive ecological views are also wedded to retrospective, specifically medievalist, literature by Daniel Helbert. In "Future Nostalgias:

Environmental Medievalism and Lanier's Southern Chivalry," Helbert interprets Sidney Lanier's editing of medieval literature as an attempt to revive values that would counter perceived problems in the 1870s, namely rampant consumerism, the increasing vulnerability of the poor, waning interest in foreign languages, and humanity's deteriorating relationship with nature. Helbert does not entirely excuse Lanier for seeking to re-establish a cultural code as laden with injustices as was chivalry in the antebellum South, but Helbert notes that Lanier often refracted this nostalgia through ecological and other concerns that contemporary readers might see as highly progressive.

Such values may still have been highly progressive in the mid-twentieth century, but they were also more common, and in "T. H. White's 'Forest Sauvage': Nostalgia and Loss," Lisa Myers joins Riley in noting that concern for the environment is very much a part of that author's Arthurian trilogy. Indeed, Myers argues that White saw human harmony with nature during the Middle Ages as a model antidote for the violence and destruction of the modern age, particularly that wrought by the World Wars. Rather than merely being a side benefit of returning to medieval values, the rewards from caring for nature were a main point of his medievalism.

One of White's near-contemporaries, J. R. R. Tolkien, also promotes environmentalism by way of medievalism and apparently does so at least in part as a response to some of the same cataclysms that motivated White, but, as Ann M. Martinez notes in "*Elvencentrism*: The Green Medievalism of Tolkien's Elven Realms," Tolkien often celebrates nature for the sake of nature. Rather than treating its care as a corollary to an idealized future via medievalism, or as a bonus for reviving chivalry and other aspects of medieval culture, or as a medieval alternative to modern violence and selfishness, Tolkien frequently shapes his medievalism in such a way as to invite sympathy for environmentalism in and of itself. While his villains inhabit and often create apocalyptic landscapes, his heroes, particularly the elves, thrive in and cultivate sylvan spaces that amply reward the considerable effort necessary to nurture and defend them. They model the behavior that more than one modern member of Greenpeace and other environmental organizations have acknowledged as inspiration for their own defense of nature.

Long before such manifestations of ecoconcerns, the natural world inevitably played a part in seventeenth-century explorations of medieval Britain, but, as Katie Peebles points out in "Fragmentary Dreams: John Aubrey's Medieval Heritage Construction," which is the first essay in the present volume's open section, Aubrey's primary focus was on human interaction with other humans, not on their relationship to nature. Throughout much of the later 1600s, he went around England, particularly his home region of Wiltshire, collecting records and stories that were later woven into a major milestone of early English medievalism – the *Monumenta Britannica*. Though this evidence and his attempts to trace it to Anglo-Saxon, British, Norman, Gothic, English, Celtic, and Roman influences were not seen by many of his contemporaries outside the Royal Society, they had a substantial influence on the antiquarians and folklorists of the next two centuries and, as Peebles notes, still endure as a reminder that "the science of antiquarian research was as much a cultural definer of early modernity as [was] the establishment of the physical sciences."

Aubrey seems to have been particularly interested in the Boarstall Horn, which, as Dustin M. Frazier Wood details in "Charter Horns and the Antiquarian Imagination in Early Modern England," is just one of numerous hunting or drinking horns that served during the Middle Ages as symbols of the transfer, ownership, or control of land. Having inherited the horn with the Boarstall estate, which passed to him by marriage, Aubrey commissioned a painting of the horn on a window in Boarstall's gatehouse and brought the horn to other antiquarians as he attempted to revive a legend that Edward the Confessor gave the estate and horn to Aubrey's ancestor-in-law for slaying a wild boar. Though the legend is almost certainly false, for the style and shape of the horn are more typical of the fifteenth than the eleventh century, the absence of inscriptions on and other early texts about the horn, as with so many of the other charter horns, invites a wide range of interpretations. And while this lack of evidence may explain why few modern scholars have discussed the horns, Frazier Wood suggests that, along with the primal physical appeal of the horns and with the importance of their general functions, the hermeneutic openness of each horn's specific function may have been a powerful lure for earlier scholars, not to mention modern tourists, as it accommodates a vast array of preconceptions about the Middle Ages in general and about the horns in particular.

Of course, even highly detailed texts from the Middle Ages may accommodate different perceptions of that era and different agendas on the part of the interpreter. As Renée Ward explains in "Giving Voice to Griselda: Radical Reimaginings of a Medieval Tale," even in nineteenth-century England, which was famously conformist, extraordinarily full narratives by revered authors could be profoundly altered to support causes that would have been thoroughly alien to those writers. Particularly by comparing Eleanora Louisa Hervey's two adaptations of the Griselda story, Ward delineates how changing circumstances in that author's life led her to reject the canonical, Chaucerian versions of the tale for a more "radical, proto-feminist retelling" that only grew in strength as Hervey became ever more dissatisfied with the social roles women were expected to fulfill and with the social systems that entrenched those roles.

Harlan Ellison, on the other hand, does not appear to have had a political agenda in mind when invoking the *Inferno*, but as Jeremy Withers argues in "Medieval and Futuristic Hells: The Influence of Dante on Ellison's 'I Have

No Mouth and I Must Scream,'" these references compound the horror of Ellison's science fiction. Though Ellison and other New Wave authors explicitly strove to depart from contemporaneous expectations for their genre, his story about a supercomputer that becomes sentient and then destroys all but the five people it has chosen to eternally torment echoes not only Dante's *contrapasso* tendency to fit the punishment to the crime, but also some details of those punishments, as when Count Ugolino in the *Inferno* and Benny in "I Have No Mouth" gnaw on someone else's head. The net effect of this medievalism, then, is to frame the computer's torture in, and perhaps contrast it to, a literary history of righteous justice and to suggest a broader horizon of suffering for the computer's victims.

Such enrichment from turning to, rather than departing from, the past is compounded in George R. R. Martin's extensive parallels to late medieval texts that may themselves be medievalism. As Carol Jamison explains in "Reading Westeros: George R. R. Martin's Multi-Layered Medievalisms," the author of *A Song of Ice and Fire* employs the narrative strategies of Malory and other Arthurian romance writers in such a manner and to such an extent as to complicate where the Middle Ages end and medievalism begins. In her reading of Martin and his sources, not only modern but also medieval people "might create a medieval past for self-understanding."

And according to Elan Justice Pavlinich, at least one modern corporation has created a medieval(ist) past to shape how consumers understand it. In "Modernity in the Middle: The Medieval Fantasy of (Coopted) Feminism in Disney's *Maleficent*," Pavlinich traces how the Disney Corporation has adapted the Middle Ages to accommodate its perception of audience values and expectations and to align itself with the most virtuous among them. Or at least to seem to. In concentrating on how *Maleficent* rewrites Disney's 1959 film *Cinderella* (not to mention the fairy tale and folklore behind those movies) Pavlinich limns some of the ways in which recent Disney films pay lip service to progressive causes like feminism yet fall short of fully embracing them and in some ways may even retreat from them, as the company suggests its new and supposedly improved version of the Middle Ages is also superior to the modernity experienced by its audiences outside of these movies.

Not that Disney is alone in such implications. As Ann F. Howey observes in "Future Medieval: (Neo)Medievalism in *Babylon 5* and *Crusade*," these television shows from the 1990s also perpetuate a patriarchal vision in their references to the Middle Ages. Though they, too, have ostensibly strong female characters, and though they, too, otherwise acknowledge feminist values, these nods to gender equality are often undermined by sexist stereotypes in the shows' attempts to establish continuity with or similarity to the Middle Ages. As, for example, the heroic rangers in *Babylon 5* are predominantly male, Howey is led to wonder whether such bias is inherent to and can ever be completely extirpated from these and other examples of neome-dievalism, from what she, like Carol L. Robinson and Pamela Clements, define as conscious impositions of contemporary ideology and comprehension on the Middle Ages.[1]

Though it is often difficult to know whether interpreters are indeed consciously imposing ideology and comprehension on the past, Kara L. McShane's "Cosmopolitan Anxieties and National Identity in the Netflix *Marco Polo*" finds multiple echoes of contemporary politics in that show. Many of the parallels play out in the tension between the emphatically masculine identity of the Mongols, as embodied by Kublai Khan, and the more effeminate portrayal of the Chinese, as portrayed by Kublai's son Jingim. But as Orientalist (not to mention sexist) as are those characterizations, even more direct references to the ugly side of contemporary politics, particularly the ever louder, ever more strident, and ever more widespread condemnation of Others, are found in the roles foreigners play relative to the Mongols and the Chinese. As McShane notes, Polo is not only tolerated by the Mongols but, like so many of his earlier incarnations in Western literature, honored and elevated above them for his wisdom and learning. Though Orientalism and related biases were certainly not lacking in the Middle Ages, nor in many places before or after that period, they are here entwined with medievalism in a modern blend that, consciously or not, manages to promote them pervasively and systemically yet so subtly as to minimize the likelihood of resistance to them.

The geographical fictions behind such very real relations are explored by Angela Jane Weisl in "Mapping Everealm: Space, Time, and Medieval Fictions in *The Quest*." Through the lens of a 2014 television program in which twelve contemporary contestants are supposedly transported into a medievalist universe to save the fictional land of Everealm from the villain Verlox, Weisl discusses how the maps employed in the show reveal some of the many ways cartographic conventions map their makers. Tracing this insight back to the Middle Ages, Weisl argues that its manifestations in the show are nevertheless, and appropriately enough, indicative of a distinctly modern self-awareness of the inevitable subjectivity inherent in all maps. Medievalism from this perspective becomes one more metaphorical, and sometimes literal, cartographic attempt to make sense of the world outside the interpreter.

And mental maps of the Middle Ages as revealed in the terminology associated with that period are precisely the subject of Paul B. Sturtevant's "Medievalisms of the Mind: Undergraduate Perceptions of the 'Medieval'

---

[1]   See for example Carol L. Robinson and Pamela Clements, "Living with Medievalism," in *Studies in Medievalism XVIII: Defining Medievalism(s) II*, ed. Karl Fugeso (Cambridge: D. S. Brewer, 2009), 55–75 (62, n. 5).

and the 'Middle Ages.'" Through a qualitative survey of nineteen students at Leeds University in 2008–9, Sturtevant explores what a reasonably well-educated, albeit fairly inexperienced audience associates with these terms and how it distinguishes between them. The distinctions that the students draw may seem quite drastic to professional scholars, but while these differences may bear little relationship to academic characterizations of the Middle Ages, they reveal much about the influence of popular medievalism and about the raw material with which teachers of medieval studies and/or medievalism often have to work.

In the volume's final article, "Mask of the Medieval Corpse: Prosopopoeia and Corpsepaint in Mayhem's *De Mysteriis Dom Sathanas*," one of the most extreme forms of this popular medievalism is dissected by Dean Swinford. While exploring how the Middle Ages are invoked by this album and by much of the rest of black metal, Swinford reveals how even, and perhaps especially, misconceptions of this era may inspire elaborate, highly non-medieval forms of expression. Dwelling on the Black Plague and other distinctly dark moments of what many black-metal followers treat as a truly dark age, Mayhem and other black-metal musicians construct a Middle Ages that revolve to an ahistorical degree around death and may be largely unrecognizable to professional scholars but clearly have a large following and may have helped legitimize a musical genre that the Norwegian government promotes as a national institution.

And with that celebration of death in the Middle Ages, particularly of death from disease and other natural causes, the volume returns to a medievalism that is intimately tied to ecology. Indeed, as Riley, Helbert, Myers, and Martinez suggest, medievalism is never far from ecoconcerns. Though many of the articles in this volume concentrate on other aspects of medievalism, and though even the essays sometimes depart from overtly addressing ecomedievalism, the natural world can rarely be far from responses to an era that was so closely tied to the natural world in fact and so much more closely tied to it in fiction. Indeed, perhaps that extraordinary proximity will ensure that this volume is not only an important catalyst for the application of ecotheory to medievalism, but also a revelation of the many ways medievalism may inform broader ecostudies, of the many ways the past may shed light on the most vital issues of the present and future.

I

Ecomedievalism: Some Perspective(s)

"A Sense of Life in Things Inert": The Animistic Figurations in Nineteenth- and Twentieth-Century Medievalist Texts

Scott Riley

One of the more predictable tropes of nineteenth- and twentieth-century medievalist literature is the animistic figurations scattered throughout those texts. Indeed, the presence of such figuration is so commonplace in the medievalist oeuvre as to seem unnoteworthy, and yet an investigation into the various forms that such figuration takes reveals a good deal of insights into both medievalism and contemporary ecocritical discourses. Whether it is Guinevere describing "the Spirits of the waste and weald" mourning her departure from Camelot in Tennyson's *Idylls of the King* or Sieur Louis de Conte in Mark Twain's *Personal Recollections of Joan of Arc* describing "The Fairy Tree" of Domremy, the natural world is represented repeatedly in these texts in animistic terms. That is, these texts routinely describe the natural world, including animals, vegetation, even rocks and water, as having some form of sentience. This figuration often occurs through anthropomorphic and zoomorphic images that blur the line between the nonhuman and human worlds. However, it also includes the depiction of the nonhuman as sacred, the representation of elemental figures such as sprites and gnomes, and the imaginative synthesis of humanity with the nonhuman, such as in mythological figures like fauns, centaurs, and sphinxes. The animistic figurations, however they are rendered, suggest that nonhuman beings are not merely inanimate objects but conscious, intelligent, willful beings.

There exist at least three ways in which medievalist texts employ these animistic figurations, the first of which relates to the Romantic medievalism so entwined with nineteenth-century political discourses. This form uses animism as a means of animating not only the constituents of a given nation but also the nation itself, as a geographical locale. It uses a particular natural object, such as an animal, a tree, or a natural landmark, as a symbol of a given nation. A clear example of this would be the representation of the Rhine in Wagner's *Der Ring des Nibelung*, in which the Rhine is anthropomorphized as three maidens who guard the golden ring central to the operas' narrative. The opening scene of the first opera, *Das Rhinegold*, begins with a prelude in which Wagner varies the E-major scale to create the sense that the Rhine itself is singing. This anthropomorphism functions, narratologically, to precipitate the allusion, which will be explored more explicitly over the course of the four operas, that the Rhine itself embodies the qualities of the German nation; utilized in a medievalist text like the libretto of *Das Rhinegold*, this figuration bolsters the Romantic Nationalism of the text by figuring a nonhuman being, in this case the Rhine River, as a symbol of Germany. The Rhine in *Das Rhinegold* becomes synecdochically Germany itself, with all of the problematic oversimplifications such a synecdoche connotes.

Another example of this nationalistic figuration would be the representation of Lake George in *The Last of the Mohicans*. That novel, modeled as it is on the medievalist text *Ivanhoe*, has been interpreted by Peter Giles as a form of "Medieval American Literature." Giles argues that, just as Walter Scott romanticized the social structures of medieval England in *Ivanhoe* in order to construct a sense of British identity, U.S. authors, writing in the mid-nineteenth century, often romanticized the social structures of Pre-Contact Native American peoples to create a similar sense of national identity.[1] Lake George (or the Horicon, as it is referred to in the novel) becomes, for Cooper, like the Rhine in *Das Rhinegold*, a symbol of the nation itself. Cooper writes that "Perhaps no district [...] can furnish a livelier picture of the cruelty and fierceness of the savage warfare of those periods [the mid-eighteenth century], than the country which lies between the head waters of the Hudson and the adjacent lakes."[2] Lake George and its surrounding environs, for Cooper, become emblematic of not only the geography of what would become the United States but also that nation's embryonic character. While Lake George is not anthropomorphized as explicitly as Wagner's Rhine, it is given an overtly religious significance. Cooper writes, "Near its southern termination [Lake Champlain] received the contributions of another lake [Lake George], whose waters were so limpid as to have been exclusively selected by the Jesuit missionaries to prefer the typical purification of baptism, and to obtain for it the appropriate title of 'Saint Sacrément,'" and later, in the following paragraph, Cooper refers to Lake George as a "holy lake."[3] Both the Rhine and Lake George, in *Das Rhinegold* and *The*

---

1   Paul Giles, *The Global Remapping of American Literature* (Princeton, NJ: Princeton University Press, 2011), 94.
2   James Fenimore Cooper, *The Last of the Mohicans: A Narrative of 1757* (New York: Penguin Books, 1986), 11.
3   Cooper, *Last of the Mohicans*, 11–12.

Last of the Mohicans, respectively, are depicted as more than simple inanimate objects; they are depicted as either anthropomorphized or sacred spaces that symbolize the nation-states to which each writer was beholden.

Another form of animistic figuration in contemporary medievalist texts does not focus on the nation-state so much as on what T. J. Jackson Lears calls "antimodernism." For Lears, the medievalism of the late nineteenth and early twentieth centuries, at least in the U.S. and Britain, was a means of opposing the rapid modernization of the world. The turn to the medieval, for Lears, was not only a means of constructing a national identity but also a means of defying the overwhelming forces of industrialization. The animistic figurations that support this understanding of medievalism represent animals and other nonhuman beings not as symbols of a nation-state but as "authentic" modes of being.[4] A popular, contemporary example of such figuration would be the use of owls as a means of communication in J. K. Rowling's *Harry Potter* series, in which owls are used in lieu of telephones, email, and postal services. A more pointed example, however, would be Henry Adams's representation of the Virgin throughout his later work. In Adams's *Mont-Saint-Michel and Chartres* (1904) and *The Education of Henry Adams* (1907), he describes "the Virgin" in naturalistic terms and "the Dynamo" in mechanistic terms – that is, he tends to use natural, pastoral imagery to discuss the Virgin and the language of machines and technology to describe the Dynamo. The poem "Prayer to the Virgin of Chartres" (1901), which Lears analyzes in *No Place of Grace* (1981) as a text that "foreshadowed" both *Mont-Saint-Michel and Chartres* and *The Education of Henry Adams*, articulates this divide between "the Virgin" and "the Dynamo."[5] In the poem, which, as the title suggests, is a prayer to the Virgin Mary's depiction in the medieval cathedral at Chartres, the penultimate stanza reads:

> Brave though we be, we dread to face the Sphinx,
> Or answer the old riddle she still asks.
> Strong as we are, our reckless courage shrinks
> To look beyond the piece-work of our tasks.[6]

In this stanza, Adams illustrates this tendency to describe the Virgin, to which the "Sphinx" corresponds, in naturalistic terms and the Dynamo, to which "the piece-work of our tasks" corresponds, in the language of technology and industrialization. The Sphinx is presented as an intelligent,

---

4 T. J. Jackson Lears, *No Place of Grace: Antimodernism and the Transformation of American Culture, 1880–1920* (New York: Pantheon Books, 1981), xix.

5 Lears, *No Place of Grace*, 279.

6 Henry Adams, *Letter to a Niece and Prayer to the Virgin of Chartres* (Boston: Houghton Mifflin, 1920), 127.

sentient creature. Following the Sophoclean reference, we can hypothesize that the "old riddle she still asks" concerns the nature of humanity, the implication being that those living within the Dynamo struggle to understand the circularity of human life, its growth and demise. The speaker "dreads to face" that Sphinx and cannot "answer" that question, which is consistently posed to him or her. Adams's implication is that, when circumscribed by synthetic, mechanistic life, one cannot deign to understand that humanity is itself circumscribed within the ebb and flow of natural existence, subject to the same principles of construction and destruction as anything else. The Dynamo forgets its indebtedness and interconnectedness with the Virgin, and the poem as a whole is a faithful "prayer" to the Virgin to help the speaker, blinded as he or she is by the power of the Dynamo, recognize that indebtedness and interconnectedness. The animistic figuration supports this theme not by presenting a symbol but rather by representing the natural world in a way that can be made intelligible to humanity. It is interesting to note that while the nationalist use of animism in medievalist texts tends to create a symbol for the given nation-state, this antimodernist use of animism ironically turns animistic figures into tools for humanity to avoid synthetic mechanization. Rowling's owls are not wild owls, free to act as they will, they are tamed to perform the deeds requested of them by their wizards. The Sphinx in Adams's poem "still asks" its riddle, suggesting that it exists primarily to enact a task for humanity. The irony is that for texts that look to oppose the "modernist aesthetic," as Lears puts it, they are remarkably implicated within figuration that makes of nonhuman beings objects for the whims of humanity.

Added to these two forms of animistic figuration is what I would like to call the ecocritical form. This third use of animistic figuration in medievalist texts represents non-human beings not as symbols of a nation-state or as a means of resisting or avoiding modernization but rather as beings unto themselves. Examples of this figuration include the education of King Arthur in T. H. White's *The Once and Future King*, in which Arthur, through the wizardry of Merlin, must live as a perch, hawk, ant, owl, wild goose, and badger.[7] Each animal reveals to Wart, the young King Arthur, a different lesson, which he presumably will need to understand in order to rule in Camelot. In these lessons, each animal that he inhabits has its own unique kind of sentience; his existence as a perch teaches him of tyranny and the dangers of absolute power. His life as an ant teaches him of the vulgarity of war. As a hawk, Wart learns of courage. The representation of these animals as sentient creatures does not make of them symbols of either Britain or Camelot, nor does it function to oppose any modernist aesthetic. Instead, Wart's lessons

---

7   T. H. White, *The Once and Future King* (New York: G. P. Putnam's Sons, 1958), 72–197.

allow him to live for a short time as these creatures, to recognize their own, unique sentiences and to learn from those experiences. Anyone versed in the discourse of contemporary ecocriticism will recognize the similarity between this explanation of Wart's education and an Object Oriented Ontology. After all, Wart becomes these animals; he learns of and must come to terms with the ontologies of the various creatures he becomes. Such a representation of animism is fundamentally different from Wagner's Rhine, Cooper's Lake George, or Adams's Sphinx. In this case, the animals teach Wart to grapple with the ontologies of others, a lesson that will make him into the conscientious, generous king he will become.

With this said, while Wart does inhabit these creatures, their representations are decidedly anthropomorphic. The ants, one might say, speak not so much to ants themselves as to humanity's desire for war. The parable of the badger speaks particularly to this point, for the badger informs Wart not about what it is to be a badger but what it is to be a human being. The presence of certain anthropomorphisms, however, should not be confused with a complete transformation of the animals' sentiences into human sentience. That is, while White surely does not completely offer us a description of what it is to be the various animals he describes, the assertion is clear: animals have something to teach human beings, and that assertion alone is enough to differentiate his animism from Wagner's or Adams's. While White is not able to offer us complete, unfiltered access to each animal's ontology, his narrations gesture toward the ability to occupy, or at least learn from, a nonhuman ontology. Indeed, the limits of White's animism gesture not so much to his own limitations as a writer as to the horizons, in the phenomenological sense, of Object Oriented Ontology itself. Can a text, using human language, ever truly offer animistic figurations that do not make of the nonhuman something at least marginally human? Object Oriented Ontology, after all, does not proclaim the ability to offer unfettered access to another object's ontology; it looks to "orient" us toward another, nonhuman ontology, and that is precisely what White's description of Wart's education does. It describes an education that allows a human being to consider nonhuman ontologies. That the narration of that education makes those nonhuman beings into something resembling human beings is a requisite: how else to make nonhuman beings intelligible to human beings? It is the gesture that matters, a gesture that looks to recognize the ontology of another, nonhuman being.

With this in mind, all three forms of animistic figuration, the nationalist, antimodernist, and ecocritical, offer a means of untangling ontology itself from *Dasein*, understood as humanity's particular ontology. The nationalist form suggests that a nation is more than a community of human beings; it is also a community of nonhuman beings. Antimodernist figurations, meanwhile, remind us of the utility of nonhuman beings. They call us to consider the arbitrary boundary we draw between synthetic and natural objects, and such a consideration necessarily illustrates, if not the complete immateriality of that boundary, at least its protean nature. Finally, ecocritical figurations attempt to represent nonhuman beings as beings subject to the same laws as humanity and worthy of the same respect.

A close reading of a particular poem might help to clarify these points. I have thus far treated the three categories of animistic figuration as if they were mutually exclusive, as if Wagner's operas only use nationalist figurations, as if Adams is solely an antimodernist, and as if White used only the ecocritical form, but texts can intertwine all three, if not more, forms of animistic figuration. Indeed, even a given figure itself, as the badger in White's novel illustrates, can operate in multiple ways, open to more than one interpretation. An example of such a text that utilizes more than one form of animistic figuration is Edith Wharton's 1909 poem, "Ogrin the Hermit." The poem tells the story of Tristan and Iseult, and especially a relatively minor episode in that tale, their encounter with a monk named Ogrin. While Iseult and Tristan are fleeing the authorities of Cornwall, Ogrin shelters them for a short while in his hermitage. In the traditional account of the story, Ogrin, at the bequest of Iseult, helps Tristan to compose a letter, in which Tristan asks King Mark, Iseult's husband, to accept the lovers back to court. Mark, guided by his barons, allows Iseult to return but does not allow Tristan to stay in Cornwall. Ogrin, in other words, mediates between the lovers and the traditional hierarchy of the court. In Wharton's account, Ogrin still plays a mediating role, but we are offered an insight into his own experience of the encounter. Namely, in the poem, Ogrin himself is transformed by the encounter with the couple. The poem, which is told from Ogrin's point of view, recounts Iseult's description of the love she and Tristan have experienced:

> For she [Iseult] said:
> "Love is not, as the shallow adage goes,
> A witch's filter, brewed to trick the blood.
> The cup we drank of on the flying deck
> Was the blue vault of air, the round world's lip,
> Brimmed with life's hydromel, and pressed to ours
> By myriad hands of wind and sun and sea.
> For these are all the cup-bearers of youth,
> That bend above it at the board of life,
> Solicitous accomplices: there's not
> A leaf on bough, a foam-flash on the wave,
> So brief and glancing but it serves them too;
> No scent the pale rose spends upon the night,
> Nor sky-lark's rapture trusted to the blue,

But these, from the remotest tides of air
Brought in mysterious salvage, breathe and sing
In lovers' lips and eyes; and two that drink
Thus onely of the strange commingled cup
Of mortal fortune shall into their blood
Take magic gifts. Upon each others' hearts
They shall surprise the heart-beat of the world,
And feel a sense of life in things inert;
For as love's touch upon the yielded body
Is a diviner's wand, and where it falls
A hidden treasure trembles: so their eyes,
Falling upon the world of clod and brute,
And cold hearts plotting evil, shall discern
The inextinguishable flame of life
That girdles the remotest frame of things
With influences older than the stars."[8]

This poem, to the extent that it has been analyzed at all, has typically been understood as an homage to Henry Adams, with whom Wharton was a close friend. Ogrin, as a stand-in for Adams, shelters the illicit love of this medieval couple, interpreting it for the modern world, just as Adams interpreted the medieval aesthetic for the late nineteenth and early twentieth centuries. The use of natural imagery connotes a sense of ancient, natural landscapes "older than the stars," and these images create a sense of antimodernism in that they suggest that this love, which allows access to "magic gifts," is no technological invention. It is a natural thing, a cup of "the blue vault of air." And yet, the naturalistic imagery also suggests that nonhuman figures like the "wind and sun and sea" have wills unto themselves; the earth has a "heart-beat" in this poem. The love Iseult and Tristan share, according to this account, is given to them, "pressed" to their lips, by the "myriad hands of wind and sun and sea." Moreover, this "cup," filled with "the blue vault of air," allows her to see the "sense of life in things inert." Not only is the love given to her by the natural world, but that love also allows her to recognize the natural world as a concatenation of living, sentient beings. There exists, in other words, in this excerpt both antimodernist and ecocritical forms of animistic figuration. The notion that there is "life in things inert" not only creates a sense of distrust for the mechanistic, modern world but also encourages the reader to orient him- or herself toward an understanding of things in themselves. Indeed, one might even say that this poem, with its assertion

---

8   Edith Wharton, *Artemis to Actaeon and More: Selected Verse* (Rockville, MD: Wildside Press, 2002), 88–89.

that the earth has a "heart-beat," partakes also of the first, nationalistic form of animistic figuration. But in this case, instead of constructing a nationalistic symbol, the figure constructs a cosmopolitanist one. By asserting that the earth has a "heart-beat," the poem suggests that there is a fundamental unity to earth that undergirds any seeming difference.

The animistic figurations found so consistently in medievalist texts are more than mere representations of a pre-humanist worldview; they are also attempts to gesture toward a post-humanist worldview, for which nonhuman beings are conscious, intelligent, and willful. All three forms of animistic figuration outlined here perform such a gesture. The nationalistic form recognizes the nation as a supra-human constellation of beings; the antimodernist form suggests that the lines we draw between natural and artificial objects are arbitrary and, therefore, mutable. The ecocritical form, meanwhile, looks to offer to human beings a window into the ontologies of nonhuman beings. In this sense, all three forms are proper subjects of ecocriticism in that all three are clear examples of how medievalist literature represents the natural world. However, of these three forms, it is the final form that at least attempts to treat nonhuman beings not as tools for humanity but as beings unto themselves. That such an attempt always turns those nonhuman beings into anthropomorphisms should be seen not so much as a failure as an inevitable result of an Object Oriented Ontology. That is, the goal of such figuration is to "orient" us toward the ontology of another, nonhuman being. One can never, necessarily, become that other ontology, but that does not imply that such an orientation has failed. Instead, for a post-humanist worldview, it might well be that a recognition of the limitations of human imagination and communication is itself an estimable goal for any ecocritical discourse, medievalist or not.

Future Nostalgias:
Environmental Medievalism
and Lanier's Southern Chivalry

Daniel Helbert

Both David Matthews, in his study of the history of medievalism, and Katey Castellano, in her study of the origins of environmentalism, cite Edmund Burke's *Reflections on the Revolution in France* (1790) as an immensely important embryonic moment in the history of these two traditions. In particular, Castellano cites the development of "environmental conservationism" (a right-of-center political movement invested in localizing communities of natural conservation) as a formative reaction to the destruction of an "intergenerational awareness" of the value of social order and the natural environment by nascent capitalism and the French Revolution.[1] Similarly, Matthews traces "a conservative appropriation of [medieval] romance" from Burke's recurring comments on the failure of chivalry to the rise of "romantic medievalism" (conservative, literary reconstructions of the past through the commonly received genre of medieval romance).[2] Though neither environmentalism nor medievalism are monolithic, "environmental conservationism" and "romantic medievalism" are important, foundational subgenres in these diverse movements. Therefore, the extensive liquidation of multi-generational land holdings (and the aristocracy who held those lands)

---

1   Katey Castellano, *The Ecology of British Romantic Conservatism, 1790–1837* (New York: Palgrave Macmillan, 2013), 1–3. For more on environmental conservatism, see Roger Scruton, *How to Think Seriously about the Planet: The Case for Environmental Conservatism* (Oxford: Oxford University Press, 2012), esp. 5–37.
2   David Matthews, *Medievalism: A Critical History* (Cambridge: D. S. Brewer, 2015), 25. For more on romantic medievalism, see Elizabeth Fay, *Romantic Medievalism: History and the Romantic Literary Ideal* (New York: Palgrave, 2002).

during the French Revolution is a logical historical springboard for both medievalism and environmentalism.

It is not only a common origin in this peculiar historical moment that environmentalism and medievalism share, however. Both were founded, and have been consistently re-imagined, by a deep-seated urge of nostalgia: nostalgia for a world where principles and common sense supposedly prevailed, for a world where humanity supposedly had a closer link with nature, or simply for a time when Progress (with its industrial-capitalist morality) did not advance so quickly. In the following essay, I consider how nostalgia, in its complex presentation of poly-temporal fantasies, formatively links environmentalism and medievalism. After first inviting readers to revisit the chronological and intellectual implications of nostalgia in medieval and environmental studies, I offer a brief reading of Sidney Lanier's early poetry as an important precursor to the current theoretical debates ongoing within these disciplines.

Eco-medieval nostalgia is often problematic: Valerie B. Johnson's exploration of the "greenwood" constructions of the twentieth-century Robin Hood adaptations in an earlier volume of this journal is an excellent example of how a fantasy of medieval primitivism can be employed to suggest a "recoverable Edenic condition" that is not merely inaccurate, but legitimizes real environmental oppression.[3] Similarly, the recent trend in Sustainable Development Agriculture that encourages the use of draft animals along with medieval farming practices and technologies is steeped in nostalgic medievalism: "The farmers of medieval Europe maintained the Two-field system [because] [...] Nature abhors open ground. The peasant farmers had faith in the powers of the wild herbs that grew up to heal and restore the land."[4] Though revisiting medieval agricultural techniques and practices as a viable alternative to mechanized, monocrop agribusiness has my full support, this spiritualistic nostalgia risks essentializing the Middle Ages as a pre-industrial paradise of organic food and permaculture peasantry; and it unwittingly overwrites the unsavory ideological baggage that was so often attached to farming and peasants in the Middle Ages.

I want to suggest, however, that the reflective nostalgias of medieval studies, and medievalism in particular, still have the potential to offer a complex and informed take on the futures of environmental justice; that the nostalgia for

---

[3]   Valerie B. Johnson, "Ecomedievalism: Applying Ecotheory to Medievalism and Neomedievalism," in *Studies in Medievalism XXIV: Medievalism on the Margins*, ed. Karl Fugelso with Vincent Ferré and Alicia C. Montoya (Cambridge: D. S. Brewer, 2015), 31–37 (32).

[4]   Stephen Leslie, *The New Horse-Powered Farm – Tools and Systems for the Small-Scale, Sustainable Market Grower* (White River Junction, VT: Chelsea Green Publishing, 2013), 171.

a "greener" medieval past is not always-already an escapist fantasy that avoids dealing with the environmental problems of the present. "Reflective nostalgias," in the sense employed by Svetlana Boym, "discover that the past is not merely that which doesn't exist anymore, but [...] the past opens up a multitude of potentialities, nonteleological possibilities of historical development."[5] As a consciously constructed fantasy of the past that invariably comments on the present and the future, environmental medievalism has the potential to provide both the historical context for our present environmental problems and the inspiration for some of their solutions.

Both environmentalists and scholars of medievalism have lately been reconsidering the role of nostalgia in critical studies;[6] but despite their similarities, these mediations have not been in conversation with one another.[7] The word "nostalgia," of Greek derivation through Latin, is often pejorative and is tinged with a sense of belittlement in English; yet these connotations do not accompany the non-Romantic approximations of the word I am aware of (Welsh *hiraeth*, High German *Heimweh*, Swiss German *Längizyti*), nor do they accompany the lofty etymons from which "nostalgia" derives (Gk. νόστος [homeward journey] + ἄλγος [pain]).[8] Nonetheless, as Carolyn Dinshaw has said, to call representations of the medieval "nostalgic" is the quickest and easiest way to devalue them: "in three syllables you achieve intellectual delegitimation as well as psychological, political and aesthetic trivialization."[9]

These same suspicions and dismissals of nostalgia are common in ecocritical studies as well, especially among those theorists deeply invested in the

---

5 Svetlana Boym, *The Future of Nostalgia* (New York: Basic Books, 2001), 50.

6 In medievalism, important recent readings include Leah Haught, "Performing Nostalgia: Medievalism in *King Arthur* and *Camelot*," *Arthuriana* 24.4 (2014): 97–126; and the entire special issue of *postmedieval* 2.2 (2011): *The Medievalism of Nostalgia*. Susan Aronstein discusses the political appropriation of nostalgia in her *Hollywood Knights: Arthurian Cinema and the Politics of Nostalgia* (New York: Palgrave Macmillan, 2005); and Renée Trilling, *The Aesthetics of Nostalgia* (Toronto: University of Toronto Press, 2009), reminds us that complex nostalgias also govern medieval texts. Within Ecostudies circles, Jeremy Davies, "Sustainable Nostalgia", *Memory Studies* 3.3 (2010): 262–68, and Alastair Bonnett, *The Geography of Nostalgia: Global and Local Perspectives on Modernity and Loss* (New York: Routledge, 2016), esp. 45–72, are particulary useful for their engagements with ecocritical nostalgias.

7 Laurie Finke and Martin Shichtman's recent article on the fascinating modern-day British "Eco-Warrior" who has renamed himself Arthur Uther Pendragon is a possible exception to this neglect, as the authors consider the complexities of Pendragon's environmental nostalgia, even if they ultimately condemn it as "retrogressive" and "authoritarian." See their "Arthur Pendragon, Eco-Warrior," *Arthuriana* 23.1 (2013): 5–19.

8 I am indebted to Christian Wuillemin for helping me to work through the linguistic subtleties of these cognates.

9 Carolyn Dinshaw, "Nostalgia on my Mind," *postmedieval* 2.2 (2011): 225–38 (225).

social constructivism of "nature" and the presentism of environmentalism. For instance, in Timothy Morton's most recent work, he writes that "[c] elebrations of deracination and nostalgia for the old ways are both fictional. […] The ecological era is the revenge of place, but it's not your grandfather's place."[10] However, Alastair Bonnett draws a distinction between, on the one hand, platforms like Morton's and, on the other, those of scholars who have embraced an environmental nostalgia that is polytemporal, multifaceted, and critical: "in talking themselves out of nostalgia, critics of the 'myth of nature' [like Morton] end up talking themselves out of environmental commitment or concern."[11] Similarly, Jeremy Davies has recently stressed that practical environmentalism is *necessarily* nostalgic, and that this environmental nostalgia is inherently futuristic: "If it describes its preferred future in terms of sustainability, as apparently it must, then environmentalism enters into nostalgia, and the characteristics of nostalgic thinking will affect the shape of that future."[12] The nostalgia of environmental medievalism need not be a monolith of *naïveté* and escapism; it has the unique capability of shaping the future with its focus firmly on the past.

This is evident in many medievalist and neomedievalist writings of our own time. Tolkien's depiction of what Matthews has called the struggle "between virtuous craft and threatening industry" has long been associated with environmentalists' concerns, much more so than Tolkien probably imagined or desired.[13] More recently, novels by Kazuo Ishiguro and Paul Kingsnorth (the former editor of Greenpeace publications and *The Ecologist*) both employ stark eco-apocalyptic settings for their medieval characters and plotlines.[14] The growing number of writers who interrogate environmental issues *through* medieval characters, settings, and themes necessitates further scholarly conversation on both the thematic links between medievalism and environmentalism, and the dualistic role that the Middle Ages can play in shaping environmental studies. In the remaining portion of this essay, however, I want to briefly offer an example of ecomedieval nostalgia that simultaneously precedes the above examples by multiple generations and, yet, anticipates the dualistic role that the Middle Ages can (and should) have in conversations about environmental justice.

---

[10] Timothy Morton, *Dark Ecology: For a Logic of Future Coexistence* (New York: Columbia University Press, 2016), 11.

[11] Bonnett, *Geography of Nostalgia*, 55.

[12] Davies, "Sustainable Nostalgia," 265.

[13] Matthews, *Medievalism*, 32. The recent environmental reading of Tolkien by Matthew Dickerson and Jonathan Evans, *Ents, Elves and Eriador: The Environmental Vision of J. R. R. Tolkien* (Lexington: University Press of Kentucky, 2006) is evidence of the continued scholarly interest in this vein.

[14] Kazuo Ishiguro, *The Buried Giant* (New York: Vintage Books, 2015); Paul Kingsnorth, *The Wake* (London: Unbound, 2014).

"Giant Trade" vs. Southern Chivalry: Sidney Lanier's Dualistic Nostalgia

In the summer of 1881, Sidney Lanier, the acclaimed transcendental nature poet, musician, literary critic, and former Confederate soldier, retreated to the thickly wooded mountains of western North Carolina in an attempt to curb yet another onset of his severely advanced tuberculosis. Though Lanier expressed optimism that he would pull through this latest episode of the recurring debilitations that had plagued him since he contracted the disease as a prisoner during the Civil War, Lanier was also well aware that his overall condition was grave. In a letter to his son that summer, Lanier wrote that he had "been for several weeks lying at the very gates of death – so close that I could almost peep in upon the marvels of that mysterious country."[15] However, despite the knowledge that he was teetering ever toward the brink of his life's end, Lanier continued to work feverishly on the project that had occupied him for the last few years: the editing of medieval chivalric literature for American – and perhaps especially *Southern* American – young boys. These editions were to be (intended or not) his final life project.

Lanier's dedication to this project in the final years of his life is not the most obvious choice for a statement of his legacy. He had, in the previous two decades, garnered much acclaim for his work as a musician and literary critic, and he left a distinct and enduring mark on American poetry, especially through his nature poetry. Indeed, "The Marshes of Glynn," his surprisingly enthralling poem about a piece of swampy Georgia coastline, has been accepted in the Southern literary canon for some time. Though Lanier's *Boy's Library* editions of Froissart (1879), Malory (1880), the *Mabinogion* (1881), and the Percy Folio (published posthumously in 1882) were very successful, scholars of his poetry have tended either to ignore Lanier's final project or write it off as "literary hackwork."[16] Similarly, while medievalists have lately begun to emphasize the peculiarity of Lanier's medievalism – his unique construction of masculinity and his presentation of the medieval as an escape and antidote to his terminal tuberculosis – Lanier's *Boy's Library* of medieval literature has nevertheless been seen as a distinct project, related only tangentially, if at all, to his remaining literary corpus.[17] I suggest here, however, that there are some important links between the *Boy's Library* and

---

[15]   Sidney Lanier, "Letter To Charles D. Lanier," 20 July 1881, in *Sidney Lanier: Poems and Letters*, ed. Charles R. Anderson (Baltimore, MD: Johns Hopkins University Press, 1969): 222–23 (222).

[16]   Edd Winfield Parks, *Sidney Lanier: The Man, the Poet, the Critic* (Athens: University of Georgia Press, 1968), 42.

[17]   Marya DeVoto, "The Hero as Editor: Sidney Lanier's Medievalism and the Science of Manhood," in *Studies in Medievalism IX: Medievalism and the Academy I*, ed. David Metzger, Kathleen Verduin, and Leslie J. Workman (Cambridge: D. S. Brewer, 1997), 148–70; Rob Wakeman, "The 'Best Breathed' Knights in a Stertorous Age: Tuberculosis and

his earlier projects, both social and literary, especially in their attempts to revive a historically informed sense of medieval chivalry to curb the cultural and environmental destruction by what Lanier perceived as the greatest evil of Reconstruction in the American South: "Trade."

The effects of "Trade" (by which Lanier means a laissez-faire, mercantilist denomination of industrial capitalism) and by four years of war (fought almost exclusively in the South) on the natural and social environment have been largely overlooked by Northern authors of the era and by many modern historians for the desirable military victory these effects entailed. Lanier, however, whose family never recovered economically from the war, did not overlook this extensive and enduring damage to the land and the impoverished multitude that had to live off of that land. In his early poem "The Symphony" (1875), Lanier details the horrors that Trade brings to the ecosystem, poor people, and human morality at large. His medieval nostalgia comes out strongly in the poem, for the days gone by when "Love thy neighbor" was the rule and when "man found neighbors in great hills and trees / And streams and clouds and suns and birds and bees."[18] Those days, when man was part of nature rather than its oppressor, are now gone, and he cites Trade as the looming enemy enforcing this division:

> But oh, the poor! the poor! the poor!
> They stand by the inward-opening door
> Trade's hand doth tighten ever more,
> And sigh their monstrous foul-air sigh
> For the outside hills of liberty,
> Where Nature spreads her wild blue sky.
> ("The Symphony" 29)

Lanier portrays Trade as an inward swinging "door" that traps the poorest of society inside its coal-smeared factory, crushing them until they heave a collective "foul-air sigh" of industrial air pollution. Lanier's attention here to "the poor" as the demographic who suffers most from environmental destruction is a remarkable anticipation of Rob Nixon's concept of "slow violence": the recognition that environmental destruction goes unnoticed because it takes place on a protracted time scale and primarily affects the abject and ignored populations of the world.[19]

Sidney Lanier's *The Boy's King Arthur*," *Arthuriana* 25.3 (2015): 98–114; Alan Lupack and Barbara Tepa Lupack, *King Arthur in America* (Cambridge: D. S. Brewer, 1999), 75–80.

18   Lanier, "The Symphony," in Anderson, ed., *Poems and Letters*, 28–29.

19   Rob Nixon, *Slow Violence and the Environmentalism of the Poor* (Cambridge, MA: Harvard University Press, 2011).

As in any good romance (or nostalgic reflection of the past), we need a hero to counteract Trade's ills, and Lanier does not disappoint. After citing further deprivations of morality that Trade causes, Lanier introduces a medieval knight into the fray to challenge this foe:

> Where's he that craftily hath said,
> The day of chivalry is dead?
> I'll prove that lie upon his head,
> Or I will die instead,
> Fair Lady.
> Is Honor gone into his grave? […]
> Will Truth's long blade ne'er gleam again?
> Hath Giant Trade in dungeons slain
> All great contempts [sic] of mean got gain
> And hates of inward stain,
> Fair Lady? ("The Symphony" 31)

It is no coincidence that Lanier allegorizes Trade as the recurring, grotesque, and Otherly enemy of many a medieval knight in chivalric romance, as a monstrous "Giant" to be slain with "Truth's long blade." The Giant, like that oppressive scourge of Nature, Trade, is a "monstrous being that is undeniably both human and something Other," to use Jeffrey Cohen's familiar terminology.[20] It is an excessive growth of the worst of humanity, a cancerous enemy that wreaks unhindered havoc on the weak and vulnerable and must be slain by the best of humanity: the chivalrous knight.

At the same time that Lanier was working on "The Symphony," he was also writing a work he thought would become his "Magnum Opus": a novel in verse called *The Jacquerie*, which was to be a historical romance covering the fourteenth-century French peasant riots of the same name.[21] As Lanier described this poem in a letter written a few months before writing "The Symphony," this particular peasant revolt was the origin of Trade's tyranny over the modern world:

The peasants learned – from the merchant-potentates of Flanders – that a man who could not be a lord by birth, might be one by wealth: & so Trade arose & overthrew Chivalry. Trade has now had possession of the civilized world for four hundred years; […] its oppressions upon the moral existence of man have come to be ten thousand times more

---

20   Jeffrey Jerome Cohen, *Of Giants: Sex, Monsters, and the Middle Ages* (Minneapolis: University of Minnesota Press, 1999), 11.

21   Lanier, "Letter to Logan E. Beckley," 15 November 1874, in Anderson, ed., *Poems and Letters*, 152–54 (153).

grievous than the worst tyrannies of the Feudal System ever were. Thus in the reversals of time, it is *now* the *gentleman* who must arise and overthrow Trade. That chivalry which every man has, in some degree, in his heart; which does not depend upon birth but which is a revelation from God of justice.[22]

To judge Lanier by the contemporary standards of economic history, his conspiratorial link between the rising Merchant Capitalism and the peasant revolts of the fourteenth century are overstated. However, the connections he makes between social unrest, the devaluation of chivalry, nascent capitalism, and environmental degradation are broadly true – as Castellano and Matthews's aforementioned emphasis on Burke's *Reflections on the Revolution in France* indicates. Lanier's comments here make explicit both the medieval theme of this particular poem and for his literary corpus at large. The Middle Ages are not simply a lyrical decoration for Lanier, a trope to capitalize on the Sir Walter Scott-induced craze for jousting knights and damsels in distress. For Lanier, the Middle Ages are a keystone to understanding the contemporary problems facing modern society and are a potential source of antidotes to those problems.

Lanier's nostalgia for the Middle Ages, here and elsewhere, is not an escapist fantasy, but rather a conscious, historically informed, "reflective nostalgia" that is didactic, revisionist, and futurist. Lanier does not long for a classist, racially stratified chivalry such as that embraced by Thomas Dixon some years later; nor does he harbor any illusions that the practice of chivalry in the Middle Ages was a homogeneous and exclusively positive construction. In the 800-line fragment of *The Jacquerie* he left (he never finished the work), Lanier goes to great length to enumerate and exaggerate the oppressive classism inherent in medieval feudalism, narrating in melodramatic detail how a (fictional) Lord Raoul considered trampling a crowd of peasants with his warhorse for entertainment.[23] He warns his adolescent male readers of Froissart to be wary of "how money is already creeping into the beautiful institution of knighthood in the fourteenth century and corrupting it," and to eschew the "Oriental luxuriance" of Gwenhwyfar (Guinevere) in *The Lady of the Fountain*.[24] The Giant Trade, and the social and environmental destruction it inevitably brings, is ever encroaching on the knightly ideal.

---

22 Lanier, "Letter to Logan E. Beckley," 15 November 1874, in Anderson, ed., *Poems and Letters*, 152–54 (153–54), emphasis in original.

23 Lanier, "The Jacquerie: A Fragment," in *Poems of Sidney Lanier*, ed. Mary Day Lanier (New York: Charles Scribner's Sons, 1898), 191–214 (203–5).

24 *The Boy's Froissart*, ed. Sidney Lanier (New York: Charles Scribner's Sons, 1879), ix; *The Boy's Mabinogion*, ed. Sidney Lanier (New York: Charles Scribner's Sons, 1881), xv.

Lanier's reintroduction of that ideal for the benefit of future generations and the nonhuman environment is inherently revisionist.

I do not contend that Lanier's medievalism is irreproachable when judged by contemporary ethical standards: his conception of chivalry is overtly masculine and is often at the expense of female individuality, for instance. I would merely counter that he is a writer of his time and that other Southern male writers of that same time and later exploited medieval nostalgia for much more egregious purposes, including to inculcate the Cult of Domesticity and to justify mob-fueled violence against African Americans.[25] Lanier's nostalgia for medieval chivalry, by contrast, is both historically informed and notably progressive. Lanier's future-oriented nostalgia for medieval chivalry was an antidote to rampant consumerism, a means of protecting the poor and vulnerable sections of society, a means of encouraging the study of modern and ancient languages, and a source for reconsidering humanity's interactions with the environment. In short, Lanier valued medieval culture for many of the same reasons we see fit to continue teaching it today.

---

[25] On the Southern appropriation of chivalry for racist and misogynist goals, see Amy S. Kaufman, "Anxious Medievalism: An American Romance," *The Year's Work in Medievalism* 23, ed. M. J. Toswell (Eugene, OR: Wipf and Stock, 2009): 5–13; and Tison Pugh, *Queer Chivalry: Medievalism and the Myth of White Masculinity in Southern Literature* (Baton Rouge: Louisiana State University Press, 2013).

T. H. White's "Forest Sauvage": Nostalgia and Loss

Lisa Myers

Written in the shadow of two World Wars, T. H. White's Arthuriad, *The Once and Future King* (1938–58), revolves around the nature of human violence and the need to control it. While White's primary source is Sir Thomas Malory's *Le Morte Darthur*,[1] Malory says nothing of Arthur's childhood in the household of Sir Ector, leaving White free, in his tetralogy's first book, *The Sword in the Stone*, to create an adolescence for the legendary king. This opening book maintains many of the aspects of chivalric romance present in Malory and constructs an idyllic boyhood filled with joy, wonder, and childhood adventures while also presenting intervening perspectives that foreshadow the ultimate failure of Arthur's desire to end violence through his reign. The perspectives of the modern, omniscient narrator and Arthur's tutor Merlyn, who lives backward through time and knows the future, create a bittersweet nostalgia that foreshadows the apocalyptic ending of Arthur's world. These elements converge in White's depiction of the Forest Sauvage surrounding Ector's estate, which becomes a location of comparison between medieval England and the modern world that both forecasts the tragedy of *The Once and Future King* and critiques the progress of White's own time.

The Sword in the Stone's Forest Sauvage, the Savage/Wild/Unspoiled Forest, replicates elements of woodlands found in Malory. While this opening book incorporates aspects of many genres, including pastoral, fantasy, and *bildungsroman*, the natural setting of the narrative closely mirrors the stereotypical romance forest. Many scholars have discussed the role of the forest in chivalric romance, including Corinne Saunders, who examines it as the location

---

[1]   White drew upon multiple sources for his work, but he most often directly cites Malory within his text. For more on White's relationship with Malory, see Elisabeth Brewer, *T. H. White's* The Once and Future King, Arthurian Studies 30 (Cambridge: D. S. Brewer, 1993), 207–25.

of adventure, love, and spirituality in a variety of texts,[2] and Robert Pouge Harrison, who articulates the connection between the forest as the location of adventure for the knight and the romance as an aristocratic genre.[3] The generic forms and motifs of medieval romance, which came to England through the Normans, are intimately bound to aristocratic values, including the depiction of the natural world as the location of adventures that support the knight's personal development and, through his success, uphold the ideology of the ruling class.

The image of the forest as strange, foreign, and dangerous dominates romance. Centered in the castle or court as the location of aristocratic values, this genre views the world beyond as its antithesis, a wild Other world that provides a contrast to civilization.[4] Typically, a chivalric romance begins in the elegant society of the court, involves a knight leaving alone and entering upon a quest in the forest lying beyond the perimeter of society, and ends when the knight returns to the court to enjoy the glory he gains from facing the dangers outside. Following Lawrence Buell's first dimension of place-connectedness in which a series of concentric circles represents a movement from the security of the home to the uncertainty of the outside world,[5] the farther the knight travels from the castle, the more strange and unsettling the setting and its occupants become. Tournaments at court display a knight's prowess, but adventures outside society prove his true worth because of uncalculated risks, such as fairies, dishonorable knights, magic, and wild and strange beasts. In *Le Morte Darthur*, despite success in many tournaments at court, Lancelot sees these as sport until he tests himself away from civilization: "Thus Sir Launcelot rested hym longe with play and game, and than he thought hymself to preve in straunge adventures [...] and rode into a depe foreste."[6] The dangers of the forest are the true test of knighthood because the physical risks of that alien environment signify a greater threat to the values of society.

In order to achieve their aims, romance authors depicted the forests of medieval England as dark and primeval, able to conceal myriad possibilities for adventure. The realities of the English countryside, however, were less exotic. At the time of Roman withdrawal from Britain (410), little woodland

2   Corinne Saunders, *The Forest of Medieval Romance: Avernus, Broceliande, Arden* (Cambridge: D. S. Brewer, 1993).

3   Robert Pogue Harrison, *Forests: The Shadow of Civilization* (Chicago: University of Chicago Press, 1992).

4   Jeff Rider, "The Other Worlds of Romance," in *The Cambridge Companion to Medieval Romance*, ed. Roberta L. Krueger, Cambridge Companions to Literature (Cambridge: Cambridge University Press, 2000), 115–31 (115–16).

5   Lawrence Buell, *Writing for an Endangered World: Literature, Culture, and Environment in the U.S. and Beyond* (Cambridge, MA: Belknap Press, 2001), 64.

6   Sir Thomas Malory, *Le Morte Darthur*, 2 vols., ed. P. J. C. Field, Arthurian Studies 80 (Cambridge: D. S. Brewer, 2013), 90.

remained[7] and the clearing of land for cultivation and grazing during the Early Middle Ages further impacted wooded areas, a situation that worsened between the Norman Conquest (1066) and the Black Death (1349) when England experienced a population boom[8] and most serviceable land not designated as royal forest was put to agricultural use.[9] In the seventh century, England was approximately 20 to 25 percent woodland,[10] dropping to 7 percent by 1350.[11] Some thick forests may have remained, but they were not extensive, nor were they "untamed wilderness."[12] Additionally, the Forest Laws controlled the remaining woodland that had not given way to agricultural needs, preserving wooded spaces for aristocratic hunting and recreation. If, as Erich Auerbach states, "A self-portrayal of feudal knighthood with its mores and ideals is the fundamental purpose of the courtly romance,"[13] then the fictional landscapes constructed to suit the ideological needs of the aristocracy reflect the reality of aristocratic control of English land, if not the actual topography.

In *The Sword in the Stone*, White creates a natural setting that not only mirrors medieval romance landscapes, but also provides a tone of mystery and wonder for his adolescent protagonist, facilitating Arthur's development as a future leader. Like the romance forest, the Forest Sauvage that surrounds Sir Ector's castle is vast and primeval, providing an appropriate sense of threatening danger beyond castle walls. Several descriptions scattered throughout the text build upon its menacing aspects:

> The most of the Forest Sauvage was almost impenetrable, an enormous barrier of eternal trees, the dead ones fallen against the live and held to them by ivy, the living struggling up in competition with each other toward the sun which gave them life, the floor boggy through lack of drainage, or tindery from old wood so that you might suddenly tumble through a decayed tree trunk into an ants' nest, or laced with brambles and bindweed and honeysuckle and convolvulus and teazles and the stuff which country people call sweethearts, until you would be torn to pieces in three yards. (91) [14]

---

7   Michael Reed, *The Landscape of Britain: From the Beginnings to 1914*, History of the British Landscape (Savage, MD: Barnes and Noble Books, 1990), 122.

8   Christopher Dyer, "Documentary Evidence: Problems and Enquiries," in *The Countryside of Medieval England*, ed. Grenville Astill and Annie Grant (New York: Basil Blackwell, 1988), 12–35 (23).

9   Reed, *Landscape of Britain*, 126.

10 Oliver Rackham, *Woodlands*, New Naturalist 100 (London: Collins, 2006), 64–65.

11 Rackham, *Woodlands*, 65.

12 Reed, *Landscape of Britain*, 122.

13 Erich Auerbach, "The Knight Sets Forth," in *Middle English Romances*, ed. Stephen H. A. Shepherd (New York: Norton, 1995), 411–27 (418).

14 References to *The Sword in the Stone* are from T. H. White, *The Once and Future King* (New York: G. P. Putnam's Sons, 1958).

It is a dangerous place, intimidating even in its lushness and nearly impossible to traverse. In addition, White locates this forest along the Welsh Marches, an area notoriously turbulent for William the Conqueror, the model for White's Uther Pendragon. While White is inconsistent regarding the temporal background of his work, the subtle link between the Normans and their difficulties with the Welsh borderlands increases the threatening aspects of the frontier setting. Not only is the forest itself an unknown space, but what lies beyond it is too. Looking out of Merlyn's tower room:

> Your eye finally wandered out over the distant blue tree-tops of the Forest Sauvage. This sea of leafy timber rolled away and away in knobs like the surface of porridge, until it was finally lost in remote mountains which nobody had ever visited, and the cloud-capped towers and gorgeous palaces of heaven. (84)

Here, the mystery of the surrounding forest spreads to the edge of the earth and into the heavens, providing a sense of isolation while also implying a limitless source of adventure. Extending this sense of a vast, unknown space, White eventually designates the countryside between the Castle of the Forest Sauvage and London as "an England without civilization" (204). While Malory never describes his forest in detail, White's depiction of the Forest Sauvage provides a sense of the romance ideology surrounding the natural world.

Just as the forest exists in romances in order to provide adventure for the hero, White's limitless tracts function appropriately for the nobility of Ector's family and inner circle. The three aristocratic adults – Sir Ector, King Pellinore, and Sir Grummore Grummursum – are all rather comic, and White describes their activities in the forest more as recreation than dangerous adventure. All participate in the boar hunt directed by master huntsman William Twyti. Sir Grummore spends his days "beknighted out questin'" (4) in the forest but his description of one day's activities includes four place-names (4). He actually seems to accomplish little except for a comic duel with King Pellinore, observed by Wart (Arthur's childhood nickname). In addition, King Pellinore's perpetual pursuit of the Questing Beast delivers a great deal of comic enjoyment rather than knightly adventure.

The exploits of Wart and his foster-brother Kay create the true romance narrative of the text as their activities provide opportunities for the young noblemen to prove themselves in trying circumstances. In these situations, the forest as an unknown wilderness gives way to a vibrant world, existing outside the nurturing safety of stone walls. While White highlights Wart's development as a future leader, even Kay experiences the ennobling effects of the forest. Both boys participate in the boar hunt and together frequently hunt for rabbits along the edges of the woodland. Both enjoy an adventure involving Robin Wood, White's version of Robin Hood, who lives with his band in a series of man-made glades in the Forest Sauvage (92). This escapade includes a daring rescue from the castle of Morgan le Fay, also situated deep within the woodlands (108). In particular, Wart's tenacity appears in his refusal to abandon the hawk Cully and his resulting night in the dark depths of the forest where he discovers his new tutor, Merlyn, living quite comfortably in a small cottage (22). While not consistent with historical English topography, the Forest Sauvage, like a romance forest, appears impenetrable but is actually full of interesting figures, locations, and adventures that exist to develop White's main character. Wart, although ignorant of his true identity, expresses the connection between chivalry and the natural world in his wish to be a knight:

> I should have called myself the Black Knight. And I should have hoved at a well or a ford or something and made all true knights that came that way to joust with me for the honour of their ladies, and I should have spared them all after I had given them a great fall. And I should live out of doors all the year round in a pavilion, and never do anything but joust and go on quests and bear away the prize at tournaments, and I should not ever tell anybody my name. (56)

Wart, in typical chivalric fashion, views knighthood as a series of deeds accomplished outside the safety of court and castle.

The other landscapes of *The Once and Future King* do not receive the same level of description as the Forest Sauvage. Alan Lupack notes that the tetralogy "grows up" with its protagonist, becoming more mature as the narrative moves toward tragedy and the optimism of Wart's youth is lost in the realities of adult life.[15] Correspondingly, the natural settings cease to serve as a source of joyful, adolescent adventure. The Orkney children's escapades on the windswept cliffs of the Out Isles are dark and foreboding, contrasting with Arthur's childhood.[16] Even the forests of the later books lose much of their fascinating aspects, functioning as tropes of romance. In the tetralogy's second book, *The Queen of Air and Darkness*, Sherwood hides Arthur's ambush for the Battle of Bedegraine instead of the outlaw hero expected by the modern audience (310–11), and in the third book, *The Ill-Made Knight*, while the forest does provide adventure for the hero as well as a number of

---

15 Alan Lupack, "*The Once and Future King*: The Book that Grows Up," *Arthuriana* 11.3 (2001): 103–14.

16 The dreary landscapes of book two were extensively revised from the original version, *The Witch in the Wood* (New York: G. P. Putnam's Sons, 1939), which employs a woodland setting. These changes in landscape appear a conscious choice to heighten the contrast between Arthur's childhood and the childhood of the Orkney faction.

hermits in the Grail section, the only true landscape descriptions are of the Fenland (374) and, interestingly, a short comment on Lancelot's difficulty in the Forest Sauvage (361) after his escape from Morgan le Fay's castle, which, in keeping with the maturing tone of the tetralogy, no longer displays the fairy aspects described in *The Sword in the Stone*. In the fourth book, *The Candle in the Wind*, the extended description of the wind outside Benwick Castle that opens chapter 13 creates a bleak setting for the tragic conclusion. These elements are all important aspects of the tone of each book, but White almost exclusively reserves extensive commentary on the landscape to *The Sword in the Stone* where it plays a leading role in the opening of his tragedy.

The relationship between White's Forest Sauvage and his use of nostalgia and time in *The Sword in the Stone* anticipates the apocalyptic conclusion of *The Once and Future King*. Prelapsarian in its boyish innocence and connection to nature, the opening setting of White's tetralogy creates a childhood paradise bound to an idealized natural world, a georgic society where Ector's serfs "were healthy, free of an air with no factory smoke in it, and, which was most of all to them, their heart's interest was bound up with their skill in labour," and, "the evil was in the bad people who abused it, not in the feudal system" (131).[17] The most memorable aspect of the text involves Wart's transformation into a variety of animals as part of Merlyn's tutelage, the purpose of which is to teach him that Might does not make Right, a concept that informs the entire series.[18] Wart's time as a perch, merlin, ant, gander, and badger serves a similar purpose as the adventures of the Forest Sauvage in preparing Wart for adulthood. Moving from Mr. P, who is the ruthless pike that rules the moat, to the utopian geese, these episodes develop the problem of violence that plagues Arthur throughout his rule.[19] In creating an adolescence for Arthur that provides an ideology behind the creation of the Round Table, White delivers a nostalgic view of childhood innocence tied to agricultural production, animals, and the forest, with the narrator's commentary on the Forest Sauvage most directly foreshadowing the apocalyptic conclusion of the text as well as commenting upon the shortcomings of the modern era.

White extends the nostalgia of his text through his modern, omniscient narrator who speaks directly to the reader from the early twentieth century, explaining concepts through modern politics and popular culture. As in his

---

17   For more on nostalgia and nature in White's idealized medieval world, see Brewer, *T. H. White*, 24–27 and 189–91.
18   See Ashley Pfeiffer, "T. H. White and the Lasting Influence of World War I: King Arthur at War," in *Baptism of Fire: The Birth of the Modern British Fantastic in World War I*, ed. Janet Brennan Croft (Altadena, CA: Mythopoeic Press, 2015), 299–310, and Lake La Jeunesse, "T. H. White, *The Once and Future King*, and the Scientific Method," *Arthuriana* 22.2 (2012): 21–36 (24).
19   Evans Lansing Smith, "The Narrative Structure of T. H. White's *The Once and Future King*," *Quondam et Futurus* 1.4 (1991): 39–52 (41).

lamentation for feudal society, the narrator emphasizes that the natural world no longer exists in its medieval form: "Wart would not have been frightened of an English forest nowadays, but the great jungle of Old England was a different matter" (12). A longing for the past becomes more pronounced in the description of the Castle of the Forest Sauvage today, where "The Society for the Preservation of This and That" (37) holds sway over the ruins of Ector's home. As already discussed, English romance authors constructed woodland settings not as realistic depictions of the forest, but according to the needs of the genre. Similarly, White's Forest Sauvage, although following his source material, is an imagined landscape masquerading as the medieval original,[20] heightening nostalgia for a simpler time.[21] While such nostalgia risks becoming overly sentimental,[22] White moderates this tendency through the narrator's winking acknowledgement of this idealism, as in the description of the perfect English seasons (137) and in the assurance that the wolves outside slathered only "in an appropriate manner" (138).

In depicting Arthur's childhood home through both the young boy's naïve innocence and the modern narrator's knowledge, White moves between an idyllic medieval England and a present one spoiled by modern industrialization and regulation, creating a post-Industrial critique of the modern world as a force for both destruction and control of the environment. While lamenting the loss of the former, the presence of the latter asserts that the world of Arthur is doomed. The explicit changes in forest and castle, key elements of medieval romance, foreshadow the end of chivalry and the apocalyptic ruin of Arthur's glorious civilization based on justice rather than violence. White underscores this poignancy through the figure of Merlyn whose life's work is to prepare Arthur, but, as John K. Crane notes, also lives backwards through time, knowing, like the modern narrator, the results of human progress, yet labors to end war and destruction.[23] As Marilyn K. Nellis observes, Merlyn's reversal of time and the many anachronisms associated with him "[suggest] the universality of human nature,"[24] furthering

---

20   For more on the interaction between the natural world and human memory, see Simon Schama, *Landscape and Memory* (London: HarperCollins, 1995).

21   On White's nostalgia, see C. N. Manlove, "Flight to Aleppo: T. H. White's *The Once and Future King*," *Mosaic* 10.2 (1977): 65–83.

22   Brewer examines didactic boys' literature of the nineteenth century as an influence upon White's connection between nature and nostalgia. She specifically names Richard Jefferies, Kenneth Grahame, E. Nesbit, and Arthur Ransome as influences, *T. H. White*, 23–24.

23   John K. Crane, *T. H. White* (New York: Twayne, 1974), 191, n. 1. See also C. M. Adderley, "The Best Thing for Being Sad: Education and Educators in T. H. White's *The Once and Future King*," *Quondam et Futurus* 2.1 (1992): 55–68 (57).

24   Marilyn K. Nellis, "Anachronistic Humor in Two Arthurian Romances of Education: *To the Chapel Perilous* and *The Sword in the Stone*," *Studies in Medievalism* 2.4 (1983): 57–77 (68). In this connection, Nellis also discusses three episodes cut from the 1958 version of

the tragedy of White's version of the legend as the collapse of Arthur's world applies to all human history. In highlighting the future spoiled state of the Forest Sauvage, White forecasts the concluding fall of Arthur's civilization.

In the idealized natural world of *The Sword in the Stone* and the apocalyptic conclusion of *The Once and Future King*, White risks infantilizing the Middle Ages, which David Matthews defines as a tendency of writers to depict the medieval period as "The remote *childhood* of modernity, a time when culture was unformed, underdeveloped, at best promising, at worst simply infantile."[25] As apocalypse is both a violent end and a new start, White concludes his tetralogy with "The Beginning," depicting Arthur as a visionary whose world is not ready for his ideas of law and order, seemingly conforming to Matthew's definition. C. N. Manlove notes that Arthur, in essence, runs out of the time he needs to find an antidote to human violence,[26] while Lupack asserts that the appearance of Thomas Malory to carry Arthur's vision into the future mitigates this problem of time by passing Arthur's values to the next generation.[27] The task of moving beyond a society based upon military power appears reserved for a later period, seemingly making Arthur's reign an immature start to a more sophisticated world that will exist in the future.

White's treatment of the Forest Sauvage and its imagery of decay, loss, and regulation in *The Sword in the Stone*, however, complicates an interpretation of Arthur's reign as a childhood to the maturity of the modern period. The narrator's movement between a past and a present England and his descriptions of the now-tamed Forest Sauvage with its crumbling castle not only foreshadow Arthur's tragic end, but also imply that the modern period has brought decay rather than enlightenment. John Howe and Michael Wolfe assert that modern representations of medieval, primordial landscapes express more about modern ideology than they do about past topography.[28] Correspondingly, White's descriptions not only express nostalgia resulting from disillusionment with the industrialized world, but also the widespread corruption of that world. The episode of the ants in *The Sword in the Stone* and Merlyn's tirade on the "young Austrian" in *The Queen of Air and Darkness* (274) both directly illustrate White's concerns with violence in his own time. Rather than a post-medieval world where justice has been achieved,

---

The Sword in the Stone: the history lesson of T. natrix, the Dream of the Trees, and the Dream of the Stones.

25 David Matthews, *Medievalism: A Critical History* (Cambridge: D. S. Brewer, 2015), 132.

26 Manlove, "Flight to Aleppo," 79–80.

27 Lupack, "The Book that Grows Up," 112. See also Adderley, "The Best Thing for Being Sad," 57.

28 John Howe and Michael Wolfe, "Introduction," in *Inventing Medieval Landscapes: Senses of Place in Western Europe*, ed. John Howe and Michael Wolfe (Gainesville: University Press of Florida, 2002), 1–10 (2).

the modern world continues to struggle with the same problems of Arthur's reign. Chapter 3 of *The Candle in the Wind* provides a long diversion on the culture of the Middle Ages, concluding with an address to the modern reader:

> Do you think that they, with their Battles, Famine, Black Death and Serfdom, were less enlightened than we are with our Wars, Blockade, Influenza and Conscription? Even if they were foolish enough to believe that the earth was the centre of the universe, do we not ourselves believe that man is the fine flower of creation? If it takes a million years for a fish to become a reptile, had Man, in our few hundred, altered out of recognition? (569)

While idealistic in his depiction of Arthur's childhood, White's narrator also resists an image of the Middle Ages as the infancy of the modern era in his assertion that humanity has failed to mature in the intervening centuries. No adulthood has been achieved. Merlyn, having lived through the centuries, seeks not only to change the medieval past, but, perhaps, also to reform the present. White's nostalgia regarding the forest of *The Sword in the Stone* not only prepares the reader for the apocalyptic conclusion of Arthur's reign, but also contextualizes the ruined present where humanity's perpetual struggle against violence and destruction continues.

Elvencentrism:
The Green Medievalism
of Tolkien's Elven Realms

Ann M. Martinez

In 1972 the eco-activist David Taggart sailed into a French nuclear testing site, in what many consider to be the foundational protest of Greenpeace. Taggart later wrote of the experience, "I had been reading *The Lord of the Rings*. I could not avoid thinking of parallels between our own little fellowship and the long journey of the Hobbits into the volcano-haunted land of Mordor."[1] It is not surprising that a medieval-inspired story of different people coming together to save their world resonated with the Greenpeace movement. Tolkien, in his work, often emphasizes the struggle to overcome adversity; however, he also gives ample attention to the importance of nature – a perfect combination for environmentalists. Accordingly, Verlyn Flieger states, "Tolkien has come more and more to be viewed as a kind of advance-man for the Green Movement."[2] Indeed, Tolkien was a staunch supporter of nature and exhibited this through his work, as he explains in a letter to the editor of the *Daily Telegraph*: "In all my works I take the part of trees as against all their enemies."[3] Additionally, he was clear about his reaction to mishandled nature. "I am (obviously) much in love with plants and above all trees, and always have been," he wrote in a letter to his publisher, "and I find human maltreatment of them as hard to bear as some find ill-treatment of

---

1 Patrick Curry, *Defending Middle-earth: Tolkien: Myth and Modernity* (New York: St. Martin's, 1997), 55.
2 Verlyn Flieger, *Green Suns and Faerie: Essays on J. R. R. Tolkien* (Kent, OH: Kent State University Press, 2012), 262.
3 J. R. R. Tolkien, *The Letters of J. R. R. Tolkien*, ed. Humphrey Carpenter (New York: Houghton Mifflin, 2000), 419.

animals."[4] Tolkien's strong sentiments about the value of nature clearly echo throughout his writings, where the landscape is as important to the story as any of the main characters.[5]

As a fantasy author, Tolkien wrote of an epic journey; as a medievalist, he situated this journey on a medieval landscape. Always vast and occasionally war-torn, the landscape of Tolkien's mythopoeic world includes, in the Elven realms, an idealized green space that echoes the royal parks of the Middle Ages. In Middle-earth's saga, I argue, this medieval-inspired idealized green space becomes ecocentric. Furthermore, the philosophical foundation of Tolkien's nature is evocative of what later is known as "deep ecology", particularly as it pertains to the Eldar Elves.[6] Coined by Arne Naess, deep ecology advocates for the intrinsic value of living things, hearkening toward "biospherical inclusiveness" while prioritizing the ecocentric over the anthro-

---

4   Tolkien, *Letters*, 220.
5   For more environmental readings of Tolkien's work, see the following: Matthew Dickerson and Jonathan Evans, *Ents, Elves, and Eriador: The Environmental Vision of J. R. R. Tolkien* (Lexington: University Press of Kentucky, 2006), conclude that, for Tolkien, environmental issues were as important as his theological beliefs; since Tolkien was a devout Catholic, the significance of such a statement is essential for understanding Tolkien's conception of nature in regard to the position of people. Patrick Curry, however, in his review of *Ents, Elves, and Eriador*, in *Tolkien Studies* 3 (2007): 238–44 [239–40, 243], critiques the authors for presenting solely a Christian environmental ethic, and for proposing that Tolkien has a fundamentally Christian view toward nature. He also criticizes them for not providing a broader environmental context, one that would have engaged with the works of other prominent ecocritics. In his own work, *Defending Middle-earth*, Curry touches on the ideas of "nostalgic pastoralism" (both in regard to the idyllic, long-lost past, where green abounds around every corner, and in regard to the Shire) and the sustainable environment created by the Hobbits; fittingly, he uses the term "radical" to describe Tolkien's ecologism in the sense of a "return to roots" (28). Alex Lewis and Elizabeth Currie state that Tolkien appears to be a "geographer or geologist, or perhaps also a biologist," based on his meticulous creation of Middle Earth; see "Realms of Ecology: Tolkien and the Physical Universe," in their *The Uncharted Realms of Tolkien: A Critical Study of Text, Context and Subtext in the Works of J. R. R. Tolkien* (Weston Rhyn, Oswestry, UK: Medea, 2002), 18–33 [18]. Verlyn Flieger discusses Tolkien's dualistic representation of trees as both good and evil entities in "Taking the Part of Trees: Eco-Conflict in Middle-earth," in *J. R. R. Tolkien and His Literary Resonances: Views of Middle-earth*, ed. George Clark and Daniel Timmons (Westport, CT: Greenwood, 2000), 147–73 [147–49]. Marcella Juhren, in "The Ecology of Middle-earth," *Mythlore* 76 (April 1994): 5–8 [5], praises Tolkien's environmental awareness and scientific exactitude and credits him with portraying "this earth with deep understanding, and with as much care for detail as an ecologist would use in […] preparing a report for his professional society."
6   Those Elves who never depart from Middle-earth are called "Dark Elves" or "Moriquendi," for they never see the light of the Blessed Realm in Valinor. I make a clear environmental distinction between the Eldar Elves and the Dark Elves (which include the Wood Elves), as the actions of the former affect Middle-earth more strongly in regard to elvencentrism.

pocentric.[7] The Elves' practice of land management and territorialization is a manifestation of deep ecology. In what I term "elvencentrism", the Eldar Elves engage in the care of nature (ecocentric land-management) but do so primarily within their own realms, establishing what appear as Elven bioregions (territorialization) that are reminiscent of medieval royal parks.[8] To be elvencentric, thus, means that the Elves have an eco-focus within their borders.[9] The Elves' attention to and nurturing of the land is a model of proper environmental behavior. Tolkien strikingly contrasts the green spaces they construct with wastelands, directly addressing a major postmedieval concern: environmentalism.

Technodominationism: A Mind of Metal and Wheels Decays the Land

The obliteration of the landscape in Middle-earth is the result of mechanized modernity.[10] The pursuit of power – unrestrained, all-encompassing power

---

7   Lawrence Buell, *The Future of Environmental Criticism: Environmental Crisis and Literary Imagination* (Malden, MA, and Oxford, UK: Wiley-Blackwell, 2005), 137.

8   A bioregion "is a geographical area of similar climate where similar ecosystems and groups of species are found on similar sites" (Buell, *The Future*, 135). Accordingly, bioregionalism "views a bioregion not only as a territory defined by natural markers, such as watersheds, but also as a domain of consciousness" (Buell, *The Future*, 135). Because the Elves apply their specific views regarding the environment on a geographical area, the terms are relevant.

9   I chose the term "elvencentrism" because the actions of the Eldar are reminiscent of Eurocentric colonialism. As Val Plumwood states in "Decolonizing Relationships with Nature," in *Decolonizing Nature: Strategies for Conservation in a Post-Colonial Era*, ed. William Adam and Martin Mulligan (London: Earthscan, 2003), 51–78 [53]:

> An encompassing and underlying rationalist ideology applying both to humans and to non-humans is thus brought into play in the specific processes of European colonization. This ideology is applied not only to indigenous peoples but to their land, which was frequently portrayed in colonial justifications as unused, underused or empty – areas of rational deficit.

The Eldar Elves see Middle-earth as "unused, underused, or empty," and they set it upon themselves to change that. The ideology behind colonization entails the "imposition of the colonizers' land forms and visions of ideal landscapes," as is seen in the Eurocentrism of European colonization (Plumwood, *Decolonizing*, 53). The elvencentric tendencies the Eldar exhibit prompt them to create the "ideal landscapes" they have envisioned, whether from their own imaginings, as replicas of Valinor, or as a combination of both.

10   Critics have long discussed Tolkien's views on modernity. He was one to condemn change when it altered the idyllic landscape of his childhood memories. During his lifetime, war greatly changed the landscape through its modern mechanizations. In a letter to his son Christopher, Tolkien talks about the "evil spirit" of the world during World War II as embodied by "mechanism, 'scientific' materialism, [and] Socialism in either of its factions [then] at war" (Tolkien, *Letters*, 110). In the mythos of Middle-earth, such mechanism and scientific materialism is held within the One Ring; as a mechanical construct, its power to dominate and obliterate makes it a seemingly invincible weapon of war.

over all the peoples of Middle-earth – prompts a disregard for the environment and requires the exploitation of natural resources. Sauron garners his
power through the One Ring and wields it through the seemingly limitless armies at his disposal. They are his soldiers and also his slaves, as they
fear him beyond reason. Through their actions he threatens the ecological
stability of the land, for any land his armies inhabit quickly degrades:

> Mordor was a dying land, but it was not dead yet [...]. [L]ow scrubby
> trees lurked and clung, coarse grey grass-tussocks fought with the
> stones, and withered mosses crawled on them; and everywhere great
> writhing, tangled brambles sprawled. The sullen shriveled leaves of a
> past year hung on them, grating and rattling in the sad airs [...].[11]

The land is in a perpetual state of decay; there is no regeneration in this
environment. Rather than green, the colors evoked are grays and browns.
The devastation is immeasurable. Yet for Sauron and his Orc armies, the evils
of environmental degradation are furthest from their thoughts – it becomes
collateral damage. Sauron's endeavors are directly antagonistic toward the
people of Middle-earth and indirectly toward the environment. However,
Saruman, while still focused on attaining power, more pro-actively damages
nature through his undertakings, to the point that nature uproots itself to
fight against him, as is seen in the Ent attack on Isengard.

Saruman has his eyes set on a mechanized modernity, is a firm believer
and practitioner of technodominationism, and could not care less about
the environment. When speaking to Merry and Pippin, Treebeard says of
Saruman, "He has a mind of metal and wheels; and he does not care for
growing things, except as far as they serve him for the moment."[12] To fuel
his war machine and his armies, Saruman ventures into Fangorn Forest for
firewood. Of all the forests of Middle-earth, he selects the one most known
for being sentient. The trees themselves are *alive* and as conscious as human
beings.[13] Ents, as herdsmen of the forest, have a cultural memory, traditions,
and rules to abide by (like the Entmoot), and they experience and express
emotion. For example, Quickbeam, although typically a "gentle creature,"
now "hates Saruman all the more fiercely" because "his people [i.e., rowan
trees] suffered cruelly from orc-axes."[14] His emotions have been stirred by

---

11   J. R. R. Tolkien, *The Return of the King*, 2nd edn (Boston: Houghton Mifflin, 1993), 198.
12   J. R. R. Tolkien, *The Two Towers*, 2nd edn (Boston: Houghton Mifflin, 1993), 76.
13   In the early days Saruman frequented Treebeard's company and learned many things
     about the forest from the Ent. Saruman is well aware that the forest is not an ordinary
     forest (Tolkien, *Towers*, 76).
14   Tolkien, *Towers*, 173.

the intentional, massive destruction of tree people to fuel Saruman's technological advances.

Through Saruman's actions, Tolkien shows the dangers and consequences of disregarding the environment by vilifying those who use nature for their own gain, destroying it in the process. After all, Saruman is labeled a *murderer* in the text. We learn that Skinbark's tree-folk were "murdered" by Orcs under Saruman's command; the word choice here carries a heavy denotation.[15] According to the *OED*, to murder is to kill someone "unlawfully, spec. with malice aforethought," and "to kill (a person) wickedly, inhumanly, or barbarously."[16] It can also refer to "slaughter in a terrible manner, to massacre."[17] Tolkien, as a word craftsman conscious of language, chooses a term that both gives the trees personhood while also underscoring the malevolence behind the act of destruction – an act so heinous that Skinbark is forever traumatized, going away "into the high places" from where "he will not come down."[18] Quickbeam, whose Elven name is Bregalad, tells the most poignant narrative about Saruman's massacres of trees:

> "There were rowan-trees in my home," said Bregalad, softly and sadly, "rowan-trees that took root when I was an Enting, many many years ago in the quiet of the world. [...] And these trees grew and grew, till the shadow of each was like a green hall, and their red berries in the autumn were a burden, and a beauty and a wonder [...]. Then Orcs came with axes and cut down my trees. I came and called them by their long names, but they did not quiver, they did not hear or answer: they lay dead."[19]

The rowan trees have a history; they are part of a community. The closing words of the passage are haunting, bringing to mind an open field strewn with dead bodies – "they lay dead."

Saruman's technodominationist expansionism leaves an indelible mark on the land. This is most apparent when members of the Fellowship, along with Theoden and other Rohirrim, arrive at Wizard's Vale. The "pleasant, fertile" land was once "fair and green," but no more.[20] What the riders encounter is a "wilderness of weeds and thorns," where "[n]o trees grew [...] but among the rank grasses could still be seen the burden and axe-hewn stumps of ancient

---

15 Tolkien, *Towers*, 78.
16 *OED* s.v. *murder* (v.) def. I.1.a.
17 *OED* s.v. *murder* (v.) def. I.3.a.
18 Tolkien, *Towers*, 78.
19 Tolkien, *Towers*, 86.
20 Tolkien, *Towers*, 159.

groves."[21] As in the previous passage, Tolkien calls attention to age. These had been *ancient* groves, like Bregalad's rowan trees, until Saruman hewed them down. The ill treatment of nature is a heinous act, according to Tolkien, but it is even more so when the vegetation is irreplaceable. Such concern calls to mind the medieval groves that survived into modern times because of proper woodland management; tragically, some ancient trees only perished recently owing to less conservative use of the land. As environmental historian Oliver Rackham explains:

> By the thirteenth century A. D. woodland management was a fully-developed art with conservation as its chief objective; its success is measured by the many medieval woods known to have lasted, often with the same boundaries, for 700 years or more. In many areas more than half the woods named in medieval documents survived into the twentieth century and are either still there or have only recently succumbed to the less conservative land-uses of our own period.[22]

In Middle-earth, the loss of ancient trees occurs at the instigation of a power-hungry antagonist, but in modern England, as Rackham states, it is through human mismanagement of the land.

Elvencentrism: Deep Ecology, Ecosophy, and Elven Bioregionalism

The deep-ecology movement prioritizes the ecocentric over the anthropocentric. Its roots can be found in the Ecological Revolution of the mid-twentieth century, which attempted a shift in "perception, values, and lifestyles […] as a basis for redirecting the ecologically destructive path of modern industrial growth societies."[23] Deep ecology unifies rather than separates. It emphasizes the links between all elements within the natural world. As Fritjof Capra explains, "[deep ecology] does not see the world as a collection of isolated objects but rather as a network of phenomena that are fundamentally interconnected and interdependent."[24] Such interconnectedness can also lead to concern, as an ecocatastrophe in one geographical location can affect those

---

21 Tolkien, *Towers*, 159.
22 Oliver Rackham, *Ancient Woodland: Its History, Vegetation and Uses in England* (Colvend, UK: Castlepoint Press, 2003), 1. One example of proper woodmanship helping preserve trees is that of the ash tree. An unattended ash tree can collapse after about 200 years. When coppiced properly it can still be alive after 500 years (3).
23 George Sessions, "Preface," in *Deep Ecology for the Twenty-first Century*, ed. George Sessions (Boston and London: Shambhala, 1995), ix–xxviii [ix].
24 Fritjof Capra, "Deep Ecology: A New Paradigm," in *Deep Ecology*, 19–25 [20].

who live far away, creating a sense of global community. The 1960s and 1970s were witness to a plethora of environmental threats (from hydrogen- and nuclear-bomb testing, to oil spills), which in turn led to various manifestations of activism, ranging from literary responses to protests and the establishment of laws.[25]

Although there is no way to directly ascertain the influence of Tolkien's writings on the environmental movement, the parallels between the environmental degradation and conservation of Middle-earth and our own Earth are present. The popularity of *The Lord of the Rings* surged precisely in the 1960s and 1970s, and showcased a world torn between good and evil, between nature and mechanization.[26] In the Elves, Tolkien gave readers a community that, as deep ecology promotes, was "fundamentally interconnected and interdependent with nature" to the point that it is hard to separate the two. For instance, Sam ponders on this connection while in Lothlórien; he says to Frodo, "[the Elves] seem to belong here, more even than Hobbits do in the Shire. Whether they've made the land, or the land's made them, it's hard to say [...]."[27] It is a relationship with the land any environmentalist would envy.

The Elves, within their secluded realms, practice stylized forms of bioregionalism where nature's aesthetic quality is emphasized. Their intent is to maintain ecological aesthetic sustainability: the Elves not only care for nature, but also prompt it to flourish in its most beautiful state. While the Hobbits, for example, live in a highly functional "organic community," which hearkens to the small, craft-based community that practices sustainable forms of agriculture and is harmonious with nature, as defined by F. R. Leavis and Denys Thompson, the Elves focus their attention on nature's aesthetic potential; and as a well-tended English garden, nature must be pleasing to the eye.[28] Matthew Dickerson and Jonathan Evans touch on a similar point when they describe the environmentalism of the Elves as the more "sophisticated" one.[29]

---

25 Some of the major ecological responses at the time included the establishment of the following organizations and laws: World Wildlife Foundation (1961), Earth Day (1970), Clean Air Act [in the United States] (1970), Environmental Protection Agency [in the United States] (1970), Greenpeace (1971), Clean Water Act [in the United States] (1972), United Nations Conference on the Human Environment (1972), Endangered Species Act [in the United States] (1973), and Earth First! (1980).

26 With an estimated 50 million copies sold worldwide, Curry calls *The Lord of the Rings* the "biggest-selling single work of fiction this century" (*Defending*, 2). For more on Tolkien's popularity, see *The J. R. R. Tolkien Encyclopedia: Scholarship and Critical Assessment*, ed. Michael Drout (New York: Routledge, 2006). In particular, see the following entries: Mike Foster, "America in the 1960s: Reception of Tolkien," 14–15, Lisa Spangenberg, "Technological Subcultures: Reception of Tolkien," 636–37, and Anthony Burdge, "Gaming," 228–30.

27 J. R. R. Tolkien, *The Fellowship of the Ring*, 2nd edn (Boston: Houghton Mifflin, 1993), 376.

28 F. R. Leavis and Denys Thomson, "The Organic Community," in their *Culture and Environment: The Training of Critical Awareness* (London: Chatto and Windus, 1948), 87–92 [91].

29 Dickerson and Evans, *Ents, Elves*, 99.

Hobbits are *earthier*, and so is their relationship to nature. They are easily seen on their hands and knees in their gardens, tending to their plants. Eldar Elves, however, create the nature that surrounds them through "enchanting" powers at their disposal, allowing them to benefit larger tracts of land. The original use given to the Elven Rings of Power is, after all, to heal the hurts of Middle-earth, and later to maintain a high level of ecological aesthetic sustainability within the Elven lands. The Elves are susceptible to Sauron's proposal because with the rings they can "ward off the decays of time and postpone the weariness of the world."[30] Accordingly, in *The Lord of the Rings* the realms that possess these Rings find their level of nature surpassing all other expressions of nature outside their borders.[31]

In warding off decay and restoring nature, the Elves call to mind ecosophy, "a philosophy of ecological harmony or equilibrium"[32] that underscores ecological wisdom and is a foundational concept within deep ecology. Inside these Elven bioregions, nature is cared for and crafted above and beyond what other native Middle-earthlings can do – even green is greener. Outside, all is bland – and brown. When the Fellowship arrives in Lothlórien, one can see the difference: "[i]n winter here no heart could mourn for summer or for spring. No blemish or sickness or deformity could be seen in anything

---

[30] J. R. R. Tolkien, *The Silmarillion*, 2nd edn (Boston and New York: Houghton Mifflin, 1999), 288.

[31] Elrond keeps Vilya, the Ring of Air, in Rivendell, and Galadriel keeps Nenya, the Ring of Water, in Lothlórien. Once the One Ring is destroyed, the power held by the Elven Rings also diminishes. It is this "enchanting" quality of the Rings that allows them not only to guard the seclusion of the realms but also to maintain the *type* of nature within. Tolkien breaks down the concept of *power* as expressed between Sauron and the Elves. He writes:

> [The Elves'] "magic" is Art, delivered from many of its human limitations: more effortless, more quick, more complete (product, and vision in unflawed correspondence). And its object is Art not Power, sub-creation not domination and tyrannous re-forming of Creation [...]. The Enemy in successive forms is always [...] concerned with sheer Domination, and so the Lord of magic and machines. (Tolkien, *Letters*, 146)

For the Elves, the power of enchantment is put to artistic use. Owing to this artistic propensity in them, Tolkien also calls them "embalmers" (Tolkien, *Letters*, 197). *To embalm* is defined as "to preserve [...] from decay by other means" and also "to preserve from oblivion" (*OED* def. I.2., and 3.a., respectively). As embalmers or preserves of Middle-earth, Elves are intent on protecting nature's aesthetic quality from decay and environmental degradation. The creation of their secure nature-preserves highlights their reluctance to socialize with other peoples, and in doing so limit the ecobenefits to particular boundaries.

[32] Arne Naess, "The Shallow and the Deep, Long-Range Ecology Movement: A Summary," in *The Deep Ecology Movement: An Introductory Anthology*, ed. Alan Drengson and Yuichi Inoue (Berkeley, CA: North Atlantic Publishers, 1995), 3–10 [8].

that grew upon the earth. On the land of Lórien there was no stain."[33] The ecological wisdom of the Elves allows them to heal and maintain the land, creating an environmentally constructed space. This space, in turn, creates awareness in outsiders. While visiting Lórien, Frodo's experience heightens his awareness of nature and allows him to see the world through new eyes. Tolkien describes the experience as follows:

> [Frodo] laid his hand upon the tree beside the ladder: never before had he been so suddenly aware of the feel and texture of a tree's skin and of the life within it. He felt a delight in wood and the touch of it, neither as a forester nor as a carpenter; it was the delight of the living tree itself.[34]

The Elves nurture nature for the sake of nature, and not because of the gains it may afford them. As a product of an agriculturally focused community, Frodo is only now learning to understand his coexistence with the green world and connect with it at a deeper emotional level.

Ecological harmony and wellbeing is at the heart of Tolkien's elvencentrism, and Lothlórien is a prime example of an ecocentric green space. When Legolas describes the woods to Aragorn and Gimli, he is very detailed:

> There are no trees like the trees of that land. For in the autumn their leaves fall not, but turn to gold. Not till the spring comes and the new green opens do they fall, and then the boughs are laden with yellow flowers; and the floor of the wood is golden, and golden is the roof, and its pillars are of silver, for the bark of the trees is smooth and grey.[35]

It is a majestic woodland, unique in its beauty. However, the landscape changes completely once the Elves depart. Years later, after Aragorn's death, Arwen returns to Lothlórien to await her own death, and she finds a very different space. The woodland is described as "silent," and the "fading" mallorn trees are losing their leaves, even though it is not spring, as Legolas had previously explained.[36] The "ecological harmony or equilibrium" that the Elves provided, their ecosophy, is gone.

However, not all perceive the loss equally, since the astounding nature within the Elven bioregions does not typically benefit outsiders. Like the royal parks of the Middle Ages, these realms are marked off and separate, forbidding entry to those beyond the community. As the archeologist Oliver H. Creighton explains, medieval parks had two primary functions, to "keep

33 Tolkien, *Fellowship*, 365.
34 Tolkien, *Fellowship*, 366.
35 Tolkien, *Fellowship*, 349.
36 Tolkien, *Return* (Appendix A), 344.

game in and people out."[37] Elven bioregions keep nature in, protected, and people out. The principal realms portrayed in *The Silmarillion* and *The Lord of the Rings* are memorable for their seclusion.[38] The Eldar Elves have successfully labored at constructing barriers around their lands (whether these are physical barriers, or based on reputation). In the end they keep the environmental boons found in their lands unavailable to outsiders.

A Greener Postmedieval World

The love that the Elves have for their land, and their creations within it, is immense. Galadriel describes the Elves' emotional attachment to their land as "deeper than the deeps of the Sea."[39] When Galadriel speaks to Frodo of the evils of the One Ring, she says:

> Do you not see now wherefore your coming is to us as the footstep of Doom? For if you fail, then we are laid bare to the Enemy. Yet if you succeed, then our power is diminished, and Lothlórien will fade, and the tides of Time will sweep it away. We must depart into the West, or dwindle to a rustic folk of dell and cave, slowly to forget and to be forgotten.[40]

---

[37] Oliver H. Creighton, *Designs Upon the Land: Elite Landscapes of the Middle Ages* (Woodbridge, UK: Boydell, 2009), 123.

[38] The land of Doriath is also known as the "Land of the Fence," guarded by an invisible belt of power enforced by Melian the Maia, queen of the realm. Set in the center of a deep valley, framed by the tall Encircling Mountains, and reachable only through secret passageways, Gondolin is known as the "Hidden Rock" or "Hidden Kingdom," and bears the protection of Ulmo the Sea Valar in his promise to Turgon: "none shall mark thy going," he said, "nor shall any find there the hidden entrance against thy will." Its location remains secret until the betrayal of Maeglin (Tolkien, *Silmarillion*, 125). While Rivendell's location is well known to travelers, the kingdom is protected by high mountains on three of its sides and has the added protection of a river with a very strong current at the disposal of Elrond (Tolkien, *Fellowship*, 236). Elrond's control of the river not only exemplifies the seclusion of his realm but also highlights the power he has over the elements of nature. Lothlórien is located at the center of a forest, with marauding Orcs and any other unwelcomed guest kept at bay by the countless Elven guards that patrol its borders. However, the one protective measure that works best is its reputation. It has tapped into Middle-earth's fear factor. Boromir gives voice to this apprehension when he is reluctant to enter the forest as they approach its borders (Tolkien, *Fellowship*, 390). He says, "of that perilous land we have heard in Gondor, and it is said that few come out who once go in; and of that few none have escaped unscathed" (Tolkien, *Fellowship*, 352). He is so assuredly convinced of the dangers of Lothlórien that he would prefer to take a "plain road, though it led through a hedge of swords" than enter the Elven bioregion (Tolkien, *Fellowship*, 352).

[39] Tolkien, *Fellowship*, 380.

[40] Tolkien, *Fellowship*, 380.

She positions the fading of the land above that of her own people, for they have grown so intertwined with it that separating themselves from their stylized nature is impossible. Once they are gone, the land will change forever, and so will the Elves. They have nurtured nature's aesthetic potential. Slowly, they have crafted over the years a realm where the tall mallorn trees grow in circles, and where grass in the evening "glow[s] still in memory of the sun that had gone."[41] The Elves' impending departure from Middle-earth is further anguished by the loss of the nature they have guarded and cultivated.

Once the Elves have left Middle-earth, their ecological wisdom is also lost. As E. L. Risden explains, "destruction of the forest means destruction of life: when Lothlórien declines, the Elves depart Middle-earth, and with them goes beauty, knowledge, wisdom, and powers to see beyond the range of human skill and intellect."[42] But they also take their powers of environmental regeneration. Risden adds, "Tolkien's landscape in some cases romanticizes, but it never sentimentalizes: vast and varied, beautiful and perilous, it extends the range of experience and choice for all sentient beings."[43] His assessment is exact. Beyond the beauty we find within the Elven bioregions, Tolkien shows a perilous nature, like the Old Forest, an agricultural world in the Shire, and a wasteland in Mordor. Not all natures in Middle-earth are perfect or even safe, but they can be.

Time and again, Tolkien showcases the "ecological depth" of his work.[44] In the constructed environment of the Elven realms we find a beautified, sustainable, off-limits green space that is unique to Middle-earth. While the seclusion of the realms might seem elitist to some readers and a safety measure to others, what readers can take away is the concept of nurturing nature for the sake of nature.

Examining Tolkien's writings from an ecocritical perspective underscores the lens through which many see the Middle Ages. Fiction that falls under the neo-medievalism label is not only about journeys, battles, and monsters. It is also about the land. Onto a distant medieval-inspired landscape our society's fears and aspirations manifest themselves: Can we avoid the wasteland in our future? Through the allure of the medieval, Tolkien told a generation (and future generations) that our own present green space matters – we just have to work at making it greener.

---

41 Tolkien, *Fellowship*, 368.

42 E. L. Risden, *Tolkien's Intellectual Landscape* (Jefferson, NC: McFarland and Company, 2015), 200–1.

43 Risden, *Intellectual*, 201.

44 Dickerson and Evans find that Tolkien reflects the ecological depth John Elder calls for in literature that has environmental vision (xvi).

II

Interpretations

Fragmentary Dreams: John Aubrey's Medieval Heritage Construction

Katie Peebles

The English antiquary John Aubrey (1626–97), deeply concerned about the fate of fragmentary artifacts and distressed by the wartime destruction of religious monuments, set out to rescue the past by collecting premodern records and stories from many villages and arranging them into patterns of national significance. Aubrey himself published very little, but he circulated his work among friends in the newly formed Royal Society who were also engaged in collecting and organizing bits of knowledge in order to explain the natural world and, implicitly, the changing social world. His reconstruction of the medieval past is directed toward his own time, but most of his material was not read widely until it was edited and published by his intellectual inheritors, the antiquarians and folklorists of the eighteenth and nineteenth centuries.[1] His work never entirely disappeared, reappearing to remind scholars that the science of antiquarian research was as much a cultural definer of early modernity as the establishment of the physical sciences.[2] Both the difficulty and the joy in reading Aubrey lie in deciphering the indexical puzzle he presents so engagingly. In order to develop a fuller recreation of English medieval heritage after the physical and cultural destruction of the English

---

1   Michael Hunter, *John Aubrey and the Realm of Learning* (London: Duckworth, 1975), 202–8.
2   Rosemary Sweet observes that "the two sciences of natural history and antiquities explicated both the past and the present using the same method of inquiry," in *Antiquaries: The Discovery of the Past in Eighteenth-Century Britain* (London: Hambledon, 2004), 8. See also D. R. Woolf, Chap. 5: "Varieties of Antiquarianism," in *The Social Circulation of the Past: English Historical Culture, 1500–1730* (Oxford: Oxford University Press, 2003), and Kelsey Jackson Williams, *The Antiquary: John Aubrey's Historical Scholarship* (Oxford: Oxford University Press, 2016), 3–7.

Civil Wars, Aubrey tried to combine manuscripts, physical ruins and land-scapes, and local popular traditions.

In the aftermath of the turmoil and change of the Civil Wars, Aubrey attempted to recuperate what remained from earlier times. The temporally determining phrase he repeats most often is "before the Civil-warres."[3] This phrase, including his own youthful recollections and those of his older friends and relatives, marks a world of traditions, church survivals, and closer social relationships. Although Great Britain did not exist as a political entity until 1707, Aubrey followed the example of William Camden and other antiquarians in using the idea of "Britain" as specifically describing the early history of the island in the time of the Celts and Roman occupation, and more generally the idea of the country's past.[4] Aubrey saw both a duty and an opportunity to memorialize the island's history. In his conceptualization of the premodern past, Celtic Britain was transformed by Roman occupation, early Britain was invaded by Anglo-Saxons, and England was changed again by the Norman Conquest, leading to a remarkable period: "the Crusades to the Holy-warres were most magnificent and glorious."[5] The transformation from medieval Britain to modern England is the most dramatic and also the change of longest duration. This last change includes the Reformation and the separation of the Church of England from Rome (1532–36), the development of humanist and Baconian philosophy, and the Civil Wars (1642–60).[6] The destructiveness of the battles between royalist and parliamentary forces ended the tenuous existence of medieval elements that had lasted until then, leaving only physical and ideational fragments. Aubrey's efforts to record these fragments and make sense of them through ancient and medieval history produced an early form of medievalism.

---

3   John Aubrey, *Remaines of Gentilisme and Judaisme*, in *Three Prose Works*, ed. John Buchanan-Brown (Carbondale: Southern Illinois University Press, 1972), 131–304 (139, 157, 169 *et passim*). See also Williams, *The Antiquary*, 128–30.

4   Graham Parry explains that Camden's choice of title "was to describe Britain as a province of the Roman Empire," in *The Trophies of Time: English Antiquarians of the Seventeenth Century* (Oxford: Oxford University Press, 1995), 23. See also Angus Vine, "Copiousness, Conjecture and Collaboration in William Camden's *Britannia*," *Renaissance Studies* 28.2 (2014): 225–41 (231).

5   Bodleian Library, MS Aubrey 3, fol. 9v. Printed in *Wiltshire Collections. The topographical collections of John Aubrey, F.R.S., A.D. 1659–70, with illustrations*, corrected and enlarged by John Edward Jackson, pub. by the Wiltshire Archaeological and Natural History Society (London: Longman, 1862), 11. A digital facsimile is also available: <https://archive.org/details/wiltshiretopogra00aubr>, last accessed 2 September 2016.

6   See Robert Tittler, *The Reformation and the Towns in England: Politics and Political Culture, c.1540–1640* (Oxford: Oxford University Press, 1998); Diane Purkiss, *The English Civil War: Papists, Gentlewomen, Soldiers, and Witchfinders in the Birth of Modern Britain* (New York: Basic Books, 2006); Richard Cust, *The English Civil War* (New York: St. Martin's Press, 1997); and Robert Tombs, *The English and Their History* (New York: Knopf, 2014).

Antiquarianism covered a much broader field of fragments than only those of the medieval period, and there was a great deal of interest in the discovery of British Roman remains in the early modern period.[7] The movement of antiquarianism as it developed in the seventeenth and eighteenth centuries covered a large field of interests that engaged professional scholars and amateurs, generalists and specialists alike.[8] Much of Aubrey's attention, however, went to fragments that he associated with prehistoric Britain and Anglo-Norman England.[9] For him, ancient and medieval thought and belief encompassed everything that was supplanted by modern scientific inquiry. As Richard Bauman and Charles Briggs point out, Aubrey constructed himself as a modern subject through his collecting of ideational relics and physical traces of the past. This opposition is possible because he "drew the intellectual framework for his antiquarian investigations from Baconian Natural Philosophy, and saw the Civil Wars as marking the point of disjunction between the old times and the new."[10] Aubrey used his position as a modern subject to justify his interest in relics of the past.

Although Aubrey subscribed to the Royal Society's principles of rational inquiry, his ongoing collections of fragments attached to past cultures and rural communities would seem to contradict the project of naturalizing modernity. However, his collecting also opened the possibility for unity through cultural memorialization. By attaching troublesome fragments to a medieval history, he put them into a heritage context where they could be safely handled by his intellectual cohort and heirs. D. R. Woolf describes how politically sensitive antiquarianism was in England from the Reformation through the seventeenth century because "the collection of artifacts from the past [...] bore a superficial resemblance to the collection and adoration of relics" and evoked deeper fears about the dangers of heterodox beliefs and practices.[11] In Aubrey's work, fragmentary artifacts must be recorded because of the threat of their disappearance, and this fragmentary state – the loss of original function – also implicitly makes it safe to record them. Kate Bennett describes how "Aubrey's manuscripts are paper museums," a characterization that suggests the complexity of purpose

---

7   D. R. Woolf, "The Dawn of the Artifact: The Antiquarian Impulse in England, 1500–1730," in *Studies in Medievalism IV: Medievalism in England*, ed. Leslie J. Workman (Cambridge: D. S. Brewer, 1992), 18–23.

8   Sweet, *Antiquaries*, xiv–xvi.

9   Williams points out that Aubrey was more interested in the ancient past and the Renaissance in his work overall than in the medieval (*The Antiquary*, 158–59). I would add to this observation that conceptualizing medieval traditions was nevertheless key to Aubrey's understanding of national heritage and the contrast with modernity.

10   Richard Bauman and Charles L. Briggs, *Voices of Modernity: Language Ideologies and the Politics of Inequality* (Cambridge: Cambridge University Press, 2003), 121.

11   See Woolf, "The Dawn of the Artifact," 13.

behind his collections.[12] Rhetorically, the present cannot be threatened by objects on the verge of disintegration, and can instead gain cultural power by collecting and archiving them.

Aubrey's imaginative distinctiveness of an exotic past allows his mining of the past for traits of cultural heritage. Barbara Kirschenblatt-Gimblett describes this process in more recent collections: "Ethnographic artifacts […] become ethnographic by virtue of being defined, segmented, detached, and carried away by ethnographers."[13] Similarly, Aubrey made his fragments "antique" and deserving of antiquarian attention by removing them from any modern context and placing them in a framework suggestive of the past. The penchant for miscellaneous detail contributes to the diversity of his antiquarian collections. The thousands of bits of information he collected all contribute to a mosaic of the English past, highlighting multiple constituencies of one nation. Aubrey's continuing appeal may come from his reading of the past in the details of the present.

Aubrey is particularly interested in Wiltshire, and attributes his antiquarianism to the region he grew up in, rich in fragments of the past that suffered visible losses during his youth.[14] Bennett characterizes Aubrey's "antiquarianism as an emotional and purposeful response to neglect and ignorance."[15] Growing up in Wiltshire, he was surrounded by the post-Dissolution, pre-Civil Wars remains of religious monuments and artifacts. In his note "To the Reader" at the beginning of *Monumenta Britannica*, he comments, "I was inclined by my genius, from my childhood to the love of antiquities: and my fate dropt me in a country most suitable for such enquiries."[16] Aubrey's story about his origin as an antiquarian scholar is defined by his ties to the region that was once the heart of the Anglo-Saxon kingdom of Wessex. He recounts how:

> in my grandfathers dayes, the Manuscripts flew about like Butterflies: All Musick bookes, Account bookes, Copie bookes &c. were covered with old manuscripts, as wee cover them now with blew Paper or Marbled

---

12   Kate Bennett, "General Introduction," in *Brief Lives* with *An Apparatus for the Lives of our English Mathematical Writers*, vol. 1, ed. Kate Bennett (Oxford: Oxford University Press, 2015), lxxvi.

13   Barbara Kirshenblatt-Gimblett, *Destination Culture: Tourism, Museums, and Heritage* (Berkeley: University of California Press, 1998), 1.

14   Ruth Scurr brings out this sense of Aubrey's motivation in her creative biography *John Aubrey: My Own Life* (London: Chatto & Windus, 2015), organizing his own letters, personal notes, and other historical sources into a diary.

15   Kate Bennett, "John Aubrey and the Rhapsodic Book," *Renaissance Studies* 28.2 (2014): 317–32 (328).

16   Aubrey, *Monumenta Britannica*, vol. 1, ed. John Fowles and Rodney Legg (Boston: Little, Brown, 1980), 17.

Paper; and the Glovers at Malmesbury made great Havock of them, and Gloves were wrapt up no doubt in many good pieces of antiquity.[17]

The young Aubrey also saw the rector of Yatton Keynel use manuscript pages as stoppers for barrels of ale, and remembered: "He sayd nothing did it so well, which me thought did grieve me then to see."[18] Ruin was inevitable, whether through human action or natural disaster, but Aubrey hoped the past could be redeemed through scholarly interest.

Aubrey expresses the appeal of the worn and distressed, formative in his approach to interpreting decayed monuments: "the eie and mind is no lesse affected with these stately ruines than they would have been when standing and entire. They breed in generous mindes a kind of pittie; and set the thoughts a-worke to make out their magnificence as they were when in perfection."[19] His project is to reconstruct antiquities through imagination, but this method is ultimately limited by everything that has been lost. In order to make up for the unavoidable presence of loss, Aubrey insists on the contemporaneous viewer's responsiveness to the prompting of the ruins. His evocation of a state of "perfection" might be understood to signify a complete, intact structure, but it even more strongly suggests the loss of a deeper perfection: the loss of the world (including a countryside and families) that the ruins were built for. Bauman and Briggs describe his purpose: "The antiquary's task is the interpretive reconstruction of the decontextualized fragment."[20] Aubrey sought a picture of a coherent past world that he could only perceive through the creative juxtaposition of fragments, giving a new context to the items he identified.[21]

Aubrey was an early member of the Royal Society (chartered in 1662) and served on many of the Society's committees and as a cataloger for its Repository.[22] His group of friends included Anthony Wood, a historian of Oxford; Robert Hooke; Sir Christopher Wren, who made several efforts to secure agreeable employment for him; and Edward Lhwyd, a Welsh antiquarian.[23] He donated books and manuscripts to the Society, as well as

17   Aubrey, *Memoires of Naturall Remarques in the County of Wilts*, Royal Society MS 92 (221); qtd. by Elizabeth Yale, *Sociable Knowledge: Natural History and the Nation in Early Modern Britain* (Philadelphia: University of Pennsylvania Press, 2016), 205–6.

18   *Memoires of Naturall Remarques in the County of Wilts*, RS MS 92 (221); qtd. by Yale (2016), 205–6.

19   Bodl. MS Aubrey 3, fol. 11 (*Wiltshire Collections*, 4).

20   Bauman and Briggs, *Voices of Modernity*, 121.

21   Williams characterizes Aubrey's methodology as "imaginative reconstruction" (*The Antiquary*, 49).

22   William Poole, *John Aubrey and the Advancement of Learning* (Oxford: Bodleian Library, 2010), 25–29.

23   Hunter, *John Aubrey and the Realm of Learning*, 15, 32.

to other educational groups and institutions. Inspired by Bacon's essays, Aubrey was committed to the Society as the engine for developing and implementing a universal and scientific system for organizing knowledge. The Society was also highly social.[24] Bauman and Briggs describe Aubrey's world as characterized by "the learned, 'ingeniose,' intellectual, 'modern' conversation [...] to be found in the elite male fellowship of the university and the coffeehouse."[25] His persistent and imaginative collection of details spread its influence among his friends and rippled out in larger circles. Richard Dorson highlighted his role as an explicit part of folklore's lineage for modern British and American folklorists in *The British Folklorists* (1968) and thus part of the use of history in the authorizing of folklore as an independent field.[26]

The scholarly figure of Aubrey nevertheless became something of an intellectual outsider, pushed out of the main current of modernization. Michael Hunter explains that Aubrey's historical writing has "something in common with the rather old-fashioned tradition of historical writing that preceded the more sophisticated antiquarian movement which reached its climax with Dugdale."[27] What Hunter refers to is the exhaustive, detailed systematization that Sir William Dugdale managed so much better than Aubrey. Antiquarians like Dugdale, John Selden, Edmund Gibson, and Thomas Tanner were an early part of shaping the discipline of modern historical scholarship through their methodical, comprehensive approach and publications.[28] Aubrey's own methods were supplanted by the increasing scientization of antiquarianism, and eighteenth- and nineteenth-century scholars and editors had an ambiguous relationship to his work.[29] On one hand, Aubrey had been an original member of the Royal Society and had left an enormous mass of largely unedited manuscript notes ready for any of the many new antiquaries looking for a project.[30] Some of his informa-

24 Bennett, *Brief Lives*, xxxi–xxxii.
25 Bauman and Briggs, *Voices of Modernity*, 80.
26 Richard M. Dorson describes the transmission of this lineage and argues, "Although not published for nearly two centuries, the *Remaines* enjoyed a considerable reputation among antiquaries [...] Aubrey directed the concept of antiquities as formulated by Leland and Camden toward local tradition and called attention to the disappearance of popular customs in the vortex of social and political revolution." *The British Folklorists: A History* (Chicago: University of Chicago Press, 1968), 10.
27 Hunter, *John Aubrey and the Realm of Learning*, 154.
28 For details of their careers, see Parry, *Trophies of Time*.
29 Scurr provides an overview of the reception and editorial history of Aubrey's work in "Aubrey's Afterlife," *John Aubrey: My Own Life*, 425–32.
30 Among these influences was the *Monumenta Britannica*, which circulated in sections, and the *Chronologia Architectonica*, partially published in *The Fashion of Windows in Civil and Ecclesiastical Buildings, Before the Conquest* (London, 1766) (Sweet, *Antiquaries*, 257); the *Miscellanies* and natural history notes also attracted attention. Aubrey donated his

tion was unique and irreplaceable due to the erosion or willful destruction of monuments. All of his material carried a certain weight of authenticity simply from its having been recorded two centuries closer to the original antiquities. On the other hand, the projects of the newer antiquaries engaged in the development of the modern social sciences required a level of systematization that is simply not present in Aubrey's work because it was not methodically designed, recorded, and analyzed in the way that most nineteenth-century historical and folkloristic projects were. The sense of dubious necessity comes through in John Edward Jackson's remark that "Aubrey may not have been always quite accurate, but [...] it is something to have copied at all."[31] Scholars like Jackson (1805–91), John Britton (1771–1857), and John Brand (1744–1806) who edited or incorporated Aubrey's work into their own were working with the vision of a systematic history, constituted by a series of local studies that would include and explain all the physical and ideational survivals throughout Great Britain. The different epistemological interests of Aubrey and Jackson become apparent in the case of Malmesbury Abbey. In a lyrical mood, Aubrey comments, "Where the Choir was, now grass grows, where anciently were buried Kings and great men." Jackson supports the statement, based on an archaeological expedition in 1853, and makes it more precise in a footnote: "The site of King Athelstan's grave is now under an asparagus bed."[32] The contrast of these two conclusions exemplifies the degree of change from Aubrey's imaginative antiquarianism to the methodical nineteenth-century science of antiquarianism. Jackson uses the irony of this contrast to dramatize a basic change in worldview, implying that a touch of medieval romance and mysticism still lingered in Aubrey's own writing. Aubrey himself had come to gain some of the characteristics of an antiquity.

In his own time, Aubrey firmly anchors medievalism in expressions of post-medieval modernity for his intellectual descendants.[33] His vision is largely defined by his sense of home in Oxford and Wiltshire; medieval examples he finds in other places are often related back to local examples. Even when Aubrey constructs an overall integrating theory explaining a particular aspect of medieval antiquities, his material is rooted in local

---

manuscripts to the Ashmolean Museum, and Bennett comments that "donation of his manuscripts, in particular his biographical manuscripts, to a safe repository, was [...] his preferred form of publication for them" (*Brief Lives*, lxxv).

31 *Wiltshire Collections*, ix.

32 *Wiltshire Collections*, 255. Aubrey's phrasing here may be inspired by a quotation from Ovid, "Iam seges est ubi Troia fuit," which he cites in *Monumenta Britannica* (Williams, *The Antiquary*, 55).

33 Parry characterizes Aubrey's view of the Middle Ages "as a time of splendid building when learning was cultivated in hospitable monasteries across the length and the breadth of the land" (*Trophies of Time*, 296).

evidence. For example, he uses Oxford churches and colleges to work out a chronology of how the styles of Gothic windows developed.[34] He notes "that the Fashions of Building do last about 100 Years, or less; the Windows the most remarkable. Hence one may give a guess about what Time the Building was. The Colleges in Oxford (by Mr Wood's Illustration) will give the best measure for this that I know."[35] He diagrams types of windows in his manuscript pages, outlining them as a standard for comparison.[36] Another university's windows are helpful for dating one at Aubrey's family home: "Mem. This kind of Cross buttonnée is in the Windows of the Gallery over King's College Chapel in Cambridge, & also in the Library Window which is at the Bottom of the Chapel, which College & magnificent Chapel was built by King Henry the Sixth [...]. Wherefore I conclude about his Reighn the Hall & Dining-Room at Easton-Pierse was built."[37] Buildings themselves could communicate stories of the past as, for example, the inn at Walsingham that still reminded local informants of a royal pilgrimage. Aubrey writes:

> King ...... and his Queen came down the Hill [...] bare-foot (for they sayd 'twas holy ground) in Pilgrimage, & lay in the chamber that is now the Hay-Loft of the <u>Falcon</u>; it was a painted roome: and I suppose it was a receptacle or Inne there for Pilgrims: or els they would have layn at the Lord Abbotts.[38]

Aubrey thinks the king was one of the Edwards, but neither he nor his source knew for sure.[39] The emphasis on the room instead of the king suggests that this local memory was kept alive by showing the inn that provided shelter to medieval pilgrims, rather than by remembering a legend associated with a particular king. These familiar connections attach meaning to a project of abstract systematization.

---

[34] See Olivia Horsfall Turner, "'The Windows of This Church Are of Several Fashions': Architectural Form and Historical Method in John Aubrey's 'Chronologia Architectonica,'" *Architectural History* 54 (2011): 171–93, for a full, illustrated analysis of his groundbreaking architectural history.

[35] Bodl. MS Aubrey 16, fol. 1 r.

[36] Hunter points out that this project was "the first attempt at a history of medieval architecture in this country." Michael Hunter, "Introduction," in *Preserving the Past*, ed. Michael Hunter (Stroud: Alan Sutton Publishing, 1996), 1–16 (3).

[37] Bodl. MS Aubrey 16, fol. 4r.

[38] Bodl. MS Top. Gen. c. 24, fol. 192r (*Monumenta Britannica*, ed. Fowles and Legg, 378).

[39] Many King Edwards visited the shrine at Walsingham; see Gary Waller, *Walsingham and the English Imagination* (New York: Routledge, 2016), 22–23. Edward IV and Elizabeth Woodville may have made a pilgrimage in 1469; see J. L. Laynesmith, *The Last Medieval Queens: English Queenship 1445–1503* (Oxford: Oxford University Press, 2005), 111.

Gothic architecture also has the advantage of visual magnificence to Aubrey's eyes: "The Normans then came and taught them civility & building: which though it was Gothiq (as also their Policy Feudalis Lex) yet they were magnificent."[40] Modernity offered a hope for political centralization and clarity that Aubrey saw as lacking in medieval England, calling Anglo-Norman polity "a Nest of Boxes."[41] Whatever the Anglo-Saxons and Normans lacked, Aubrey takes pride in a past complexity, a source of richness for a more rational modern system. As part of his reconstruction of medieval society, he has an idyllic view of the lord's hall and the idea of close feudal relationships touching everyone in the community. His introduction to "An Essay towards a Description of the North Division of Wiltshire" presents a lyrical description of what he imagined as feudal life.[42] While Aubrey idealized certain aspects of the medieval past, he disapproved of what he understood as the absolute power of individual lords, recounting their powers of punishment and death through the surviving machinery now turned into curious antiquities. The point that seems most alien to Aubrey, though, is the idea that secular and religious lords could execute their subjects without interference or correction from any kind of law.[43] In Aubrey's worldview, the king is the central figure of Law – the ideal self-regulating regulator. This emphasis on the legal exercise of power creates another dimension of distance between the present and the medieval past, which may have been particularly important to Aubrey after living through a tumultuous period of wars with competing sides arguing for the authority of law. Aubrey's own family was subjected to a high fine levied by Parliament in 1646.[44] Arbitrary local lords were replaced by parliamentary fees and charges.

Aubrey admires a type of feudalism he calls the "Gothic method" defined by "knight service."[45] In his prospectus for an ideal plan for primary education, he wants the boys to model themselves after Chaucer's Knight and to understand that feudalism is the best method of expansionist government, "of settling government after conquests," a concern that was even more pressing in Aubrey's time than in the medieval past he imagines.[46] An element he identifies as a feature of this "settling" was a tradition of tournaments, from Roman circuses to Gothic tilts and King Arthur's tournaments,

40 Bodl. MS Aubrey 3, fol. 10v (*Wiltshire Collections*, 7). Williams points out that Aubrey preferred Roman and Roman-inspired architecture (*The Antiquary*, 82–84). Nevertheless, he was impressed by Gothic buildings and made extensive notes on their details.
41 Bodl. MS Aubrey 3, fol. 10v (*Wiltshire Collections*, 7).
42 Bodl. MS Aubrey 3, fol. 9 (*Wiltshire Collections*, 8–10).
43 *Remaines of Gentilisme and Judaisme*, 303; *Wiltshire Collections*, 7.
44 David Tylden-Wright, *John Aubrey: A Life* (London: HarperCollins, 1991), 55.
45 *Aubrey on Education: A Hitherto Unpublished Manuscript by the Author of Brief Lives*, ed. J. E. Stephens (London: Routledge, 1972), 129.
46 *Aubrey on Education*, 132, 129.

ending with the departure of Charles I from London. He explains, "After the comeing-in of the Gothes, these Roman Games and Cirques, were turned into Tilts and Tournaments: *e.g.* the Annuall solempnity of the Knights of King Arthur's Round Table at Pentecost – &c. Tilting breath'd its last when King Charles 1ˢᵗ left London."[47] The tradition survives the departure of Roman culture, rejuvenated by an Arthurian tradition that avoids Aubrey's more usual distinction of Saxon and Norman cultural succession, but cannot be preserved in the royal vacuum created by the Civil Wars. In describing a more destructive form of combat, Aubrey notes that "the very words of Trepeget and Mangonel, I find nowhere but in Sir Geoffrey Chaucer's Tale of ...... They were engines of battery before the invention of cannons."[48] The reference is to the *Romaunt of the Rose*, where False Semblant is explaining the danger of hypocrisy undermining "Holy Churche" from within so that "without stroke it mote be take / of trepeget or mangonel," a concern also relevant to Aubrey's culture.[49] He also quotes from Chaucer's *Treatise on the Astrolabe* in justifying the study of the astrolabe in his educational plan, as a way to interest young boys in mathematics.[50] Aubrey cites this medieval author as part of his description of premodern defenses and warfare, and as a way to interest modern students in higher mathematics, incorporating the medieval into the modern.

Aubrey was also interested in modern uses of natural resources, describing them in *The Natural History of Wiltshire*.[51] The most obvious sign of cultural disruption between historical periods is the transformation of physical landscapes. What is lost when the Celts are displaced by the Saxons foreshadows the major losses Aubrey saw in the modern world's succession to Anglo-Norman culture. One kind of loss is framed in terms of scientific exploitation, even though it refers to a medieval resource; this is rhetorically different and in a more practical register than his reflections on church windows and superstitions. Aubrey comments that around the village of Seene is a high natural density of rich iron ore and evidence of early metalworking, but that this resource was neglected and that now the ore cannot be exploited since "the forest was destroyed about 1630, and now no wood left in the parish to melt it."[52] The project of modernity actively disrupts itself; a technological

---

[47] *Remaines of Gentilisme and Judaisme*, 301.
[48] Bodl. MS Top. Gen. c. 24, fol. 212r (*Monumenta Britannica*, ed. Fowles and Legg, 431).
[49] Geoffrey Chaucer, *Romaunt of the Rose*, ll. 6271, 6278–79, in *The Complete Poetry and Prose of Geoffrey Chaucer*, 3rd edn, ed. John H. Fisher and Mark Allen (Boston: Wadsworth Cengage Learning, 2012), 801.
[50] *Aubrey on Education*, 100.
[51] See Yale, *Sociable Knowledge*, especially Chap. 4.
[52] *Wiltshire Collections*, 45.

capacity available in the Middle Ages is no longer accessible. In another case, the natural resource remains while its social use has disappeared:

> in the hedges of the Priory-downe are yet a great number of Berbery-trees which 'tis likely the Nunnes used for Confection, and they taught the young ladies that were bred-up there; for in those dayes the women were bred at Nunneries; no such schools as at Hackny & Sarf for women till since the Reformation.[53]

However, seventeenth-century receipt books still give instructions for preserving barberries.[54] Because of Aubrey's focus on the medieval past and its lost community of women, he omitted or missed seeing continuing uses of the fruit.[55]

Destruction could result even from restoration. In 1660, the towns-people of Malmesbury shot off cannons to celebrate the birthday of the newly restored King Charles II. Later that night, the west tower of the abbey collapsed. Aubrey reports:

> When the great rejoicing was on the King's birth-day, 1660, for the return of King Charles 2ᵈ., viz. 29ᵗʰ May, here were so many and so great vollies of shot, by the inhabitants of the Hundred, that the noise so shook the pillars of the Tower, that one pillar and the two parts above fell down that night.[56]

The east tower had already fallen, between 1500 and 1510, and the abbey had already been converted into a parish church in 1541, during the Reformation. But the tower collapse marks the most dramatic moment of physical transformation in the abbey's history. It is ironic that the building, and even a little of the stained glass, survived the depredations of the recent wars, only to suffer at the hands of those celebrating the restoration of the old order.

---

[53] Bodl. MS Aubrey 3, fol. 67v.

[54] Danille Christensen discussed early modern barberry preservation with sugar or brine in her talk (July 19, Library of Congress, <https://www.loc.gov/folklife/events/BotkinAr-chives/BotkinArchives.html>, last accessed 2 September 2016). Examples included Mary Mott, "Manuscript Cookery Book," 1679 (Katherine Golden Bitting Collection on Gastronomy, Library of Congress, Rare Book and Special Collections) and Mary Hellier, "To Make Paste of Barbery's," in "Mary Hellier Cookery Book," Recipe Books Collection (MMC-1644), 1740 (Library of Congress, Manuscript Division).

[55] Aubrey does note the survival of some medieval recipes, probably medicinal: "The Monks were good Chemists, & invented many good Receipts: which they imparted to their Peni-tents: & so are handed downe to their great-grandchildren, a great many varieties." Bodl. MS Aubrey 3, fol. 11r (*Wiltshire Collections*, 12).

[56] *Wiltshire Collections*, 255.

The building could not be fully restored, and neither could the town return to a cultural point preceding the regicide of Charles I. Although Aubrey does not specifically remark on this collapse, it is emblematic of the antiquary's hopeless longing: even in the moment of the king's return, which would indicate a return to an earlier world, the monument of the earlier world, necessary for its restoration, is finally destroyed.[57]

Malmesbury was a particularly significant place for Aubrey because it was the home of two men he identified as intellectual ancestors. William of Malmesbury exemplified the best of medieval learning, and Thomas Hobbes, born within sight of the abbey, was an emblematic part of the birth of the new, modern philosophy. Aubrey explains William's service to the study of history:

> This great Historian, wrote the History of his Times, and dedicated it to a naturall son of William the Conqueror. He wrote also the Historie of the Abbey of Glastonbury, which is in the Librarie of – College in Manuscript. He says himselfe, that he was the next that wrote after Venerable Bede.[58]

Aubrey uncritically accepts William's claim to have inherited Bede's mantle, but simultaneously frames it as indirect speech rather than his own assertion. The reporting of the claim ties Bede and William more closely together, in the same cultural period and across the division of the Norman Conquest, for Aubrey. The theme of indebtedness to previous scholars for historical recording, creating a debt that can only be repaid through gratitude, comes through strongly from William to Aubrey. Aubrey may himself hope to become part of this chain of historians, to eventually have his own work repaid with gratitude by future readers. Aubrey also uses his imagination of William's method as a warrant for collecting local, contemporary accounts. He explains that, since William supposedly had few written histories to draw from, William "added that he was fain to pick up his History out of old Traditional Songs."[59] This connection of source and material continued in the development of British

---

57   Abbey preservationists are still adapting to changes resulting from the seventeenth century. New damage in the fabric of the building was discovered only recently. The deterioration of the extraordinary Norman sculptural program that covers both the exterior and interior of the south porch is now believed to have been caused not only by modern air pollution, but also by corrosion seeping down from the armaments that were stored in the parvise (the room over the porch) over 300 years ago (*The Guide to Malmesbury Abbey* [Derby: English Life Publications Ltd, 1994]). Some changes, cultural as well as physical, become apparent very slowly.

58   Bodl. MS Aubrey 3, fol. 36r (*Wiltshire Collections*, 254).

59   Bodl. MS Aubrey 11, fol. 14v. See Adam Fox, "Remembering the Past in Early Modern England: Oral and Written Tradition," *Transactions of the Royal Historical Society*, Sixth Series, 9 (1999): 233–56, for a fuller discussion of this traditional chain of authority.

folkloristics: the history in old songs authorizes their preservation, but the songs must be marked as traditional in order to certify the history.

An implicit inheritor of the "great Scholars" was Thomas Hobbes, by virtue of his birthplace just west of Malmesbury Abbey. The schoolboy Aubrey met Hobbes when he returned to Wiltshire in 1634 to visit their mutual school-master Robert Latimer, and they were friends until Hobbes's death.[60] Hobbes published *Leviathan*, his most famous work, from France in 1651, and its universalizing vision of contemporary political forces applies to local as well as national forces. The town of Malmesbury, as well as the rest of Great Britain, had to adapt to new perspectives and new interpretations of political systems. Hobbes's theory problematizes the relationship between polities within a larger organization, predicting, "And as for very little Common-wealths, be they Popular, or Monarchicall, there is no humane wisdom can uphold them, longer then the Jealousy lasteth of their potent Neighbours."[61] Aubrey's work was based on a cumulative premise that the description of each place's medi-eval past adds up, with others, to describe the nation. Hobbes's understanding that a place's self-definition depends on a resistance to its neighbors, a distinc-tion formed from both an unavoidable distance and a competitive desire, is reflected in Aubrey's attention to the particularity of each place.

Changes in local government had their own impact on Aubrey's antiquities and his response to them. Aubrey critiques the land enclosures of the previous century, asserting that they made more people dependent on the parish.[62] In this case, medievalism anticipated contemporary political culture – enclosures only became a serious political issue in the late eighteenth century.[63] Aubrey frames the problem of enclosures in terms of the present economic complica-tions for each village. However, enclosures also represented a dramatic change from what he imagined as the feudal model existing throughout the Middle Ages, in which a lord was dependent on peasants who helped to till the land he administered in return for protection of their own fields and common pasturage. Aubrey's imagined peasants were independent workers, not hired laborers, and had their own responsibilities. Regarding the formerly common park and allocated plots in his childhood village of Kington St. Michael, Aubrey identifies the source of the villagers' losses:

---

60 Bennett, *Brief Lives*, xxxiv–v, xci.
61 Thomas Hobbes, *Leviathan*, ed. C. B. MacPherson (New York: Penguin Books, 1982), II: 25.
62 "Since the Reformation and Inclosures aforesaid, these parts have swarmed with poore people. The Parish of Calne pays to the poore (1663) £ 500 per annum: and the Parish of Chippenham little lesse, as appears by the Poor's bookes there. Inclosures are for the private, not for the public good. For a shepherd and his dogge, or a milk mayd, can manage that land, that upon arable employed the hands of severall scores of labourers" (*Wiltshire Collections*, 11).
63 Tombs, *The English and Their History*, 492–93.

Nicholas Snell (formerly Reeve to the Lord Abbot, who bought the Inheritance with the Areares of Rent detained in his hands, foreseeing the Destruction of Church Lands) [...] taken from them by their new landlord Snell, so heretofore they were able to keep a whole plough: But since having but worke enough for halfe a plough they live poorely, & needily.[64]

The Dissolution had a destructive effect on the traditional economy of village society. Before the selling of church lands, the ill-effects of Nicholas Snell's corruption were at least confined to the officials whose rents he was skimming.

As part of the "modernization" of agriculture, other medieval remnants are assigned new uses. In Biddeston, the change is particularly excruciating. Aubrey often cites the deterioration in the fabric of church buildings since the wars, but in this village the changes in religious and agricultural practices conspire together. Aubrey describes how St. Peter's Church had been subjected to sordid practical need: "Here are two parish churches – that at the lower end of the village is St Peters church, formerly a prettie little church, but now lamentably ruined, and converted to a barne, and nothing of antiq. there."[65] Only the ghost of its past charm interests Aubrey. He directly attributes other changes to the destruction of the Civil Wars. Aubrey refers to coats of arms and stained glass broken by "barbarous soldiers."[66] The soldiers spoiled not only the beauty of the stained-glass windows, but also a significant part of the village history Aubrey sought. The loss of such a large material part of its heritage threatens the continuity of the village. Is an extra barn more important to physical survival than a medieval church is to community survival? Aubrey makes no mention of a new church. The soldiers destroyed the medieval ornamentation of the church, but local inhabitants completed the destruction of its religious and historical significance by turning the church into a barn. Aubrey does not consider the possibility that the inhabitants could have been trying to make the best of a bad situation, after the soldiers' destruction. It seems too irreligious, especially for rural villagers whom Aubrey normally sees as the conservative holders of superstition. He regretted the loss of what he saw as a medieval uniformity of religion, while dismissing that particular religion as superstitious.

In addition to the widespread damage to physical monuments and landscapes, the Civil Wars also destroyed elements of ideational folklore: "Warres

---

64 Bodl. MS Aubrey 3, fol. 76v (*Wiltshire Collections*, 131).
65 Bodl. MS Aubrey 3, fol. 106v (*Wiltshire Collections*, 53).
66 Aubrey remarks that people in Bedwyn Magna "tell in the windowes of this aisle were more escutcheons and painted glasse which the barbarous soldiers spoyled." *Wiltshire Collections*, 374.

not only extinguish Religion and Lawes: but Superstition: and no suffimen is a greater fugator of Phantosmes, than gunpowder."[67] In the *Remaines of Gentilisme and Judaisme*, a collection of superstitions and country traditions, this comment is ambiguous. Superstitions and phantasms inhibit the scientific progress Aubrey the Fellow of the Royal Society was engaged in promulgating, but their disappearance would emphasize the dramatic and destructive changes English society had undergone. Aubrey also imagines how the disappearance of this last vestige of medieval belief affects education, informal and formal:

> When I was a Child (& so before the Civill Warrs) the fashion was for old women & mayds to tell fabulous stories nightly and of Sprights, and walking of Ghosts etc.: this was derived downe from mother to daughter &c [...] for the Divines say, deny spirits, you are an Atheist. When the Warrs came with the Liberty of Conscience & Liberty of Inquisition – the phantoms vanished. Now children fear no such things, having heard not of them, and are not check'd with such fancy.[68]

Aubrey categorizes the contemporary superstitions he found around him as premodern through a rhetoric of destruction and disappearance.

While the destroyed forest of Seene and St. Peter's Church could not be easily resurrected, Aubrey takes it upon himself to bring the standing stones of Avebury to the public attention. "This old Monument does as much exceed in greatness the so renowned Stoneheng, as a Cathedral doeth a parish Church: so that by its grandure one might presume it to have been an Arch-Temple of the Druids." [69] In the *Monumenta Britannica*, he sets out his position for their precedence among British religious monuments as the greatest and least ruined, although strangely neglected by scholars.[70] The earthworks had been noted in records for centuries, and the 1610 edition of William Camden's *Britannia* by Philemon Holland mentions the stones, but Aubrey was the first visitor to record the monumental relics in detail. [71] In the history of archaeology, Aubrey is best known for his work on Avebury in which he illustrated some features that have since disappeared, and for his

---

67 *Remaines of Gentilisme and Judaisme*, 207. See also Henk Dragstra, "'Before woomen were Readers': How John Aubrey Wrote Female Oral History," in *Oral Traditions and Gender in Early Modern Literary Texts*, ed. M. E. Lamb and Karen Bamford (Aldershot: Ashgate, 2008), 41–56 (43–44).

68 Bodl. MS Aubrey 3, fol. 30r (*Wiltshire Collections*, 15). See also Fox, "Remembering the Past in Early Modern England," 234.

69 Bodl. MS Top. Gen. c. 24, fol. 32v (*Monumenta Britannica*, ed. Fowles and Legg, 36).

70 Bodl. MS Top. Gen. c. 24, fol. 31r (*Monumenta Britannica*, ed. Fowles and Legg, 33).

71 Peter J. Ucko, Michael Hunter, Alan J. Clark, and Andrew David, *Avebury Reconsidered: From the 1660s to the 1990s* (London: Unwin Hyman, 1991), 8–9.

insistence that, contrary to Inigo Jones's architectural judgment that Stone-henge was built by the Romans, the groups of standing stones were built by early Britons for religious purposes.[72] Many stones were knocked down and buried circa 1300–30, but most of the irreparable destruction was done in the seventeenth and early eighteenth centuries, when stones were deliberately shattered and used to build houses and a Nonconformist chapel.[73]

Aubrey frames his largest antiquarian discovery as the result of a hunting trip with friends: "the chase led us (at length) thorough the village of Aubury, into the closes there: where I was wonderfully surprized at the sight of those vast stones, of which I had never heard before."[74] His narrative completely encapsulates his first exploration of the stone circles of Avebury within the formula of a gentlemen's hunt. He sets off with his friends in pursuit of a fox, then leaves them to explore the remains of this gigantic monument, and finally rejoins them for dinner when he, "(steered by the cry of the hounds) overtook the company, and went with them to Kynnet, where was a good hunting dinner provided."[75] The outcome of the fox hunt remains undetermined, but Aubrey satisfies the reader with the success of his antiquarian hunt.

Although Aubrey does not consider the Avebury monuments themselves to be medieval, he finds it useful to interpret them through analogy to medieval structures, what we now see as the lens of medievalism:

> When a Traveller rides along by the Ruins of a Monastery, he knows by the manner of building, *sc.* Chapell, Cloysters &c., that it was a Convent, but of what Order, *sc.* Benedictine, Dominican, &c., it was,

---

72 Avebury is now dated to approximately 2600 BCE, much earlier than Aubrey's imagined construction by Druids (Aubrey Burl, *Prehistoric Avebury* [New Haven, CT: Yale University Press, 1979]).

73 Burl, *Prehistoric Avebury*, 36–40, 46. Aubrey also notes that in Amesbury, "The inhabitants about the Amesburys have defaced this piece of antiquity since my remembrance: one large stone was carried away to make a bridge. It is generally averred hereabout, that pieces (or powder) of these stones put into their wells, do drive away the toads, with which their wells are much infested, and this course they use still" (*Monumenta Britannica*, ed. Fowles and Legg, 87). Stonehenge was only preserved because of its undesirability as building material: "Mr... Conyers Apothecary at the White Lyon in Fleetstreet hath an old manuscript Roll of the time of Henry VI, which confirms, that Aurelius Ambrosius was buried at Stoneheng. Those times were troublesome, and by that meanes there might not be erected for him any magnificent Regal monument: but had there been one of marble or freestone, the country people would have converted it to their use; and had not this antiquity of Stonehenge consisted of such an extreme hard and ill coloured stone, that it is hardly fit for any use, without much trouble, this venerable Temple had long since been erased and forgotten" (*Monumenta Britannica*, ed. Fowles and Legg, 93).

74 *Monumenta Britannica*, ed. Fowles and Legg, 18.

75 *Monumenta Britannica*, ed. Fowles and Legg, 18–19.

he cannot tell by the bare View. So it is clear, that all the monuments, which I have here recounted, were Temples. Now my presumption is, That the Druids being the most eminent Priests (or Order of Priests) among the Britaines; 'tis odds, but that these ancient Monuments, *sc.* Aubury, Stonehenge, Kerrig y Druidd &c., were Temples of the Priests of the most eminent Order, viz. Druids, and it is strongly to be presumed, that Aubury, Stoneheng, &c., are as ancient as those times. This Inquiry I must confess is a gropeing in the Dark: but although I have not brought it into a clear light; yet I can affirm, that I have brought it from an utter darkness to a thin Mist: and have gonne farther in this Essay than anyone before me.[76]

Aubrey is not suggesting the Druids were part of an English Middle Ages but rather claims that the medieval model of culture is distinct enough to provide an interpretive standard for a monument of ancient Britain. He uses medievalism to form a scientific hypothesis that he and several following scholars continued to test and refine. Aubrey's completion of his research was cut short by the deaths of two kings. He first encountered Avebury during the hunt described above on 7 January 1649, during the second stage of the Civil Wars and shortly before the execution of Charles I. Much later, in the summer of 1663, Aubrey showed Avebury to Charles II, who "commanded me to write a description of it, and present it to him."[77] He finally prepared a document for publication (advertised for 18 shillings); when Charles II died, Aubrey altered the dedication, but never succeeded in publishing it.[78] A short portion of Aubrey's work on Avebury in his *Monumenta Britannica* manuscript was printed in the 1695 edition of Camden's *Britannia*.[79] For this impressive translation and revision, Edmund Gibson had contributions from other scholars, including Thomas Tanner, who added material from the *Monumenta* with Aubrey's permission.[80] However, William Stukeley (1687–1765), who wrote the first published book studying Avebury, read a manuscript copy of the *Monumenta*.[81] Aubrey has a continuing influence on

---

76 Bodl. MS Aubrey Top. Gen. c. 24, 25v–26r (*Monumenta Britannica*, ed. Fowles and Legg, 24–25).

77 *Monumenta Britannica*, ed. Fowles and Legg, 21. The labor of turning research into manuscript into print is suggested by Aubrey's note that, "In September following, I surveyed that old monument of Aubury with a plain-table and afterwards took a review of Stonehenge; and then I composed this following discourse in obedience to his Majesty's command: and presented it to Him: which he commanded me to put in print" (*Monumenta Britannica*, ed. Fowles and Legg, 22).

78 Tylden-Wright, *John Aubrey*, 69–79. See also Bennett, *Brief Lives*, xxxix–xl.

79 William Camden, *Britannia* (London: ed. E. Gibson, 1695), 81, 108–11, 618, 637.

80 Parry, *Trophies of Time*, 332–37.

81 Hunter, *John Aubrey and the Realm of Learning*, 206.

later archaeologists through his careful mapping recording of details like the Aubrey holes at Stonehenge that did, indeed, later disappear.[82]

Aubrey's work on the details of the past of specific places, especially in Wiltshire, also led him to find national significance in the medieval family histories of the region. He clearly saw intangible family inheritances as part of the local heritage of the particular village or hundred the families belonged to. This connection from familial to local to national history became especially significant after the Reformation, as Jan Broadway argues: "local historians [...] strove to use their antiquarian learning to establish a link between their new sense of national and local identity and the world of their medieval ancestors."[83] She also explains that both cultural and educational changes provided members of gentry families with the ability to research the past and an interest in protecting their family's social identity and prerogatives.[84] In 1659, a group of interested gentlemen in Devizes commissioned Aubrey to survey the northern half of Wiltshire "in Imitation of Mr. Dugdale's Illustration of Warwickshire," and Aubrey set out to look for items of local cultural heritage.[85]

Some of Aubrey's favorite fragments were stories about families that he collected from his friends and in exploring around Wiltshire churches. One long story, with several installments that appear in different places in Aubrey's manuscripts, relates the failures of a family through the preceding two centuries of change. The Stradlings family of Dauntesey collapses after a reported fifteenth-century mass murder and is only saved by the marriage of the one surviving daughter. The destruction of the past foreshadows a seventeenth-century destruction by three brothers, descendants of the Stradlings. Henry Danvers, the first earl of Danby, kills a man; Sir Charles Danvers joins the revolt by the Earl of Essex and is executed; and Sir John Danvers becomes one of the regicides who signs the warrant for Charles I's execution and is later attainted by Charles II, leading to the confiscation of

---

82   Sweet notes that much had disappeared as soon as the early eighteenth century: "When Stukeley began his researches at Avebury a number of the features described by Aubrey had already been lost, and during his lifetime the remaining stones were blown to pieces in order to clear the land for agriculture" (*Antiquaries*, 128). These losses would have also given Stukeley more scope for developing his interpretations of what remained on the ground and in Aubrey's text.

83   Jan Broadway, *"No historie so meete": Gentry Culture and the Development of Local History in Elizabethan and Early Stuart England* (New York: Manchester University Press, 2006), 7.

84   Broadway, *"No historie so meete"*, 240; See also Fox, "Remembering the Past in Early Modern England," 250.

85   *Wiltshire Collections*, 2. See also Broadway, *"No historie so meete"*, 51–53, for the power of William Dugdale's 1656 *Antiquities of Warwickshire* to inspire similar works.

the Stradlings' estate.[86] This really is a family tragedy: Aubrey attributes Sir John's decision to participate in the Parliamentary judgment to a desire to win political favor in order to overturn the will of his brother Henry, and resentment of his inheriting sister.[87] Nevertheless, Aubrey, a cousin of the Danvers family, remembers Sir John fondly, often referring to "my cousin" and their pleasant companionship. Instead, he uses the story of old murders to express the unutterable trauma still disturbing the nation even after the end of the Civil Wars.

Medieval inheritances can affect the present in potentially destructive ways, as the Danvers family experienced after inheriting the murders of the Stradlings. Aubrey writes:

> Here was a Robbery committed at the Mannour howse, on the family of the Stradlings: he [Sir Edward], and all his servants, except one plowboy who hid himself, were murthered: by which means, this whole estate came to Anne his sister, and heire. She married after to Sir John Danvers a handsome gentleman, who clapt up a match with her before she heard the newes, he, by good fortune lighting upon the Messenger first.[88]

The crime is revealed when none of the Stradlings' household comes to church on Sunday and the concerned congregation goes to find out why. The surviving plowboy identifies the parson as one of the murderers. This is one of Aubrey's most dramatic family stories; he is usually content to record the marriages and children of a few generations of each local landed family, along with their coats of arms. However, this story fits into Aubrey's larger theme of social continuity by emphasizing the attempted destruction of a family by the rapacious local clergyman and its reincarnation under a new name, the same family name that held the manor house until the Restoration and its confiscation by the Crown from Aubrey's cousin Sir John. Even though marriage appears to revitalize a threatened family lineage, the inheritance of violence breaks out again generations later in an even more destructive threat to cultural lineage.

The Dauntesey murder case is particularly relevant as a medievalizing connection to the wars of Aubrey's recent past. Because this tale explains the origin of the family that later produced one of the men who signed the warrant for Charles I's execution, we, as Aubrey's audience, know that the family carries the taint of murder in its blood. On the surface, the story

---

[86] *Brief Lives*, 568–71.
[87] *Brief Lives*, 570. Additionally, three other members of the Danvers family had been exiled for murder and executed for complicity in revolt (*BL* 568–69).
[88] Bodl. MS Aubrey 3, fol. 44v (*Wiltshire Collections*, 218).

explains how the local family of the gentry changed names through a sole heiress. But Aubrey gets thoroughly involved in the story, explaining the details and presenting them in the order that, he implies, it was told to him by the villagers he met. This suggests that the details and the whole shape of the story have a continuing resonance, one of the signs of the opportunity for and use of medievalism. Even though the original family was the victim of the murder, and the first Sir John Danvers is not supposed to have had any involvement in the murder other than deliberately acting to marry the heiress before she could learn of the event, the violent event still pushes the family in a new direction.

Aubrey selects the Danvers family heritage as emblematic of medieval Wiltshire and of his own family. He traces it forward from its medieval roots in the past and backward from its relevance to events in the present. He emphasizes its personal relevance by including the Danvers' device in a quarter of his own coat-of-arms. One of his great-grandfathers was a Danvers, and Aubrey considered contemporary Danvers family members cousins. By considering events of both local and national significance together, he shows that the Danvers family seems to have been frequently involved with controversy and violence. The interrelationships of families that can be gleaned from densely packed coats of arms give Aubrey hints about networks of families stretching back into the past. He comments that, despite the drudgery of the work, "it shews a kind of gratitude and good nature, to revive the Memories and memorialls of the pious and charitable benefactors long since dead and gonne."[89] The benefactors need Aubrey's attention to tell a wider audience about their service and donations, especially since many of them had contributed to a religion that was then rejected in the Reformation.

The daughter Anne represents the continuity of the Stradling family. She transmits its earlier medieval heritage to the Danvers line and shapes its early modern future. But she cannot represent the family itself in the public world; she carries instead the responsibility for its maintenance. Even though material inheritance like land and money was usually transmitted from fathers to sons, cultural heritage was built on the foundations laid and maintained by women, or, by extension, by family members and mentors performing the roles often assigned to mothers. Transitions between families often created conflicts for women. In the Welsh ancestry of George Herbert is the memory of a woman who was taken from one class to another in a medieval marriage: "Vpon this Match with the Millers daughter are to this day recited; or sung by the Welsh, these verses [...]. To this sence, Ô God! Woe is me miserable, my father was a Miller, and my mother a Milleresse,

---

[89] *Wiltshire Collections*, 17.

and I am now a Ladie."[90] Her social self was split. The physical memorials for George Herbert's own mother, Magdalene, were divided because her second marriage was to Sir John Danvers of Wiltshire. In death, her allegiances to two husbands was represented through the placement of her effigy next to that of her first husband, Richard Herbert, in the church at Montgomery Castle with a "great freestone monument," but her body "lies interred at Chelsey church but without any monument."[91] This division seems to reflect her two roles: the Herbert materfamilias is publicly memorialized but physically absent, and the Danvers wife was physically absorbed by her second home. Aubrey's account of these women slides between past and present, indicating how medieval family stories are representative of formative Englishness.

The eclectic nature of Aubrey's collections reflects the composite sense of his medievalism. The medieval past was Anglo-Saxon, British, Norman, Gothic, English, with Celtic and Roman inheritances of monuments, language, and traditions. It was unified and parochial, superstitious and learned, and magnificently complex above all. Like other medieval antiquaries in his period, Aubrey drew in rich details and worked to organize them in order to reconstruct the time before the Reformation and the Civil Wars. He sought to draw rational conclusions from medieval fragments and framed the remains as distinctively part of a shared British past, thus simultaneously affirming and quarantining them. Aubrey's work emphasized the significance of cultural memorialization to the development of modernity: rather than rejecting the past, it classified reminders of the past as heritage.

---

[90]   *Brief Lives*, 692. Aubrey gives four lines in Welsh before translating into English; one of his close friends was Edward Lhwyd, an expert in Welsh and Celtic antiquities and keeper of the Ashmolean Museum, who may have provided assistance with this song.

[91]   *Brief Lives*, 690–91. Aubrey notes, "This stately Castle was demolished since the late Warres," a political casualty to punish the owner (*Brief Lives* 692, 1652).

Charter Horns and the Antiquarian Imagination in Early Modern England

Dustin M. Frazier Wood

On Thursday, 20 February 1755, William Stukeley presented "An Historical Dissertation upon the antient Danish Horn, kept in the Cathedral Church of York" to the Society of Antiquaries of London. The essay was probably familiar to some of the older Fellows, having been read to the Society in 1718 by its author, Samuel Gale. Its subject was the Horn of Ulf, then on display in the sacristy of York Minster. According to Gale, "of all the curiosities which a traveller sees, in visiting the great church of York, nothing can more merit the sedulous notice of the Antiquary, than that large vessel of ivory."[1]

Stukeley's 1755 rereading of Gale's essay sparked renewed interest in charter horns among English medievalist antiquaries. The "Dissertation" was deemed interesting enough to be included in the first issue of *Archaeologia* in 1770. The third issue, printed in 1775, opens with a further seven articles on horns ranging from a drinking horn from Corpus Christi College, Cambridge, to a pair of mammoth tusks at Carlisle Cathedral, which Charles Lyttelton partly confused with a hunting horn known to have been given to the cathedral by Henry I.[2] For the rest of the century, references to charter horns continued to appear in the Society's minute books, in periodicals such as *Archaeologia*, and in a series of popular prints sold to historically minded collectors. According to two modern historians, both before and after Gale "a constant trickle of curious tourists" were "gratified by the sight of Ulphus's horn," from Celia Fiennes and Daniel Defoe in the seventeenth century to

---

1   [Samuel Gale], "An Historical Dissertation upon the antient Danish Horn, kept in the Cathedral Church of York. Anno Domini MDCCXVIII. By Samuel Gale, Esquire. Presented by Dr. Stukely to the Antiquarian Society, February 20, 1755; together with a Runic Plate," *Archaeologia* 1 (1775): 168–82 (169).

2   Charles Lyttelton, "Account of Certain Charter Horns in the Cathedral of Carlisle. By Bishop Lyttelton," *Archaeologia* 3 (1775): 22–23.

the Duke of York in 1766.[3] This particular antiquarian curiosity was also a notable tourist attraction.

Mostly uninscribed, and almost entirely without accompanying documentary evidence that is contemporary or near contemporary with their creation, charter horns have been largely forgotten by academic medievalists. The wealth of family tradition and local lore that surround charter horns – which made them so appealing to early modern antiquaries – seems to have had almost the opposite effect on twentieth- and twenty-first- century scholars.[4] By contrast, their display in popular galleries such as the British Museum, Victoria and Albert Museum, and York Minster has led to a renewed interest in medieval charter horns on the part of curators and the museum-going public, who seem to recognize their power to evoke imaginative and intellectual responses to the medieval pasts they purport to represent.

This article takes as its focus three horns that have been the subjects of renewed interest in recent years, and which were the subjects of ongoing discussion and debate among early modern antiquaries: the Horn of Ulf, the Boarstall Horn, which is linked to the village of Boarstall in Oxfordshire and is now in the Buckinghamshire County Archives, and the Pusey Horn, which is traditionally associated with the Pusey family of Berkshire and is now on display in the silver gallery of the Victoria and Albert Museum. All three horns were believed to pre-date the Norman Conquest and were therefore frequently touted as examples of native English cultural and legal practices that had survived the shock of conquest and the imposition of Norman law on the Anglo-Saxon legal system. In addition to their inherent interest as well-preserved artifacts and works of medieval art, and as remarkable forms of legal evidence, charter horns also seem to have represented (and might still represent for twenty-first-century tourists) links to an increasingly well-developed narrative of England's essentially pre-Conquest cultural and institutional origins.

---

3   *A History of York Minster*, ed. G. E. Aylmer and Reginald Cant (Oxford: Clarendon, 1977), 258. According to Celia Fiennes, "There is a large hunters horne tipt with Silver and Garnish'd over and Engrav'd ffinely all double Gilt wth a Chaine, the same given by a Gentleman that also gave his Estate to add to the revenues of ye Church, on a dislike to disobedient Children; he used the horne When he hunted and drank in it too." Celia Fiennes, *Through England on a Side-Saddle, in the Time of William and Mary*, ed. Emily Griffiths (London: Field & Tuer, 1888), 60.

4   For late seventeenth- and early eighteenth-century antiquarian interests and practices, see, inter alia: Rosemary Sweet, *Antiquaries: The Discovery of the Past in Eighteenth-Century Britain* (London: Hambledon, 2004), esp. chaps. 1, 3 and 6; D. R. Woolf, "The Dawn of the Artifact: The Antiquarian Impulse in England, 1500–1730," in *Studies in Medievalism IV: Medievalism in England*, ed. Leslie J. Workman (Cambridge: D. S. Brewer, 1992), 5–35.

Charter Horns: Function and Symbolism

In the simplest terms, a charter horn is a hunting or drinking horn that replaces a written charter as a symbol of the transfer, ownership, or control of land. Writing in 1772, Samuel Pegge classified the commonest types of horn tenure as frank almoigne (a grant of land to a religious foundation in exchange for perpetual prayers for the donor's soul), fee (a common tenure with no requirement of service, often made by a royal or noble grantor), or serjeanty (tenure in exchange for performing a specified non-military duty for the monarch).[5] Of the horns discussed here, the Horn of Ulf is of the first type, and the Pusey Horn of the second or third. The Boarstall Horn, linked to a forest serjeanty, is of the third type and seems also to have served as a badge of office. Other examples of horns associated with forest serjeanties include those from Savernake, Carlisle, Wirral, and Delamere.[6]

Like the knives used as accompaniments to or surrogates for charters by Norman rulers in Normandy and England, charter horns were both symbolic and functional objects.[7] As John Cherry has written, "the moment of greatest importance for a symbolic object" such as a charter horn "was at the time of the ceremony of transfer or investiture."[8] In that moment a charter horn functioned as a symbol in multiple ways. Jacques le Goff's classification of medieval symbols of vassalage as socio-economic, socio-cultural, and/or socio-professional in nature provides a helpful starting point for understanding the possible *original* symbolism of a charter horn, though, as Cherry and Shalem have argued, such classifications are less solid and more slippery and overlapping than le Goff allows.[9] More importantly in the current context, however, is the fact that in many cases charter horns have experienced remarkable histories that follow the moment at which they were transferred from one owner to another as symbols of tenurial investiture. As they have been discussed, valued, interpreted, curated, and preserved over time, charter horns have also changed. In some cases this change has been physical, for example through the addition of a decorative chain to the Horn of Ulf in the thirteenth century, the horn's removal from York Minster in the sixteenth century, and its restoration in the

---

5   Samuel Pegge, "Of the Horn, as a Charter or Instrument of Conveyance. Some Observations on Mr. Samuel Foxlowe's Horn; as likewise on the Nature and Kinds of these Horns in general," *Archaeologia* 3 (1775): 1–12 (1).

6   John Cherry, "Symbolism and Survival: Medieval Horns of Tenure," *The Antiquaries Journal* 69 (1989): 111–18 (112–14).

7   Michael Clanchy, "The Norman Conquest and Anglo-Saxon Literacy," *Past and Future* 3 (2008): 6–7; and *From Memory to Written Record: England 1066-1307*, 3rd edn (Oxford: Wiley-Blackwell), 38–39.

8   Cherry, "Symbolism and Survival," 111.

9   Cherry, "Symbolism and Survival," 111; Avinoam Shalem, *The Oliphant: Islamic Objects in Historical Contexts* (Leiden: Brill, 2004), 120.

seventeenth century. In other cases the change has been symbolic, the result of passing from one owner or family to another and thereby acquiring new associative and genealogical significance. Over the course of centuries complex historical–biographical narratives have developed around each charter horn, so that the significance of any given horn in any given historical present has derived and continues to derive from the persons and events to which it is connected in contemporary popular memory.[10] The biography of any charter horn is the biography of a legal document, of an *aide-mémoire*, of a touchstone for folk history, of a family badge, of a record of active office, of a representation of a religious agreement and exchange, and of numerous individuals and the places they call their own.

Reconstructing the object biographies of these three horns reveals that each one has been a focus for medievalizing consistently over the course of its existence. Remarkably polyvalent symbols, they possess the power to engage in what Keith Thomas calls "chartering": telling and retelling narratives of history, place, and family that "call in the past to ratify the present."[11] As symbols of land ownership, charter horns ratified the right of the current possessor to the land while simultaneously shoring up the incumbent's claims to a historically grounded right of ownership, and thus to the historical significance of a particular family or institution and its historical association with a particular corner of the English landscape. Whether or not a horn was authentic in the sense that it was "the original" was in most cases taken for granted. Where questioning arose, however, the horn was assumed to be authentic in the sense that it was "the authorized version" and was possessed of "believability or verisimilitude."[12] It is essential to remember that each of the charter horns discussed here was believed by medieval and post-medieval commentators to be genuine, and to represent a moment in medieval time in which the political-geographical boundaries of a commentator's lived landscape had been drawn. Moreover, it is worth remembering that charter horns remained legal proofs long after the period under discussion. Only with the passage of Lord Birkenhead's Act in 1922 were the customary tenures – for example, cornage tenure, or tenure by virtue of a horn – abolished.[13]

---

[10]   Chris Gosden and Yvonne Marshall, "The Cultural Biography of Objects," *World Archaeology* 31.2 (1999): 169–78 (170).

[11]   Keith Thomas, *The perception of the past in early modern England: The Creighton Trust Lecture 1983, delivered before the University of London on Monday 21 November 1983* (London: University of London, 1983), 3.

[12]   Pam Clements, "Authenticity," in *Medievalism: Key Critical Terms*, ed. Elizabeth Emery and Richard Utz (Cambridge: D. S. Brewer, 2014), 19–26 (19).

[13]   Arthur Underhill, *A Concise Explanation of Lord Birkenhead's Act (The Law of Property Act, 1922) in Plain Language* (London: Butterworth & Co., 1922), 37–38.

Historical Evidence

The earliest account of the use of charter horns comes from the *Historia Croylandensis*, published in a well-known edition by William Fulman in 1684. According to the *Historia*, during the first years of Anglo-Norman rule, "at first many estates were transferred simply by word of mouth, without writing or charter, and only with the lord's sword, helmet, horn, or cup; and many tenements [were transferred] with a spur, scraper or bow; & some with an arrow."[14] Believed by early modern scholars to have been written by Ingulph, abbot of Croyland from 1087 to 1109, the *Historia Croylandensis* provided historians and antiquaries with a highly detailed source for the history of late eleventh-century England. Orderic Vitalis provided a sketch of Ingulph's life; and the contents of the *Historia* seemed to align with work by later historians. Its mention of the use of horns in place of charters, then, provided early modern antiquaries with proof that the stories attached to surviving charter horns were more than simply entertaining legends.[15] As the only written reference to the use of charter horns available to antiquaries, this passage served as the starting point for most commentaries on English charter horns. It also complemented the evidence for early medieval use of charter horns by the Danes provided by the continental antiquaries Jean Mabillon and Ole Wormius.[16] To the work of Fulman, Mabillon, and Wormius early eighteenth-century antiquaries added the evidence provided by commentaries on the Horn of Ulf, and the Pusey and Boarstall Horns by their sixteenth- and seventeenth-century predecessors, most notably George Hickes's "Dissertatio Epistolaris," arguably the most important work of premodern scholarship on Anglo-Saxon and Old Norse grammar, philology, diplomatic, and manuscript studies.[17]

By the time Samuel Gale wrote his "Dissertation," then, he had access to a wide range of scholarship that led him to two conclusions. The first was

---

[14] [Conferebantur etiam primo multa prædia nudo verbo, absque scripto, vel charta, tantum cum domini gladio, vel galea, vel cornu, vel cratera; & plurima tenementa cum calcari, cum strigili, cum arcu; & nonnulla cum sagitta.] *Rerum Anglicarum Scriptorum Veterum. Tom. I. Quorum INGULFUS nunc primum integer, cæteri nunc primum prodeunt*, ed. William Fulman (Oxford: Sheldonian Theatre, 1684), 69.

[15] While twentieth-century historians have largely dismissed the *Historia* as too suspect to be a useful source for medieval historiography following its identification by W. G. Searle as a late fourteenth- or fifteenth-century compilation by a "Pseudo-Ingulph," more recent scholarship has argued that the text needs to be reassessed as a well-researched and valuable source in its own right. See, for example, Marjorie Chibnall, "Introduction" to *The Ecclesiastical History of Orderic Vitalis, Volume II: Books III and IV* (Oxford: Clarendon, 1969), xxv–xxix, and David Roffe, "The Historia Croylandensis: A Plea for Reassessment," *The English Historical Review* 110 (February 1995): 93–108.

[16] Jean Mabillon, *De Re Diplomatica Libri VI.* (Paris, 1681); Ole Wormius, *Danicorum monumentorum libri sex: e spissis antiquitatem et in Dania ac Norvegia extantibus ruderibus eruti* (Copenhagen, 1643).

[17] George Hickes, *Linguarum veterum septentrionalium thesaurus grammatico-criticus et archaeologicus* (Oxford: Sheldonian Theatre, 1703).

that it was "very certain, that this manner of endowing was usual among the Danes here in England, and especially in the time of King Cnute," as evidenced by the story of the Pusey Horn and Horn of Ulf. Second, the practice had continued in use in the late Anglo-Saxon period, when "the like donation [was] made by King Edward the Confessor," a reference to the Boarstall Horn.[18] Armed with this knowledge, Gale set about a close examination of the history of the Horn of Ulf.

The Horn of Ulf

Twenty-eight inches long and just over five inches in diameter at the mouth, the Horn of Ulf (Fig. 1) is unquestionably the most striking charter horn in England. The decorative band around its wider end depicts dogs, lions, griffons, and unicorns in a woodland setting. Its mix of Arabic, Persian, and Italian stylistic elements has led to its classification as one of the so-called "Byzantine" group of oliphants (horns made from a single elephant tusk) probably produced in an eleventh-century workshop in Amalfi or Salerno.[19] Both were port cities with long histories of trade to and from the Arabic and Scandinavian worlds, and both came under Norman rule at about this time, Amalfi in 1075 and Salerno a year later. It has been suggested that the horn was carved in a workshop that also produced the stylistically similar oliphants now in the Museum of Fine Arts in Boston, Muri Abbey in Vienna, and the Chartreuse de Portes in Bénonces.[20]

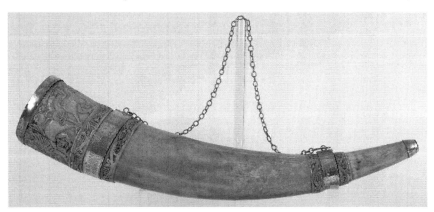

Fig. 1: The Horn of Ulf (© Chapter of York: Reproduced by kind permission)

18   Gale, "Dissertation," 176.
19   Otto von Falke, "Elfenbeinhörner: II. Byzanz," *Pantheon* 5 (1930): 39–44; Shalem, *Oliphant*, 9–11; Thomas D. Kendrick, "The Horn of Ulph," *Antiquity* 11 (1937): 278–82.
20   Hanns Swarzenski, "Two Oliphants in the Museum," *Bulletin of the Museum of Fine Arts* 60, 320 (1962): 34.

According to the earliest detailed account, the horn was given to St. Peter's, York, by Ulf, son of Thorald, who held lands in the western parts of Deira in Northumbria. Angered by a disagreement that arose between his sons over which would inherit their father's estates and titles after his death, Ulf "took the horn from which he drank, filled it with wine and carried it to the altar, and going on his knees gave all of his lands to blessed Peter, prince of the Apostles."[21] For good measure he also donated the horn, his most valuable moveable, as a symbol for and evidence of his gift.

More than simply augmenting the church's holdings, the lands given by Ulf represented the first major benefaction to the dean and chapter rather than to the archbishop. It was precisely these lands – known throughout the medieval period as *terra Ulfi* – that came to the fore in the course of a royal inquest "into the liberty of St Peter within York and its suburbs" in 1276, a year that saw increasing levels of conflict between the mayor and citizenry of York, and their ecclesiastical landlords.[22] In the same year the dean and chapter "negotiated a special agreement whereby the lands of Ulf would be regarded as part of the Liberty of St. Peter and would be exempted from husgabel (a house-tax) and other tolls due to the crown in return for an annual payment of 6*s.* 8*d.* to the mayor and citizens of York."[23] Shortly thereafter, the arms of Ulf were displayed on a spandrel in the north side of the nave of York Minster, "a prominence [...] equalled only by those of the crown."[24] For a community that enjoyed unprecedented wealth and status within both the ecclesiastical and political spheres, while simultaneously facing potential threats from an increasingly powerful citizenry, the celebration of such an important early medieval donor served as a rehearsal of the basis of their authority over significant portions of the very fabric of the city. The elevation of Ulf to a place of especial prominence within the decorative scheme of the Minster served to reinforce visually the importance of the chapter and the benefactor whose gift marked the origin of its wealth and independence.

Late in the fourteenth century Ulf and his horn were celebrated in a metrical chronicle written at York, in a subsection detailing "*De libertatibus possessionibus date per adelstannum et alios*" ("Of the liberties and possessions given by Athelstan and others").[25] Here Ulf appears as "*consul* [...] *et comes*" ("an official and a nobleman"), the only non-royal in a list of benefactors

---

21   William Camden, *Britannia; sive Florentissimorum Regnorum, Angliæ, Scotiæ, Hiberniæ, et Insularum Adiacentium ex intima antiquitate Chorographica descriptio* (London: George Bishop, 1607), 573.

22   D. M. Palliser, *Medieval York 600–1540* (Oxford: Oxford University Press, 2014), 148.

23   Sarah Rees Jones, *York: The Making of a City 1068–1350* (Oxford: Oxford University Press, 2013), 142.

24   Rees Jones, *York*, 142 n. 21.

25   "Consul et insignis eboracensis comes Ulfus / Predia prebendis prebuit ille sua / Tradens ex ebore cornu petroque sigillum / Investituram constituit solidam / Cornea buccina

that includes Athelstan and later Anglo-Saxon kings such as Edwyn, Edgar, Æthelred, Canute, and Edward the Confessor. Ulf's horn, which "testified with clear light the munificence and exemplary largesse of that count," is described at some length. In the context of the chronicle, the horn's existence and its history draw attention to the fact that *terra Ulfi* belonged by right and tradition to the dean and chapter, and more particularly to the prebendary supported by the income it produced.

In the sixteenth century Ulf came to the attention of William Camden. During a visit to York, Camden was shown "an ancient book […] which elucidated the donations to the church," probably the *Liber Albus* (or *Magnum Registrum Album*), a fourteenth-century volume detailing the early estates, rights, and privileges of the archbishop and chapter.[26] The first edition of Camden's *Britannia* included the much-expanded version of Ulf's story outlined above, and firmly linked Ulf to the historical and modern geography of York in the first chorographical history of England, a foundational text in the emergence of early modern antiquarian studies of the remains of England's medieval past.

Camden's thinly substantiated tale seems never to have been doubted. Over the next two centuries antiquaries struggled to identify the historical Ulf and the lands he granted with the horn. Writing in or around 1666, William Dugdale offered additional details of Ulf's life in a history of York Minster that was published posthumously in the second edition of his *History of St Paul's*.[27] He might have come across the story first while collaborating with Roger Dodsworth to prepare *Monasticon Anglicanum*, where the horn appears as part of a pre-Reformation inventory of the treasures of the Cathedral Church at York: "Item, one great horn of ivory decorated with silver gilt, a gift of Ulf son of Thorald, with a chain attached, a gift of Master John Newton Treasurer."[28]

The fact that Newton, appointed treasurer in 1393, added a gold chain to the horn at roughly the same time that it was being commemorated in the metrical chronicle suggests that in the late fourteenth century the chapter once

---

candida lucida testificatur / Munus et eximium largisem comitis […]" BL Cotton Cleopatra C IV, fol. 16r.

26 William Camden, *Britannia*, 2nd edn (London: George Bishop, 1600), 637–38.

27 William Dugdale, *A Brief Historical Account of the Northern Cathedrals of York, Durham, and Carlisle; as also of the Principal Collegiate CHURCHES in the Province of YORK Extracted from Authentick Records, and other Authorities* (London: Jonah Bowyer, 1715), 6–7.

28 [Item unum magnum Cornu de ebore ornatum cum argento deaurato, ex dono *Ulphi* filii *Thoraldi*, cum Zona annexa, ex dono Magistri *Johannis Newton* Thesaurarii.] William Dugdale, *Monastici Anglicani, Volumen Tertium et Ultimum: Additament* […] *necnon Fundationes, sive Dotationes diversarum Ecclesiarum Cathedralium ac Collegiatarum continens; Ex Archivis Regiis, ipsis Autographis, ac diversis Codicibus Manuscriptis decerpta* (London: Savoy, 1673), 173.

again sought to reiterate its status and ancient rights and liberties. This was perhaps connected with the completion in 1405 of a centuries-long series of rebuilding works, over the course of which the Norman cathedral was largely demolished and replaced by the current Gothic structure. If so, the rehearsal of benefactors to the dean and chapter would have served as a reminder of the early medieval traditions that underlay the impressive new cathedral.

Dugdale certainly studied the horn at first hand during a visit to the collection of Thomas Fairfax. According to Dugdale, the horn had been removed from the Minster during the reign of Edward VI and "sold to a Goldsmith, who took away from it those Tippings of Gold wherewith it was adorned, and the Gold Chain affix'd thereto" by Newton. Fairfax had rescued the horn and preserved it during the Civil War, and showed it to Dugdale in 1666. Eleven years later Fairfax's son Henry returned it to York Minster, having added a plate commemorating his restoration.[29]

Dugdale was not the only antiquary interested in the Horn of Ulf, however. When the horn came to the attention of Samuel Gale, it likely did so via his father, Thomas, who became Dean of York in 1697. Thomas was himself a notable antiquary with a keen interest in the early Middle Ages. After providing William Fulman with a transcript of the *Historia Croylandensis* from the Cotton Library, he went on to publish an additional volume of early medieval chronicles that included the works of Gildas and Nennius, and Eddius' *Life of St Wilfrid*.[30] Samuel Gale's essay on the Horn of Ulf contained references to the metrical chronicle, the published works of Camden, Dodsworth, and Dugdale, and additional manuscript evidence from the library of York Minster and his father's antiquarian collections.

Tellingly, Gale begins and ends his dissertation with references to the horn's contemporary symbolism. For Gale, the horn represents a "venerable piece of Antiquity," and no treasure in York Minster could "more merit the sedulous notice of the antiquary."[31] His discussion of the horn concludes with encomia to Thomas and Henry Fairfax, the former a "lover of Antiquities [...] whose memory is still deservedly honoured" for his safeguarding of the horn "during the confusions of the civil war," as well as for his support of Roger Dodsworth's antiquarian studies, his donation of manuscripts to the Bodleian, and his efforts to keep the cathedral at York from being despoiled after the city's capitulation to Parliamentarian forces in 1644. Following Henry Fairfax's restoration of the horn to York Minster, it gained new symbolic meaning as "a noble

---

29   Dugdale, *Historical Account*, 6–7; Gale, "Dissertation," 182.

30   Fulman, *Rerum Anglicarum*, "Lectori"; Thomas Gale, *Historiae Britanicae, Saxonicae, Anglo-Danicae, Scriptores XV*. (Oxford: Sheldonian Theatre, 1691). Gale almost certainly sent Fulman the copy from MS Cotton Otho B xiii.

31   Gale, "Dissertation," 167, 169.

monument of modern, as well as ancient piety."[32] For Gale, the importance of the Horn of Ulf no longer lay solely in its value as a legal instrument, nor as a symbol of the power and stature of the dean and chapter (though this might not have been the case for his father, who would have had a vested professional interest in the horn's legal and symbolic significance). Rather, the Horn of Ulf had become an object worthy of reverence on account of its status as an artifact, the enduring legal function of which only served to highlight its power to draw closer together the pious Ulf, the canons of St. Peter's, benefactors such as Newton and Fairfax, and Gale and his fellow members of the Society of Antiquaries. In Gale's "Dissertation," the Horn of Ulf becomes a symbol of a medieval moment that continues to shape his own lived present.

Gale's presentation was warmly received, and "it was orderd unanimously that a Drawing [...] be printed," along with copies of the dissertation.[33] Engraved by George Vertue, prints of the horn (Fig. 2) were completed and sold to members of the Society the following year.[34]

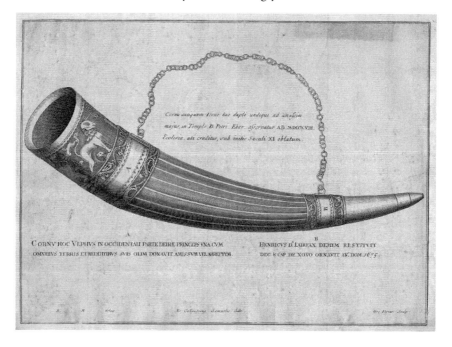

Fig. 2: George Vertue, The Horn of Ulf, engraving, 1718
(© Trustees of the British Museum)

[32] Gale, "Dissertation," 182.
[33] Society of Antiquaries of London, Minute Books, 1:11.
[34] Society of Antiquaries of London, Minute Books, 1:19, 21.

Learned and well received though it was, Gale's was not the final version of the story of Ulf and his horn. Just over a decade later, the surgeon-cum-historian Francis Drake discovered in the York Minster archives five volumes of manuscript notes and histories written by the seventeenth-century ecclesiastical antiquary James Torre, on which Drake drew extensively in writing *Eboracum*, a successful and highly regarded history of the city. Citing Torre's identification of Kekolthorp, Newbald, Goodmundham, Barneby, Pokelington, Millington and Beneldale, and Alvesthorpe as *terra Ulphi*, Drake theorized that Ulf "must have lived very near *York*; and probably at *Aldby*."[35] The comment was anything but off-hand. Then as now, Aldby Park, a hilltop site not quite ten miles northeast of York, was associated with Anglo-Saxon royalty. According to legend, Aldby had been the site of the coronation of King Edwin, who was converted to Christianity in 627 by Paulinus of York. Bede gives a vivid account of Edwin's conversion in Book 2 of the *Ecclesiastical History*, which also describes the destruction of a pagan temple at Goodmanham by the priest Coifi.[36] By overlaying the story of Ulf on Bede's narrative of Anglo-Saxon Christian piety, Drake concretized the legend and fixed both Ulf and *terra Ulfi* in the historic and modern landscape. In doing so, Drake was attempting to unite identifiable artifacts and their associated legends with medieval literary sources and specific geographical locations, a method that characterized antiquarian medievalism from the early sixteenth to the late eighteenth century. Similar motivations characterized all future reappearances of the horn in the eighteenth century, including Stukeley's rereading of Gale's dissertation and its publication in *Archaeologia*, the surge in interest in charter horns over the subsequent three decades, and the interest in the Boarstall and Pusey Horns, believed by many antiquaries to be close contemporaries with Ulf's.

The Boarstall Horn

Like the Horn of Ulf, by the early modern period the Boarstall Horn had accumulated an elaborate and well-known biographical narrative, though one that was traced back to Edward the Confessor. According to an account by White Kennett:

35 Francis Drake, *Eboracum: or the History and Antiquities of the City of York, From its Original to the Present Time, Together with the History of the Cathedral Church and the Lives of the Archbishops of that See* [...] (London: William Bowyer, 1736), 544.
36 *Bede's Ecclesiastical History of the English People*, ed. Bertram Colgrave and R. A. B. Mynors (Oxford: Clarendon, 1969), 175–87.

This pious King [...] had a Royal Palace [at Brill], to which he retir'd for the pleasures of hunting in his forest of *Bernwood*. [...] The Forest of *Bernwood* was much infested by a wild Boar, which was at last slain by one *Nigel* a Hunstman, who presented the Boar's head to the King, and for a reward the King gave to him one hyde of arable land call'd *Derehyde*, and a wood call'd *Hulewode*, with the custody of the forest of *Bernwood*, to hold to him and his heirs from the King, *per unum cornu quod est charta prædictæ Forestæ* [...]. Upon this ground the said *Nigel* built a lodge or mansion house call'd *Borestalle*, in memory of the slain Boar.[37]

A grant of land at Boarstall to William Fitz-Nigel from Fulco de Lisuris dated to c. 1170–76 represents the earliest known verifiable reference to the family of Nigel at Boarstall. William Fitz-Nigel's name also appears in the Pipe Roll for Michaelmas 1176, probably as a result of the grant.[38] A hint of an earlier connection appears in Henry III's confirmation in 1266 of the formal grant of the bailiwick of Derehyde to John Fitz-Nigel, which refers to the familial forestership as having been held "of the king and his ancestors from the conquest of England," though it is worth noting that neither the inquisition of 1230 nor that of 1265 mention this fact.[39] Despite what appears at first glance to be a fabulous family story, it is possible that the tale of the Anglo-Saxon Nigel, forester of Bernwood, contains a seed of truth.

Evidence for the existence of the surviving Boarstall Horn (Fig. 3), however, does not appear until several centuries later. In 1435 Edmund Rede inherited the manor of Boarstall. A lineal descendant of the Fitz-Nigels, Rede's family had risen to a position of local prominence as a result of successful legal careers and strategic, lucrative marriages. Boarstall came to Edmund through his mother, Cristina, who also added land and houses in Oxfordshire, Buckinghamshire, and Berkshire to her husband's existing Oxfordshire holdings at Checkenden, Standhill, and Gatehampton.[40] As a result of this union and his parents' careful husbandry of their cumulative holdings, Edmund Rede witnessed his family's rise from local to regional importance, and to greatly increased wealth. Even before coming into his inheritance Rede had served as sheriff of Oxfordshire in 1430, and would hold the office again in 1450, before being knighted on 26 May 1465.

---

[37]   White Kennett, *Parochial Antiquities Attempted in the History of Ambrosden, Burcester, and other adjacent parts in the Counties of Oxford and Bucks.* (Oxford: Sheldonian Theatre, 1695), 51–52.

[38]   Boarstall Cartulary, fol. 1v; *The Great Roll of the Pipe for the Twenty-Second Year of the Reign of Henry II*, Pipe Roll Society XXV (London: Spottiswoode, 1904), 21.

[39]   *The Victoria County History of Buckingham*, ed. William Page, vol. 4 (London: Archibald Constable, 1928), 11; *Calendar of the Patent Rolls Preserved in the Public Record Office. Henry III. A. D. 1266–1272* (London: HM Stationery Office, 1913), 15.

[40]   H. E. Salter, *The Boarstall Cartulary* (Oxford: Clarendon, 1930), viii–x.

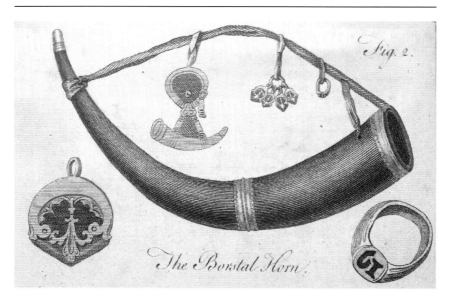

Fig. 3: James Basire, The Boarstall Horn, engraving, c.1775. The ribbon, ornaments, and ring are of unknown date. The ornaments and fragments of the ribbon remain with the horn in the Buckinghamshire County Archive. (By kind permission of the Spalding Gentlemen's Society)

In 1444, Rede commissioned the Boarstall Cartulary, which brought together copies of all of the extant deeds to his family's recently expanded holdings in one volume. By far the largest section was given over to Boarstall, Rede's primary seat. Continually added to until c. 1499 by at least three scribes in addition to the first, the cartulary contains 294 folios decorated with rubrications, ornamented blue capitals, and a red filigree pattern. Measuring 13 by 9 inches and still bound in its original boards and white chamois, the volume was and remains a conspicuous status symbol. But it was more than that. For Edmund Rede, the Boarstall Cartulary also provided a vehicle for validating his family's status by asserting – or fabricating – a myth of pre-Conquest origins.

Preceding the largest section of the cartulary is a map of Boarstall (notable in its own right as the earliest extant map of a medieval English village), followed by the earliest known version of the story of Nigel and the Boarstall Horn. At the bottom of the map Nigel, in a white tunic and red hose, kneels and presents the still-bleeding boar's head on a sword to the king, who appears crowned and wearing a red, fur-trimmed robe and blue hose. Behind the king, two or three frightened courtiers peer out from behind stylized trees or bushes. In exchange for the boar's head, the king presents Nigel with arms (two red crescents above, and a green horn below, a red bar, all on a silver field) and with the horn, depicted dangling from the king's wrist. Above this group appears the village of Boarstall as it probably appeared in

Rede's time, with the impressive moated, crenellated gatehouse erected in 1312 opposite the church, the bell-tower of which had been built in 1391.

On the following folio the arms of Nigel reappear beneath the narrative of his hunt and the king's grant, the first in a succession of shields that emphasize the royal grant of arms and the fundamental identity of the horn and the lordship of Boarstall. At about the same time he commissioned the Boarstall Cartulary, Rede seems to have resurrected the horn as his personal badge. A deed of 1450/6, now in the Buckinghamshire County Record Office, bears the only known surviving seal of Edmund Rede, which consists of a horn and baldric identical to the one depicted in the cartulary.[41] Rede might also have commissioned a bedstead, now lost, on which was carved "the same figure of a boar's head."[42] The generally accepted dating of the Boarstall Horn's silver gilt mountings to the fifteenth century comes as little surprise, given the sudden explosion of horn iconography following Edmund Rede's inheritance of the lordship of Boarstall. The horn itself could well have been produced at the same time. There is no evidence of modification to accommodate the fifteenth-century fittings, and the horn's overall shape and style suggest a similar date of manufacture. It seems likely that Rede began the process of resurrecting and embellishing a narrative of familial origins to match his newly elevated position in society. If so, he was an early participant in a "broader tradition of gentry self-fashioning linking chivalric ideals of prowess and bravery to the possession of land," a landowner who sought to achieve self-promotion through a conscious, deliberate process of self-medievalizing.[43] The authenticity of Rede's proofs and their correctness in all their particulars almost certainly mattered less than that they were believable enough to ratify the Rede family's place in the socio-economic hierarchy of fourteenth-century England.

Whether or not some version of the story of Nigel that was in circulation in Rede's day included a specific reference to Edward the Confessor is unknown, but is not unlikely, given the appearance of the crowned king on the map of Boarstall. Royal figures notwithstanding, the tale of Nigel and the Boarstall Horn seem to have faded into local legend when Boarstall passed out of Rede hands in the fifteenth century. In 1691, however, Sir John Aubrey, a baronet with antiquarian leanings, became lord of Boarstall by marriage. With a suddenly expanded income and attendant rise in social status, Aubrey set out to revive his wife's family legend once again. He added painted glass depicting the arms of Edmund Rede and the horn to the windows of

---

[41] Buckinghamshire County Record Office D/AF 3/2.
[42] Kennett, *Parochial Antiquities*, 52.
[43] Christian D. Liddy, "Land, Legend and Gentility in the Palatinate of Durham: The Pollards of Pollard Hall," in *North-East England in the Later Middle Ages*, ed. Christian D. Liddy and R. H. Britnell (Woodbridge: Boydell, 2005), 75–96 (93).

Boarstall's fortified gatehouse, and brought the horn and cartulary to the attention of the highly respected antiquary and vicar of Ambrosden, White Kennett, whose *Parochial Antiquities* (1695) announced the Boarstall Horn to England's growing antiquarian community. The ninth chapter, entitled "Saxons Restored," opens with a lengthy narrative describing Edward the Confessor's birth at Islip and his subsequent affinity for the royal manor at Brill in the forest of Bernwood. According to Kennett, or perhaps Aubrey speaking through Kennett, "it is to this Prince, and to his diversion at this seat, that we must ascribe the traditional story of the family of *Nigel*, and the Mannor of *Borstall* on the edge of the said Forest."[44]

Parochial Antiquities quickly became a standard reference for successive generations of antiquaries. Kennett's reputation for first-hand research and frequent use of primary sources lent weight to his claim that "most part of the tradition is confirm'd by good authority," and meant that Edmund Rede's story as embellished by Kennett and Aubrey became accepted as historical fact.[45] Their narrative receives additional reinforcement from the engraving of Boarstall by Michael Burghers that appears between pages 678 and 679 of *Parochial Antiquities*. Paid for by Aubrey, the engraving depicts clearly the divisions of fields and forests, the centrality of the gatehouse and church to the village, and the medieval road layout (which had since been converted into fashionable garden paths) of the map included in the Boarstall Cartulary; indeed, the two versions are strikingly similar when viewed side by side. Though Burghers' engraving does not incorporate the Boarstall Horn, its border traces the descent of the lordship of Boarstall, beginning with "Nigellus de Borstall temp. Ed. Confess." in the upper left and continuing counterclockwise around the scene until it reaches "Iohanni Aubrey Baronetto."

In 1703, George Hickes repeated Kennett's assertion that the Boarstall Horn had been given to Nigel by Edward the Confessor in his discussion of charter horns in the first volume of his *Linguarum veterum septentrionalium thesaurus grammatico-criticus et archæologicus*.[46] Kennett's account also provided Samuel Gale with evidence for the use of horns as charters in England before the Norman Conquest, and in turn for his attribution of an early eleventh-century date to the Horn of Ulf. In 1773 the Boarstall Horn and Cartulary were exhibited at a meeting of the Society of Antiquaries. As with the Horn of Ulf, the Fellows were so impressed that they "caused to be engraved this very interesting memorial and instrument of ancient conveyance, and the curious plan of the manor taken at the time of compiling the cartulary" for inclusion in *Archaeologia*.[47]

---

44 Kennett, *Parochial Antiquities*, 51.
45 Kennett, *Parochial Antiquities*, 51.
46 Hickes, *Thesaurus*, "Dissertatio Epistolaris," 84.
47 Anon. [Mr Southouse?], "Of the Borstal Horn," *Archaeologia* 3 (1775): 15–18 (16).

The Pusey Horn

The Society also commissioned an engraving of the Pusey Horn, based on a drawing (Fig. 4) by Jane Allen, sister of John Allen Pusey, the recently deceased lord of the manor.[48] This too was printed in the third volume of *Archaeologia*, accompanied by a brief essay by Daines Barrington.[49]

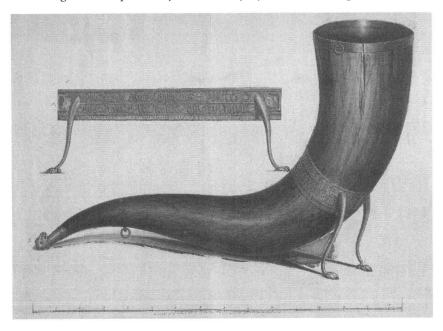

Fig. 4: Jane Allen, The Pusey Horn, pencil and watercolor, 1782.
(By kind permission of the Society of Antiquaries of London)

A somewhat hazy tradition held that the manor of Pusey was "still held by a horn" that had been given to an unnamed Pusey ancestor by King Canute.[50] Just as the tale of Nigel and Edward the Confessor, the story of Canute and the Puseys was embellished by later commentators. When Jacob, Second Earl of Radnor, presented his "Observations" on the Pusey Horn to a meeting of the Society of Antiquaries in 1790, he described it as a reward made to William Pusey by Canute for having warned the king of the approach of an enemy army, though he did not specify the date or

48   *The Victoria County History of Berkshire*, ed. P. H. Ditchfield and William Page, vol. 4 (London: Archibald Constable, 1927), 471–74.
49   [Daines Barrington], "Of the Pusey Horn," *Archaeologia* 3 (1775): 13–14.
50   William Camden, *Britannia* (London: George Bishop, 1609), 203.

location of this episode.[51] Earlier attempts to date the horn itself had fixated on the inscription running around the silver band to which its claw feet are joined. In a script probably intended to appear old-fashioned – or perhaps even "medieval" – at the time of its creation, the text reads: "I Kyng Knowde geve Wyllyam Pewt[s?]e / Yys horne to holde by yy lond." Though treated with some wariness in most published accounts, the inscription's first-person voice led early modern viewers to the conclusion that the horn was either the original given by Canute, or at least a very good copy. In fact, the inscription and claw feet suggest a mid-fifteenth-century date of manufacture for the Pusey Horn, making it roughly contemporary with the Boarstall Horn. Given the fact that at precisely this time a "William Wattes *alias* Richard" came into possession of the manor of Pusey by marriage to an unnamed Pusey widow, it is tempting to speculate that similar motives lay behind the creation of both horns.[52]

Nevertheless, all of the evidence available to early modern antiquaries pointed to an eleventh-century provenance. Domesday Book records the existence of a manor at Pusey in the time of Edward the Confessor, a small tract of two hydes held by Gilbert and before him by Alfred, though of the abbot of Abingdon rather than the king.[53] The better-known Boarstall Horn with all its corroborating evidence suggested that individual families and manors could well retain early medieval charter horns, and the Horn of Ulf seemed to antiquaries such as Gale, Pegge, and Barrington to high-light a connection between early medieval charter horns and the Danes in England. Antiquarian precedent was also on their side: William Camden had mentioned the horn and its legend in *Britannia* and, more recently, Hickes had cited the Pusey Horn alongside the Boarstall Horn as positive evidence of the pre-Conquest practice of cornage tenure.[54]

Undoubtedly the best evidence for the pre-Conquest origin of the Pusey Horn, however, came from a seventeenth-century courtroom. In 1684 Charles Pusey appeared in Chancery to recover the manor, presumably from a rival from another branch of the family. With him he brought one piece of evidence: the Pusey Horn. In the *Thesaurus*, Hickes describes how Lord Chancellor George Jefferies and his fellow judges "with universal admira-tion, received, admitted, and proved [it] to be the identical horn by which, as by a charter, Canute had conveyed the Manor of Pusey."[55] The case was

---

51   Jacob, Earl of Radnor, "Observations on the Pusey Horn," *Archaeologia* 12 (1796): 397–400.
52   Ditchfield and Page, *Berkshire*, 471–74.
53   *Domesday Book*, ed. Ann Williams and G. H. Martin (London: Penguin, 1992), 144 (Domesday fol. 59v).
54   Camden, *Britannia*, 203; Hickes, *Thesaurus*, xxv.
55   [Barrington], "Of the Pusey Horn," 13.

settled in Charles Pusey's favor, and versions of Hickes' description (the only known account of the judges' reaction) of the Pusey Horn's appearance in court as evidence were repeated within and beyond Britain for more than two centuries.[56]

Charter Horns and the Antiquarian Imagination

Charles Pusey's experience provides the most dramatic illustration of the reasons that charter horns possessed the appeal they did for early modern antiquaries. As proxies for legal documents, charter horns served the same documentary function of attesting to the historical patterns of the lordship and ownership of particular pieces of land. If, as the author of the *Historia Croylandensis* claimed, horns were given in place of written charters, Charles Pusey's appearance in Chancery provided antiquaries with the only substantiated instance of a charter horn fulfilling its intended symbolic and legal function. The immediacy and notoriety of this act conferred a kind of seal of authenticity on the Pusey Horn and, by extension, on all other charter horns. Pusey relied on the medievalism of the family legend, embodied in the horn, to prove his claim; by legally authenticating both the legend and the physical horn, Jefferies in effect wrote that medievalism into legal precedent.

Charter horns also provided antiquaries with proofs of individual families' historical rights to land and authority that pre-dated the imposition of Norman laws and tenures. Sixteenth-, seventeenth-, and eighteenth-century jurisprudence increasingly took for granted the Anglo-Saxon origins of English common law, as well as the geographic divisions of the English landscape that informed and underpinned that law. Among the great legislators of early medieval English history, only Alfred the Great occupied a position equal to Canute and Edward the Confessor.[57] For Charles Pusey or John Aubrey, the possession of a charter horn and the accumulated weight of centuries of story telling linking that horn to Edward or Canute conferred legitimacy and respect. For the dean and chapter at York, the Horn of Ulf symbolized not only the historical origins of their wealth and prestige, but also their relevance to contemporary life as the time-honored landlords of significant swathes of a modern, urbanized, civilized city still dominated by their cathedral.

---

[56] For a twentieth-century example from Australia, see: "HEIRLOOM SOLD – Pusey Horn Brings £1,900 – Gift from King Canute," *The Canberra Times* (25 July 1935): 4.

[57] Simon Keynes, "The Cult of King Alfred the Great," *Anglo-Saxon England* 28 (1999): 225–356 (269–74); Colin Kidd, *British Identities Before Nationalism* (Cambridge: Cambridge University Press, 1999), 83–98; Hugh MacDougall, *Racial Myth in English History: Trojans, Teutons, and Anglo-Saxons* (Hanover, NH: University Press of New England, 1982), chaps. 2–3; Dustin M. Frazier Wood, "John Fortescue-Aland, Old English and the Study of the Common Law" (forthcoming in *Huntington Library Quarterly*).

Early modern legal studies contributed to an increasing interest in and improved scholarly and popular sentiment toward England's Anglo-Saxon and Saxo-Danish past, a result of the fact that antiquaries tended to be lawyers or clergy, or members of the gentry, all groups with personal and professional interests in genealogy and the history of tenures. After 1688, and with increasing volubility from 1714, English historians encouraged their contemporaries to conceive of themselves as the descendants of noble and admirable Anglo-Saxon ancestors. The increasing importance of the early Middle Ages to a sense of English national identity owed much to the efforts of those antiquaries who brought surviving manuscripts and artifacts to the attention of the reading public. The minutes of antiquarian meetings and the frequent appearance of antiquarian publications concerned with local history suggest that for many antiquaries the map of England had begun to acquire a pre-Conquest historical overlay, as often as not a composite of scholarly and imaginative engagement with medieval remains. For example, Samuel Gale's analysis of the Horn of Ulf combines Camden's vivid and almost certainly apocryphal story with an account of the lands given to York by Ulf that has recently been substantiated by Sarah Rees Jones.[58] Similarly, modern scholarship on later medieval horns from Tutbury, Wirral, and Savernake suggests that Edmund Rede's story of Nigel the huntsman and the Boarstall Horn, like the Pusey family legend, is one of many in a tradition of what might be called "horn narratives" that originated in the Middle Ages and that participated in a process of conscious medievalizing of family and place.[59]

Though their association with legal tenure almost certainly led to the survival of the Boarstall and Pusey horns, and in part to the survival of the Horn of Ulf, it is clear that such associations are not the only reasons for the enduring appeal of charter horns.[60] Their dual nature as art objects and archaeological evidence demands, as Avinoam Shalem has written, "that we observe them carefully in order to find out the history marked on their surface [...] to retrieve through [them] the lost world of the past."[61] Charter horns served much the same purpose for their creators as for their subsequent beholders: evoking actual, desired, or imagined cultural memories of family, place, tradition, and identity rooted in a medieval past always anterior to the point of their first recorded appearances as instruments of investiture.

58   Rees Jones, *York*, 51–52, 142, and Map 13.
59   See, *inter alia*: R. Camber and J. Cherry, "The Savernake Horn," *British Museum Yearbook* 2 (1977): 201–11; Cherry, "Symbolism and Survival"; Liddy, "Land, Legend and Gentility"; Shalem, *The Oliphant*, 116–23; *A History of the County of Stafford, Volume X: Tutbury and Needwood Forest*, ed. Nigel J. Tringham (London: Institute of Historical Research, 2007), 19.
60   Cherry, "Symbolism and Survival."
61   Shalem, *Oliphant*, 3.

As one of the few types of early medieval artifact that antiquaries believed they could date with some certainty, and as further support for an increasingly well-developed historical narrative of the history of England's landscape and cultural institutions, charter horns exerted an almost irresistible draw on the antiquarian intellect. Perhaps more importantly, they exerted an equally powerful draw on the antiquarian and the popular imagination; it is a testimony to their power as foci for medievalizing that they continue to do so. Interpretative panels accompanying the Pusey Horn at the Victoria and Albert Museum in London, and the Horn of Ulf at York Minster, continue to recite the horns' legendary associations with Canute and Ulf the thegn. The Horn of Ulf rests in a pair of cast hands, inviting viewers to imaginatively revisit the precise moment when Ulf made his gift at the altar in York Minster, to imagine themselves as recipients of Ulf's largesse or even as Ulf himself. Although the Boarstall Horn now sits largely unseen in the Buckinghamshire County Record Office, visitors to Boarstall Tower are told the story of Nigel, Edward, and the horn by the caretaker, and escorted to the second floor to view the painted panes of glass installed by John Aubrey in the seventeenth century. For modern historical tourists as for early modern antiquaries and medieval landowners, charter horns retain their appeal. With their tangibility and compelling stories rooted in particular events and locales, charter horns continue to evoke in viewers a feeling of immediate medievality, in which each modern moment of viewing and the horns' own medieval moments of investiture are drawn closely, imaginatively together.

Giving Voice to Griselda: Radical Reimaginings of a Medieval Tale*

Renée Ward

In recent decades, scholars of medieval literature have increasingly turned their attention to post-medieval interpretations and adaptations of medieval texts, including editions and adaptations of Chaucer's works. Numerous studies, such as those by Steve Ellis and Stephanie Trigg, consider the ways in which authors have reimagined and responded to Chaucer's corpus, from the Early Modern period to the present, in various media.[1] Similarly, Candace Barrington and Jonathan Hsy are expanding critical awareness of Chaucer's dissemination in other cultures through the public nature of their *Global Chaucers* project.[2] Their growing online database of post-1945 and non-Anglophone adaptations of the poet's works suggests that his influence is considerably more widespread than previously understood. Other studies, including those by David Matthews, Velma Bourgeois Richmond, and Mary Flowers Braswell, examine adaptations and editions of Chaucer's

---

* I am grateful to my colleagues Elyssa Warkentin, Sheila Christie, and Kathy Cawsey for their comments on this project at various stages, as well as to the *Studies in Medievalism* editorial readers, who provided helpful feedback during the revision process.

1 Steve Ellis, *Chaucer at Large: The Poet in the Modern Imagination*, Medieval Cultures 24 (London and Minneapolis: University of Minnesota Press, 2000); Stephanie Trigg, *Congenial Souls: Reading Chaucer from Medieval to Postmodern*, Medieval Cultures 30 (London and Minneapolis: University of Minnesota Press, 2002). Other notable studies on Chaucer and his influence exist, including *Rewriting Chaucer: Culture, Authority and the Idea of the Authentic Text 1400–1602*, ed. Tom Prendergast and Barbara Kline (Columbus: Ohio State University Press, 1999); Tom Prendergast, *Chaucer's Dead Body: From Corpse to Corpus* (New York: Routledge, 2004); and Candace Barrington, *American Chaucers* (New York: Palgrave Macmillan, 2007).

2 See the *Global Chaucers* homepage, <http://globalchaucers.wordpress.com>, last accessed 11 August 2015.

works aimed at primarily child readers during the Victorian and Edwardian periods, and highlight the now well-known adaptors Charles Cowden Clarke (1787–1877) and Mary Eliza Haweis (1848–98). Such studies often herald the volumes by Clarke and Haweis as forerunners of the nineteenth- and early twentieth-century popular editions of Chaucer's works,[3] and Haweis in particular receives frequent acclaim as an early and potentially proto-feminist female adaptor. According to Siân Echard, Haweis's *Chaucer for Children* (1877) provided for turn-of-the-century audiences a "tantalizing" alternative to more traditional editions of Chaucer's works through its textual commentary, which articulates dissatisfaction with the medieval poet's portrayal of female figures.[4]

Critics, however, frequently overlook writers who adapted and published individual Chaucerian narratives outside of the more familiar and frequently moralizing male-narrated framework of editions or collections, primarily of *The Canterbury Tales*. They also almost entirely overlook female writers prior to Haweis whose adaptations are progressive, even radical, in their treatment of women. This article introduces one such neglected writer – Eleanora Louisa Hervey (née Montagu; 1811–1903) – and her poetic responses to the Griselda story, including post-medieval editions of Chaucer's *Clerk's Tale* that were popular in the middle decades of the nineteenth century. Hervey published two unique adaptations of the medieval tale. The first, "Griseldis, with her Children" (1850), appeared in one of the foremost publications of the era, *The Athenaeum: Journal of English and Foreign Literature, Science, and*

3   David Matthews notes that the success of Clarke's and Haweis's volumes "produced many imitators in the late-Victorian and Edwardian periods in England and in America." "Infantilizing the Father: Chaucer Translations and Moral Regulation," *Studies in the Age of Chaucer* 22 (2000): 94–114 (104). For similar studies, particularly those that emphasize editions and adaptations for children, see Velma Bourgeois Richmond, *Chaucer as Children's Literature: Retellings from the Victorian and Edwardian Eras* (Jefferson, NC, and London: McFarland, 2004); Mary Flowers Braswell, "The Chaucer Scholarship of Mary Eliza Haweis (1852–1898)," *Chaucer Review* 39.4 (2005): 402–19; Miriam Youngerman Miller, "Illustrations of the *Canterbury Tales* for Children: A Mirror of Chaucer's World?," *Chaucer Review* 27.3 (1993): 293–304; Charlotte C. Morse, "Popularizing Chaucer in the Nineteenth Century," *Chaucer Review* 38.2 (2003): 99–125; Steve Ellis, "Children's Chaucer," in *Chaucer at Large*, 46–57; and Siân Echard, "Bedtime Chaucer: Juvenile Adaptations and the Medieval Canon," in *Printing the Middle Ages* (Philadelphia: University of Pennsylvania Press, 2008), 126–61.

4   Echard points out that Haweis's illustrations of the Madonna-like Griselda do not match the bluntness of her narrative, which "tells a horrific story […] in which children are apparently murdered." *Printing the Middle Ages*, 130. Echard also highlights Haweis's commentary on Griselda's behavior, in which she suggests "such submission in a woman of the present civilization would be rather mischievous than meritorious. If a modern wife cheerfuly consented to the murder of her children by her spouse, she would probably be consigned to a *maison de santé*, while her husband expiated her sins on the scaffold." Quoted in Echard, *Printing the Middle Ages*, 132.

the Fine Arts; the second, "Griselda" (1869), appeared in Hervey's volume *Our Legends and Lives: A Gift for All Seasons*.

Hervey diverges from the mainstream interpretations of Griselda and her story, and presents instead a radical, proto-feminist retelling. Although she participates in the Chaucerian branch of Victorian medievalism, she boldly rejects canonical and more widely known versions of the tale. In short, she eradicates the framework within which Griselda's story traditionally appears. The majority of the medieval versions, for instance, relay the story through a male narrator: Boccaccio, in *The Decameron*, assigns her tale to his last male story-teller, Dioneo; Petrarch, in *A Fable of Wifely Obedience and Devotion*, presents it within an epistolary narrative guided by his own voice; and Chaucer, in *The Canterbury Tales*, has his Clerk convey and comment upon her story.[5] Later adaptors and editors follow this pattern. Charles Cowden Clarke, for example, embeds Griselda's story within the larger, moralizing

---

[5]   Boccaccio included the story in his *Decameron* (1353), as the tenth tale of the tenth day; Petrarch, in his *Epistolae Seniles* (*Letters of Old Age*, 1373), translated the tale from Italian into Latin, calling it *De obedientia ac fide uxoria mythologia* (*A Fable of Wifely Obedience and Faithfulness*); Chaucer, drawing heavily on Petrarch, reworked the story as the *Clerk's Tale* (1392–95), one of the narratives belonging to the marriage group of Chaucer's *Canterbury Tales*. Christine de Pizan also includes the story in *Le Livre de la Cité des Dames* (*The Book of the City of Ladies*, 1405), but while her narrative emphasizes multiple female voices, Griselda's tale remains at a distance. That is, her story is not a first-person narrative, even if the frame narrative has shifted to a female voice. See Giovanni Boccaccio, *The Decameron*, 2nd edn, trans. G. H. McWilliam (London: Penguin, 1995); Francis Petrarch, *A Fable of Wifely Obedience and Devotion*, in Robert Dudley French, *A Chaucer Handbook*, 2nd edn (New York: F. S. Crofts, 1947), 291–311; Geoffrey Chaucer, *The Canterbury Tales*, in *The Riverside Chaucer*, 3rd edn, ed. Larry D. Benson (Boston: Houghton Mifflin, 1987); and Christine de Pizan, *The Book of the City of Ladies*, trans. Rosalind Brown-Grant (London: Penguin, 1999). Much critical work on the medieval tales exists, especially on their relationships to each other and on the moral questions they raise, including (but by no means limited to) J. Burke Severs, *The Literary Relationships of Chaucer's Clerkes Tale*, Yale Studies in English 96 (New Haven, CT: Yale University Press, 1942; Hamden, CT: Archon Books, 1972); Robin Kirkpatrick, "The Griselda Story in Boccaccio, Petrarch and Chaucer," in *Chaucer and the Italian Trecento*, ed. Piero Boitani (Cambridge: Cambridge University Press, 1983), 231–48; Anne Middleton, "The Clerk and His Tale: Some Literary Contexts," *Studies in the Age of Chaucer* 2 (1980): 121–50; Charlotte C. Morse, "The Exemplary Griselda," *Studies in the Age of Chaucer* 7 (1985): 51–86, and "Critical Approaches to the Clerk's Tale," in *Chaucer's Religious Tales*, ed. C. David Benson and Elizabeth Robertson (Cambridge: D. S. Brewer, 1990), 71–83; Kathryn L. Lynch, "Despoiling Griselda: Chaucer's Walter and the Problem of Knowledge in The Clerk's Tale," *Studies in the Age of Chaucer* 10 (1988): 41–70; Robert R. Edwards, "'The Sclaundre of Walter': The 'Clerk's Tale' and the Problem of Hermeneutics," in *Mediaevalitas: Reading the Middle Ages*, ed. Piero Boitani and Anna Torti (Cambridge: D. S. Brewer, 1996), 15–41; Robin Waugh, "A Woman in the Mind's Eye (and not): Narrators and Gazes in Chaucer's *Clerk's Tale* and in Two Analogues," *Philological Quarterly* 79 (2000): 1–18; and Amy W. Goodwin, "The Griselda Game," *Chaucer Review* 39.1 (2004): 41–69.

discourse of his *Tales from Chaucer* (1833), explaining his hope that child readers "might become wise and good by example of the sweet and kind creatures" they will encounter in his text, such as Griselda.[6]

Hervey, however, favors the female voice. No male narrator guides the reader, and no male interlocutor provides introductory or moralizing discourse on the story's content. Only one voice appears throughout the poem, that of Grisledis.[7] Hervey uniquely reimagines Griselda's story from a female perspective, and, in doing so, presents a negative view of male authority and patriarchal social structures. She sharply critiques the heavily polarized views of women popular in the Victorian period, that they are either angels or monsters, which recall similar dichotomous views from the medieval period of women as either virgins or whores.

This politicization of Griselda's tale derives directly from Hervey's professional and personal experiences. Not only was she a female writer in a male-dominated profession, but also – through her marriage to Thomas Kibble Hervey (1799–1859) and his connections to *The Athenaeum* – she was immersed in an active and critical literary circle, one greatly shaped by the reformist politics of the day. Hervey's later widowhood likewise impacts her writing. Her status as a widow and as the sole provider for her family contributes to the revisions her Griselda poem underwent for publication in *Our Legends and Lives*, a volume in which she expresses explicit concern for control over her previously published works and in which she criticizes publishers who have printed these works without her permission. Hervey's concerns about her own authorial autonomy link her directly to her subject.

The following discussion thus explores how Hervey employs Griselda in texts geared toward adult, female, and child readers, as well as the different media and contexts within which she presents her adaptations of this medieval figure. Further, through its examination of Hervey's unique and proto-feminist retellings, it provides new perspectives on how writers and audiences in the nineteenth century received, reimagined, and appropriated

---

6   Charles Cowden Clarke, Preface to *Tales from Chaucer in Prose. Designed Chiefly for the Use of Young Persons. Illustrated with Fourteen Wood Engravings* (London: Effingham Wilson, 1833), iii. In his later edition, Clarke describes Griselda's conduct as "a fervid hymn in praise of patience, forebearance, and long suffering." *The Riches of Chaucer. Illustrated with wood engravings by W. H. Mott and S. Williams* (London: Effinghman Wilson, 1835), 1.48.

7   In this she aligns herself closely with contemporary female writers such as Elizabeth Barrett Browning, whose "The Complaint of Annelida to False Arcite" (1841) is an adaptation of Chaucer's *Anelida and Arcite* (1380–87). Barrett Browning removes from this poem the male-narrated framework of Chaucer's original, and focuses primarily on Anelida's voice and complaint.

this medieval figure and her story. It also simultaneously restores a "forgotten and neglected" female author to the public and academic realms.[8]

In the 1850 "Griseldis, with her Children" (Appendix A), Hervey condenses the story of Griselda into a narrative of fifty-six lines: a brief poem of fourteen quatrains, each quatrain consisting of two rhyming couplets with the rhyme scheme *aabb*. The poem has two parts, with eight quatrains in the first part and six in the second, and takes the form of a dramatic monologue, a genre popular in the Romantic and Victorian periods that emphasizes the viewpoint of a single speaker at a moment crucial to the speaker's story. The title of the poem's first part, "Griseldis, The Childless," announces Hervey's emphasis on her protagonist's experience of loss and foregrounds a key element of the narrative with which readers familiar with the story would be aware: a husband's cruel testing of his wife through the abduction and supposed murder of their children.

From the poem's opening lines, Hervey's Griseldis appears as a figure of perpetual mourning. Loss and grief impair her will to live, as well as her view of herself, and she informs readers of her imminent demise:

> Sound, sound again the muffled bell, – toll for another dead,
> And heap – heap high, the coals of fire – not ashes – on my
>   head!
> Ye have mocked me with my patience; – let no more such
>   incense rise.
> For here, of women most accursed, the lost Griseldis lies! (1–4)

The sound imagery of these lines evokes the very funeral dirge they represent, and announces that the poem is, in fact, Griseldis's self-crafted eulogy, a lament for her life and for her choices. The stanza's repeated "s" sound, created through initial and internal alliteration, mimics the hiss of flames as a fire is stoked or fed fuel. The emphasis on fire or flames likewise highlights Griseldis's negative view of herself. As she faces her mortal end, the speaker self-identifies not just as a sinner, but also as a soul fully deserving and fully desirous of the fires of hell. She sees herself as someone for whom redemption does not exist, and she willingly faces her fate, even if it is worse than her grim existence in the earthly realm.

---

8   The author borrows this expression from Alan Lupack and Barbara Tepa Lupack, who, in their discussion of Hervey's Arthurian work *The Feasts of Camelot and the Tales that Were Told There* (1863, 1877), identify the poet as one of the "forgotten and neglected" female authors "who never achieved canonical status or whose Arthurian works, by deviating from convention, place them outside the main tradition." *Arthurian Literature by Women*, ed., Alan Lupack and Barbara Tepa Lupack (New York and London: Garland, 1999), 3.

Griseldis welcomes death and demands for herself the tolling bell and the funeral pyre, burial rituals that would not go unnoticed by her audience. Indeed, Hervey's poem has strong overtones of Robert Browning's "The Bishop Orders his Tomb at Saint Praxed's Church Rome, 15 –" (1845), one of the most famous dramatic monologues of the period. Browning's Bishop, like Hervey's Griseldis, lies on his deathbed "dying by degrees" (11) and entreats his children to approach him as he fades from the earth. He also repeatedly instructs those he leaves behind to memorialize him through an elaborate tomb and epitaph, the material replacements for his decaying physical body.[9] As Michael Wheeler explains, during the Victorian period, "highly conventionalized social customs and funerary rituals eased the transition from the deathbed to the bed that is the grave."[10] Funerary rituals formalized and commemorated all aspects of an individual's passing, from confession and the last visit, to the funeral procession and burial itself, "giving shape and thus possibly some meaning" to death.[11] Against more traditional deathbed scenes or funerary practices, Griseldis's requests are unusual. By denying herself burial or a resting place such as the tomb Browning's Bishop requests, Griseldis deprives herself of the type of meaning and memorialization typically associated with Christian funerary rituals. Death will thus erase all vestiges of her physical presence from the earth, as she leaves behind no material or human (children) reminder of her existence. She clearly sees herself as an ultimate sinner and social outsider, one worthy only of a non-Christian burial, cremation.[12]

9   In the Victorian period, as Prendergast explains, monuments or memorials functioned as "material replacements for the lost body" of the deceased. Browning's Bishop, for instance, initially requests a "slab of basalt" (25) with "nine columns round me, two and two" in "Peach-blossom marble" (27, 29), but then later demands "antique-black" (54), along with a "bas-relief in bronze" (56). See Prendergast, *Chaucer's Dead Body*, 75, and Browning, "The Bishop Orders His Tomb at St. Praxed's Church," in *The Works of Robert Browning*, ed. F. G. Kenyon, 10 vols. (London: Smith, Elder, & Co., 1912), 4: 125–28.

10   Michael Wheeler, *Heaven, Hell, and the Victorians* (Cambridge: Cambridge University Press), 5.

11   As Wheeler explains:

Social and literary conventions relating to the deathbed included the visit from a doctor or priest, the presence of a loving attendant to whom a dying confession could be made or of a family on whom a dying blessing could be bestowed, the laying out of a corpse in a darkened room, the "last visit" of the bereaved, and the closing of the coffin. Those associated with the grave included the funeral procession, the funeral itself, the burial, the erection of a memorial stone, and subsequent visits to the grave made by the bereaved. These conventions formalized the different stages of death and bereavement, giving shape and thus possibly some meaning to a transitional phase between one state and another.

See *Heaven, Hell, and the Victorians*, 30–31.

12   Mary Elizabeth Hotz notes that cremation was a focal point for Victorian social and political reformers and became an increasingly popular choice in the last two decades of the nineteenth century, even though the Cremation Act itself was not passed in England

The second stanza shifts the narrative's focus to its medieval origins. Griseldis, reflecting upon her youth, describes her former self:

> I was a shepherd's daughter, and I used to watch the fold
> At eve beside a little cairn upon a lonely wold;
> And I wept to see the new-yeaned lambs how close they lay at rest
> 'Neath the parent breath that fanned them like a soft wind from the west. (5–8)

These images, especially the references to an isolated, rural setting and to the act of shepherding, contribute to the nostalgic and pastoral feel of the stanza, and to the sense that Griseldis's past life was simpler and happier than her current existence. Further, these lines paint an idyllic scene highly evocative of the world that Chaucer's protagonist inhabits, and align Griseldis with the most famous shepherd of all, Christ. Hervey reinforces Griseldis's connection to both the medieval tale and the divine when she links her protagonist to the Marian figure. Like Chaucer's Grisilde, who "A few sheepe, spyn-nynge, on feeld she kepte; / [and] wolde noght been ydel til she slepte" (IV, 223–24), Hervey's speaker spends her time tending the flock.[13] As Larry D. Benson notes, Grisilde's activities align her closely to the Virgin, who was "often pictured both as a shepherdess and as a spinner."[14] Hervey's emphasis on shepherding extends this alignment to her Griseldis, and the combined focus on her purity, industriousness, and maternity marks her as an example of the "domestic angel" who provided for Victorians a secular descendant of the medieval Catholic Madonna.[15] Yet the poem's sudden movement to a pastoral setting underscores the contrast between the first and second stanzas, subtly reminding readers that despite moments of similitude this poem is not the tale with which they are familiar. Likewise, the reference to

---

until 1902. Hotz, Chapter 5: "'The Tonic of Fire': Cremation in Late Victorian England," in *Literary Remains: Representations of Death and Burial in Victorian England* (Albany: State University of New York Press, 2009), 141.

13 All citations of Chaucer's works indicate fragment and line numbers.

14 Benson, "Explanatory Notes," in *The Riverside Chaucer*, 881.

15 "In the Middle Ages [...] mankind's great teacher of purity was the Virgin Mary. [...] For the more secular nineteenth century, however, the eternal type of female purity was represented not by a madonna in heaven but by an angel in the house. Nevertheless, there is a clear line of literary descent from divine Virgin to domestic angel, passing through (among many others) Dante, Milton, and Goethe." See Sandra M. Gilbert and Susan Gubar, *The Madwoman in the Attic: The Woman Writer and the Nineteenth-Century Literary Imagination*, 2nd edn (New Haven, CT, and London: Yale University Press, 2000), 20.

the cairn, itself a symbol of death, recalls the protagonist's opening eulogy and her utter despair.

The second stanza also identifies the major theme of Hervey's poem – motherhood – and establishes the standard by which Griseldis judges her own behavior. Motherhood, in Griseldis's view, consists primarily of the nurturing and protection of one's young, and her experiences as a shepherdess expose her to what she considers the paragon of mothering in the natural world. She notes the tender and protective manner with which the ewes treat the lambs, and renders their relationship sublime. The ewes are as gentle with the lambs as is a soft breeze upon their fleece. Griseldis idealizes both the pastoral setting of her past and its associated depiction of motherhood, and, through her self-identification as a shepherd's daughter, aligns herself with these nurturing figures. She sees herself, in youth, as a maternal figure of purity and love. This is a far cry from the despairing sinner of the poem's opening.

Griseldis's contemplation of motherhood continues in the third stanza, where she emphasizes the connection between instinctual behavior and correct or appropriate mothering. "Motherhood," she declares, "is strong as life" (9). That is, for the female of a species the urge to mother is as strong as the very instinct to live. Further, this urge is "strongest in the least, / [and] findeth out sweet channels in the poor four-footed beast" (9–10), in the creatures or beasts that lack the capacity of reason accessible to humans. Drawing again on the example of her sheep, Griseldis explains how the ewe's instinct to mother is so strong that it "giveth suck to the strange kid if it waileth for its dam" (11). The protection and survival of the lamb, even if not one of its own, is the most important thing for the ewe, demonstrating that instinctual behavior is natural, perfect even, when connected to motherhood. Griseldis, though, falls short of the example she presents, and emphasizes this point by aligning one of her own children with the lambs. She confesses to her audience: "But I, my bird to the kite I gave and to the wolf my lamb" (12). Rather than protect her young, as do the ewes the lambs, she relinquishes the care of her children to a known predator. The instincts to nurture and to protect are more manifest in the lesser beings of her flock than they are in her, a member of the human species. Her sin is thus twofold: she sins because she acts against her instincts and gives away her children, and she sins because as a rational being she should know better than to do so. Griseldis becomes, in her own eyes, a monster because she fails as a mother and as a human being. Here, then, is the root of her anguish.

Griseldis's belief that her decisions and actions result in the loss of her children's lives persists in the following two stanzas, which recount her transition from shepherdess to wife. She explains that upon meeting her husband, she "took him for [her] lord" (15) and "left the young sheep bleating and the cottage by the fold" (16). Hervey's use of the verbs "took" and "left" emphasize her speaker's sense of agency, while the bleating of the lambs, a sound that evokes a sense of distress, reinforces the identification of Griseldis as an unnatural being ill-suited to motherhood. Through language, Hervey renders Griseldis's marriage an active abandonment of both her former self and the first children for which she was responsible, the sheep. She also foreshadows the later abandonment of the human children that occurs when Griseldis acquiesces to her husband's demands and allows them to be removed from her care and purportedly killed.

However, Hervey ultimately suggests that her protagonist's agency is an illusion. She draws attention to the complex and contradictory reality of married life for Victorian women when Griseldis declares that in the act of marriage she "vowed obedience" (20). As a woman under the legal doctrine of coverture, like her medieval counterpart, she must subordinate her will first to that of her father and then to that of her husband. The legal doctrine of coverture, as Ben Griffin explains, extended from the medieval period well into the nineteenth century, and even mid-century, "married women had no independent legal identity in the eyes of the law: husband and wife were deemed to be one person, and that person was the husband."[16] Indeed, "It is the will of the two men, not the will of the daughter, that counts."[17] Regardless of how culpable Griseldis believes herself to be, by performing her duties as a wife – by being the obedient and virtuous domestic angel – she dooms herself to failure as a mother. While one of her primary roles as a wife is to provide heirs for her husband, in order to achieve wifely obedience she must abandon her instincts as a mother. In the patriarchal system, male (and therefore supposedly rational) authority supersedes female instinct (emotion or passion), and marriage (obedience to the husband) is the ultimate undoing of the female figure.

Griseldis bemoans her union and the misery that it brings, for married life is a life without relief, a loveless life of darkness. She declares that, since marrying, "No cool draught [...] these parching lips have touched in all the land" (14), and describes the ensuing years as "the darkest ever womanhood beheld" (17). Grief overcomes Griseldis, and she slowly forgets how to love: "the shaft of love was shivered, and the shriek of anguish quelled: / I sometimes think my brain swam round in that sorrow-flood" (18–19). The nurturing young shepherdess disappears, and the resultant domestic figure becomes increasingly passive and silent, unable to act or to voice her discontent and grief. Additionally, the prominent "s" sound of these lines patterns itself after the poem's opening stanza, reconnecting the speaker to

---

16 Ben Griffin, *The Politics of Gender in Victorian Britain: Masculinity, Political Culture and the Struggle for Women's Rights* (Cambridge: Cambridge University Press, 2012), 4.
17 Gerald Morgan, "The Logic of the Clerk's Tale," *Modern Language Review* 104.1 (January 2009): 1–25 (11).

the flames of the funeral pyre. Griseldis, it seems, was fated for such a death the moment she married.

Hervey's treatment of the key male figures in the story, Griseldis's husband and father, reinforces her criticism of patriarchal authority and increases the distance between her poem and its literary antecedents. Specifically, Hervey drastically minimizes her individualization of the male characters. In "Griseldis, with her Children," the husband and father are both nameless and voiceless. The use of the dramatic monologue form eradicates any perspective other than that of Griselda, and eliminates any chance for the reader to experience a nuanced encounter with the male figures. As such, they signify a type of every-husband or every-father, and operate more broadly as critiques of all male authority within the patriarchal system. Only their actions speak for them, and these actions are cruel.

The opening line of stanza four provides a staccato list of verbs that emphasize the scopophilic nature of the husband's gaze. Griseldis tells readers, "He came – he stopped – he saw me with the pitcher in my hand" (13). The husband-to-be does not dwell upon his future wife's patient and virtuous character, a detail central especially to the medieval narratives by Chaucer and Petrarch. Instead, a voyeuristic perspective that emphasizes only the external, physical appearance of the woman replaces the concern for female industriousness and humility. Hervey's narrative, in this instance, evokes Boccaccio's story more than any other medieval source, building upon the husband Gualtieri's realization that his wife-to-be is "very beautiful," and his thought that "a life with her would have much to commend it."[18] Further, the verbs through which Hervey recounts this scene underscore the male gaze's complete objectification of Griseldis, undermining any previous sense of female agency within the narrative.

Hervey's depiction of Griseldis's father, an original and striking addition to the tale, increases the objectification of the female figure. Griseldis explains to her audience that, as she departed from the shepherd's cottage for her new life, her father "clutched his gold" (15). This gold, which passes from husband to father, identifies marriage as an entirely economic transaction, one that renders the female body a commodity to be bought and sold at the whim of men. Unlike Chaucer's Janicula or Petrarch's Janicola, both of whom express considerable emotion concerning Griselda's condition, Hervey's father figure is an emotionless shell. In Chaucer's *Clerk's Tale*, for instance, when the Marquis puts his wife aside, Janicula, echoing Job, "curseth" (IV, 902) his existence, and then escorts his daughter home "ful sorwefully wepynge" (IV, 914).[19]

---

18 Boccaccio, *The Decameron*, 785.
19 Janicula "Curseth the day and tyme that Nature / Shoop hum to been a lyves creature" (IV, 902–3), echoes Job 3:3: "Let the day perish wherein I was born, and the night in

Griseldis's father expresses no such concern for his daughter's well-being. Rather, by clutching his money, he demonstrates only his greed. Hervey's critique of the male objectification of women, like other aspects of her poem, recalls Browning's "The Bishop," in which the dying Bishop repeatedly refers to the long-dead mother of his children as an object to be gazed upon and desired, as something that earned him the envy of his rival, Gandolf. He describes her, for instance, as "fair" (5, 125), a "True peach, / Rosy and flaw-less" (32–33), and, significantly, as "the prize" (33). Likewise, in Hervey's poem, men view women as objects to be acquired, nothing more.

Hervey confirms male culpability and the powerless state of the female through her protagonist's exclamation, "I have vowed obedience, and the bond was sealed – in blood!" (20). This line, which evokes the cultural practice in which blood on the marriage-bed sheets proves both consum-mation of the relationship and the virginity of the bride, links the death of Griseldis's children explicitly to wifehood and to female submissiveness. It suggests that Griseldis's bride-price extends beyond the gold that her father clutches, even beyond her maidenhead. For Griseldis, marriage costs her the lives of her children, as well as the ability to act or speak as a woman, especially as a mother.

The remaining stanzas of the poem's first part return to Griseldis's under-standing of motherhood as instinctual and as part of the natural world. Once again, she contrasts her own behavior to that of the sheep in the fold, drawing on the previously established link between the pastoral and the divine when she declares that she seeks her (human) children in the "pasture-lands" (22). The inhabitants of this space, those creatures she has already identified as the paragon of motherhood, become "angels true to motherhood, whose robes are God's own light" (23). Mothers, she suggests, do God's work when they fulfill their natural role: they protect their young, just as Christ protects his followers (his flock). Griseldis, however, fears she cannot share in God's light. As a sinner – as a mother who fails to protect her young – she denies herself the right to such bliss. Griseldis even fears that her sins will prevent reunion with her children in the afterlife. The angels, she declares, the sheep that embody motherly perfection, "Would meet my step on heaven's floor, and shut me from your sight" (24).

Griseldis further diminishes her motherhood by suggesting that lower life forms such as insects are more successful parents than she is:

> The Ant, that airiest thing that haunts the meadows circling rings,
> To do her mother-task assigned rends off her very wings, –

which it was said: A manchild is conceived." Benson, "Explanatory Notes," in *The Riverside Chaucer*, 883.

> But I, to whom a holier sense and higher gifts were given,
> The wings that *I* have torn away had wafted me to heaven.
> (25–28)

Personal pain and suffering are less important to this insect than its responsibilities to its unborn young, and, to fulfill its reproductive duties, the ant
readily mutilates its own body.[20] Not so Griseldis, who contrasts herself
directly to the ant. Despite being human, and therefore the supposed
greater of the two species, Griseldis acts unnaturally: she tears off her wings
(her children) when instead she should protect them. She fails to fulfill the
natural and necessary motherly duties that normally would earn her a place
in heaven.[21]

The concluding stanza of the first part reinforces the grim tone of the
opening stanza while it simultaneously reminds the audience that this narrative is entirely removed from other versions of the story with which they
are familiar, medieval and post-medieval. Specifically, it maintains Griseldis's
belief that her children no longer live, and it erases the family reunion with
which the medieval authors and their redactors conclude the tale. As she
faces her demise, Griseldis seeks comfort through an imagined reunion with
her dead children:

> Close round me now in spirit while I yield me to my rest;
> Kiss – clasp me, if ye may, – that I may feel at last in death
> The phantom of that joy which died when ye gave up your
> breath! (30–32)

Here, Hervey subtly evokes the language of Chaucer's text, specifically the
reunion scene in which Grisilde repeatedly swoons as if dead and clasps her
children so fiercely that it is only "with greet sleighte and greet difficultee"
(IV, 1102) that they emerge from her embrace.[22] As Barry Windeatt suggests,
"a swoon distinguishes itself from other reactions to feelings or events by

---

20 The ant's rending of its wings is a biological process called "dealation" common among
certain ant families. See, for example, S. N. Burns, R. K. Vander Meer, and P. Teal, "Mating
Flight Activity as Dealation Factors for Red Imported Fire Ant (Hymenoptera: Formicidae)
Female Alates," *Annals of the Entomological Society of America* 100.2 (2007): 257–64; or G.
Castella, P. Christe, and M. Chapuisat, "Mating Triggers Dynamic Immune Regulations in
Wood Ant Queens," *Journal of Evolutionary Biology* 22.3 (March 2009): 564–70.

21 I am extremely grateful to the comments received on these lines via the VICTORIA listserv,
specifically those made by Herbert Tucker, Michael Wolff, and Clemence Schultze. I am also
grateful to my colleague Elyssa Warkentin for her assistance in soliciting their comments.

22 Chaucer describes Grisilde's swoons at IV, 1079, 1087, and 1099–1100. During the latter
swoon, she "so sadly [tightly] holdeth" (IV, 1100) her children that they have difficulty
disentangling themselves from her.

being such an absolute response that further ability to think and feel is temporarily overpowered."[23] In short, a swoon is akin to death in that it is a suspension of life and action. Griseldis, on her deathbed, occupies a suspended state, hovering between life and death. Further, the intensity of Griseldis's outcry parallels the silence of her medieval predecessor, whose swoons would denote to a medieval audience the overwhelming power of her emotional response.

This scene reminds readers that the memorialization Hervey's protagonist desires diverges from Victorian practices by playing upon the motif of the last visit between the dying and the bereaved, a moment that should bring closure and comfort. As an imagined experience, Griseldis's reunion fails to fulfill this traditional consolatory goal. It also increases the distance between Hervey's narrative and its antecedents. Instead of providing resolution through reunion and comfort, Hervey highlights Griseldis's joyless life and her failure to protect her young, and presents her children's deaths as real rather than imagined. The only moment of relief occurs when Griseldis, in death, finds the voice she lacks in life, and can finally give shape to her loss.

The title of the poem's second part, "Griseldis, With her Children," suggests to its audience a turn in the narrative that should align it more closely with the widely known medieval and Victorian versions in which Griselda reunites with her family. Yet despite its evocation of such a turn, the second part reinforces a reading of Hervey's adaptation as an entirely different narrative. It also confirms her intent to eradicate resolution. Reunion, when it happens, brings no love or joy, for Griseldis and her children are capable of neither. Drawing again upon images of the natural world, Griseldis compares her children to flora, although this time she does not evoke the idyllic, pastoral world that features earlier in the poem and in the medieval tales. Instead, she compares her children to the plant life of a neglected garden. She likens her children to buds that have not fully bloomed, and suggests that because of the damage previously done to them they never will. When she embraces the children, she notes how loosely their arms "twine" (39) around her, "like tendrils long since riven from a crushed and trampled vine" (40). The tendrils, her children, cannot help their current almost lifeless condition because the larger plant from which they stem, their mother, is equally damaged. To reach its potential, plant life, like the lambs in the fold, requires nurture; Griseldis's relationship with her children, though, what she refers to as "Nature's […] bond" (52), is beyond repair.[24] Reunion only perpetuates her sense of loss.

23 Barry Windeatt, "The Art of Swooning in Middle English," in *Medieval Latin and Middle English Literature: Essays in Honour of Jill Mann*, ed. Christopher Cannon and Maura Nolan (Cambridge: D. S. Brewer, 2011), 211–30 (211–12).
24 These lines recall Shakespeare's *King Lear*, which similarly focuses on the bond between

Upon meeting her children, Griseldis notes in them the very darkness that characterizes her own existence. She describes them as "shadowy forms" (33) with eyes "cold and passionless and lids without a tear" (35), and says that their faces remind her of her own upon her wedding day (36). A loveless marriage, she suggests, creates loveless children, especially if the mother subordinates the needs of her children to the needs of her husband. Griseldis even reads her guilt in the children's faces:

> Your glances say I slew you; and alas! ye seem to stand
> All shrinking and in horror – though no blood is on my hand; –
> There may be other pangs as keen from which no power can save,
> But these are as sharp thorns to bind the turf upon my grave.
> (45–48)

That her children live makes Griseldis no less culpable. By neglecting her responsibilities as a mother, she condemned her children to emotional and psychological deaths, if not to physical ones. Her reference to thorns, which evokes the Christ figure once again, reminds the reader that she views herself as a sinner and suggests that the condition of her children is a burden she must bear, in and beyond death.

The poem's final stanzas suggest that reunion is an anticlimactic ending, but one appropriate for the ills of Griseldis's life. She concludes that while "life hath no more sweetness left," death also "has no more sting" (50). The knowledge that her children live provides a degree of comfort, for she no longer fears being barred from their sight in the afterlife, and, although she still welcomes death, she does so now for a different reason. She beseeches her children to embrace her in hopes that close contact in her final moments will engender in them at least one fond memory of their mother. She hopes that, perhaps, because of such a moment, "The blossoms and the stricken tree shall grow together yet" (54). The poem's closing lines voice her dying wish: "And the sweets that failed me living shall cleave to me in my fall, / As the bind-flower to the bramble and the moss-root to the wall" (56). Although she still sees herself as a sinner (like Adam and Eve, she falls, or

---

parents and their children, as well as on natural and unnatural behaviors. The motif of the natural bond informs the relationships between Gloucester and his sons, Edgar and Edmund, but is most prominent in Lear's relationships with his daughters, Cordelia, Goneril, and Regan. For instance, when Lear queries how much his daughters love him, Cordelia responds that she does so "According to [her] bond; no more nor less" (1.1.90). Lear, dissatisfied with her response, disowns his daughter, a folly that ultimately leads to the loss of his children, most especially of Cordelia, as well as to the loss of his own self and life. William Shakespeare, *The Tragedy of King Lear: The Folio Text*, in *The Norton Shakespeare: Tragedies*, 2nd edn, ed. Stephen Greenblatt et al. (New York and London: Norton, 2008), 587.

sins), Griseldis hopes that in death she can accomplish what she could not in life: to teach her children to love and to bond with others, including herself. In doing so, she may find redemption.

Hervey's narrative is a radical departure from its literary antecedents, and, from the outset, she rejects the framework and male narrator or guide of more widely known versions of the tale. She also refuses readers the ending that they would anticipate: the resolution offered by the medieval texts and their adaptations.[25] What she offers is a new reading of Griselda's story, one that emphasizes the female perspective and female experience, and that renders maternity and female emotion superior to male or patriarchal authority. Consequently, Hervey both aligns herself with and takes up the challenge presented by Chaucer's Wife of Bath, who questions how representations of men and women would differ if written by the latter gender. Indeed, Hervey's depiction of male figures fulfills the Wife's prediction that if women wrote texts, "They wolde han write of men moore wikkednesse / Than al the mark of Adam may redresse" (III, 701–2).

These changes allow Hervey, as a writer and as a woman, to explore Griseldis's passivity and her complicity in the abduction and supposed murder of her children, along with the effects this passivity has on her emotional and psychological states. They also simultaneously allow her to gesture to the inadequacy of the more widely known medieval and post-medieval versions of the story, those told by male authors and editors, to represent women and female experiences. Hervey thus fashions her Griselda, to a degree, after Chaucer's Wife. As Theresa Tinkle suggests, "Chaucer clearly designs his feminine persona [Alison] to engage unsettled contemporary debates [...]. The persona allows [him] to enter the debates behind a mask."[26] Although Tinkle's point concerns primarily Chaucer's engagement with debates surrounding "vernacular scripture and lay hermeneutics," the point transfers readily to the current argument.[27] What matters is Chaucer's construction of a female character through which he engages in debates that ultimately concern women in society, and his use of the voice of that female figure to challenge established beliefs and practices.

Hervey does no less with her Griseldis. The dramatic monologue form especially allows her to explore more fully the conflicts between the roles of mother and wife that women were expected to fulfill in Victorian society,

---

25 This is not to say that each medieval writer does not problematize his tale's conclusion. Indeed, all accounts are fraught with moral issues. However, these accounts ultimately restore the familial and social structures that order the societies of the respective tales.

26 Theresa Tinkle, "The Wife of Bath's Marginal Authority," *Studies in the Age of Chaucer* 32 (2010): 67–101 (70).

27 Tinkle, "The Wife of Bath's Marginal Authority," 70.

and to critique the socially prescribed gender roles and behaviors that relegate women to the domestic sphere and demand that they be saint-like paragons of virtue. In particular, she criticizes the obedience a woman must show her father and especially her husband, for her protagonist's success in this area leads to her "deep sorrow-flood" (19), the loss of her children. Hervey's reimagining of Griselda and her story subverts gender stereotypes that negatively associate women with emotion and instinct. Griseldis's words suggest that motherhood derives from natural and instinctual behaviors, and that such emotions are positive experiences to be embraced rather than denied. Hervey sees patriarchal and economic systems of power that rely upon the maintenance of gendered social roles as ultimately to blame for Griseldis's condition. Such systems, which put women "totally under the control of their husbands, who manag[e] their money and determin[e] the lives of their children," pit wifehood against motherhood, with disastrous results.[28] Indeed, Griseldis's description of her loss suggests that her children's lives are meaningless to her husband and that her life equals nothing more than monetary gain for her father. In her eyes, negative appetites and desires drive these men; consequently, she and her children suffer.

Initially, the 1869 "Griselda" (Appendix B) appears to be a carbon copy of "Griseldis, with her Children." The poem maintains Hervey's eradication of the masculine framing narrative, as well as the earlier poem's criticisms of patriarchy and the entrenched gender roles and stereotypes upon which it relies. In fact, with the exception of minor word-swaps and a few changes to punctuation, the second version reproduces most of the original poem's first part, "Griseldis, the Childless." Word changes occur in line 1 ("once more" for "again"), line 16 ("wold" for "fold"), and line 24 ("bar me" for "shut"), but the language of stanzas 1 through 6 is otherwise unchanged. Several minor alterations to punctuation likewise occur, but the only notable edit appears in line 12, where a question mark replaces a comma ("But I? – My bird to the kite I gave, and to the wolf my lamb!"). The addition of the question mark, however, significantly alters the function of this line. Whereas, in the original, Hervey presents a statement of fact, here, through punctuation, she emphasizes reader interaction. The line now focuses attention on the dialogue between the speaker and her readers, suggesting that the line responds to an audience-based query concerning the fate of Griselda's children. Interestingly, Hervey's edit aligns her story closely with Chaucer's *Clerk's Tale*. The increased connection between speaker and audience parallels the Ellesmere manuscript's inclusion of an envoy, which Stephanie Trigg

---

[28]   John R. Reed, *Victorian Conventions* (Athens: Ohio University Press, 1975), 44.

describes as "a direct address to the audience," one that increases audience interest in the tale.[29]

More importantly, in "Griselda," Hervey removes all vestiges of her protagonist's reunion with her children by omitting entirely the second half of the earlier poem. This omission diminishes the narrative's focus on the consequences of her wifely obedience, particularly those visited upon Griselda's innocent children. The disturbing images of her young as damaged tendrils, and as vacant, loveless husks, disappear, as does Griselda's despairing declaration that she reads her guilt in their faces. The absence of both lessens Griselda's culpability and gives greater weight to the first part's commentary on the male figures and their actions. It likewise diminishes any evocations of medieval and post-medieval Griselda stories in which reunion and resolution occur, along with audience expectations of such closure, and reminds readers that Hervey's poem is unique.

Although the recast ending of the shorter poem renders Griselda's loss a permanent one, it simultaneously moves away from the earlier poem's lament for a grim existence toward an expression of spiritual salvation. In addition to shortening the poem, Hervey eliminates the original final stanza of the first part (lines 29–32) and rewrites the penultimate stanza, which now operates as the poem's conclusion. While the last two lines of the stanza (27–28) remain the same and can still be read as Griselda's lament for her inability to enter heaven in the afterlife, the first two lines problematize such a reading. The stanza now reads:

> The lowly ant whom motherhood to earth unerring brings,
> To Nature's instinct blindly true, rends off her clay-bound wings;
> But I, to whom a holier sense of higher gifts were given,
> The wings that *I* have torn away had wafted me to heaven!
> (25–28)

Hervey's description of the ant's wings as "clay-bound" (26) evokes biblical accounts of creation (in which God forms Adam and Eve out of dust) and renders the ant's removal of her wings a similar act: it is the first step in procreation.[30] Further, her description of the "unerring" ant being brought "to earth" evokes the Immaculate Conception and the Virgin's subsequent loss of her own child on the crucifix. In a single couplet, Hervey metaphorically links the ant to humanity, and, by extension, reinforces Griselda's connection to the idealized medieval Marian figure. Such a move provides room for an understanding of Griselda's death as ultimately redemptive. Despite her

---

29 Trigg, *Congenial Souls*, 80.
30 Specifically, it recalls Genesis 2.7: "And the Lord God formed man of the dust of the ground, and breathed into his nostrils the breath of life; and man became a living soul."

fears to the contrary, Griselda will ascend and enter heaven precisely because virtuous qualities (devotion, constancy, and obedience) inform her actions. She ultimately becomes, in death, the domestic angel.

In the second poem, then, Hervey maintains her emphasis on the female perspective and experience: Griselda condemns blind obedience in women to male authority; insists that wifely obedience conflicts with the responsibilities of motherhood; and questions the social structures that commodify the female body and existence. However, Hervey's revisions create a tension within the narrative that previously did not exist, and that potentially undermine her criticism of patriarchal authority. The confirmation of loss and utter despair present in the original gives way to an expression of hope in final redemption. The initial poem's emphasis on Griselda's failures as a mother, which result in her inability to access heaven, now exists alongside revisions that align the protagonist's behavior with the medieval pinnacle of female behavior. In short, the revised ending reinforces the social message that both versions so vehemently speak out against, that motherhood should be subservient to wifehood. "Griselda" is a strikingly different poem from its predecessor.

The use of a medieval narrative to give voice to discontent with contemporary circumstances was not uncommon in the nineteenth century. In fact, it features prominently in what Clare Broome Saunders identifies as a specifically "female" type of Victorian medievalism.[31] In a period during which women who strayed outside of the domestic sphere were often seen as barbaric or even whorish, the vehicle of medievalism, through its historical distance, provided a reasonably safe space for social criticism. In this, Hervey practices a technique familiar to medieval writers, including Chaucer, who often sets his tales in "distant times and distant lands rather than fourteenth-century England."[32] Indeed, female writers of the late Romantic and Victorian periods frequently employed "medieval motifs, forms, and settings to enable them to comment on contemporary issues, such as war and gender roles, areas where women's more open comment had often met with career-destroying censure."[33]

Griselda's story, which remained popular in European countries in the post-medieval period, was particularly attractive to many Victorians, who valued its presentation of the ideal woman as a patient and obedient wife.[34]

---

[31]   Clare Broome Saunders, *Women Writers and Nineteenth-Century Medievalism*, Nineteenth-Century Major Lives and Letters (New York: Palgrave Macmillan, 2009), 1.

[32]   Jill Mann, *Feminizing Chaucer*, Chaucer Studies (Cambridge: D. S. Brewer, 2002), xv.

[33]   Saunders, *Women Writers and Nineteenth-Century Medievalism*, 1.

[34]   By the mid-nineteenth century Griselda was revered as a saint-like or angelic domestic figure, "the wife who courageously endures intolerable conditions." See Reed, *Victorian Conventions*, 40. For a brief survey of the major nineteenth-century editions and adap-

In fact, the name "Griselda" carried considerable weight in the nineteenth century. Maria Edgeworth, for instance, demonstrated the social currency of Griselda's figure when she named a novel, *The Modern Griselda: A Tale* (1805), and its protagonist after her, while three decades later the Austrian writer Baron Münch-Bellinghausen, under the pseudonym Friedrich Halm, reworked her story as a dramatic text.[35] Versions of her story appeared frequently, sometimes serialized, in popular Victorian periodicals, many of which sold cheaply, "for a penny or a penny and a half."[36] For instance, in 1836, *Chambers's Edinburgh Journal* published the prose "Tale of the Patient Griselda," and a year later *Blackwood's Edinburgh Magazine* printed "Griselda, The Clerke's Tale," with the subtitle "re-made from Chaucer."[37] Similarly, *The Penny Magazine* ran two series on Chaucer by John Saunders, "one on the pilgrims from the *General Prologue* in 1841 and another on the *Canterbury Tales* in 1845," the latter of which included a three-part publication of the *Clerk's Tale*.[38] These serialized excerpts later appeared in Saunders's popular two-volume *Canterbury Tales from Chaucer* (1845).

As a prolific and respected writer – Hervey had an expansive and financially successful literary career from her early twenties until her early seventies[39] – and as a regular contributor to widely circulated venues such as *Chambers's*

tations of Griselda's story, albeit one that omits Hervey's poems, see Judith Bronfman, *Chaucer's Clerk's Tale: The Griselda Story Received, Rewritten, Illustrated* (New York and London: Garland, 1994), 61–72.

35 Edgeworth highlights Chaucer's *Clerk's Tale* when the characters read the story at a dinner party. She also names her protagonist, Griselda Bolingbroke, after the medieval figure, although Edgeworth's Griselda demonstrates none of the patience and humility of her literary predecessor. Halm not only dramatizes the story, but also, more incredibly, renders it an Arthurian narrative in which Walter becomes Percival and in which Arthur's queen, Guinevere, bears the blame for Griselda's misfortunes. See Maria Edgeworth, *The Modern Griselda* (London: J. Johnson, 1805), and Friedrich Halm [Baron Eligius Franz Joseph von Münch-Bellinghausen], *Griselda: A Drama in Five Acts*, trans. Ralph A. Anstruther (London: Black and Armstrong, 1840).

36 Walter Graham, *English Literary Periodicals* (New York: Octagon Books, 1966), 296 n. 1.

37 "Tale of the Patient Griselda," *Chambers's Edinburgh Journal* 257 (31 December 1836): 390; "Griselda, The Clerke's Tale. Re-Made from Chaucer," *Blackwood's Edinburgh Magazine* 41.259 (May 1837): 655–67.

38 Morse, "Popularizing Chaucer in the Nineteenth Century," 105. For the serialized version of Saunders's edition, see "Chaucer's *Canterbury Tales. The Clerk's Tale*," *Penny Magazine of the Society for the Diffusion of Useful Knowledge*, 14.856 (2 August 1845): 300–2; 14.857 (9 August 1845): 310–11; and 14.859 (23 August 1845): 323–24.

39 In 1839, one reviewer identifies Hervey as a talented and well-known writer, as "a lady whose smaller pieces have now been some years before the public, as contributions to our periodical literature. They are characterized by more vigour of thought and more independent action of mind than are common with lady poets." "*The Landgrave, a Play, in Five Acts; with Dramatic Illustrations of Female Character*. By Eleanora Louisa Montagu. Smith, Elder, & Co.," *The Athenaeum* 616 (17 August 1839): 607.

Edinburgh Journal and *The Penny Magazine*, Hervey likely encountered many periodical versions of Griselda's story.[40] As a mother (Hervey's son, Frederic James Hervey, was born in 1845), she also probably knew other incarnations of the tale directed toward child readers, such as those by Clarke. Further, as the wife of T. K. Hervey, the recently appointed editor of *The Athenaeum*, Hervey likely encountered Saunders's serialized excerpts and his subsequent two-volume edition, as well as the lukewarm review the latter received in *The Athenaeum*.[41]

It is also possible that Saunders's commentary on Chaucer's treatment of Griselda provided an impetus for Hervey's own adaptations. In his "Remarks on the Clerk's Tale," Saunders praises Chaucer's version of the story, stating that the medieval poet, "while apparently making little or no attempt to show the state of Grisilde's feelings, is in truth constantly revealing depth beneath depth of the heart of this divine woman."[42] Although Saunders questions the moral nature of Walter's testing of his wife, he purports that the aspects of the tale that might shock a contemporary audience (such as the husband's tests) would not have shocked a medieval one, which, he suggests, would recognize the behaviors of both Griselda and her husband as characteristic of their roles within the feudal system. In Saunders's opinion, Griselda, and her medieval audience, see her subjugation to Walter as "a mark of honour rather than humiliation" and as part of the "goodness" of the social system in which they existed.[43]

Hervey's reimagining of Griselda's story speaks directly to these points. Her poems, like Chaucer's, highlight the emotional state of the distraught mother, albeit in different ways, but most especially through the use of the female voice. Through their critique of patriarchal authority and social structures, they also provide a view of the relationship between Griselda and her husband that opposes the one put forth by Saunders, suggesting that his opinion – a male opinion – is inadequate as commentary upon the condition of the female and her experiences. Hervey's poems highlight themes within

---

40 Graham notes that the *The Penny Magazine*, established in 1832, "soon reached a circulation of 200,000 in weekly numbers and monthly parts." *English Literary Periodicals*, 296 n. 1.

41 The reviewer, William Hepworth Dixon, writes:

> Mr. Saunders has undertaken the, in our opinion, very needless – and certainly unprofitable – task of preparing an edition of the Canterbury Tales. [...] We agree generally with Mr. Saunders that any attempt to improve a great work of Art must prove a failure, [...] and we only wonder that the argument and the examples did not lead Mr. Saunders to carry the warning one step further" [i.e., to his own work].

See "*Canterbury Tales, from Chaucer*. By John Saunders. 2 vols.," *The Athenaeum* 1037 (11 September 1847): 951. For Saunders's volume, see *Canterbury Tales from Chaucer*, 2 vols. (London: Charles Knight and Co., 1845).

42 Saunders, *Canterbury Tales from Chaucer*, 1.216.

43 Saunders, *Canterbury Tales from Chaucer*, 1.217.

the medieval Griselda story that Saunders minimalizes in his commentary: the protagonist's specific responses to marriage, motherhood, and the loss of her children.[44] They also speak directly to the two basic assumptions out of which Victorian "domestic ideology" arose: "The first was that men would always use their domestic authority wisely; the second was that a wife would happily submit to her husband's wishes."[45] Both of Hervey's versions of Griselda's story make it clear that these assumptions are untenable.

As a writer and as a woman, Hervey was not alone in her explorations of such social issues. Through her career and marriage, she participated in a wide and progressive literary circle that included prominent Victorians such as long-time and influential Secretary for the Royal Literary Fund, Octavian Blewitt (1810–84), and the well-known writer for *The Illustrated London News* and *The Times*, Charles Mackay (1814–89).[46] Her connections to *The Athenaeum*, which, from the 1830s onward, was a well-established and prosperous literary journal that "exceeded, in circulation, any other similar paper,"[47] no doubt directly influenced the concerns she expresses in

---

44   Modern critics provide more nuanced understandings of Chaucer's representation of Griselda. Carolyn Dinshaw, for example, suggests that Chaucer's Clerk expresses considerable sympathy for her figure and recognizes that, as a woman, she is "one who is fundamentally left out of patriarchal society." *Chaucer's Sexual Poetics* (Madison: University of Wisconsin Press, 1989), 154. For discussions that similarly emphasize Griselda's strength or complex position within the tales, see also Jill Mann, *Geoffrey Chaucer*, Feminist Reading Series (Atlantic Highlands, NJ: Humanities Press International, 1991); Elaine Tuttle Hanson, "The Powers of Silence: The Case of the Clerk's Griselda," in *Women and Power in the Middle Ages*, ed. Mary Erler and Maryanne Kowaleski (Athens: University of Georgia Press, 1988), 230–49, and *Chaucer and the Fictions of Gender* (Berkeley: University of California Press, 1992); Elizabeth D. Kirk, "Nominalism and the Dynamics of the *Clerk's Tale*: *Homo Viator* as Woman," in *Chaucer's Religious Tales*, ed. David Benson and Elizabeth Robertson, Chaucer Studies (Cambridge: D. S. Brewer, 1990), 111–20; and John A. Pitcher, "The Martyr's Purpose: The Rhetoric of Disavowal in *The Clerk's Tale*," in *Chaucer's Feminine Subjects: Figures of Desire in the Canterbury Tales*, New Middle Ages Series (New York: Palgrave Macmillan, 2012), 81–107.

45   Griffin, *The Politics of Gender*, 38.

46   Letters between T. K. Hervey and Octavian Blewitt suggest that the two, and their wives, were quite friendly. Hervey addresses letters to Blewitt as "My dear Blewitt," as opposed to the more common and more formal "My dear Sir," and their exchanges reference social meetings and express warm wishes between the two families. See, for example, T. K. Hervey to The Secretary [Octavian Blewitt] of the Royal Literary Fund, 6 June 1848, 96 RLF 1/1207: 3, British Library. Correspondence exists as well between the Herveys and Charles Mackay, mostly in response to his requests to include some of their works in volumes he edited. Eleanora L. Hervey to Charles Mackay, 19 February 1857, and Thomas Kibble Hervey to Charles Mackay, 20 February 1857, RP 7536/1, British Library.

47   Graham, *English Literary Periodicals*, 318. Leslie A. Marchand likewise notes that once editors dropped the price of *The Athenaeum* "to 4d. in 1831" circulation exploded from approximately 3,000 issues to 18,000 issues. Marchand, *The Athenaeum: A Mirror of Victorian Culture* (New York: Octagon Books, 1971), 45.

her adaptation of Griselda's story. While in its early decades the publication maintained a "custom of strict neutrality in politics," under the stewardship of T. K. Hervey it voiced "a lively interest in social reform movements" and published "paragraphs and short articles or editorial notes" on topics such as "prison reform, workmen's housing, factory legislation, [and] the curbing of child labour."[48]

These interests represent only a portion of the social issues of the day, and their emphasis on disenfranchised or marginalized populations parallels closely the contemporary political reforms that emphasized women's rights, including the Aggravated Assaults, or Women's Protection, Act (1853), which increased fines and jail terms for individuals who assaulted women and children, and provided for women a modicum of protection from domestic abuse; the Divorce Act (1857), which granted women both a legal identity and the right to the property with which they entered their marriage; and the Married Women's Property Acts (1870, 1874, 1882), which granted married women the rights to inherit property and to own the earnings they made from employment.[49] The Athenaeum's remarkably high level of female participation, which increased as the century progressed and was especially notable during T. K. Hervey's editorship, suggests that such issues would be of interest not only to the journal's readers, but also to its contributors.[50]

"Griseldis, with her Children" is therefore a timely adaptation, and it is no surprise that it found a home in this prominent publication. The poet's husband was the editor for almost a decade, and the publication welcomed female contributors. More importantly, the liberal political views that permeated The Athenaeum's pages under T. K. Hervey's editorship matched the progressive nature of the poem's content. As one of the most widely circulating publications of the nineteenth century, The Athenaeum presented social issues to a sizable audience constituted primarily of adult, middle-class

---

48   Marchand, The Athenaeum, 77.
49   For more on such political advances for women during the nineteenth century, see, for instance, Griffin, The Politics of Gender in Victorian Britain; Mary Poovey, "Covered but Not Bound: Caroline Norton and the 1857 Matrimonial Causes Act," Feminist Studies 14.3 (1988): 467–85; Dorothy M. Stetson, A Woman's Issue: The Politics of Family Law Reform in England (Westport, CT: Greenwood Press, 1982); or Mary Shanley, "'One Must Ride Behind': Married Women's Rights and the Divorce Act of 1857," Victorian Studies 25 (1982): 355–76.
50   Marysa Demoor remarks that even though female contributions increased significantly in the latter part of the nineteenth century, they were still remarkable in the early and mid-decades, and she attributes to T. K. Hervey "the recruitment of possibly the most prolific woman reviewer of the middle decades of the century: Geraldine Jewsbury." Demoor, Their Fair Share: Women, Power and Criticism in the Athenaeum, from Millicent Garrett Fawcett to Katherine Mansfield, 1870–1920 (Burlington, VT: Ashgate, 2000), 1–2, 88.

readers.[51] Hervey's primarily adult and progressively minded readers would not be unfamiliar with or unused to the critique of the cultural and social hegemonies that her first version of the Griselda story articulates.

The shifts in tone and message between "Griseldis, with her Children" and "Griselda," coupled with Hervey's inclusion of the latter poem in her volume *Our Legends and Lives*, suggests that she envisioned a different audience and more didactic purpose for the revised poem than for the original. Her description of this collection of poems as a book "Especially Offered / to a Son / by his Mother" identifies her son as the initial audience. Indeed, advertisements for the volume's publication coincide with Frederic's birthday.[52] Although in 1869 he was twenty-four, his age does not preclude him from being viewed by his mother as a child reader worthy of instruction. The two remained close throughout Hervey's life, a bond likely strengthened by her widowhood, and Frederic, who never married, lodged with his mother until her death in 1903.[53] A gift book aimed at child readers was also a lucrative endeavor for the widowed Hervey, as the genre remained popular throughout the century.[54] Hervey's additional identification of the volume as "a Gift for All," however, anticipates a wider audience than just her son or other children. Families frequently engaged in shared reading practices in the domestic sphere, and adults, as the income earners, were considered the primary consumers of the gift-book genre. More specifically, middle-class female consumers were considered the target market for these highly ornamental material objects.[55] The ornamental nature and female readership of these volumes, though, did not lessen their didactic message. As Frederick W. Faxon notes, while these volumes "might ornament the drawing-room

---

51 Most Victorian periodicals were "literary reviews or magazines oriented to a general adult readership," according to Anne H. Lundin, in "Victorian Horizons: The Reception of Children's Books in England and America, 1880–1900," *Library Quarterly* 64.1 (Jan. 1994): 30–59 (33).

52 Advertisements for the forthcoming volume appeared shortly after Frederic's birthday (11 March) in the *Sheffield Daily Telegraph* and the *Bath Chronicle and Weekly Gazette*. *The Examiner*, approximately two months later, includes the publication under "Books Received." *Sheffield Daily Telegraph*, 17 March 1869, 4d; *Bath Chronicle and Weekly Gazette*, 18 March 1869, 6e; *The Examiner*, 22 May 1869, 12c.

53 Census documents list Frederic as residing with his mother in 1861, 1871, 1881, and 1901. It seems safe to assume that he lodged with her until her death, which was only two years after the 1901 census. *Census Returns of England and Wales*, The National Archives of the UK (TNA): Public Records Office (PRO), RG 9 PN 591; RG 10 PN 995; RG 11 PN 1117; and RG 13 PN 959.

54 Lundin, "Victorian Horizons," 34.

55 Eleanore Jamieson, "The Binding Styles of the Gift Books and Annuals," in Frederick W. Faxon, *Literary Annuals and Gift Books: A Bibliography, 1823–1903* (1912; repr. Old Woking, Surrey: Private Libraries Association, 1973), 15.

table," they were to do so "without offense to mind or eye."[56] That is, they were to present content that was simultaneously aesthetically pleasing and socially conservative.

Hervey's revisions of her Griselda story thus fit its movement from a politically minded newspaper to a more conservative and didactic medium. Although Hervey did not entirely erase the harsh criticisms of the 1850 poem in its later form, she reduced much of the disturbing imagery, especially the material that describes the lifeless and loveless forms of the speaker's children, which might be upsetting to younger readers. The new ending in which Griselda's wifely obedience is rewarded renders the poem less radical to its audience and reinforces the socially normative expectations of obedience in women and children common in other gift books. While the revised poem still voices criticism of patriarchal systems and figures, and questions whether women should be as blindly obedient as Griselda, it suggests that they should strive toward wifely obedience. The message of the 1869 poem is therefore more suitable for the genre with which it is associated.

Significant changes in Hervey's personal situation also provide insight as to why she would revise and republish her poem. "Griseldis, with her Children" appeared during the early decades of Hervey's career, when she had considerable renown, especially as a writer for children. Her *Juvenile Calendar and Zodiac of Flowers*, for example, published the same year as her first Griselda poem and richly decorated by famous *Punch* illustrator Richard Doyle, received acclaim as a "dainty and delicate child's book" and earned the poet, according to one reviewer, a status equal to that of famous children's writer Mary Howitt (1799–1888).[57] In the early decades of her career, then, Hervey's reputation, along with her literary connections, particularly those that arose from her marriage, provided a modicum of freedom to express progressive, even radical social commentary. Widowhood, however, limited this freedom as she now depended upon the income she derived from writing as a means by which to support herself and her son. Hervey could not risk her reputation, especially as her status as a female writer had already been questioned in the public realm. In 1837, the poet and journalist Leigh Hunt included Hervey in his satirical account of female writers, "Blue Stocking Revels; or, The Feasts of the Violets." Although Hunt remarks that Montagu (Hervey) "hath merit" and "the right inward spirit," his inclusion of her within this satirical poem potentially undermines her authority and position as a female

---

56 Faxon, *Literary Annuals and Gift Books*, xxi.
57 "*The Juvenile Calendar; or, Zodiac of Flowers: a Gift Book,*" *The Athenaeum* 1156 (22 December 1849): 1303b. Mary Howitt is the author of one of the most famous children's poems, "The Spider and the Fly" (1829).

writer.[58] Yes, Hervey was a prolific writer, and, yes, she was popular, but by Victorian standards she was still a woman engaging in what many considered unseemly (public) behavior. Her work, although produced under "conditions of pressing need," still needed to adhere to certain social conventions in order to be acceptable and therefore profitable.[59]

The financial pressures of widowhood had an additional influence on Hervey's poetic revisions. *Our Legends and Lives*, the volume in which "Griselda" appears, marks two crucial moments in Hervey's career. First, with this volume, Hervey alters her literary identifier, her byline. In the early years of her career, when she established herself as a poet, Hervey published under her full forename and maiden surname, Eleanora Louisa Montagu. Once married, and during the first decade of widowhood, she primarily published as "Mrs. T. K. Hervey," highlighting and presumably garnering some authority from her connection to a prominent male literary figure. Yet the Preface and byline to *Our Legends and Lives* suggests that by 1869 full identification with her deceased husband was no longer advantageous. Hervey retained her married surname, but reverted to her full forename, and, for the remainder of her career, she published as "Eleanora Louisa Hervey," firmly reconnecting herself and her later works to her reputation and corpus prior to marriage.

The opening pages of *Our Legends and Lives* also shed light on Hervey's decision to revise her byline. In the Preface, she voices specific concerns over the unauthorized circulation of her poems, which, for a writer dependent upon the income earned from such works, is of paramount importance. The collection includes, she explains, selections from "leading periodicals – several of such poems having, moreover, been pirated to include among the contents of Christmas gift-books."[60] Hervey counters the pirated circulation of her works and re-establishes her authorial position by compiling a gift book of her own. In short, she reclaims her poetic works from those who have usurped and benefited from them. She reaffirms her ownership over the volume's contents by highlighting that it includes, alongside the already known poems, "some new lyrics and legends."[61] Readers can expect

---

58 Leigh Hunt, "Blue Stocking Revels; or, The Feasts of the Violets," in *The Poetical Works of Leigh Hunt*, ed. Thornton Hunt (London and New York: Routledge, Warne, and Routledge, 1860), 211.

59 Hervey is a perfect example of Gilbert and Gubar's point, "For though literature by women was not encouraged, it was generally understood in the nineteenth century that under certain conditions of pressing need a woman might have to live by her pen. [...] A talented but impoverished woman might in fact have to rescue herself, and maybe even her whole starving family, by writing novels." *The Madwoman in the Attic*, 545.

60 Hervey, Preface, *Our Legends and Lives: A Gift for All Seasons* (London: Trubner and Co., 1869).

61 Hervey, Preface, *Our Legends and Lives*.

a new experience as they peruse her gift book's pages, one with guaranteed authorial intent. This new experience, of course, extends to her Griselda poem, and, interestingly, while she tones down the politics of the second poem, her bold assertions of authorial control evoke the potentially subversive content of both the 1850 and 1869 versions, creating a parallel between herself and her protagonist. Hervey, like her Griselda figure, speaks out against patriarchal structures that subordinate women to men.

Overall, then, Hervey's poems can be read as an expression of dissatisfaction with the contemporary social roles women were expected to fulfill and with the social systems that entrenched these roles. Additionally, her choice to reshape the Griselda story from the female perspective, along with its harsh criticisms of patriarchal systems, can be read as one female writer's dissatisfaction with the nineteenth-century adaptations and editions that perpetuated problematic content from the medieval versions of the story, including Chaucer's *Clerk's Tale*. By rejecting the traditional framework of the male narrator or interlocutor, Hervey gives voice to Griselda. She presents a radical new version of the story, one that demonstrates how this medieval figure can be employed in post-medieval periods to render female experiences and female emotions equal to, perhaps even more important than, male authority.

Appendix A

Eleanora L. Hervey, "Griseldis, with her Children,"

The Athenaeum 1179 (1 June 1850): 583.

Griseldis,
The Childless.

Sound, sound again the muffled bell, – toll for another dead,
And heap – heap high the coals of fire – not ashes – on my head!
Ye have mocked me with my patience; – let no more such incense rise.
For here, of women most accursed, the lost Griseldis lies!

I was a shepherd's daughter, and I used to watch the fold
At eve beside a little cairn upon a lonely wold;
And I wept to see the new-yeaned lambs how close they lay at rest
'Neath the parent breath that fanned them like a soft wind from the west.

O motherhood is strong as life, – and strongest in the least,
It findeth out sweet channels in the poor four-footed beast;
She giveth suck to the strange kid if it waileth for its dam, –
But I, my bird to the kite I gave and to the wolf my lamb.

He came – he stopped: – he saw me with the pitcher in my hand,
(No cool draught, since, these parching lips have touched in all the land);
Alas! I took him for my lord, – my father clutched his gold, –
And I left the young sheep bleating and the cottage by the fold.

Then, years drew on, – the darkest ever womanhood beheld,
When the shaft of love was shivered, and the shriek of anguish quelled:
I sometimes think my brain swan round in that deep sorrow-flood, –
But I have vowed obedience, and the bond was sealed – in blood!

My darlings! shall I dare to seek the eyes ye turn away
In those pasture-lands that lie afar in the purpling of God's day?
There, angels true to motherhood, whose robes are God's own light,
Would meet my step on heaven's floor, and shut me from your sight.

The Ant, that airiest thing that haunts the meadow's circling rings,
To do her mother-task assigned rends off her very wings, –
But I, to whom a holier sense and higher gifts were given,
The wings that I have torn away had wafted me to heaven.

Oh! dear ones, ye that nestled once so closely to my breast, –
Close round me now in spirit while I yield me to my rest;
Kiss – clasp me, if ye may, – that I may feel at last in death
The phantom of that joy which died when ye gave up your breath!

Griseldis,
With her Children.

O memory, O memory! – what shadowy forms are here,
With eyes so cold and passionless and lids without a tear?
Like the face that in my bridal hour I turned upon their sire,
Beside an altar's ashes pale in which there lived no fire!

Do I dream? – are these my children? – does the ground wheron I tread
Yet echo to the footsteps I only should have led?
Draw nearer – clasp me round: – alas! your arms how loose they twine,
Like tendrils long since riven from a crushed and trampled vine.

My buds! – whose first unfolding bloom these eyes have never seen,
I cannot paint ye as ye were, – for the blank that lies between;
And my face is to your gazing like the faces in the stone –
For ye may not trace its fondness in the days that ye have known.

Your glances say, I slew you; and alas! ye seem to stand
All shrinking and in horror – though no blood is on my hand; –
There may be other pangs as keen from which no power can save,
But these are as sharp thorns to bind the turf upon my grave.

Is this the meeting love should crown? – Is this the joy ye bring?
Then, life hath no more sweetness left and death has no more sting;
And the years that we have cast behind, and the hours that lie beyond,
Time's hand shall mark as blotted scrolls in Nature's broken bond.

Yet, once again embrace me: – though Love's fruit may never set,
The blossoms and the stricken tree shall grow together yet;
And the sweets that failed me living shall cleave to me in my fall,
As the bind-flower to the bramble and the moss-root to the wall.

Appendix B

Eleanora Louisa Hervey, "Griselda," in *Our Legends and Lives: A Gift for All Seasons*

(London: Trübner and Co., 1869), 223–24.

Griselda

Sound, sound once more the muffled bell: toll for another dead;
And heap, – heap high, the coals of fire, not ashes, on my head!
Ye have mocked me with my patience: let no more such incense rise;
For here, of women most accursed, the lost Griselda lies!

I was a shepherd's daughter; and I used to watch the fold
At eve beside a little cairn upon a lonely wold;
And I wept to see the new-yeaned lambs how close they lay at rest
'Neath the parent breath that fanned them like a soft wind from the west.

O! motherhood is strong as life; and strongest in the least:
It findeth out sweet channels in the poor four-footed beast.
She giveth suck to the strange kid if it waileth for its dam:
But I? – My bird to the kite I gave, and to the wolf my lamb!

He came; – he stopped: he saw me with the pitcher in my hand.
No cool draught since, these parching lips have touched in all the land!
Alas! I took him for my lord: my father clutched his gold;
And I left the young sheep bleating, and the cottage by the wold.

Then years drew on, the darkest ever womanhood beheld,
When the shaft of love was shivered, and the shriek of anguish quelled.
I sometimes think my brain swam round in that deep sorrow-flood:
But I had vowed obedience; and the bond was sealed – in blood!

My darlings! shall I dare to seek the eyes ye turn away
In those pasture-lands that lie afar in the purpling of God's day?
There angels true to motherhood, whose robes are God's own light,
Will meet my step on heaven's floor and bar me from your sight.
The lowly ant whom motherhood to earth unerring brings,

To Nature's instinct blindly true, rends off her clay-bound wings;
But I, to whom a holier sense of higher gifts were given,
The wings that *I* have torn away had wafted me to heaven!

Medieval and Futuristic Hells: The Influence of Dante on Ellison's "I Have No Mouth and I Must Scream"

Jeremy Withers

Even though some scholars have identified important precursors to science fiction (hereafter abbreviated as sf) in premodern genres such as epic, the fantastic voyage, and utopia, pre-Enlightenment eras are mostly absent in many critical discussions of the origins of – and the important influences on – recent sf.[1] Additionally, many sf scholars and authors often emphasize the futurity of the genre, not its orientation and links to the past. For example, Harlan Ellison (whose story is a main focus of this essay) once defined sf as: "Anything that deals in even the smallest extrapolative manner with the *future* of man and his societies, with the *future* of science and/or its effects on us."[2]

However, earlier time periods such as the Middle Ages have indeed been quite fruitful for contemporary sf.[3] This essay explores the many ways in which one of the most well-known works of medieval literature – Dante Alighieri's early fourteenth-century poem *Inferno* – served as a powerful influence on one of the more famous texts to come out of the 1960s New Wave movement in sf: Harlan Ellison's fascinating and disturbing 1967 short story "I Have No Mouth and I Must Scream." With its violent imagery,

---

1   On premodern predecessors to sf, see *The Road to Science Fiction: From Gilgamesh to Wells*, ed. James Gunn (New York: Mentor, 1977); Adam Roberts, *The History of Science Fiction* (Basingstoke: Palgrave, 2005), 21–31.

2   Ellison's definition appears in the entry "Science Fiction" in Gary K. Wolfe's *Critical Terms for Science Fiction and Fantasy: A Glossary and Guide to Scholarship* (Westport, CT: Greenwood Press, 1986), 108–111 (110), emphasis added.

3   One obvious example of the medieval influence on sf is Walter M. Miller, Jr.'s celebrated *A Canticle for Leibowitz*, a 1960 post-apocalyptic novel depicting a nuclear war that causes society to revert to something akin to the Christian Middle Ages where monastic orders again flourish and help preserve civilization's knowledge.

frank sexuality, unconventional metaphors, and experimental form, Ellison's story is a quintessentially New Wave text.[4] Many writers and scholars also associate the New Wave with a conscious attempt by the authors of that era to stop looking only to previous sf authors for inspiration, and to instead begin drawing upon avant-garde artists like the Surrealist painter Salvador Dalí and the Beat novelist William S. Burroughs.[5] This new iconoclastic attitude toward previous sf is well represented by the New Wave author J. G. Ballard's quip that "[g]reat author though he was, I'm convinced that H. G. Wells has had a disastrous influence on the subsequent course of science fiction."[6] But even though in a preface for the story "I Have No Mouth" Ellison declares that he "had to go into the future to write the story," what he actually had to do was go into the medieval past to write it.[7] Thus, even though the Middle Ages might be perceived by many to be nowhere near as fertile a ground as Dalí or Burroughs for inspiring experimental works of sf, for Ellison (as this essay will show) a medieval masterpiece like Dante's *Inferno* indeed provides ample inspiration when crafting bold new sf works.[8] And it is Ellison's repeated invocations of *Inferno* (at the same time that he rejects all of that poem's underlying sense of divine order and possibility for redemption) that helps make "I Have No Mouth" as chilling and memorable a story as it is.

---

[4]   Adam Roberts sums up the New Wave as "a loose affiliation of writers from the 1960s and 1970s who, one way or another, reacted against the conventions of traditional SF to produce avant-garde, radical or fractured science fictions," and then goes on to quote Damien Broderick as defining the New Wave as "a reaction against genre exhaustion." Roberts, *History*, 230–31.

[5]   On the influence of Dalí and Burroughs on key New Wave figures like J. G. Ballard and Michael Moorcock, see the following: the essays "The Coming of the Unconscious" and "Myth Maker of the Twentieth Century," both in J. G. Ballard, *A User's Guide to the Millennium: Essays and Reviews* (New York: Picador, 1996); "'To Write for the Space Age': Interview with Michael Moorcock by Mark P. Williams," *Reality Studio*, 8 December 2008, <http://realitystudio.org/interviews/michael-moorcock-on-william-s-burroughs>, last accessed November 2015.

[6]   J. G. Ballard, "Which Way to Inner Space?," in *A User's Guide*, 195–98 (197).

[7]   Harlan Ellison, "Forward: How Science Fiction Saved Me From a Life of Crime," in *I Have No Mouth & I Must Scream* (New York: Edgeworks Abbey, 2009), 6.

[8]   In a short chapter from his history of science fiction, titled "Interlude: 400–1600," Roberts argues that the overt religiosity and the emphasis on non-material worlds of much literature written in the Middle Ages (including Dante's *Divine Comedy*, which Roberts specifically discusses) renders such works void when it comes to precursors to science fiction. See Roberts, *History*, 32–35. However, at least one scholar has suggested there is indeed something proto-sf about Dante's *Inferno*. Merritt Abrash argues that Dante's hell serves as a precursor for the fully mechanized environments that eventually become standard fare in much sf. See Merritt Abrash, "Dante's Hell as an Ideal Mechanical Environment," in *Clockwork Worlds: Mechanized Environments in SF*, ed. Richard D. Erlich and Thomas P. Dunn (Westport, CT: Greenwood Press, 1983), 21–25.

As many readers have been quick to realize, Ellison's "I Have No Mouth" is a richly intertextual work. For example, the story is quite blatant about its borrowing from world literature through such images as a gigantic bird conjured from Norse mythology, as well as through its inclusion of Descartes' famous dictum "cogito ergo sum" within the computer "talk-fields" that periodically rupture the text. Several aspects of its plot – like the long journey in search of food and the captivity in the belly of a beast – are clearly lifted from biblical sources such as Exodus and Jonah. Furthermore, scholars like Joseph Francavilla perceive in "I Have No Mouth" a borrowing from the Prometheus myth, and Darren Harris-Fain argues that readers might note additional literary echoes in Ellison's story, ranging from Mary Shelley's *Frankenstein* to Hesiod's *Theogony*, and from John Bunyan's *Pilgrim's Progress* to H. G. Wells's short story "The Country of the Blind."[9]

However, one text strikingly absent from in-depth discussions of intertextuality in Ellison's story about a supercomputer named AM who becomes sentient, then destroys almost all of humanity except five people it preserves to torment for eternity, is *Inferno*, Dante's canonical poem about justice and torment. There are, of course, significant divergences between Dante's and Ellison's texts, not the least of which is Ellison's own insistence that (unlike Dante's devout text) his own story is not interested in God *per se*, but rather in "the dichotomous nature of the human race," a nature that "includes the demon in us."[10] But as this article argues, there are multiple interesting and illuminating overlaps between these two texts' depictions of a hellish underworld. Put simply, something strikingly Dantesque permeates the story, as Ellison himself acknowledges when in a preface he describes the story as about "five poor bastards living in a kind of Dante's Inferno inside the belly of a computer."[11] Particularly, it is in significant aspects of the story such as the way in which AM metes out its punishment to the five surviving humans and in certain details of the story's climactic ending set within an ice cavern that Ellison betrays an intentional invocation of *Inferno*.

However, the only explicit references to Dante in scholarly analyses of Ellison's "I Have No Mouth" that I have found are the following two brief, overly general references. First, John B. Ower states that the "similarity [between AM and Satan] is emphasized by [...] the infernal imagery

---

9   Joseph Francavilla, "Mythic Hells in Harlan Ellison's Science Fiction," in *Phoenix F from the Ashes: Literature of the Remade World*, ed. Carl B. Yoke (New York: Greenwood, 1987), 157–64; Darren Harris-Fain, "Created in the Image of God: The Narrator and the Computer in Harlan Ellison's 'I Have No Mouth, and I Must Scream,'" *Extrapolation* 32.2 (1991): 143–55.
10   Harlan Ellison, "Memoir: I Have No Mouth, and I Must Scream," *Starship* 39 (Summer 1980): 6–13 (10).
11   Ellison, "Forward," 6.

which makes Ellison's story reminiscent of Dante or Hieronymus Bosch."[12] Secondly, Ellen Weil and Gary K. Wolfe observe: "Although AM falls short of the godlike power to resurrect the dead, part of his Dantesque punishment consists of altering his victims' minds and bodies."[13] Neither of these two studies, however, mentions nor analyzes in any detail the deep borrowings Ellison makes from Dante in his famous story.

Yet, Ellison's *oeuvre* betrays a career-long fascination with depicting infernal underworlds, both literal and metaphorical.[14] Philip M. Rubens argues that Ellison, ever the eclectic and wide-ranging reader, demonstrates throughout his writings (but particularly in a collection like *Deathbird Stories*) "a set of circumstances, a group of characters, and a specific landscape that echo many of the traditional journeys to hell – from patristic literature to Norse myth."[15] Although Rubens does not go into any detail in pointing out specifically Dantean influences on Ellison, he affirms that, when describing hellish worlds, "one can hardly ignore the epic descents that pervade Western literature from the Greek Eleusinian Mysteries to Dante's *Inferno*."[16] Furthermore, Ellison himself specifically references Dante's epic poem elsewhere in his *oeuvre*. For example, in *Watching*, a 1989 compilation of his film essays and film reviews, Ellison describes a memory from his youth in which a woman working a movie theater ticket booth was so attractive "that merely laying down a dime for a ducat became an act of sexual congress intense enough to send the Rev. Jimmy Swaggart to the eighth and innermost circle of Dante's inferno."[17] Such a reference suggests a familiarity with *Inferno* that goes beyond a shallow, popular culture under-

---

12   John B. Ower, "Manacle-Forged Minds: Two Images of the Computer in Science-Fiction," *Diogenes* 85 (1974): 47–61 (58).

13   Ellen Weil and Gary K. Wolfe, *Harlan Ellison: The Edge of Forever* (Columbus: Ohio State University Press, 2002), 143–44.

14   Regarding the metaphorical variety, we can mention here *Memos from Purgatory*, a book Ellison describes in his prologue as telling "of two periods in my life: ten weeks in purgatory […] and 24 hours in hell." The former describes his stint in a youth gang while researching his first novel; the latter describes a brief experience he had with incarceration for firearm possession in Manhattan's infamous jail known colloquially as "the Tombs." Harlan Ellison, *Memos from Purgatory* (New York: Pyramid Books, 1975), 26.

15   Philip M. Rubens, "Descents into Private Hells: Harlan Ellison's 'Psy-Fi,'" *Extrapolation* 20.4 (1979): 378–85 (378). In a surprising omission, Rubens refrains from discussing "I Have No Mouth" in relationship to Ellison's overall interest in hellish landscapes, choosing instead to focus on the stories "Delusion for a Dragon Slayer," "Adrift Just off the Islets of Langerhans," "The Place with No Name," and "The Deathbird."

16   Rubens, "Descents into Private Hells," 379.

17   Harlan Ellison, *Watching* (Los Angeles: Underwood-Miller, 1989), vii. In a further possible connection between Dante and Ellison, Weil and Wolfe suggest that the onyx mountain that rises "out of hell" in Ellison's story "The Deathbird" is influenced by the mountain in Dante's *Purgatory*. See Weil and Wolfe, *Harlan Ellison*, 176.

standing of the medieval work. In short, for anyone like Ellison who is interested in contributing to the cultural history of representing hell, Dante clearly represents an unavoidable influence.[18]

Moving into the story itself, let us first examine the similarities between God's logic of punishment as depicted in Dante's *Inferno*, and the logic of punishment discernible in AM's methods in "I Have No Mouth." In Dante's vision of Hell, the retributive logic works according to the principle of *contrapasso*, that is, by means of a punishment that is often either analogous to or resembles the sin committed, or that is the direct antithesis of the sin committed.[19] The word *contrapasso* itself only occurs in Canto XXVIII of *Inferno*, when the renowned Troubadour poet Bertran de Born declares: "In me you see the perfect *contrapasso*!" (line 142).[20] Earlier in this canto, the pilgrim Dante and his guide Virgil have discovered Bertran in a state of eternal decapitation and carrying around his own head, a punishment meted out for his sin of "cut[ting] the bonds of those joined," that is, because Bertran sowed discord between such people as Prince Henry and his father, King Henry II of England. Bertran's punishment neatly parallels the crime: just as he severed the natural bond that should exist between father and son, and between prince and king, his head is now unnaturally and ghoulishly severed forever from his body. For an example of antithetical punishment with the *contrapasso*, we might recall the depiction of the sorcerers and soothsayers in Canto XX, who owing to their sin of claiming to have a God-like ability to see ahead into the future, must now suffer eternally the torment and indignity of having "their faces [look] down on their backs / [...] the tears their eyes [shed] / stream[ing] down to wet their buttocks at the cleft" (lines 13, 23–24). Arrogantly claiming an ability to look ahead in time, the soothsayers must now forever look grotesquely behind in space.

---

18   One other text demonstrating that people have often noted a continuity between Dante and Ellison is an anthology titled *Dante's Disciples* that includes a story by Ellison called "Chatting with Anubis." The book's introduction states that the genesis of this anthology was the book's editors asking a group of sf, fantasy, and horror writers to "write stories inspired by Dante's 'Inferno,' in other words, to use Dante as a muse in this waning, sputtering, terrifying century of ours" (vi). Ellison's particular contribution, however, makes no direct references to Dante or *Inferno*, and is instead about a brief encounter two people have with the Egyptian god Anubis during an underground archeological expedition. See *Dante's Disciples*, ed. Peter Crowther and Edward E. Kramer (Clarkson, GA: White Wolf Publishing, 1995).

19   For further discussions of *contrapasso*, see *The Dante Encyclopedia*, ed. Richard Lansing (New York: Garland Publishing, 2000), 219–22; and Peter Armour, "Dante's *Contrapasso*: Contexts and Texts," *Italian Studies* 55 (2000): 1–20.

20   Dante Alighieri, *Dante's Inferno: The Indiana Critical Edition*, ed. and trans. Mark Musa (Bloomington: Indiana University Press, 1995). All quotations from *Inferno* are from this edition.

As with the sprawling population of sufferers in *Inferno*, the torment inflicted upon Ellison's five main characters in "I Have No Mouth" follows a retributive logic similar to Dante's *contrapasso*. Put another way, the punishment that the characters in "I Have No Mouth" receive from AM is not inscrutable and random. However, the one clear difference that we need to point out is that Dante clearly depicts his sinners as being punished for sins they have directly committed themselves. God, enacting His strict form of divine justice, punishes the denizens of hell for having broken His laws and commandments. But as Harris-Fain points out, a biblical misquotation by the narrator Ted in "I Have No Mouth" alludes to the Old Testament notion of a wrathful God willing to "[visit] the iniquity of the fathers upon the children unto the third and fourth generation," a harsher view of justice that ignores direct personal culpability and with which Dante obviously does not sympathize.[21] Rather than alluding to specific sins each character trapped in AM's "belly" has committed, Ellison instead depicts AM as subjecting his five survivors to Dantesque torments despite any direct, personal involvement in what we would (theologically speaking) perceive as sin. In fact, the demented God-figure AM appears to be tormenting the humans under its[22] control because of the "sins of their fathers," that is, because the five survivors are paying the horrible price for previous human beings having created the individual supercomputers that eventually linked up to form AM, and hence they are paying the price for other people having created the sentience that AM so abhors.

However, even though Ellison does not depict punishments as directly caused by personal guilt, the punishments he does depict still follow a certain logic of the *contrapasso*, in that the characters are subjected to a punishment that, most often, perversely inverts that person's personality or defining characteristic in some way. For example, Benny, a character who we are told was a brilliant, handsome scientist, has been reduced by AM's incessant torture into a drooling lunatic. That is, like the soothsayers in Dante who claim to see far forward but are now reduced to looking backward, Benny has been changed into his antithesis: AM reduces this once-eloquent and beautiful genius into a slobbering fool. Furthermore, we are told in the story that Benny is homosexual, but that he has been changed by AM into an ape-like creature "big in the privates" (470) who must constantly

---

21   The biblical quotation is from Exodus 20:5. Harris-Fain discusses Ted's oblique reference to this biblical passage, and the implications it has for summoning forth an image of AM as a jealous God-figure in his article, "Created in the Image of God."

22   Even though the story's narrator, Ted, often uses the masculine pronoun "he" when referring to AM, I find it makes more sense to use "it" throughout this essay, since AM is a computer (albeit one that has achieved sentience).

service the only female in the group, Ellen.[23] AM, apparently insane with jealousy over the sexuality it can never possess, torments this homosexual character by making him forever engage in a form of sexuality to which he is fundamentally averse.

Ellen, if we can take her at her word, claims at one point to the other survivors to have been sexually inexperienced and mostly chaste in her life before AM's torture began. As with Benny, AM metes out an antithetical form of *contrapasso* punishment to her: the formerly modest woman has been altered into the harlot. Again, owing to AM's ungovernable jealousy over human sexuality and human forms of closeness that it can never possess, the ruthless supercomputer perhaps punishes Ellen for her "sin" of not embracing the privilege of human sexuality enough.[24]

The character of Garrister, we are told, was at one time a conscientious objector and antiwar activist. He was a person who stood up passionately for the causes he believed in. As with Ellen and Benny, AM transforms Garrister into his antithesis. In "I Have No Mouth," we glimpse him now only as a "shoulder shrugger" (474). In fact, this punishment of Garrister appears to have found its inspiration in a direct inversion of a scene from Canto III of Dante's *Inferno*, a scene set in the vestibule that leads to Hell proper. Here, the pilgrim-character Dante and his guide Virgil encounter the place for people who lived a life "with no blame and with no praise" (line 36) and a life "neither faithful nor unfaithful to their God" (line 38). In other words, they lived as constant fence-sitters and non-committers, or in the words of Ellison when describing his character Garrister, as perpetual "shoulder shrug-gers." As punishment, Dante's God commands that his shoulder shruggers chase, in perpetuity, a banner "rushing ahead, whirling with aimless speed" (line 53). In Garrister, therefore, Ellison gives us an inversion of Dante's scenario that is itself an inversion.

What we see, then, as the significant difference between Dante's and Ellison's use of the *contrapasso* form of punishment is that, for Dante, God exists and provides a sense of divine order behind the many forms of punishment that Virgil and the Pilgrim witness. Furthermore, the vengeance embodied by *Inferno* is counterbalanced by the mercy, divine love, and redemption found in *Purgatorio* and *Paradiso*, the next two parts of the tripartite *Commedia*. Thus, as Valerie Allen has written of another noteworthy modern

---

23 Harlan Ellison, "I Have No Mouth and I Must Scream," originally published in *IF: Worlds of Science Fiction* (March 1967), reprinted in *Science Fiction: An Historical Anthology*, ed. Eric Rabkin (Oxford: Oxford University Press, 1983), 467–83. All quotations are from this reprinted version of the text.

24 Ower argues that "AM's degradation of the sexual lives of his subjects reveals his jealousy of the physical pleasure and the spiritual fulfillment of human love." See Ower, "Manacle-Forged Minds," 59–60.

retelling of *Inferno*, David Fincher's 1995 film *Seven* (sometimes written as *Se7en*): "Dante's theme is redemption, a quality Fincher's movie noticeably lacks."[25] Ellison's story, like Fincher's film, also lacks redemption (with the possible exception of Ted's final action in the story, discussed below). His story depicts a world in which humanity is made to pay the horrible price for putting too much faith in their technology and for giving themselves over too much to their violent tendencies when they started the world war that ultimately led to the creation of AM. What Allen has written of *Seven* can apply equally to "I Have No Mouth," as she writes, "[r]etribution replaces mercy."[26] Likewise, the harsh, retaliatory justice meted out by AM for the crime for which the five human survivors are not even personally responsible (i.e., the creation of AM) bespeaks a grim world indeed, one in which no real sense of purpose or mercy lies behind the violent, perverse punishments.

Despite a key difference between Ellison's and Dante's punishments discussed above, one additional similarity between the forms of punishment meted out in *Inferno* and in AM's "belly" is that both possess a tendency to eradicate the identity and individuality of the sufferer. For example, in Canto XVII Dante the pilgrim encounters the usurers who are recognizable only by means of a pouch "around each sinner's neck [...] / [and] each of a different color, with [their family's] coat of arms" (lines 55–56). As Mark Musa explains in a footnote to lines 55–56: "Apparently the usurers are unrecognizable through facial characteristics because their total concern with their material goods has caused them to lose their individuality." Even when Dante meets fellow Florentines in hell and some people that he personally knew before their death, he often cannot recognize them immediately, for their punishment has so distorted their appearance. As a further instance of this, we might recall how in hell's third circle, which comprises the gluttons, the Pilgrim encounters the Florentine Ciacco. But Dante does not recognize his fellow countryman, and says to him: "The pain you suffer here perhaps / disfigures you beyond all recognition: / I can't remember seeing you before" (Canto VI, lines 43–45).

Whereas God decrees that Dante's sufferers lose their individuality as a form of *contrapasso* punishment for the unchecked willfulness and individualism that led them to sin in the first place, AM takes away individuality and identity out of a misplaced and perverse vengeance against the humans for the "crimes of their fathers." Noteworthy examples of AM's desire to efface the identity of his captured humans include the above-mentioned alteration of Benny's face to become more simian, as well as AM's curious fondness for giving bizarre new names to people, such as when AM gives one character the name of Nimdock,

---

25　Valerie Allen, "*Se7en*: Medieval Justice, Modern Justice," *The Journal of Popular Culture* 43.6 (2010): 1150–72 (1154).

26　Allen, "*Se7en*," 1157.

a "name the machine had forced him to use, because AM amused itself with strange sounds" (468). We never learn this character's former name; hence, his real identity has been thoroughly expunged by AM.

But the most salient example of Ellison's depiction of torment that obliterates the person's former identity in a Dantesque way is surely Ted's chilling alteration at the end of the story for his role in killing the other humans, an action that robbed AM of its "toys." More than any of Dante's sufferers, Ted becomes a thoroughly inhuman thing, for he is transformed by AM into "a great soft jelly thing" with "no mouth," "rubbery appendages," "legless humps," and "white holes filled by fog" (482) where his eyes once were. In fact, Ted's gruesome punishment here at the end of the story appears to carry a *contrapasso* logic of its own, for Ted throughout the narrative suffers from a paranoid narcissism of sorts, as evidenced by his conviction that the other survivors are constantly thinking about and plotting against him. As Ellison himself claims, Ted's killing of Ellen and the others in the ice cave is intended to represent "an act of transcendent heroism,"[27] a sort of redemptive moment for humanity, but to AM such a heroic and redemptive act by Ted surely constitutes an unpardonable act of individualism and self-autonomy. As punishment for this act, Ted "has lost his distinctive 'differences' and identification with humanity and has regressed into an undifferentiated blob inside the belly of AM."[28] Put simply, it is altogether fitting, in a *contrapasso* kind of way, that in retribution for Ted's individualistic and defiant killing of the others, AM erases so thoroughly Ted's cherished sense of self and individuality.

It is also significant and noteworthy that for both Ellison and Dante their respective visions of hell overlap by being distinctively multi-sensory in their visions of the persecution of the damned. That is, the horrific place imagined by each author offends and assails as many of the senses as possible. For characters who function mainly as observers, such as Dante's pilgrim and occasionally Ellison's five survivors, it is most often visual forms of torment that distress and chasten them, such as in the opening scene of "I Have No Mouth" when four of the survivors stumble upon the disturbing illusion created by AM of Gorrister's body. This harrowing visual tableau depicts the body hanging upside down, drained of its blood by "a precise incision made from ear to ear under the lantern jaw" (467). Dante's *Inferno* also brims with strikingly visual forms of torment that the Pilgrim must bear witness to, such as the sight of people being eternally boiled in hot pitch (Canto XXII). Of course, from the perspective of the damned who are actually submerged in this boiling pitch, this torment represents not a visual one but a tactile one.

---

27 Ellison, "Memoir: I Have No Mouth," 9.
28 Joseph Francavilla, "The Concept of the Divided Self in Harlan Ellison's 'I Have No Mouth and I Must Scream' and 'Shatterday,'" *Journal of the Fantastic in the Arts* 6.2–3 (1994): 107–25 (118).

Such tactile forms of punishment are found in abundance in both texts, such as when AM scorches Benny's eyes into "two soft, moist pools of pus-like jelly," leaving him "crying piteously" (471), or when fierce winds batter people in Canto V of *Inferno*.

It should be noted that this latter form of tactile and visualized torment – people being buffeted by fierce winds – finds a direct counterpart in "I Have No Mouth." In *Inferno*'s Canto V, powerful winds constantly sweep up the lustful – Dido, Cleopatra, Helen of Troy – in a manner that resembles how such people gave over their lives and their volition to sexual passion. In such a way "all those who sin in lust have been condemned," Dante writes, "those who make reason slave to appetite" (38–39). Similarly, Ted describes how the captives in Ellison's tale are hit by a hurricane "with the force of a glacier thundering into the sea" and by winds "that tore at us, flinging us back the way we had come, down the twisting, computer-lined corridors of the darkway" (475).

Interestingly, this punishing maelstrom singles out the character of Ellen for affliction, for the winds lift her up, toss her around, bloody her face, and eventually separate her from the others. This buffeting of Ellen (and the others) by the hurricane is a significant moment of Dantean allusion in the story, yet ultimately an ambiguous one. For if in Dante the winds lashed the lustful, AM's meting out of this punishment most severely to Ellen lends some credence to Ted's suggestion that Ellen is being dishonest when she insists that "she had been a virgin only twice removed before AM grabbed her and brought her down here" (474). On the other hand, perhaps AM is just once again displaying its perversity and the lack of any order beneath its punishments by penalizing Ellen for being something it has turned her into, that is, for becoming "more of a slut than she had ever been" (474) after she is forced to be the last living female amid four male survivors.

In addition to the above visual and tactile torments, Dante and Ellison both portray their respective hells as assaulting additional senses as well. Rank and offensive smells also waft through their underworlds. For example, when Dante and Virgil are entering the sixth circle, they must actually pause at one point in order to "grow accustomed to [the] vile fumes," fumes described a few lines earlier as a "disgusting overflow of stench / the deep abyss was vomiting" forth (Canto XI, lines 4–5, 11–12). Similarly, as Joann P. Cobb has recognized, Ellison's futuristic hell is also strikingly olfactory, for its smells include "the stench of matted wet fur, charred wood […] rotting orchids, sour milk, sulphur, rancid butter," and so forth.[29] Furthermore, Dante and Ellison's underworlds both share horrific auditory elements, as glimpsed by Ellison's references to sounds like "the shriek of babies being ground

---

[29]   Joann P. Cobb, "Medium and Message in Ellison's 'I Have No Mouth, and I Must Scream,'" in *The Intersection of Science Fiction and Philosophy: Critical Studies*, ed. Robert E. Meyers (Westport, CT: Greenwood Press, 1983), 159–67 (163).

beneath blue-hot rollers" and "the lunatic laugh of a fat woman," or to AM's disturbingly juvenile snicker as it voyeuristically spies on sexual acts between the surviving humans. As a complement to its visual and olfactory repugnance, Dante's hell also includes references to "[w]eird shrieks of lamentation pierc[ing] through [the Pilgrim] / like arrow-shafts whose tips are barbed with pity" (Canto XXIX, lines 43–44), as well as to the mighty blasts of the giant Nimrod's horn, a sound "which would have made a thunder-clap sound dim" (Canto XXXI, line 13).

Ellison even appears to be trying to surpass Dante. This attempt to out-Dante Dante is performed by depicting torment via abhorrent tastes as well, such as when AM sends down manna to the five survivors that tastes "like boiled boar urine" (469) and when the humans, near the point of starvation, are forced to consume worms that are "[t]hick" and "ropey" (468) in order to avoid starvation. In sum, both Dante's and Ellison's hells constitute an all-out attack on the senses of their denizens, visitors, and readers, with Ellison's attack going a bit further through the inclusion of repulsive tastes as well.

Yet one of the most striking parallels between Dante's and Ellison's texts is their ghoulish and memorable depiction of cannibalism occurring in their respective underworlds. In Dante, as the Pilgrim approaches the end of his journey through the nine circles of hell, he finds himself on the frozen lake of Cocytus, a region in which the traitors are punished. There, as described in Cantos XXXII and XXXIII of the poem, Dante encounters Count Ugolino, a figure who the Pilgrim and Virgil witness viciously attacking another person, having "sunk his teeth / into the other's neck, just beneath the skull," like "a man with hungry teeth tears into bread" (XXXII, 127–29). Archbishop Ruggieri, the victim being consumed by Ugolino, incurs the latter's wrath because of having betrayed Ugolino and then subsequently imprisoning him in a tower along with his sons and grandsons.

Count Ugolino may tend to engrave himself upon the minds of readers of *Inferno*, for his gruesome gnawing upon his enemy has long been seen as an unforgettable image of a man who, albeit depicted in the act of consuming, is himself utterly consumed by his own wrath and lust for vengeance. As William Franke has argued, what is especially ironic and tragic about Ugolino is how the story of his imprisonment and death includes a reference to how his own sons selflessly (and in a symbolically sacramental fashion) offered themselves up as food to their starving father. Franke asserts, however, that Ugolino reveals himself to be a person "unable to respond with any genuine human emotion to his sons' deeply moving offer" and remains instead "forever blinded by hatred and vengefulness."[30] As soon as

---

[30] William Franke, "The Death and Damnation of Poetry in *Inferno* XXXI–XXXIV: Ugolino and Narrative as an Instrument of Revenge," *Romance Studies* 28.1 (2010): 27–35 (32, 33).

Ugolino concludes the short narration of his life, imprisonment, and death to the Pilgrim and to Virgil, and immediately after referencing how his sons selflessly offered up their bodies as nourishment, Ugolino "glar[es] down in rage, / attack[ing] again the wretched skull [of Archbishop Ruggieri] with his teeth / sharp as a dog's, and as fit for grinding bones" (XXXIII, lines 76–78).

Ellison depicts a similar instance of cannibalism near the end of the journey of his "pilgrims," a journey that was long and exhausting yet undertaken in the hopes of finding a rumored cache of food hidden in some ice caves. It turns out that food does indeed reside in these caves in the form of a stack of canned goods; however, AM, in its typically creative and cruel way, has left the humans no tool with which to open the cans. As a result, Benny goes "completely mad with rage" (480), and begins "eating Gorrister's face [...] his hands locked around Gorrister's head like a nutcracker, and his mouth ripping at the tender skin of Gorrister's cheek" (481). Although we might initially expect Benny's bestial act to have been brought on by the maddening effects of hunger, in his reference to Benny becoming "mad with rage" Ellison appears to have something more Dantesque in mind. That is, a compulsion for vengeance (similar to Ugolino's) appears to be the catalyst for Benny's actions here, and since AM exists as essentially impervious to human attack, Benny unleashes his fury and rage upon whatever target he can. Gorrister, unfortunately, was simply standing too close by and in the wrong place at the wrong time.

As many scholars have pointed out, AM's own penchant for cruelty and vengeance appears to be merely an extension of the cruelty and vengeance humans initially created their supercomputers to mete out on a global scale.[31] As "I Have No Mouth" informs us, the individual supercomputers that eventually linked up by themselves and became sentient (thereby creating AM) were initially created by people to carry out "a big war, a very complex war" (472) that had grown too vast and complicated for humans themselves to oversee. Thus, engendered by humans working in a spirit of utmost malice and vengeance, AM (unsurprisingly) functions only in a similarly malicious and vengeful spirit. It is altogether fitting, therefore, that with a sly wink to the informed reader, Ellison references here Dante's image *par excellence* of uncontrollable, unmitigated retaliation and anger: Ugolino's eternally cannibalistic eating of his despised enemy, Archbishop Ruggieri. Such a revelation of Benny's deeper self showcases the violence and the thirst for vengeance at

---

[31] For example, this is a point H. Bruce Franklin makes when he observes that "instead of mechanically carrying out its orders to exterminate the human race, AM develops an emotion appropriate to its purpose: it infinitely *hates* its human creators." H. Bruce Franklin, *War Stars: The Superweapon and the American Imagination* (New York: Oxford University Press, 1988), 210 (emphasis in the original).

all costs lurking at humanity's core and which led to the expanding world war that tragically led to AM's eventual creation.

Another parallel between the endings of Dante's poem and Ellison's story is that both texts culminate in a forbidding icy landscape: as mentioned above, *Inferno* ends on the frozen lake of Cocytus, and "I Have No Mouth" concludes in the ice caverns, a desolate setting consisting of "[h]orizonless thousands of miles in which the ice had formed in blue and silver flashes" (480). For Dante's readers, arriving at hell's lowest and deepest point only to discover ice, instead of the burning sulphur and fire of the popular tradition of hell, might come as something of a surprise. But here, in the prison-house of traitors whose crimes Dante finds the most abominable and most retrograde to the essence of humanity, these sinners are "as far from the warmth of divine love as [they] can get,"[32] and therefore the icy setting is altogether appropriate. In addition to Count Ugolino and his gruesome meal, the Pilgrim and his guide encounter here on Cocytus's ice sufferers who are deprived of the ability to find emotional release for their grief in crying, for it is so frigid that their tears freeze into icicles upon their eyes.

The frosty setting functions appropriately for the climax of Ellison's tale as well. Here, we see the five human survivors at their most exhausted, enraged, and desperate in the story. Like Dante's traitors wedged into the lowest depths of hell, the five humans in "I Have No Mouth" appear now as utterly hopeless and forsaken. Salvation of any kind seems far away indeed for Ellison's characters, thereby increasing the parallelism with Dante's poem. In other words, Dante and Ellison's frozen settings complement one another with both of these frigid landscapes symbolizing an utterly loveless, Godless, unredemptive place.

Interestingly, however, the ice caverns exist not just as Godless for the suffering *humans*, for it is here that AM, too, experiences an absence of God, by which I mean that it is here in the ice caves that AM learns it is not God (as much as it might pretend otherwise). After Ted and Ellen complete their swift mercy-killings of the other three characters via improvised "huge ice-spear[s]," Ted muses: "Three of them were dead, could not be revived. [AM] could keep us alive [...;] but he was *not* God. He could not bring them back" (481). Just as Dante's Cocytus represents a state as far removed from God as possible, surely at this moment after AM's "toys have been taken from him" (481) by Ted (with Ellen's help) and AM experiences its own lack of power to revive the dead, the malevolent supercomputer – like Dante's frozen-eyed sufferers – is forced to confront its own painful distance from God.

The 1960s New Wave movement with which Ellison's name is often associated earned much of its notoriety for its boasts of reinventing sf and

---

32 Robert J. Di Pietro, "*Inferno* XXXIII," *Lectura Dantis* 6 (1990): 419–27 (419).

of performing something wholly new within the genre. Spokesmen for the New Wave, such as J. G. Ballard writing at the dawn of the movement, envision a new type of sf that will "jettison [sf's] present narrative forms and plots."[33] Similarly, the influential New Wave editor and writer Michael Moorcock expressed hope in the early 1960s that authors would begin submitting manuscripts to sf magazines that do not "imitate slavishly what has gone before."[34] But when some sf movements (and arguably all artistic movements) proclaim they are doing something radically new, they often are not.[35] The New Wave writer Ellison, despite the shocking newness of a story like "I Have No Mouth and I Must Scream," walks a well-worn literary path and participates in a long artistic tradition of depicting hellish underworlds when he borrows so heavily from a medieval predecessor like Dante. Like the soothsayers of *Inferno* discussed above, Ellison might claim to be looking into the future, but his story reveals him destined to look backwards, backwards into the medieval past for guidance, insight, and inspiration.

33   Ballard, "Which Way to Inner Space?," 197.
34   Michael Moorcock, "Play With Feeling," *New Worlds Science Fiction* 43/129 (April 1963): 2–3, 123–27 (124).
35   For a discussion of how 1980s cyberpunk – despite its claims, similar to the New Wave's, regarding its newness and originality – also borrows deeply from its predecessors, see Gary Westfahl, "'The Gernsback Continuum': William Gibson in the Context of Science Fiction," in *Fiction 2000: Cyberpunk and the Future of Narrative*, ed. George Slusser and Tom Shippey (Athens: University of Georgia Press, 1992), 88–108.

Reading Westeros:
George R. R. Martin's
Multi-Layered Medievalisms

Carol Jamison

Hans Robert Jauss defines modernity as "the self-understanding of our era from the past."[1] For scholars of medievalism, modernity typically refers to "the contemporary perspective from which a medievalist writer ponders, and attempts to create, a fictional Middle Ages."[2] Most assume that medievalism is "a modern invention."[3] However, in his preface to the 1996 edition of *Studies in Medievalism*, Leslie Workman defines it as "the continuing process of creating the Middle Ages." Even some medieval writers, including Chrétien de Troyes, the *Pearl* poet, and Sir Thomas Malory, created a fictional Middle Ages as a method of self-understanding the contemporary concerns of their era. In the Jaussian sense, these writers of Arthurian romance might themselves be considered to write from "modern" perspectives, and their literary creations, as Nicholas Haydock points out, could be considered medievalism (or medievalistics, in Haydock's terminology).[4] In other words, medievalism

---

1   Hans Robert Jauss, "Modernity and Literary Tradition," *Critical Inquiry* 31.2 (Winter 2005): 329–64 (329). He explains, "If one looks back over its literary tradition, it seems evident that it has always already forfeited, through historical repetition, the very claim it sets out to make. It was not coined specially for our period, nor does it seem in the least capable of designating, unmistakably, the unique features of an epoch" (329).
2   Tom Shippey, "Modernity," in *Medievalism: Key Critical Terms*, ed. Elizabeth Emery and Richard Utz (Cambridge: D. S. Brewer, 2014), 149–55 (149).
3   Shippey, "Modernity," 149.
4   Nicholas Haydock, "Medievalism and Excluded Middles," in *Studies in Medievalism XVIII: Defining Medievalism(s) II*, ed. Karl Fugelso (Cambridge: D. S. Brewer, 2009), 17–30 (17). Haydock writes that "Sir Thomas Malory's widespread influence on later forms of medievalism need not prevent us from nominating his works – especially the Caxton redaction published in the watershed year 1485 – as a classic of medievalism" (18–19). According to Haydock, "Even the medievalism of *Beowulf* is not a patent absurdity" (18).

is not necessarily a post-medieval construct. Rather, it is a process of engaging with a fictionalized medieval past, and this process is possible not only within recent medievalist texts, but also within texts from the Middle Ages. In *A Song of Ice and Fire*, George R. R. Martin embraces the narrative strategies of Arthurian romance writers, particularly Chrétien, the *Pearl* poet, and Malory, complicating our notions that medievalist narrative is dramatically different from medieval narrative. In his creation of a complex, multi-layered world, Martin vividly illustrates how both modern and medieval populations might create a medieval past for self-understanding.

According to Tom Shippey, "no literary work of medievalism can avoid some interaction with modernity."[5] Medievalist texts, either intentionally or not, reflect the contemporary concerns of their authors, but so do some medieval texts. The romance writers noted above intentionally drew upon pre-existing legends to create a fictionalized past that served to illustrate their contemporary concerns. These writers sometimes used this fictive medieval past as a point of comparison against the ills of their own society. For example, in the opening lines of his version of "The Knight of the Cart," Malory compares the debased love of his own time to pure love in the fictionalized Arthurian past: "But the olde love was nat so; for men and women coude love togyders seven yerys, and no lycoures lustis was betwixte them – and than was love trouthe and faythefulness."[6] In "The Poisoned Apple," Malory attributes to this same fictionalized past the tradition of a trial by combat that could lead to Guenivere's death by fire: "For such custom was used in tho dayes, for favoure, love, nother affinité there sholde be none other but ryghtuous jugemente, as well upon a Kynge as upon a knight, and as well upon a queen as upon another poure lady."[7] Additionally, in a direct appeal to his contemporary audience, Malory uses the Arthurian past for contemporary political purposes:

> Lo, ye, all Englysshemen, se ye nat what a myschyff here was? For he that was the moste kynge and nobelyst knight of the worlde, and most loved the felyshyp of noble knyghtes – and by hym they all were upholdyn – and yet might nat thes Englyshemen holde them contente with hym. Lo, thus was the olde custom and usayges of thys londe; and men say that we of thys londe have nat yet loste that custom.[8]

The key for Haydock lies in "continuities and alterities in any particular evocation of the medieval" (19).

5   Shippey, "Modernity," 149.

6   Sir Thomas Malory, *Le Morte Darthur*, ed. Stephen H. Shepherd (New York: W. W. Norton & Company, 2004), 624–25.

7   Malory, *Le Morte Darthur*, 595.

8   Malory, *Le Morte Darthur*, 680.

Megan Leitch explains that "At a time when England was particularly trou-
bled by civil strife, Malory's text re-shaped familiar romance material to both
comment upon, and seek to renew, faltering social commitments."[9] In other
words, Malory shaped an Arthurian past as a means of self-understanding
for his own contemporary society.

Malory writes at the end of the Middle Ages; however, the tendency to
manipulate an Arthurian past is also evident in earlier medieval romances.
Chrétien de Troyes, writing in the twelfth century, begins *Yvain* with nostalgia
for the golden age of Arthur:

> But today very few serve love [...]. Now love is reduced to empty
> pleasantries, since those who know nothing about it claim that they
> love, but they lie, and those who boast of loving and have no right
> to do so make a lie and a mockery. But let us look beyond those
> who are present among us and speak now of those who were, for
> to my mind a courteous man, though dead, is more worthy than a
> living knave.[10]

Later in *Yvain*, Chrétien makes a similar nostalgic remark: "there are those
who would be quick to say I speak of idle tales, for people no longer fall
in love, nor do they love as once they did, nor even want to hear love
spoken of."[11] Similarly, the fourteenth-century author of *Sir Gawain and the
Green Knight* opens his work with an account of a fictionalized and glori-
fied Arthurian heritage for England. Many in medieval England believed
in an actual, historical Arthur distinct from the "idle tales" of romance.
The romance, however, served primarily to model chivalric behavior, not to
record history. Medieval authors used their visions of an Arthurian past to
achieve this purpose.[12]

Thus, the creation of a fictional medieval past to reflect contemporary
concerns spans from the works of Chrétien to current writers of medievalism. Numerous articles and blogs are devoted to exploring how Martin's
medievalism reflects the concerns of today's society. For example, Benjamin
Breen believes that, despite Martin's heavy reliance on medieval themes,
"Martin has created a fantasy world that chimes perfectly with the destabi-

---

9   Megan Leitch, "Speaking (of) Treason in Malory's *Morte Darthur*," *Arthurian Literature*
    27 (2010): 103–34 (110).
10 Chrétien de Troyes, *Arthurian Romances*, trans. William W. Kibler (New York: Penguin,
    1991), 295.
11 Chrétien de Troyes, *Arthurian Romances*, 362.
12 Even medieval chronicles might draw upon a fictionalized past. Geoffrey of Monmouth's
    Historia Regum Britanniaei, written largely to promote his Welsh patriotism, is filled with
    "fictionalized history."

lized and increasingly non-Western planetary order today."[13] Robert Tracinski finds that Martin's creation both mirrors our society and challenges today's audiences "to do better, to make discovery, invention, production, and the quest for freedom and justice seem even more interesting and compelling."[14] And John Blake explores a variety of ways in which Martin's work "reflects contemporary America," including politics, finance, and racial issues.[15]

Clearly, Martin's medievalism resonates with contemporary readers. The overwhelming success of Martin's fully visualized creation of an alternate medieval world promises to match in popularity those of J. R. R. Tolkien, C. S. Lewis, and, more recently, J. K. Rowling.[16] Norman Cantor describes the medievalism of the great modern fantasy-writers Tolkien and Lewis: "Out of the medieval Norse, Celtic, and Grail legends, they conjured fantasies of revenge and recovery, an ethos of return and triumph. As Chaucer said in *Troilus and Criseyde*, they aimed to 'make dreams truth and fables histories.'"[17] Martin's novels follow in this tradition. I argue, however, that Martin's work is distinguished by the comprehensiveness of his medievalism. In an interview with *Rolling Stone*, Martin himself notes the thoroughness of his medieval world in comparison to Tolkien's:

> Tolkien can say that Aragorn became king and reigned for a hundred years, and he was wise and good. But Tolkien doesn't ask the question: What was Aragorn's tax policy? Did he maintain a standing army? What did he do in times of flood and famine? And what about all these orcs?[18]

Martin provides meticulous details about governance, historical background, and even the literature of Westeros, creating a comprehensive pseudo-medieval world.

---

[13] Benjamin Breen, "Why 'Game of Thrones' Isn't Medieval – and Why that Matters," *Pacific Standard* (June 2014), <http://www.psmag.com/books-and-culture/game-thrones-isnt-me-dieval-matters-83288>, last accessed 8 August 2016.

[14] Robert Tracinski, "Our Sick National Obsession with *Game of Thrones*," *The Federalist* (11 April 2014), <http://thefederalist.com/2014/04/11/our-sick-national-obsession-with-game-of-thrones/>, last accessed 8 August 2016.

[15] John Blake, "How 'Game of Thrones' Is Like America," *CNN* (24 May 2014), <http://www.cnn.com/2014/05/24/showbiz/game-of-thrones-america/>, last accessed 8 August 2016.

[16] I refer in particular to Tolkien's *The Lord of the Rings* (Boston: Houghton Mifflin, 2003), Lewis's *The Chronicles of Narnia* (New York: HarperCollins, 2010), and Rowling's *Harry Potter* series (New York: Arthur A. Levine Books, 2009).

[17] Norman Cantor, *Inventing the Middle Ages: The Lives, Works, and Ideas of the Great Medievalists of the Twentieth Century* (New York: William Morrow, Co., 1991), 210–11.

[18] Mikal Gilmore, "George R. R. Martin: The *Rolling Stone* Interview," *Rolling Stone* (23 April 2014), <http://www.rollingstone.com/tv/news/george-r-r-martin-the-rolling-stone-interview-20140423>, last accessed 8 August 2016.

Shippey explains that both Tolkien and Lewis "bring the modern into contact with the medieval" in obvious ways; Shippey gives as example Bilbo Baggins, who is initially "in the identifiably Victorian/Edwardian world of the Shire [...], but who moves steadily into a fairy-tale world."[19] The same is true for the characters in *The Chronicles of Narnia* and for Harry Potter, who leave their familiar worlds to enter fantastic medieval realms. Martin's Westeros, in contrast, is medieval from the opening pages. Embedded within Martin's novels, however, are "inside jokes" that could only be appreciated by contemporary audiences well-versed in contemporary works of medievalism. For example, attentive readers might recognize shades of Tolkien's Samwise Gangee in the character of Samwell Tarly. Oberyn Martell's obsessive chanting about vengeance not only evokes the significance of the blood feud in medieval heroic literature, but also parodies the chant of Inigo Montoya from *The Princess Bride*.[20] Martin gives a nod to Rowling by naming two of Brienne of Tarth's tormentors Harry Sawyer and Robin Potter,[21] and elsewhere in his novels, he alludes to *Monty Python and the Holy Grail*[22] and *The Black Adder*.[23] Scattered throughout his novels, references such as these not only delight the astute readers who recognize them, but also add layers of complexity to Martin's medievalism.

This complexity can be traced to Martin's childhood. At a young age, he immersed himself in medieval lore and history and developed a childhood fascination with physical medieval models. He describes his inspirations on his website: "I had a Marx castle and some plastic toy knights as a kid, watched Robin Hood and Sir Lancelot on television, and went to the movies to see Ivanhoe [...] and Prince Valiant."[24]

As an adult writer of fantasy, he studied the Middle Ages extensively before shaping his fictionalized version of them, including in his research historical accounts by Barbara Tuchman, Joseph and Frances Gies, and Richard Barbara, as well as the chronicles of Froissart.[25] He also resurrected

---

19   Shippey, "Modernity," 154.
20   *The Princess Bride*. Dir. Rob Reiner. Perf. Robin Wright and Cary Elwes. Twentieth Century Fox Film Corp., 1987. DVD.
21   J. K. Rowling, *Harry Potter* series.
22   *Monty Python and the Holy Grail*. Dir. Terry Gilliam and Terry Jones. Perf. Graham Chapman, John Cleese, Terry Gilliam, Eric Idle, Terry Jones. Columbia Tri-Star Home Video, 2002. DVD.
23   *The Black Adder*. Perf. Rowan Atkinson. BBC Home Entertainment, 2009. DVD. A discussion of Martin's references to other works of literature, including works of medievalism, can be found on this wiki: http://iceandfire.wikia.com/wiki/Tributes_and_homages>, last accessed 8 August 2016.
24   George R. R. Martin, <http://www.georgerrmartin.com/for-fans/knights/>, last accessed 8 August 2016.
25   Martin describes on his website his use of history to create fiction: "I like to use history to flavor my fantasy, to add texture and verisimilitude, but simply rewriting history with the

his interest in collecting models, explaining that "in 1996, deep in the throes of writing my fantasy series, my old passions reawakened, and I started buying toy knights once again." The collections are, he claims, "only the first step. Some collectors actually keep their figures in their original boxes, but that makes no sense to me. My own preference is to use them to create scenes and dioramas that help them come alive."[26] These physical medieval models are then reproduced, or reflected, in Martin's novels, which in turn serve as models for the HBO series and the ever-growing industry of games and products derived mostly from the HBO series. The (largely technologically based) empire created around Martin's novels represents what Cory Lowell Grewell calls "an eleventh Middle Ages."[27]

Martin not only transfers his medieval visions from physical models to his novels, but he also includes references to physical models within his novels, thereby creating multi-layered, and multi-textured, medievalism. Consider the scene where Sansa Stark, in the Vale, constructs a snow model of Winterfell.[28] That the "real" Winterfell is a fictionalized creation makes Sansa's model of it "further independent, further detached," qualities that, according to Carol L. Robinson and Pamela Clements, constitute neo-medievalism.[29] A similar scene occurs in *A Feast for Crows*, when an artist repaints the shield Brienne has borrowed. The artist bases her artwork solely on visions formed from the legends of Westeros: "I made [the image of the castle] in my head, what a castle ought to look like. I never seen a dragon neither, nor a griffin,

---

names changed has no appeal for me. I prefer to re-imagine it all, and take it in new and unexpected directions," <http://www.georgerrmartin.com/for-fans/knights/>, last accessed 8 August 2016.

26   George R. R. Martin, <http://www.georgerrmartin.com/for-fans/knights/>, last accessed 8 August 2016.

27   Cory Lowell Grewell, "Neomedievalism: An Eleventh Little Middle Ages?" in *Studies in Medievalism XIX: Defining Neomedievalism(s)*, ed. Karl Fugelso (Cambridge: D. S. Brewer, 2010), 34–43. Grewell uses the concept of an Eleventh Middle Ages to define neomedievalism, which is, for him, "a form of medievalism that is intrinsically influenced by postmodern ideology, that is integrally linked to late twentieth- and twenty-first-century advances in technology, and that is distinguished from previous forms of medievalism by its multi-culturalism, its lack of concern for history, and its habit of imagining the medieval world through the lens of previous medievalisms" (40).

28   George R. R. Martin, *A Song of Ice and Fire*, 5 volumes (New York: Bantam Books, 2013). Citations will be to individual novels in the series. This reference is to *A Storm of Swords*, 1101.

29   Carol L. Robinson and Pamela Clements, "Living with Neomedievalism," in *Studies in Medievalism XVIII: Defining Medievalism(s) II*, ed. Karl Fugelso (Cambridge: D. S. Brewer, 2009), 55–75 (56). *Studies in Medievalism* has devoted several recent volumes to defining the slippery new concept of neo-medievalism. Robinson and Clements' definition appears to be emerging as the most popular. They describe neo-medievalism as "purposefully, and perhaps even laughingly reshaping itself into an alternate universe of medievalism, a fantasy of medievalisms, a meta-medievalism" (56).

nor a unicorn."[30] Further, Martin's novels frequently reference mummer's shows, plays within the larger narrative that reenact both the legends and the political happenings of Westeros.

Despite his originality in creating such a thoroughly visualized and multi-layered fictional past and despite the immense commercialization of his crea-tion, Martin's medievalism is, in essence, the continuity of the medievalism found in some literature from the Middle Ages, which can also be multi-layered and multi-textured. For example, Chaucer's narrative framework in *The Canterbury Tales* (fictional characters reciting fiction) and the stories told by minstrels within chivalric and heroic literature build fiction upon fiction. A physical model appears in *Sir Gawain and the Green Knight* when Gawain first comes upon Lord Bertilak's castle and finds that it resembles a model more than an actual castle: "pared out of papure purely hit semed."[31] The notion of this "real" castle resembling a model matches the hyper-reality of Sansa's snow castle and challenges our notions of neo-medievalism as a postmodern concept. Additionally, just as Martin's Westeros has inspired an HBO televised series, games, and products, Nigel Saul explains that "Knights of the fourteenth and fifteenth centuries, soaked in the legends of Arthurian romance, sought to act out the fictions in their own lives. The worlds of reality and imagination overlapped."[32] Thus, the immensely popular medi-eval romance inspired real-life modeling as the medieval populace sought to emulate the fictional past in tournaments and pageantry.

Robinson and Clements note that "the matter of medievalism, including that of neo-medievalism, includes thousands of collectively owned tropes [...]."[33] Malory's vision of a medieval past is a bricolage, a compilation of Arthurian tropes that he assimilates, or cuts and pastes, into a comprehen-sive (and new, by medieval literary standards) work. Similarly, the intricately woven world of Westeros incorporates myriad medieval tropes.[34] Lesley Coote, in "A Short Essay about Neomedievalism," writes that "Deconstructing the text is postmodern, but cutting and pasting it to make something new is

---

30 Martin, *A Feast for Crows*, 187.
31 "Sir Gawain and the Green Knight," in *The Poems of the Pearl Manuscript*, ed. Malcolm Andrew and Ronald Waldron (Berkeley: University of California Press, 1982), line 802.
32 Nigel Saul, *For Honour and Fame: Chivalry in England 1066–1500* (London: Pimlico, 2012), 157.
33 Robinson and Clements, "Living with Neomedievalism," 62.
34 Martin randomly, yet skillfully, assimilates and reworks an impressive array of tropes and folk legends. Consider the ring of familiarity of just a sampling of the legends that are deeply embedded in the lore of Westeros: the Rat King, who served the Andal king his "prince-and-bacon pie" (*A Storm of Swords* 756) ; a woman dressed as a knight to shame her cowardly husband (reminiscent of the motif in the Old French fabliau *Le Sot Cheva-lier*); and the trickster pig of "a thousand ribald stories" (*A Feast for Crows* 10) with whom a novice at the Citadel, Pate, sadly shares a name.

neo-medieval – and it brings the cut-and-paster surprisingly close to medi-eval reading practices. Medieval readers were also expected to read on many levels."[35] Whereas the *Pearl* poet's tale of Gawain mirrors fourteenth-century England and Malory's *Le Morte D'Arthur* seems to reflect fifteenth-century England, Martin's Westeros clearly mimics medieval England but is outside of any specific time reference. Thus, he creates what Shippey terms "a permanent anachronistic stew," an expansive and somewhat random incorporation of "the medieval imaginary."[36] Craig Bernthal compares Martin's expansive world to Malory's and Spenser's, but Bernthal argues that the many layers of narra-tive and the open-endedness of Martin's novels are features that make them postmodern.[37] He describes Martin's work as an "endless struggle for power," denying the possibility of a definite conclusion. However, just as Malory brings his *Le Morte D'Arthur* to an end, Martin has promised to bring his vast work to conclusion. Thus, despite the non-specificity of Martin's settings, both Martin and Malory assimilate myriad medieval tropes into comprehensive works. Their similar methodology narrows the perceived gulf between them.

Martin layers fiction upon fiction as the characters of Westeros relate the legends of their past, legends that mimic the Arthurian legacy in their intricacy. In his book on Tolkien's rich mythology, Shippey writes that, with Tolkien, readers get "a sense that the author knew more than he was telling, that behind his immediate story there was a coherent, consistent, deeply fascinating world about which he had no time (then) to speak."[38] Martin, on the other hand, takes time within his novels to explore the fascinating heritage that undergirds his primary matter. He makes frequent references and allusions to the stories behind the immediate story, creating many layers of medievalism within his medievalist text. As characters and singers recall stories from the past, Martin's readers can reconstruct much of the backstory. Westeros is so rich in legend that it has merited its own volume, *The World of Ice and Fire*, told from the perspective of a Maester of the Citadel who seeks to document his learning and assimilate the lore available to him.[39] The expansive pseudo-literary tradition of Westeros, both oral and written,

---

35 Lesley Coote, "A Short Essay about Neomedievalism," in *Studies in Medievalism XIX: Defining Neomedievalism(s)*, ed. Karl Fugelso (Cambridge: D. S. Brewer, 2010), 25–33 (30).
36 Shippey, "Modernity," 149.
37 Craig Bernthal, "Endless Game of Thrones," Review of *A Song of Ice and Fire* by George R. R. Martin, in *The University Bookman* (June 2012), <http://www.kirkcenter.org/index.php/bookman/article/endless-game-of-thrones/>, last accessed 8 August 2016.
38 Tom Shippey, *The Road to Middle Earth: How J. R. R. Tolkien Created a New Mythology* (New York: Mariner Books, 2003), 230.
39 Published posthumously by Tolkien's son Christopher, *The Silmarillion* provides a compa-rable background to Tolkien's mythopoeic world. I find that storytelling and references to (pseudo-) history are much more frequent, and more critical to the narrative, in Martin's novels than Tolkien's.

authenticates Martin's mythopoeic world. Martin fills his novels with references to, and even some examples of, medieval genres: histories, chronicles,
romances, songs, and poems. In this respect, if we concede that Malory's
work might be considered "modern," Martin's novels are remarkably "medieval." He vividly illustrates how a medieval population, through its production of both oral and written literature, might use a fictional medieval past
as self-understanding.

For example, Martin makes several references to a valuable guidebook for
kings of Westeros, *Lives of Four Kings*. This pseudo-history book is doubly
fictionalized in that the author, Grand Maester Kaeth, intends it more as
an instructional manual than a history and appears to shape its contents
accordingly. Tyrion Lannister, a self-professed bibliophile, gives his nephew
Joffrey this extremely valuable book, which Joffrey subsequently destroys.
Acknowledging that this book might have helped Joffrey in his reign, Tyrion
laments, "He might have learned a thing or two if he'd read it."[40] Whereas
Joffrey rejects the notion of using (pseudo-)history as a model for his own
reign, his uncle Jaime, once he loses his hand and returns to the Kingsguard
as Lord Commander, seriously considers his own responsibility as contributor to the White Book: "Within the White Book was the history of the
Kingsguard. Every knight who'd ever served had a page, to record his name
and deeds for all time [...]. *My duty, now*."[41] This book not only records the
feats and exploits of former members of the Kingsguard, but, in doing so,
serves as a sort of handbook of chivalry for subsequent generations. Unlike
his depraved nephew Joffrey, Jaime Lannister uses the past, as Jauss describes,
"for self-understanding."[42] Jaime determines to use the White Book as a
model for his future behavior and, in time, to himself become a model for
others through its pages. Similar literature in the Middle Ages (romance and
chivalric handbooks such as those by Raymond Lull and Christine de Pizan)
also functioned as models for ideal behavior.

Martin not only embraces some of the narrative techniques of medieval
romance writers, but he also includes references to romances within his
novels. In Chrétien's *Yvain*, the titular hero of the romance comes upon a
maiden who is herself reading a romance. Martin echoes this moment in
his references to several characters who are influenced by reading or hearing
chivalric stories, such as the fanciful stories that fill Sansa Stark with unre-
alistic expectations, and the book Ser Jorah Mormont gives to Daenerys
as a gift. Upon dismissing Ser Jorah from her service and banishing him,
Daenerys wants to read this book as an escape from the heart-breaking task
she has just completed: "She wanted to lose herself in the words, in other

---

40 Martin, *A Storm of Swords*, 807.
41 Martin, *A Storm of Swords*, 913–14.
42 Jauss, "Modernity and Literary Tradition," 329.

times and other places. The fat leather-bound volume was full of songs and stories from the Seven Kingdoms. Children's stories, if truth be told, too simple and fanciful to be true history. All of the heroes were tall and handsome, and you could tell the traitors by their shifty eyes. Yet she loved them all the same."[43] Daenerys's pseudo-collection of entertaining, romance-like tales set in a doubly fictional past is another example of the richly layered medievalism of Westeros. These narratives, by portraying ideal heroes, serve to shape the chivalric ethos of Westeros, again mimicking the purpose of medieval romance.

Martin embeds songs and oral narratives throughout his series. These oral sources effectively mimic, in their multiple versions, the many-versioned Arthurian narratives of the Middle Ages. For example, Malory acknowledges that a number of narratives offer speculation about the death of Arthur:

> Yet som men say in many partys of Inglonde that kynge Arthure ys nat dede, but had by the wyll of Oure Lorde Jesu into another place; and men say that he shall com agayne, and he shall wynne the Holy Crosse [...]. And many men say that there ys wyitten uppon the tumbe thys [vers]: Hic iacet Arthurus, Rex quondam Rexque futurus.[44]

Similarly, in his recollections of Old Nan's stories about the Night's King of the Night's Watch, Bran Stark notes that many versions of the tale exist: "Some say he was a Bolton [...]. Some say a Magnar out of Skagos, some say Umber, Flint, or Norrey. Some would have you think he was a Woodfoot [...]." Bran, not unlike Malory, molds a many-versioned legend to his own purpose, in this case, self-identity: "He never was. He was a Stark, the brother of the man who brought him down."[45]

The many singers found throughout Martin's saga build narrative upon narrative as they capture and craft the lore of Westeros to suit their various Westerosi audiences. Martin's singers thus mirror the medieval minstrel who not only preserves history, but also shapes it creatively through song. At Joffrey's wedding, Tyrion fumes over a singer's recounting of the Battle of Blackwater Bay, which seems, for political reasons, unlikely to credit him with the victory: "If I am ever Hand again, the first thing I'll do is hang all the singers."[46] Tyrion realizes that, in the doubly fictionalized songs about the battle he helped to win, his own role will be erased and a new, "false," version will emerge in its place. The citizens of Westeros are challenged in their attempts to discern which elements of their rich heritage are "real"

43 Martin, *A Storm of Swords*, 991.
44 Malory, *Le Morte Darthur*, 689.
45 Martin, *A Storm of Swords*, 762.
46 Martin, *A Storm of Swords*, 832.

and which are, like the minstrel's account of the Battle of Blackwater Bay, (pseudo-)fictional. When he is sent to Mance Rayder's camp to kill Mance, Jon Snow spies what he believes to be the Horn of Winter, which he knows from legend. He wonders if the legends might hold true: "If I sound the Horn of Winter, the Wall will fail. Or so the songs would have me believe."[47] Similarly, novices at the Citadel discuss the rumors of dragons told by various sailors: "'The tales are *not* the same,' insisted Armen. 'Dragons in Assahai, dragons in Qarth, dragons in Meereen, Dothraki dragons, dragons freeing slaves … each telling differs from the last."[48] Martin's own narrative about Daenerys' dragons is redoubled by the multi-layered fictional accounts of dragons that make their way across the Narrow Sea to Westeros.

At least so far in the series, Martin downplays the role of magic and the supernatural. Westeros is largely a rationalized world; its inhabitants are mostly skeptical about their own (doubly) fictionalized history and certainly skeptical about the possibility of living dragons. In a council at King's Landing, Maester Qyborn mocks the role of the Night's Watch in defending the realm from the supernatural that reportedly lies beyond the Wall: "The Night's Watch defends us all from snarks and grumkins."[49] Much of the narrative tension results from characters' denials of the existence of magic. Those who do believe in magic generally perceive it as something that took place in the past or takes place across the Narrow Sea and beyond the Wall. Westeros itself is inhabited by ordinary humans; the dwarf Tyrion is seen as an anomaly. Thus, Martin's medievalism is decidedly less fantastic than can be found in Tolkien, Lewis, or Rowling, who populate their novels with hobbits, centaurs, giants, orcs, and other magical creatures.

At a glance, Martin's skepticism might be attributed to contemporary forms of rationalization believed to be absent from medieval writers. However, in *Le Morte Darthur*, Malory, too, downplays magic and the supernatural. Eugène Vinaver describes Malory's de-emphasis of magic compared to his sources: "Nothing is more characteristic of Malory's attitude to the French tradition than his frequent refusal to explain unusual occurrences in purely supernatural terms."[50] Even for Chrétien de Troyes and the *Pearl* poet, magic and the supernatural function practically, as obstacles or challenges, and then typically disappear or are explained once the hero has faced them. For example, in Chrétien's *Le Chevalier à la Charrette*, the sword-bridge that Lancelot must cross disappears once he has rescued Guinevere. Despite the fact that

---

47 Martin, *A Storm of Swords*, 1019.
48 Martin, *A Feast for Crows*, 6.
49 Martin, *A Feast for Crows*, 355.
50 Eugène Vinaver, "Introduction," in *King Arthur and his Knights: Selections from the Works of Sir Thomas Malory*, ed. Eugène Vinaver (New York: Oxford University Press, 1956), vii–xxi (xvii).

much of the action in *Sir Gawain and the Green Knight* occurs in Bertilak's enchanted kingdom, the *Pearl* poet has Bertilak explain the cause and reason for his supernatural transformation into the Green Knight after Gawain has faced his challenge, and then Gawain returns to the decidedly less magical realm of Arthur's court. As Martin's series progresses, the boundaries between the rationalized world of Westeros and the supernatural world beyond its borders promise to be breached, and once (if) this happens, literary perceptions in (and of) Westeros will likely change as works believed to be fiction prove fact. [51] Readers can only surmise how Martin's medievalism will evolve in his final novels once Others breach the Wall and dragons make their way back to Westeros. Regardless of the outcome, Martin has created the richest of medievalist texts by embracing romance narrative techniques and layering medievalisms. Martin illustrates how medievalism can be possible within a medieval text and also how multi-layered medievalisms can exist in a medievalist text.

---

[51] The reception of Arthurian literature tended to take the opposite path, from fact to fiction. For example, Geoffrey of Monmouth's fictionalized history of King Arthur, one of the most influential texts of the Middle Ages, was believed by many in the Middle Ages to be a true account. Though criticized by some of his own generation, famously by Wace, his work was not completely debunked until the sixteenth century by Polydore Vergil.

Modernity in the Middle:
The Medieval Fantasy of (Coopted) Feminism in Disney's *Maleficent**

Elan Justice Pavlinich

In 2014, *Maleficent* revisited the 1959 Disney animated classic *Sleeping Beauty*.[1] An early production for the emerging company, *Sleeping Beauty* is foundational to the Disney corpus; it represents the values upon which the Disney kingdom is constructed. *Maleficent*, released over half a century later, signifies Disney's introspective turn toward its own heritage, a heritage rooted in medieval fantasy. Challenging audiences' familiarity with popular fairy tales and the Disney corpus, the narrator proposes, "Let us tell an old tale anew, and we will see how well you know it." *Maleficent* suggests a progressive, feminist conclusion that clashes with audiences' present circumstances, rendering modernity a "dark age" by comparison. *Maleficent* is a revision that inflects the older *Sleeping Beauty* with contemporary social concerns and the emerging progressive values of a more inclusive Disney kingdom.

The film opens with two opposing realms: the moors, which are a dense natural realm inhabited by diverse mythical creatures, versus the kingdom, which is composed of bleak dingy spaces, dimly lit by fire, and inhabited by humans. Within the moors, young Maleficent, played by Isobelle Molloy, is a happy fairy dressed in earth tones, with a pleasant smile and playful nature. Her immense wings carry her over edenic spaces with breakneck speed. She

* I would like to thank Karl Fugelso, Nicole Guenther Discenza, Diane Price-Herndl, Gwendolyne Knight Keimpema, and the anonymous readers for *Studies in Medievalism* for their insightful comments on multiple drafts. Also, I am deeply grateful to Richard Utz for his direction and encouragement.
1 *Maleficent*, directed by Robert Stromberg (2014; Burbank, CA: Buena Vista Home Entertainment, 2014); and *Sleeping Beauty*, directed by Clyde Geronimi (1959; Burbank, CA: Buena Vista Home Entertainment, 2014).

is a healer, maintaining the health and well-being of the moors. But there is an intruder here. Stefan, a human boy, has ventured into the wilderness that his people typically fear. During their exchange, we learn two things: Stefan has attempted to take a stone from the moors as a token, and fairies like Maleficent are burned by the touch of ironworks forged by humans. Maleficent and Stefan cultivate a relationship that verges on romance, but they are eventually separated as Stefan grows older and is overcome by ambition. Fearing the mythical creatures, and seeking to commodify the natural realm, the king of the humans, Henry, launches an assault against the moors, which is vanquished by Maleficent, now played by Angelina Jolie. King Henry decrees that any subject who slays Maleficent will succeed him to the throne. Relying on their previous intimacy, Stefan lures Maleficent to a private meeting, severs her wings from her body, and presents them to the king as a token of her demise. Soon after, Stefan is crowned and Aurora, his first child, is born. On the day of Aurora's christening, Maleficent interrupts the festivities to deliver the iconic curse: on her sixteenth birthday the princess will prick her finger on the spindle of a spinning wheel and fall into a death-like sleep that only true love's kiss can relieve. Driven by hatred, Maleficent maintains vigilance over Aurora to ensure that her curse comes to fruition. Maleficent's affection for the young girl, now played by Elle Fanning, develops as Aurora matures. She becomes Aurora's protector, but she cannot keep the girl from the fateful curse. Aurora pricks her finger, falls asleep, and Maleficent's quest to awaken Aurora begins. A kiss from the handsome Prince Phillip proffers the traditional remedy, but he fails to awaken her. Heartbroken by Aurora's death-like slumber, Maleficent kisses her apologetically, whereupon the princess serendipitously revives. Their peril, however, is far from over. Having fallen prey to his own paranoia, King Stefan ensnares Maleficent in iron, bent on murdering her once and for all. But Aurora discovers Maleficent's purloined wings in a secret chamber and frees them, whereupon they are restored to Maleficent's body. King Stefan is then overwhelmed by Maleficent, but left alive, and in one final, desperate attempt he lunges at her, only to topple to his death from the spires of the castle. With the details of the Sleeping Beauty legend having been dramatically revised, the film concludes with the kingdom of humans harmoniously united with the natural realm of the moors under the rule of Queen Aurora and her magical advisor, Maleficent.

This updated Sleeping Beauty narrative suggests that the medieval English kingdom of *Maleficent* was potentially more progressive than Western cultures are today. *Maleficent*'s "happily ever after" revolves around the patriarch's demise, the concomitant death of the kingdom's social hierarchy, and presumably the liberation of women and people of color, who had been exploited to serve the kingdom's industrialization. If Maleficent's victory over forces of oppression, including patriarchal capitalism, occurred in the medieval past, then the modern Western tradition that historically follows this medieval past has failed to maintain that victory. This disparity between fantasy and historical reality may alienate some postmodern audiences from the social conditions in which they are immersed. Typically, modernity is privileged as an age that is distinct from, and triumphant over, the Middle Ages. Glenn Burger observes that "the *pre* of premodern or the *middle* of medieval is so often employed to indicate a stabilizing sequentiality[, but] medievalism can function as a [...] coming and going rather than a start or finish to some organized narrative of origins."[2] Accordingly, *Maleficent* disrupts linear notions of social progress by situating feminist ideals in the medieval past, inviting comparison between the social politics projected by the film and audiences' lived experience. Between an ideal medieval past and an optimistic future of "happily ever afters," the postmodern condition is rendered comparatively inferior in terms of social equality. By imposing postmodern ideologies on *Sleeping Beauty*, *Maleficent* situates feminist politics within the medieval past, creating disorientation between medieval fantasy and contemporary reality. Modernity is identified as a dark age for feminism.

The opening sequence seeks to moderate this disorientation, easing audiences into the medieval setting by means of the Disney trademark castle, a signifier that renders Disney's brand name synonymous with medievalisms.[3] Disney has fabricated an enduring medieval heritage that reverberates with the continued employment of castles, most significantly featured in the various permutations of the Disney trademark logo. Looking at early productions, Jay P. Telotte observes the aesthetic of Disney castles and the construction of medieval space, particularly in *Sleeping Beauty*:

> The [cartoon's] primary castle, that of King Stefan, clearly recalls the richly colored and ornately designed structures depicted in [the Limbourg brothers' illuminated manuscript] *Tres Riches Heures*, a look that sets this structure in stark contrast to the dark, forbid-

---

2   Glenn Burger, "Shameful Pleasures: Up Close and Dirty with Chaucer, Flesh, and the Word," in *Queering the Middle Ages*, ed. Glenn Burger and Steven F. Kruger (Minneapolis: University of Minnesota Press, 2001), 213–35 (218).

3   *Snow White and the Seven Dwarves*, *Sleeping Beauty*, and *Cinderella* are just a few of the early medievalisms of Disney that feature castles as touchstones between the fantasy of the films, and tangible monuments at locations such as Disney World and Disney Land. The castle trademark is employed to mark the parameters of the Disney kingdom, one that claims actual spaces internationally, and that stretches temporally into the past to claim folklore and fairy tales as origin narratives for contemporary Western culture. Disney cites the Middle Ages as a cultural origin to which the production company lays claim with its enduring use of the castle trademark logo. In this way, Disney fabricates a medieval heritage.

ding, and indeed crumbling castle inhabited by the evil fairy
Maleficent and her half-animal servants, the "forces of evil," as she
terms them. If the former structure suggests the vitality, richness,
and indeed openness of medieval culture [...], the other, perched
precariously atop one of the "Forbidden Mountains," surrounded
by gloom, its only entry a guarded, gargoyle-adorned bridge over
a deep canyon, points to the culture's other potential, for repression, violence, and enclosure. [A short while later, as Maleficent]
places a curse on Aurora, she also effectively transforms the castle
from an open, brightly-colored, and inviting realm to a kind of
green-tinged fortress [...]. Appropriately, this shift is marked by the
disappearance of the multiplane shots in favor of a flat manuscript
page, with time and space becoming a function of its words that
simply note, "Many sad and lonely years passed by for King Stefan
and his people."[4]

Maleficent maintains this same dichotomous construction of space, but
the distinction between good and evil realms, which contrasts the masculine kingdom with the feminine moors, is reversed. The natural realm
is altered from the dark and forbidden territory of *Sleeping Beauty* to a
lush and playful panorama in *Maleficent*, while the castle of the human
kingdom, which is dim, dingy, and isolated, suggests that, within its
domain, capitalist forces oppress humans and nature alike. In spite of
this alternative perspective that identifies the human realm as the site
of corruption, this castle maintains affinities with the Disney trademark.
The castle of the human kingdom corresponds to the Disney heritage,
suggesting that the present film is a critical reflection upon the production
company's earlier ideologies.

In accordance with convention, the Disney trademark castle opens
Maleficent: a sweeping aerial view of a diverse landscape, under a gloaming
sky, punctuated by the iconic Sleeping Beauty's Castle. In this opening
sequence, just after the Disney brand name fades and leaves the ivory
castle to dominate the shot, the vibrant colors of the Disney castle degrade
to the dull earth tones of a dimly lit functional fortification. The trademark logo transforms into an establishing shot of the human kingdom.
This kingdom remains nameless through the film, befitting the ambiguity
of the medieval period in the modern imagination. Suddenly, the visual
frame veers off in the exact opposite direction of the castle to show a dense
and thriving natural panorama: the moors. Here dragons, fairies, and

---

4   Jay P. Telotte, "Flatness and Depth: Classic Disney's Medieval Vision," *The Year's Work
    in Medievalism* 30 (2015), <https://sites.google.com/site/theyearsworkinmedievalism/all-
    issues/30-2015-1>, last accessed 5 May 2016.

wallerbogs (small mud creatures with trunks and antennae) rely on one another. They have no need for a ruler, nor the oppressive apparatus of capitalism. Consequently, the castle represents both the Disney tradition and the nameless patriarchal kingdom of humans that stands in opposition to nature and the marginalized beings of the moors. *Maleficent*'s audience, polyvalently reminded by the opening sequence that they are viewing a Disney production, has been conveyed into the medieval setting by means of the trademark Disney castle. A crane shot turns viewers toward the moors, or the natural realm, as it appears from the point of view of the (Disney) castle. The film has only just begun, but the perspective imposed on viewers by this establishing shot claims the audience as denizens of the Disney kingdom.

Modern capitalism, working across multiple planes, is hailing audiences as subjects of the Disney kingdom, and modern capitalism is responsible for much of the conflict within the film's medieval setting. In the medieval fantasy of *Maleficent*, capitalist forces are depicted with a modern register, and this familiarity extends their presence beyond the boundaries of the film. In the opening segment, woodland guards corner young Stefan for having removed a stone from its natural setting. Influenced by a capitalist society, Stefan attributes extrinsic value to the stone to increase his own worth. Similarly, when the king offers a reward to any subject who vanquishes Maleficent, Stefan severs Maleficent's wings from her body; he renders her appendages a token for his personal prosperity and social advancement. Stefan is motivated by capitalism to acquire wealth by commodifying and oppressing others, particularly the others who inhabit the natural realm. Furthermore, King Henry orders his knights to conquer the moors for the purpose of expanding his dominion and profiting from the resources therein. After his death, Stefan succeeds him as the patriarch. While King Stefan appears to be more eager to isolate the human kingdom from the natural realm, he governs a social hierarchy that maintains the capitalist apparatus of oppression, reducing people to the value of their labor for the purpose of privileging the patriarch. This is evident in the few depictions of disempowered people in *Maleficent*.

First, the queen of the kingdom, Stefan's wife, is oppressed by capitalist forces in spite of her social status. She gives birth to Aurora, and she dies some years later, alone, not even to be comforted by her partner, the king. She is merely a means of production. Having begotten Stefan's heir, she has fulfilled her obligation to the kingdom's economy. Similarly, other women are charged with domestic labor that is suppressed from public view: the fairies – Flora, Fauna, and Merryweather – care for Aurora in a distant cottage, and teams of women labor in the underground laundry rooms. People of color are also marginalized; no people of color are visible amid nobles or even gentry at court, and the only black man with a speaking role serves as a night watchman. In accordance with capitalist forces that serve to maintain the patriarch's power, women and people of color are reduced to the value of their labor. They are commodified and kept out of sight.[5] The labor of these marginalized people benefit a select few, who maintain their social standing via these capitalist forces of oppression. For the most part, white people with power dominate the focus of the film: Stefan, Aurora, and even Maleficent, who adopts patriarchal strategies of power when she is motivated by vengeance to assume a central throne from which she imposes her authority over the previously serene moors. Each of these subjects exercise a degree of autonomy through their power.

Resolving the drama, Maleficent defeats the patriarch, and Aurora is subsequently crowned. Resolving the realm to Aurora's rule promises the harmonious integration of the kingdom with the moors, of humans with nature. The patriarch's capitalism is deposed and replaced by a relationship between humans and nature under the rule of Aurora. *Maleficent's* medievalism is more progressive than audiences' postmodern condition, because the medieval fantasy results in the patriarch's demise, women's empowerment, and the suggestion of legally enforced respect for nature.

The "happily ever after" suggested by this conclusion frustrates synthesis with some audiences, who are conscious of contemporary issues that could not logically follow from reconciliation between humans and nature under a benevolent matriarch. Women and people of color continue to be discriminated against and denied opportunities to exercise autonomy. Wealth and power are disproportionately and unjustly distributed. The environment is commodified, perverted, and diminished to support capitalism. Contradicting the Sleeping Beauty narrative with which most postmodern audiences are familiar, the narrator reveals herself to be Aurora. Her personal experience opposes and exposes the corrupt, misogynist *Sleeping Beauty*, and thus authorizes *Maleficent* as the true, unadulterated account.[6] This very revelation, that the narrator is Aurora, subordinates modernity because this suggests that contemporary audiences, whose cultural memory supports the misogynist Sleeping Beauty narrative, must

---

5   Sandra Harding observes that marginalized people generally perform manual labor that, in order to be considered "good work," will also render those who perform this work invisible to the people whom they serve. Sandra Harding, *Is Science Multicultural?: Postcolonialisms, Feminisms, and Epistemologies* (Bloomington: Indiana University Press, 1998), 152.

6   I argue that Disney manipulates visual rhetoric and appeals to experience, constructing a textual authority that overrides its animated predecessor in my article, "The Chaucerian Debate of *Auctorite* versus Experience in Disney's *Sleeping Beauty* and *Maleficent*," in *The Year's Work in Medievalism* 30 (2015), <https://sites.google.com/site/theyearsworkinmedievalism/all-issues/30-2015-1>, last accessed 18 December 2016.

have eventually lost the idealized equality and harmony that was made possible by Maleficent and Aurora. Attempting to fit the fantasy of *Malefi- cent* as an origin narrative into our historical narrative necessitates that at some point in the modern era the patriarchal forces resumed control and perverted the account authorized by Aurora, leaving audiences with a fairy tale that affirms modern strategies of power, *Sleeping Beauty*. Gwendolyn Morgan explains, "conscious recreations of the [medieval] era have bred further *un*conscious re-imaginings, beginning a chain of self-perpetrating self-deception in justifying contemporary beliefs by non-existent medieval roots."[7] In the case of *Maleficent*, the film invites a feminist hermeneutic, suggesting to audiences that social conditions of equality were achieved, then corrupted, and that feminist ideals are rooted in the medieval past. Through this disjuncture between the film's rendition of the medieval past and the realities of the postmodern condition, *Maleficent* underscores the inequities of capitalism and puts pressure on some of the distinguishing features of modernity.

Maleficent invites a feminist reading because it is a gynocentric film that concludes with women being empowered, and because the title char- acter exhibits a feminist visual rhetoric by means of her horns, lips, and wings. The spectacle of Maleficent emphasizes the character's womanhood and bolsters her autonomous power, but all of this is a veneer. It is the trappings of feminism without content. Posing a feminist visual rhetoric, *Maleficent* polyvalently invites audiences to perform a feminist reading of the text without insisting that they do so. To begin with, Maleficent's red lips contrast with the color scheme of the *mise-en-scène*. The earth tones of the moors emphasize the brightness of her painted lips. The audi- ence is accustomed to cosmetic enhancement as a signifier of femininity, and so her lips function as a symbol of womanhood.[8] Next, Maleficent's horns mark her as the Other within a heteronormative, male-dominated social context. Her horns, an observable biological feature, resonate with women's bodies and the subsequent marginalization of women in patri- archal societies. They constitute a familiar feature that originates with the *Sleeping Beauty* villainess, but in *Maleficent* they have an emphasized tripartite curvature, as if to signify an opening much like the two lips of

7   Gwendolyn Morgan, "Authority," in *Medievalism: Key Critical Terms*, ed. Elizabeth Emery and Richard Utz (Cambridge: D. S. Brewer, 2014), 27–33 (33).

8   Some third-wave feminists have argued that lips painted brightly red are an indication of feminine autonomy because lipstick obscures the distinction between authenticity and artifice, and this is an act of rebellion against hegemonic gender. See Linda M. Scott, *Fresh Lipstick: Redressing Fashion and Feminism* (New York: Palgrave Macmillan, 2005), 302; and Karen Lehrman, *The Lipstick Proviso: Women, Sex & Power in the Real World* (New York: Doubleday, 1997), 1–6 and 65–96.

labia.[9] Furthermore, her horns, combined with her bright red lips and her enormous wings, as signifiers of her womanhood, lend themselves to such an interpretation in light of the sexual implications of her stolen wings. Threatened, the king declares that the first man to kill Maleficent shall succeed him and rule the kingdom. So, Maleficent's lover, Stefan, severs her wings from her body, rendering them tokens that buy his way into nobility. As Maleficent weeps with horror at her defilement, younger audiences may see a woman who has been harmed by a man whom she trusted, while mature audiences may read the circumstance as rape.[10] Having been perverted by masculine strategies of oppression, the wings signify her sexuality and her autonomy. They not only convey her to skies that are unreachable by other creatures, but they also enable her to vanquish multiple knights with a single blow in the first combat scene. In a patriarchal society, women are disciplined by ideology and social practices to be sexually restrained, petite, and feeble, explains Sandra Lee Bartky, whereas men are empowered by signifiers of the phallus that express expansion and encourage the domination of space.[11] The knights, with swords drawn, are enfeebled by the aspect ratio of a crane shot. Maleficent's wings expand and dominate the screen, threatening the phallic swords. Her wings are a source of power, and they facilitate her resistance to the patriarchy. Maleficent's lips, horns, and wings signify her womanhood not only as they constitute her character, but also as her physical attributes are interpreted and reinscribed by other characters in the film.

The visual rhetoric of Maleficent's embodiment encodes her womanhood in such a way that over the course of the film, as her body is threatened, commodified, or even recontextualized, she signifies certain aspects of women's experiences that invite a feminist reading. This is not meant to suggest that Maleficent signifies every woman, or that women's experiences are reducible to these events or the general feminine embodiment depicted by the film. Such essentialist paradigms are to be avoided because they simply reify the identity categories of the patriarchy that are so problematic. Women's experiences, and woman as an identity category, are far broader than the biologi-

---

9   Sexuality in Disney productions has been a matter of debate, and in some instances, these have been confirmed by the artists. Audiences have noticed a golden penis hidden in the pillars of the castle on the VHS cover of *The Little Mermaid*, a topless woman in the background of *The Rescuers Down Under*, and "sex" spelled out in *Pocahontas* and *The Lion King*, to name a few.

10   Hayley Krischer, "The *Maleficent* Rape Scene That We Need to Talk About," in *The Huffington Post*, 6 June 2014, < http://www.huffingtonpost.com/hayley-krischer/the-maleficent-rape-scene_b_5445974.html >, last accessed 27 October 2014.

11   Sandra Lee Bartky, "Foucault, Femininity, and the Modernization of Patriarchal Power," in *Feminism and Foucault*, ed. Irene Diamond and Lee Quinby (Boston: Northeastern University Press, 1988), 66.

cally observable features described above. Maleficent resonates with women's experiences and general political issues that feminists continually combat in that she is marginalized and threatened by multiple patriarchal powers, who target her because of her observable biological features, which a man deliberately commodifies to gain power for himself and to exert mastery over Maleficent and the natural realm.

Maleficent's victory over the corrupt patriarch implies that all women will be freed from the oppressive forces of capitalism that marginalize their lives and silence their voices. In light of this interpretation, *Maleficent* presents a medieval past that indicates the possibility of achieving a feminist ideal of equality – an ideal that modernity has yet to realize and maintain. Still, *Maleficent* merely hints at the potential for a feminist reading. The "happily ever after" is not resolved to postmodern social circumstances, and a closer investigation of the film's ideology and power dynamics, as they relate to gender, reveals the polyvalent nature of the characters, which compromises the integrity of a feminist moral.

Older oppressive identity politics are not revised; they are repackaged and represented with a modern register. The capitalist forces that *Maleficent* depicts as having been vanquished extend beyond the film's conclusion; therefore, the "happily ever after" frustrates synthesis with audiences' contemporary social circumstances. This disjuncture between medieval fantasy and postmodern reality suggests that feminist forces within the narrative have been coopted to serve the very patriarchal forces that maintain subjugation within both the fantasy of the film and within the very real experiences of the audience. *Patriarchal equilibrium* describes the adaptability of forces of oppression in response to social changes for the purpose of maintaining the status quo. As activists successfully promote change, strategies of oppression evolve in response to preserve the social hierarchy.[12] Patriarchal equilibrium is most commonly exhibited as cooption: ideas and actions that are promoted by activist groups are appropriated to serve the very structure that such groups rally against.

While this retelling of *Sleeping Beauty* from the antagonist's point of view claims to tell an old tale anew, Maleficent is violently made to inhabit the dichotomous roles that are generally imposed upon women by patriarchal forces. Misogyny typically limits women to one of two roles: either the virgin saint or the monstrous whore. According to this binary, which is reified by popular entertainment and patriarchal forces of oppression, a woman is either an analogue of Mother Mary, or the fallen Eve.[13] Considering the evolution of Maleficent's character, from the villain of *Sleeping Beauty* to

---

[12] Judith M. Bennett, *History Matters: Patriarchy and the Challenge of Feminism* (Philadelphia: University of Pennsylvania Press, 2006), 4.

[13] For the ways in which Old English poets explain these secular binary categories of woman

the vengeful fairy of *Maleficent*, her persona is shaped by this patriarchal dichotomy: as long as she threatens the social hierarchy of the kingdom by cursing the king's heir she is evil personified, but over the course of the film her malicious vigilance over Aurora is turned to maternal affection. In trailers advertising the film, Maleficent was portrayed as a monster.[14] Audiences were enticed by the spectacle of Disney's dark side, not an enlightened portrait of a vilified woman. Taglines in trailers and movie posters read, "Evil has a beginning," suggesting that Maleficent is like Eve: the cause of all our woe, for it was she who introduced evil into the Disney canon, just as Eve is often ridiculed for having been the first to taste of forbidden fruits. Associations of Maleficent with the fallen Eve gain little traction in the film itself. Instead, audiences encounter Maleficent as a feminine creature whose interactions with patriarchal forces coerce her into the role of a virgin mother. Her character is reconceived in the image of Mother Mary. Over the course of the film, Maleficent is not recuperated to a self-determined woman; rather, she only finds happiness within the social order when she realizes her role as godmother to Aurora. The visual register of the film hints at Stefan's rape of Maleficent without admitting of any overt sexual acts; and so, by means of allusion, the film maintains Maleficent's virginity. By accepting her role as godmother within the normative identity categories of the patriarch, Maleficent's happiness hinges on her resolve to virgin and mother; thus she conforms to the subject position maintained by misogynistic ideals – even when these ideals conflict with the cultural memory of *Sleeping Beauty*.

The monster–whore dichotomy that informs Maleficent's characterization may have also influenced decisions to cast Angelina Jolie in the lead role. In the early days of her acting career, Jolie was eroticized by tabloids, focusing on a bizarre display of affection with her brother, in addition to her sexual practices. Media has manipulated her image to conform to the deviant whore persona. Now, with the ample media attention given to her family life, her political views, and her charity work, Jolie is portrayed as a maternal figure. Considering that Maleficent is depicted as both a monstrous whore and a virgin maternal figure, it would seem that Jolie's media persona had considerable influence on casting decisions. This also suggests that the monster–whore dichotomy has significant consequences beyond the fictions of the silver screen.

Furthermore, Maleficent is coopted by the ensemble of oppressive forces when she imposes her own monarchical regime onto the moors. Preceding

by using Germanic and Christian concepts, see Jane Chance, *Woman as Hero in Old English Literature* (New York: Syracuse University Press, 1986).

14   For an in-depth discussion of the monstrous feminine in popular culture, see Barbara Creed, *The Monstrous Feminine: Film, Feminism, Psychoanalysis* (New York: Routledge, 1993), 3–7.

Stefan's betrayal, the moors operated as a place of mutual respect, in which all members contributed equally to the harmony of the environment. After being stripped of her wings, Maleficent shifts from the guardian who lives contentedly in a tree to the ruler who governs from a centralized throne. For the purpose of defeating the patriarch, she adopts the patriarch's apparatus of oppression, effectively becoming the enemy. She exercises her power over nature in a similar fashion to the very patriarch whom she opposes. Illustrating this, Maleficent exercises her powers a number of times over the bodies of beings who she seems to regard as inferior to herself. Diaval, a crow transformed into a man by Maleficent to save his life from hunters, is obliged to serve her. Normally he does her bidding without hesitation, but during one scene he begs her not to change him into a wolf for the purpose of terrifying and tormenting humans. His pleas fall on deaf ears; Maleficent disregards his feelings, and she exercises her might against the body of an animal who originates outside of the human realm, and whom she has transformed into a man, to fulfill her whim. Similarly, when Maleficent encounters Prince Phillip, she incapacitates him to fulfill her quest and deliver him to Aurora to break the spell. Previously, Maleficent had levitated Aurora supinely into the air with her composure connoting sleep, but when she performs the same spell on Phillip, she lifts him into the air by his hindquarters, resulting in a comically absurd pose. Phillip, a man whose title as prince firmly locates him within the patriarchal social hierarchy, is treated differently than Aurora. Under Maleficent's control, his buttocks are elevated over his head, and he is forced into a bodily orientation of masculine submission. Maleficent's control over masculine bodies, whether they are associated with the natural realm or the kingdom of humans, is deliberately demeaning. The opposition that Maleficent enacts against the human kingdom merely renders her an extension of patriarchal powers.

In spite of the sympathy that the narrative garners for Maleficent – who is portrayed as a wounded and vengeful woman requiring compassion and love, rather than an evil monster who ought to be vanquished – the film falls short of promoting a truly feminist system of ethics. Representations of women have been altered, but to the extent that women perform and maintain patriarchal forces of oppression. The gender of the agents of oppression is reversed, but the power structure remains the same. Superficially, women appear to be empowered by the end of the film: Maleficent overcomes her oppressor and restores her physical integrity, and Aurora assumes leadership of the natural and human realms. But Maleficent's emotional integrity was traumatically ruined in the process, and Aurora merely enacts the directives of her forefathers: to dominate the natural realm. Just because women now perform the dominant roles once maintained by men does not mean that *Maleficent* has overturned the patriarchy that governs fairy tale traditions. The updated *Sleeping Beauty* narrative of *Maleficent* dons a feminist ideology that aims at equality with traces of inclusiveness, as if to amend the misogynistic cartoon predecessor. Identifying both texts, *Sleeping Beauty* and *Maleficent*, as representative of the Disney tradition extends the realm of the Disney kingdom, attempting to encompass not only every time and place but also every ideology. As a result, the Disney canon polyvalently supports numerous conflicting political agendas.[15]

Audiences have access to greater resources and perspectives to inform their understandings and interactions with various texts and ideologies. Simply reversing the power dynamic associated with traditional gender roles, therefore, is not sufficient to promote a feminist system of ethics. The conclusion of *Maleficent*, for all of its consciousness of the Disney heritage and audiences' cultural memory, straddles a misogynistic tradition and contemporary audiences' familiarity with progressive identity categories. The film polyvalently appeals to not only conventional sex–gender roles but also the potential for a feminist interpretation; and it is this compromise that complicates the morality of the fairy tale.

Revising a misogynistic text like *Sleeping Beauty* requires an explicitly feminist narrative. By merely suggesting a feminist hermeneutic, *Maleficent* succumbs to patriarchal equilibrium by depicting an empowered woman whose actions reify the patriarchal order. Betsy Hearne argues that, for all of the criticism leveled at Disney, Disney productions are successful because they accurately reflect the social conditions from which they are issued. According to Hearne, these cartoons are not meant to animate an earlier text with any authenticity, nor are they supposed to posit revolutionary ideologies; instead, Disney productions merely reflect contemporary social values.[16] Given the scope of Disney's cultural influence, I sympathize with the compulsion to defend the Disney heritage. Critically, however, Walt Disney had a distinct vision: he wanted to influence the world to conform to his values. For example, Epcot at Disney World was constructed as an ideal that would inform later models of the American city.[17] Early criticism of Walt Disney claimed that he evacuated fairy tales of their original cultural content. For all of his innovations, Walt "employed animators and technology to stop thinking about change, to return to his films, and to long nostalgically for neatly ordered patriarchal realms."[18] In the early Disney Animated Classics,

---

15 Disney represents an amalgamation of temporalities and cultures without social conflict. See Henry Giroux and Grace Pollock, *The Mouse that Roared: Disney and the End of Innocence* (Lanham, MD: Rowman & Littlefield, 1999), 148.
16 Betsy Hearne, "Disney Revisited, Or, Jiminy Cricket, It's Musty Down Here!," *The Horn Book Magazine* 73.2 (1997): 137–46.
17 J. I. Baker, *LIFE: Walt Disney: From Mickey to the Magic Kingdom* 16.7 (New York: Time Inc., 15 April 2016): 79.
18 Jack Zipes, "Breaking the Disney Spell," in *From Mouse to Mermaid: The Politics of Film,*

the princesses were white, beautiful, noble songstresses. While *Snow White and the Seven Dwarfs* (1937), *Cinderella* (1950), and *The Little Mermaid* (1989) focus on women, they are often passive and they require the actions of men or wicked characters, who subvert sex–gender ideals, to advance the narrative. Furthermore, according to Nicholas Sammond, Walt Disney composed himself as a paternal figure for the very purpose of marketing his corporation as a parental substitute.[19] It is the essence of patriarchy that the father imposes order as he deems fit. In fact, a preliminary study, the results of which were released in June 2016, studied the effects of Disney's princess culture on 198 five- and six-year-olds, to find that increased engagement with princess culture resulted in increased female gender-stereotypical behavior performed by girls and boys alike. Additionally, the study concludes that media is influential in motivating these gender-stereotypical behaviors.[20] From its very foundations, Disney exerts, and intends to exert, power to impose ideologies. The narratives produced by Disney convey these ideologies, and these ideologies continue to influence cultural memory and social practices across generations of media consumers.

Now, Disney is a company that empowers numerous artists, working in diverse media, to express the core values of the Disney brand. Among these values, Disney touts a policy of inclusion, explaining that "our characters appeal to children across gender, ability, and experience because they're defined by kindness, loyalty, humor, courage, wit and other traits that make a good friend."[21] Recent additions to the Disney canon appear to respond to, or at least avoid criticism for having previously failed to model inclusiveness. In 2007, *Enchanted* delivered a princess who stepped out of the cartoon fantasy and into the realities of present-day New York to fight her dragon for herself. Still, in spite of the film's feminist potential, it continues to limit women's roles to shoppers and caregivers in a capitalist society.[22]

Gender, and Culture, ed. Elisabeth Bell, Lynda Haas, and Laura Sells (Bloomington: Indiana University Press, 1995), 40.

19   Nicholas Sammond, *Babes in Tomorrowland: Walt Disney and the Making of the American Child, 1930–1960* (Durham, NC: Duke University Press, 2005), 3.

20   Sarah M. Coyne, Jennifer Ruh Linder, Eric E. Rasmussen, David A. Nelson, and Victoria Birkbeck, "Pretty as a Princess: Longitudinal Effects of Engagement with Disney Princesses on Gender Stereotypes, Body Esteem, and Prosocial Behavior in Children," *Child Development* (18 June 2016) <http://onlinelibrary.wiley.com.ezproxy.lib.usf.edu/doi/10.1111/cdev.12569/abstract;jsessionid=35099661B01687F67014BD4A8E7E39EC.f02t03>, last accessed 27 June 2016.

21   "Policy and Approaches: Our Stories and Characters," *The Walt Disney Company*, <https://thewaltdisneycompany.com/citizenship/policies/our-stories-and-characters>, last accessed 5 September 2015.

22   Maria Sachiko Cecire, "Reality Remixed: Neomedieval Princess Culture in Disney's *Enchanted*," in *The Disney Middle Ages: A Fairy-Tale and a Fantasy Past*, ed. Tison Pugh and Susan Aronstein (New York: Palgrave Macmillan, 2012), 254.

Next, in 2009, *The Princess and the Frog* introduced Tiana, a black woman, into the ranks of Disney princesses. This cartoon also proved to be problematic because Tiana spent the majority of her screen time in the green skin of an amphibian.[23] Currently, Disney continues developing alternative perspectives from the Disney animated classics: *Alice in Wonderland* (2010), *Once Upon a Time* (2011–present), and *Maleficent* revisit the fairy tales from the inception of the Disney heritage, challenging the older versions with narratives that invite feminist readings. Adding to the princess collection, Disney has released *Brave* (2012), a film that empowers Princess Merida to claim her independence while mending her frustrated relationship with her mother. This was quickly followed by *Frozen* (2013), which repeatedly undermines the traditional Disney princess narrative, replacing the salvific kiss of a chivalrous man with the true love that is fostered between sisters. This brave new moral, however, is undermined by the unnatural representation of women's bodies.[24]

Most recently, *Zootopia* (2016) takes up themes of cultural diversity and prejudice, and some have connected the movie to issues that concern Black Lives Matter. *Zootopia* is not a princess fairy tale, but it is worth mentioning because the narrative follows the development of a young woman, Judy Hopps, who moves to the city to become the first bunny police officer. Hopps is a strong female lead who calls out the assumptions made by her peers because of her small stature and gender, while negotiating her own biases against predatory mammals. Relying on the structure of the animal fable, *Zootopia* cleverly traverses controversies surrounding racial profiling and economic disparity that limit the opportunities of marginalized people, which Disney cleverly presents in terms of the animal identity categories: predatory mammals versus prey mammals. If indeed *Zootopia* is a product of contemporary social justice issues related to Black Lives Matter, however, it is problematic that only a few people of color provide voices for the film.

Still, Disney continues to exert considerable influence on popular culture. In 2008, marketing analysts estimated that consumers spend roughly 13 billion hours per year in contact with Disney media.[25] These numbers have

23 Sophia A. Nelson observes a number of problematic issues of representation that intersect with race, class, and gender in *The Princess and the Frog*, in "Disney's First Black Fairy Tale: More Frog than Princess," in *The Huffington Post*, 25 May 2011, < http://www.huffingtonpost.com/sophia-a-nelson/disneys-first-black-fairy_b_406226.html>, last accessed 4 May 2016.

24 Philip Cohen, "'Help, My Eyeball is Bigger than My Wrist!' Gender Dimorphism in *Frozen*," in *The Society Pages*, 17 December 2013, <http://thesocietypages.org/socimages/2013/12/17/help-my-eyeball-is-bigger-than-my-wrist-gender-dimorphism-in-frozen/>, last accessed 23 June 2015.

25 Michael Santoli, "The Magic's Back: Disney's Bright Future," in *Barron's*, 26 February 2008, <http://www.barrons.com/articles/SB120372700801387237>, last accessed 2 June 2016.

increased tremendously now that Disney has acquired Pixar, Marvel Entertainment, ESPN, ABC, and Lucasfilm. Now that Disney controls a significant portion of the market, Disney also controls a significant amount of representations that media consumers encounter on a daily basis. Considering the immensity of Disney's power within a capitalist society, Henry A. Giroux and Grace Pollock argue that:

> [c]orporate culture uses its power as an educational force to redefine the relationships between childhood and innocence, citizenship and consumption, civic values and commercial values [...] in a society in which power is increasingly held by megacorporations, [there exist few safeguards against] market logic that provides neither a context for moral consideration, nor a language for defending vital social institutions and policies as a public good.[26]

In a capitalist society, Disney's control over the market bears a direct correlation to Disney's control over culture. The company maintains the paternalistic image cultivated by its founder; it upholds its authority as a source for revered historical folklore and the kernels of our cultural memory; and it panders to contemporary social movements without explicitly empowering revolutionary social reform. By increasing dominion of the Disney kingdom, polyvalently appealing to various interpretive strategies, and authorizing its own brand as the definitive source for cultural narratives, Disney teaches audiences to return to Disney. Ultimately, Disney is manufacturing consumers.

Rather than mending the misogyny of *Sleeping Beauty*, *Maleficent* coopts feminism and reorients the audience to the medieval period, remapping the power dynamics of *Sleeping Beauty* on to the capitalist relationship between Disney and consumers. Consequently, the patriarch must win. Capitalism conquers. It is, after all, the misogynistic version of *Sleeping Beauty* that informs the greater cultural memory. If we locate the events of *Maleficent* within a sequential historical narrative of cause and effect, then regardless of the "happily ever after" that depicts women assuming power, the present audience is unable to reconcile a feminist moral to their contemporary cultural memory. It could only mean, if we accept the fantasy of the film, that eventually the patriarchy resumed power; or worse, Maleficent and Aurora are only empowered to the extent that they maintain the patriarchal, capitalist hierarchy.

At the intersection of scholarship and activism, it is important to not only criticize a text that fails to meet feminist ideals, or blatantly violates them, but also to think about what an authentically feminist narrative

---

26 Giroux and Pollock, *The Mouse that Roared*, 20.

would look like. The roles of critics are vital for realizing feminist ideals so that we can imagine, and even practice, freedom. We need to think critically about whether it is even possible to create a narrative that is free from patriarchal conventions, and that is also accessible to audiences living amid these forces of oppression. Otherwise, we run the risk of maintaining the Möbius strip that defends Disney productions as mirrors of society, rather than agents complicit in capitalism, and conscious of the pacifying effects of polyvalently pandering.

I am confident that a feminist narrative is not only possible in postmodern media and recognizable to postmodern audiences, but also that such a narrative has the potential to resolve conflict with a satisfying "happily ever after" that promotes critical engagement with contemporary audiences. A feminist conclusion would have returned Maleficent to the natural realm of the moors, where she and the other mythical creatures could continue their autonomous, symbiotic relationships. It is not necessary to bend the natural realm to Aurora's rule; nor is it necessary for Maleficent to conform to a maternal role. The conclusion would have been more satisfying if the moors were respected and maintained, apart from the human kingdom. A feminist narrative would have permitted Maleficent to cultivate a relationship with Aurora without having to assume a maternal role to squelch her feelings of rage, nor would Aurora require a maternal figure to fill the absence left by the death of her birth mother. Women's relationships do not need to fit coherently into hegemonic identity categories in order to be recognizable and valid. Allowing these two women to share affection without signifiers of a hierarchical mother–daughter relationship would accurately portray and promote the complexities of women's intersections. Moreover, the complexity of a feminist "happily ever after," which resists subjugating deviant characters like Maleficent to traditional roles within a capitalist system, might also inspire critical reflection upon our own contemporary social politics among audiences.

Retellings of familiar fairy tales, like *Maleficent*, suggest revisions that progress social justice, but *Maleficent* is not a radically feminist text, for it maintains the problematic sex–gender identity categories and representations that govern its misogynistic predecessor. Locating Disney films chronologically along a continuum, beginning with the early misogynistic cartoons like *Sleeping Beauty* and *Cinderella*, and then looking forward to the progressive morals of *Zootopia* and the liberal representations of nonconforming individuals in *Finding Dory*, *Maleficent* signifies transition for the Disney Company. With *Maleficent*, Disney artists reflect on their own heritage, and they compose a retelling that challenges the very foundations of their production company. *Maleficent* does not promote a sound feminist ethic, but it signifies a key moment in Disney's productions, in which turning backwards toward Disney's medievalisms as a point of origin is necessary to revise the past and to advance a new ideology of inclusion. Medievalism is the means by which *Maleficent* critiques contemporary social practices, and the means by which Disney artists critically engage with the ideological foundations of their production company. The fantasy of the Middle Ages, a time of historical ambiguity in the postmodern cultural memory, provides a creative space in which identities and ideologies are composed, criticized, and reconstituted, so that in turning toward the Middle Ages artists and audiences identify origin narratives that cultivate social change in the present.

Future Medieval:
(Neo)Medievalism in *Babylon 5*
and *Crusade*

Ann F. Howey

Early in "The Long Road," the second episode to be aired of J. Michael Straczynski's short-lived television series *Crusade* (1999), a character refers to the way of life of the inhabitants of a planet as "practically medieval."[1] It is a small comment, possibly used merely to indicate an ancient as opposed to contemporary way of life or level of technology; furthermore, since the series is set in 2267 CE, the human colony is an example, not of the medieval period, but of medievalism. Despite its brevity, this comment draws attention to medievalism (and neomedievalism) within this science-fiction series and its parent – *Babylon 5* – and to the debate that "The Long Road" specifically enacts regarding what form of (neo)medievalism is productive.[2] The moments of (neo)medievalism in *Babylon 5* and *Crusade* exemplify categories at debate in scholarly journals such as *Studies in Medievalism* and demonstrate the usefulness to popular culture of the medieval as a contrast to the present. *Babylon 5* and "The Long Road" tend to use such contrasts to question the opposition of past and present in order to suggest continuity and similarity, sometimes to celebrate perceived medieval ideals of justice and sometimes to comment on violence, past and present. However, resolving the past–present dichotomy, particularly in "The Long Road," perpetuates

---

[1]   "The Long Road," dir. Mike Vejar, writ. J. Michael Straczynski, *Crusade*, 16 June 1999. Babylonian Productions / Warner Bros. Television, 2004. Further references will be in text.
[2]   As the next paragraph demonstrates, there are distinctions between medievalism and neomedievalism, and as I will show, *Crusade* and *Babylon 5* contain examples of both categories; I will use "(neo)medievalism" to talk collectively about all forms of medievalism and neomedievalism.

a patriarchal vision, raising questions about the inherent gender politics of (neo)medievalism.

As four volumes (namely, numbers 17 to 20) of *Studies in Medievalism* explicitly attest, defining "medievalism" and "neomedievalism" has been a matter of scholarly discussion. The history of the terms and their use over time – from Leslie Workman or Umberto Eco to the contributors to the volumes of *Studies in Medievalism* just mentioned – suggest more than just that scholars have different opinions. Although all the scholars are concerned in some way with commenting on the "post-medieval attempt to *re-imagine* the Middle Ages, or some aspect of the Middle Ages,"[3] the sheer variety of post-medieval engagements with the medieval make multiple definitions possible, depending on which factors – media, purpose, audience, among others – are emphasized in creating a definition. Nevertheless, one of the key factors defining what I see as the continuum of medievalism to neomedievalism is the approach taken to medieval materials. As M. J. Toswell argues, "medievalism implies a genuine link – sometimes direct, sometimes somewhat indirect – to the Middle Ages,"[4] that is, to the period in Western European history spanning from 500 to 1500 CE. Carol L. Robinson and Pamela Clements associate neomedievalism, on the other hand, with "the postmodern techniques of fragmentation: anachronism, pastiche, bricolage";[5] the inaccuracies of neomedievalism are deliberate, "an act of taking care to consciously impose contemporary ideology and comprehension" on to the medieval tropes.[6] Replicating the past or playing with the past – and the innumerable combinations between these poles – suggest the scope of (neo)medievalism(s).

Regardless of its innumerable variations, (neo)medievalism offers popular culture a way of holding past and present in dialogue, and *Babylon 5* and *Crusade* use their moments of (neo)medievalism for just this purpose. The two series are set in the future, and the relationship of past and future is a subtle (and sometimes not so subtle) thematic thread throughout both. *Babylon 5* in particular emphasizes its temporal setting, as the voice-over for the title sequence of each episode contains the information, "The year is [...]."[7] The repetition of this information episode after episode reinforces the

---

3   Tom Shippey, "Medievalisms and Why They Matter," in *Studies in Medievalism XVII: Defining Medievalism(s)*, ed. Karl Fugelso (Cambridge: D. S. Brewer, 2009), 45–54 (45), emphasis in original.

4   M. J. Toswell, "The Simulacrum of Neomedievalism," in *Studies in Medievalism XIX: Defining Neomedievalism(s)*, ed. Karl Fugelso (Cambridge: D. S. Brewer, 2010), 44–57 (44).

5   Carol L. Robinson and Pamela Clements, "Living with Neomedievalism," in *Studies in Medievalism XVIII: Defining Medievalism(s) II*, ed. Karl Fugelso (Cambridge: D. S. Brewer, 2009), 55–75 (64).

6   Robinson and Clements, "Living," 62 n. 5.

7   The title sequences vary from season to season, but always end with a statement of the year and the place. My discussion of the title sequence uses as an example the one from

distance of the story from the viewers' present: these are events of humanity's imagined future. At the same time, earlier parts of the title sequence
use the past tense, as in these opening words: "It was the dawn of the third
age of mankind […]" ("Grail" title sequence). From the first season, then,
the voice-over frames the series as a historical record of the future. Because
"This is the story of the *last* of the Babylon stations" ("Grail" title sequence,
emphasis added), the narrative voice positions audiences to view the imagined future as history: the only way to know it is the last station is to speak
from a time beyond that of the station itself. "The Deconstruction of Falling
Stars," the final episode of season four, extends this conceit; different future
centuries provide recorded segments that the audience, along with a far-
future human, watches.[8] *Crusade* structures its title sequence differently, so
there is no invocation of historical record; however, its use of questions and
answers evokes the Arthurian legend. The openings of both series thus play
with our often neat, orderly divisions of time, bringing past into imagined
future and situating future as past.

Instances of (neo)medievalism within the narratives of individual episodes
of *Babylon 5* and *Crusade* do similar work, bringing past, present, and future
together. Significantly, (neo)medievalism in the two series is not simply a
matter of using medieval-inspired costume and dress to represent alien
species and cultures, although that does happen. (Neo)medievalism is shown
as a human impulse, a continual negotiation of the past in relation to the
present that happens at the meta-level (the creators of the show employing
it in the late twentieth century) and within the narrative itself (characters in
the show employing it in the imagined twenty-third century). (Neo)medie-
valism, then, connects viewers' present with the narrated future as a recurring
human activity. The consequences to gender representation in both series
when (neo)medievalism is most explicit, however, suggest the problems of
the recurring past.

"The name of the place is Babylon 5*"*: *Futuristic Medieval Moments*

The series *Babylon 5* takes place on a space station, designed to act as a
military, diplomatic, and commercial meeting place for humans and alien
races (such as the mysterious, ancient Vorlons, the technologically advanced

---

"Grail," dir. Richard Compton, writ. Christy Marx, *Babylon 5*, 6 July 1994. *Babylon 5:
Grail / Eyes*, Columbia House, 1997. Further references will be in text.

8   "The Deconstruction of Falling Stars," dir. Stephen Furst, writ. J. Michael Straczynski,
Babylon 5, 27 October 1997. *Babylon 5: The Complete Fourth Season*, Babylonian Productions / Warner Bros. Television, 2004. Further references will be in text.

9   "Grail" title sequence. See note 7.

Minbari, the violent yet philosophical Narns, and many others). The five-year story arc includes different alliances, most notably against the Shadows, a sinister, older race that foments conflict among different groups. The series' imagined future includes space-travel technology, improved medical and communications devices, and human colonies on various planets and moons. Despite its science-fiction premise and visual elements, the show also includes moments of medievalism, such as its Arthurian allusions; Arthurian material creates major plot threads in two episodes – "Grail" from season one and "A Late Delivery from Avalon"[10] from season three – although as Kristina Hildebrand notes, "Arthurian references abound even outside the explicitly Arthurian episodes."[11] In addition, a group of elite warriors and spies designed to fight the Shadows and keep the interstellar peace provide visual and narrative elements of medievalism. These Rangers wear cloaks and fight with a technologically enhanced version of a quarterstaff, so their costuming and weaponry are reminiscent of medieval characters such as Robin Hood.[12]

The medieval past that such allusions and characters evoke contrasts to the futuristic world that makes up the main characters' quotidian reality. Visually, the seeker of the Grail (Aldous, played by David Warner) in "Grail," or the man calling himself King Arthur (played by Michael York) in "A Late Delivery from Avalon," or any of the human Rangers stand out among the Earthforce personnel of the space station. In one scene of "A Late Delivery from Avalon," King Arthur and the Ranger, Marcus (Jason Carter), face each other wearing flowing cloaks; they are surrounded by security personnel and Dr. Franklin (Richard Biggs) who wear square-cut military uniforms. In addition to the visual contrast this scene creates, the actors' accents also provide contrast; as Arthur points out, Marcus speaks like "a Briton," as does Arthur himself, whereas the others do not.[13] Hildebrand argues that

---

10   "A Late Delivery from Avalon," dir. Mike Vejar, writ. J. Michael Straczynski, *Babylon 5*, 22 April 1996. *Babylon 5: The Complete Third Season*, Babylonian Productions / Warner Bros. Television, 2004. Further references will be in text.

11   Kristina Hildebrand, "Knights in Space: The Arthur of *Babylon 5* and *Dr. Who*," in *King Arthur in Popular Culture*, ed. Elizabeth S. Sklar and Donald L. Hoffman (Jefferson, NC: McFarland & Company, 2002), 101–10 (102).

12   Note that the quarterstaff-like weapon is of Minbari origin, making it an example of the series' use of medieval-themed objects to characterize an alien species. The Rangers are introduced in the second-season episode, "The Coming of Shadows," but they become more prominent from the third season onward, with the arrival of Marcus (Jason Carter) on the space station and as a series regular in seasons three and four. "The Coming of Shadows," dir. Janet Greek, writ. J. Michael Straczynski, *Babylon 5*, 1 February 1995. *Babylon 5: The Complete Second Season*, Babylonian Productions / Warner Bros. Television, 2003.

13   In the world created by Straczynski, national divisions remain to a certain extent, but Earth is united under a global president and Earthforce draws from all regions of the planet in staffing its military / exploration forces. Use of "Briton" thus suggests Arthur's location in the past.

"contrasts introduce a feeling of incongruity";[14] in the context of a returning Arthur, such incongruity "serves to remind viewers that the return of Arthur is unlikely. The return of Arthur from the dead would contradict the laws of nature, which *Babylon 5* normally avoids violating; that Arthur looks like a medieval king further emphasizes that he is out of place."[15] The medieval draws attention because it does not belong, and that allows the series to hold up the act of medievalizing for commentary.

Babylon 5 rationalizes its Arthurian and medieval matter, at least to some extent, because of this commentary; medievalism must be explained and justified. Aldous is aware of his anachronistic and impossible quest, and his clothing seems deliberately chosen (by the character, as well as by the episode's creative team) to represent his rejection of the typical twenty-third-century lifestyle in order to embrace medieval values of the spiritual quest ("Grail"). "Arthur" is a persona created by ex-Gunnery Sergeant David McIntyre to cope with his guilt over the start of the Earth–Minbari war ten years previously; apparently unaware of his real identity, he retreats to the medieval to realize a vision of a just and good society ("A Late Delivery"). The Rangers' clothing and fighting style distinguish them, deliberately, from the species-specific military units, so they can be a force for interplanetary peace. Replicating past quests, past kings, or past clothing styles is presented by the series as an attempt to create distance from the assumptions of one's own time in order to pursue more fully ideals of compassion, truth, and justice. Being "out of place," or more accurately, outside of time, seems to be necessary to deal with the problems of the series' present. In a scene right after the title sequence of "A Late Delivery from Avalon," Marcus guides Dr. Franklin "Down Below" to rescue the station's homeless population (called lurkers) from a potentially deadly flu. As the doctor notes, few people would bother trying to save the lurkers; the episode thus associates the visually medieval Ranger with justice and compassion for all regardless of status. In the scene immediately following, Marcus, this representative of medievalist charity, encounters King Arthur. The medieval past may, as Hildebrand claims, be rejected "as a route to salvation" in *Babylon 5*, but the association of the medieval with spiritual quests and justice, and King Arthur's association with "compassion and responsibility" are shown to be useful for characters seeking to facilitate self-actualization and communal action.[16] The medieval is necessary, if only as inspiration.

At the same time, that role of the medieval as inspiration means that *Babylon 5* suggests continuity between past and present, particularly in "A Late Delivery from Avalon" and in the equation created between the Rangers

14   Hildebrand, "Knights in Space," 108.
15   Hildebrand, "Knights in Space," 108.
16   Hildebrand, "Knights in Space," 109.

and Arthurian knights in "The Deconstruction of Falling Stars." As Hildebrand notes, the rational explanation for "Arthur" in "A Late Delivery" is
counterbalanced by mysteries left unresolved about his character, such as his
possession of a sword and the appearance of the Vorlon ambassador at his
departure: "he may not be Arthur, [but] he is more than McIntyre."[17] As a
result, the medieval analogue does not disappear with McIntyre's healing,
although his delusion of being Arthur ends. Marcus concludes the episode
by remarking on a number of parallels between characters on *Babylon 5*
and Arthurian personalities: Captain John Sheridan (Bruce Boxleitner) is
Arthur; the Minbari ambassador, Delenn (Mira Furlan), is the Lady of the
Lake; Commander Susan Ivanova (Claudia Christian) is Gawain; Marcus
himself is Galahad, and so on. Moreover, he speculates about whether the
Arthurian characters or the twenty-third-century characters are the origi-
nals: Vorlon technology and their habit of visiting planets and traveling in
time might mean that *Babylon 5* inspired the Round Table rather than the
other way around, he suggests, creating a cycle rather than a chronological
progression.[18] The possibility of a cycle is reinforced, along with the Arthurian parallels, in "The Deconstruction of Falling Stars." One segment of that
episode is set a thousand years after *Babylon 5*'s main storyline, when the
"Great Burn" has destroyed Earth's cities and civilization, and in the abbey
that acts as a Ranger base, monks illustrate texts, including stories of *Babylon
5*'s characters. In the series, the medieval past as inspiration for particular
ideas of justice and service is both separate from and continuous with the
present, depending on whether that inspiration is seen as anachronistic or as
a continuous cycle; it is often presented as simultaneously both.

The Arthurian parallels that Marcus proposes, however, raise the issue of
(neo)medievalism and gender. Susan Ivanova's Arthurian avatar is Gawain,
a cross-gender identification unique in Marcus's list. Ivanova is second-in-
command of the space station and thus an administrator, diplomat, and
warrior. Although medieval Arthurian legend includes female warriors, such
as Spenser's Britomart, that character is not as central to the legend (and
presumably not as well known to modern audiences) as Gawain. Gawain's
record of service, close ties to Arthur, and, in some texts, sacrifices for Arthur
make him a better parallel for Ivanova.[19] Delenn's Arthurian avatar – the Lady

---

[17] Hildebrand, "Knights in Space," 107.
[18] In the most explicit example of time travel in the series, Jeffrey Sinclair (Michael O'Hare),
      former commander of the station, goes back in time to become the Minbari prophet
      Valen. See "War Without End Part Two," dir. Mike Vejar, writ. J. Michael Straczynski,
      Babylon 5, 20 May 1996. *Babylon 5: The Complete Third Season*, Babylonian Productions
      / Warner Bros. Television, 2004.
[19] I am thinking of texts where Gawain volunteers for a dangerous encounter in order to
      prevent that danger from reaching his king, as in *Sir Gawain and the Green Knight*. Ivano-

of the Lake – results from events unique to "A Late Delivery"; Delenn might also, as Sheridan's love interest and wife in later seasons, be seen as Guinevere. Neither of these Arthurian characters, however, adequately account for her roles: she is mystic, priest, lover, politician, and war-leader in *Babylon 5*. It is not that the male characters match their Arthurian avatars exactly, but the parallels are closer; there are more similarities between roles for men in Arthurian romance and roles for men in this television series, whereas female roles in medieval romance provide inadequate scripts for these twenty-third-century female characters. (Neo)medievalism in *Babylon 5*, therefore, tends to focus on relationships between male characters: Aldous inspires a young man to become a seeker in "Grail"; Arthur interacts primarily with Marcus, the Narn ambassador G'Kar (Andreas Katsulas), and Dr. Franklin, with Delenn appearing only in the final minutes of "A Late Delivery from Avalon"; in "The Deconstruction of Falling Stars," the Rangers are "brothers," monk-like guardians of history and scripture. "Medieval" in this series is used to contrast past and present and to represent particular ideas of justice, but in the process it is coded masculine; *Crusade*'s "The Long Road" makes even more apparent both the usefulness, to popular culture texts, of the idea of the "medieval" and the potential problems of its gender politics.

"Sounds quite charming": Crusade*, the Medieval, and the Arthurian Alternative*

The contrast and similarity of past and present are more explicit in "The Long Road" of *Babylon 5*'s spin-off *Crusade*, a series that aired for only thirteen episodes. *Crusade*'s premise is that Captain Matthew Gideon (Gary Cole) and the crew of the starship *Excalibur* are tasked with exploring known space for a cure to a plague with which aliens have infected Earth; the aliens are the Drahk, allies of the Shadows who acted as the enemy in seasons two through four of *Babylon 5*. A made-for-television film, *A Call to Arms*,[20] sets up *Crusade*'s storyline by showing the attempt of Sheridan (now President of the Interstellar Alliance) to stop the Drahk from attacking Earth. He does destroy the aliens' worst weapon, but the fleeing Drahk release a virus into Earth's atmosphere, and the quest for a cure for this virus takes the *Excalibur* and its crew to different locations in each episode of *Crusade*. In "The Long Road," they are called to Regula 4, a planet that ninety years previously was settled by humans who wanted to return to an agrarian life.

---

va's service to her captain at times includes physical combat, but also instances where she takes on administrative or diplomatic duties to help or protect him.

[20] *A Call to Arms*, dir. Mike Vejar, writ. J. Michael Straczynski, 1999. *Babylon 5: The Movie Collection*, TNT / Warner Bros. Television, 2004.

The planet produces a natural anti-viral mineral, and the Earthforce ship *Medusa* has been assigned to strip-mine the planet to procure the mineral quickly, in hopes that it will help Earth; it is the *Medusa*'s first officer, Lieutenant Meyers (Scott Paetty), who refers to the settlers as "medieval." The *Excalibur*'s assistance is requested when tensions escalate between the settlers and those responsible for the mining.

If that farmer-versus-miner conflict sounds more Old West than medieval, the costumes and sets also look inspired by westerns. The broad-brimmed hat that Gideon wears when he visits the village closest to the mine evokes the western, as does his explanation that he has brought cattle to market. He and the techno-mage Galen (Peter Woodward) stop at an inn, but the long bar and small round tables of its interior would be equally at home on location in a saloon. In the American context of the show's production, much of its casting, and its initial broadcast, referring to the colony as "like something out of the Old West" would have been perfectly intelligible, yet the word "medieval" is used instead; moreover, although there are other races less technologically advanced that are encountered in the course of the series and other human groups who seek to escape the technologically driven Earth norm, none of these groups are referred to as medieval.[21] How, then, does the word "medieval" function in this episode?

The descriptor "medieval" establishes an absolute opposition between settlers and starship crew (both miners and military personnel) regarding technology; "medieval" as Meyers uses it connotes alterity, the "primitive" Other to the technologically advanced "norm." Meyers's intent, given the actor's tone of voice and facial expression as the line is delivered, is to distance himself and his companions as far as possible from the attitudes of those he is describing.[22] Whereas Old West settings often include symbols of industrialization and technological progress such as railways and trains, and thus gesture toward the possibilities of twentieth-century capitalism's fast-paced travel, communications, and commerce, "medieval" connotes a level of technology removed from such ideas of progress. Medieval society

---

[21]   The sixth episode shows Max Eilerson (David Allen Brooks) in his quarters reading Chaucer's *The Canterbury Tales*, but that is the only other explicitly medieval reference I have found in the series. That same episode includes ex-soldiers who want to stay on Theta 49 to escape modern Earth ideas of progress, but they are not referred to as "medieval," perhaps because an Earthforce program that experimented on them has left them with cybernetic enhancements. "Patterns of the Soul," dir. Tony Dow, writ. Fiona Avery, *Crusade*, 7 July 1999. Babylonian Productions / Warner Bros. Television, 2004.

[22]   The distance might also be geographical. The Old West is American, while "medieval" is more likely to be perceived as Western European, if not exclusively British. That Galen and Alwyn (Edward Woodward), who defend the settlers' way of life, are played by British actors might encourage this geographical interpretation, but the accents of the other settlers do not maintain the division.

tends to be seen as more rural, connected to land and nature rather than
technology, and to be, as a result, slower-paced. The lieutenant's description of the settlers refers to their use of "wood stoves" and "hand tools";
the latter evokes what Toswell has identified as one of the tropes of medievalism: namely, handmade artifacts.[23] The settlers are an "agrarian society,"
and thus to Meyers, "practically medieval" ("The Long Road"). As Meyers
delivers his speech about the settlers, he guides Gideon and Galen through
the brightly lit, busy corridors of the *Medusa*; his surroundings vividly
contrast the way of life he describes, and his tone and body language
convey disdain for the medieval. Galen's comment that it "Sounds quite
charming" challenges the lieutenant's use of "medieval" as an insult, by
suggesting other perspectives are possible.

The episode represents the choice of the settlers to reject technology as
a rejection of violence (at least in part). They have no weapons comparable
to those carried by the starship crew. *Medusa*'s Captain Daniels (Marshall
R. Teague) observes that the attempt to impose order will be "a skeet
shoot"; the villagers, without technology, will be simply targets, at the
mercy of advanced weaponry. By recognizing this vulnerability – indeed
it is debated by the settlers themselves – the episode critiques the use of
weapons technology to force compliance: representatives of technology,
such as Captain Daniels and Lieutenant Meyers, are portrayed as hypo-
critical and cowardly. Both speak enthusiastically about military conflict;
neither wants to lead the charge into battle. The Captain's rank allows him
to escape the duty and to send Meyers instead, but their dialogue and the
expression on Meyers's face when he realizes he will have to fight amount
to implicit criticism of modern military technology and its distancing of
those who give orders from the consequences of those orders. The episode
suggests that such distance only begets more violence, as well as exploitation and an unwillingness to see reason.

If the settlers have rejected technology, they are associated instead with
magic, and the use of "medieval" gestures to this association. Magic is first
represented in the episode by the gold dragon with red eyes. In one early
scene, it towers above the mine itself. Reactions of Earthforce personnel
reinforce that the dragon is an anachronism, that it does not belong in a
universe of technology and science. Toswell identifies the dragon as a particularly powerful trope of medievalism, given its associations with "awesome
power and aggression,"[24] and the miners indeed view it in this way; one mine
worker's response to the dragon's appearance is to request that Earthforce
"send troops, ships, anybody with a gun" ("The Long Road"). Meyers, again

---

[23] M. J. Toswell, "The Tropes of Medievalism," in *Studies in Medievalism XVII: Defining
    Medievalism(s)*, ed. Karl Fugelso (2009), 68–76 (70).
[24] Toswell, "Tropes," 70.

representing a modern rather than medieval mindset, refuses to believe in the dragon's corporeality, which leads to the revelation that it is a holograph. Magic, therefore, would seem to be illusion, "smoke and mirrors," as Meyers says. The source of these illusions, Alwyn the techno-mage (played by Edward Woodward), acts as another of Toswell's tropes of medievalism: the warlock. Although the dragon is shown to be hollow, another of Alwyn's spells has more bite, literally, as the holo-demons he conjures batter the lieutenant's forces into submission. Thus, although Alwyn is a techno-mage, producing magical effects with technology, that technology remains unseen and unexplained except in some vague references to programming, and the physicality of the holo-demons in particular seems to be less tech and more mage. Arthur C. Clarke's dictum that "Any sufficiently advanced technology is indistinguishable from magic" applies here,[25] and the villagers never indicate that they know or question the source of Alwyn's effects; they simply accept them.[26]

The episode's conflict thus embodies an opposition – set up to be perceived by characters and thus pointed out to viewers – between the medieval as non-technological, magical, outmoded Other and the technologically advanced, scientifically logical representatives of the show's present (that is the viewers' future). While dialogue and imagery establish this binary, it is also invoked with the word "medieval," suggesting that viewers of the episode are presumed to recognize both the binary and what "medieval" means in that context. Which side of the opposition has (or should have) the most power forms the tension of the episode. Captain Daniels and Lieutenant Meyers do not have to negotiate at the beginning: they have the power of advanced weapons. By the middle of the episode, similarly, the villagers believe, "we don't have to be reasonable," as long as they have Alwyn – the power of magic – on their side. As a result, although the episode creates a binary between technology (future) and magic (medieval), it collapses that binary, first in the supposed technological sources of Alwyn's magic and more importantly in the revelation that whatever the source of power (technology or magic), the attitudes of Daniels, Meyers, and the villagers are identical: use power to force your opponents' complete submission.

If the Earthforce personnel of the *Medusa* and the settlers are two extremes that nonetheless become identical in their relationship to power and willingness to abuse it, the episode endorses a third position, an Arthurian alternative represented by Galen, Gideon, and the *Excalibur*; as with

---

[25]   Arthur C. Clarke, "Hazards of Prophecy: The Failure of Imagination," *Profiles of the Future: An Inquiry into the Limits of the Possible* (New York: Harper & Row, 1973), 12–21 (21).

[26]   Alwyn talks about one of the villagers in a way that suggests, jokingly, her supernatural powers: "The vegetable chowder made by Mrs. Sims just down the road stays blisteringly hot for at least half an hour after it is drawn from the pot. Don't know how she does it. It defies at least two of the laws of thermodynamics, I just can't decide which two" ("The Long Road").

the Arthurian episodes of *Babylon 5* already discussed, "The Long Road" represents this alternative as a blending of past and future, associates it with compassion, truth, and justice, and codes it masculine. As a techno-mage, Galen consciously fuses the supposed opposites of technology and magic, thus questioning attitudes that would see them as separate categories since, inevitably, such categorization privileges one over the other. Of course, Galen is not the only techno-mage; besides Alwyn, other techno-mages are mentioned. Galen, however, seems to be unique, as suggested by the fact that others of his order asked that he leave them. Unlike Alwyn, who has become caught up in the settlers' dream of a simpler, "medieval" life, and unlike the other techno-mages, who have withdrawn to preserve themselves and their knowledge for the future, Galen fuses past and future, just as his vocation fuses magic and technology. His presence on the *Excalibur* values past ties (he once saved Gideon's life) and engages him in specific present actions to create (not merely wait for) the future: Earth saved from the plague.

Captain Gideon's Arthurian avatar can be easily seen as Perceval, given the series of questions that he answers (or does not answer) in the show's title sequence,[27] and given his task of healing the wasteland that Earth is (or will be). In this episode, however, he is an Arthur-figure. He brings his knights to the aid of others, and like the idealized Arthur of Alfred, Lord Tennyson's idyll "Gareth and Lynette," he hears the case and seeks justice.[28] This justice-seeking–compromise approach is not exactly what the previous episode would lead viewers (or his superiors) to expect: when he is assigned his task in "War Zone" he declares, "I'll do whatever is necessary. If that means turning the entire galaxy upside down and shaking its pockets to see what falls out, that's what I'll do. I'm not subtle, I'm not pretty, and I'll piss off a lot of people along the way. But I'll get the job done."[29] Like Sheridan in the earlier *Babylon 5* series (himself an Arthur-figure, as mentioned earlier), Gideon only appears to be an unthinking blunt instrument of military force. He is instead a leader determined to see justice done, whether in assigning a telepath as his first officer ("War Zone") or investigating both sides of the conflict on Regula 4 before taking action ("The Long Road"). Moreover, he, like Arthur, wields an Excalibur; Gideon's Excalibur is a ship,

---

27 The title sequence of each episode features a voice-over in which questions are asked by Galen and answered by Gideon. The questions are: "Who are you?" "What do you want?" "Where are you going?" and "Who do you serve and who do you trust?" The last question is unanswered, except perhaps by images of the main characters of the series, as music swells through the rest of the sequence ("The Long Road," title sequence).

28 When Gareth first arrives at Camelot, Arthur listens and gives judgment on several cases (see lines 310 to 430). Alfred, Lord Tennyson, "Gareth and Lynette," in *Tennyson: A Selected Edition*, ed. Christopher Ricks (Harlow: Pearson Education Limited, 2007), 693–735.

29 "War Zone," dir. Janet Greek. writ. J. Michael Straczynski, *Crusade*, 9 June 1999. Babylonian Productions / Warner Bros. Television, 2004. Further references will be in text.

but as Marcus says in "A Late Delivery from Avalon," "Well, a ship, a sword, what's the difference?"[30]

Gideon's *Excalibur* represents future technology; designed and built from an amalgamation of alien and human technology, it is the most advanced starship humans have ever constructed, making the *Medusa*, the only other Earthforce ship in "The Long Road," seem outdated.[31] However, Excalibur as a name reaches back to the medieval, and to the legendary: to pastness outside historical time. The name Medusa also alludes to a mythic past, but the Arthurian allusion includes associations of sovereignty and justice, whereas the Medusa allusion connotes destruction, mirroring the way Gideon listens to the settlers' grievances while Captain Daniels and Lieutenant Meyers lack any concern for the villagers' fate. The Arthurian allusion is also unemotional in contrast to the common association of Medusa with rage. The *Excalibur*, like the *Medusa*, is associated with violence – it is a destroyer-class vessel after all – but unlike the *Medusa* it is also associated with exploration, science, and healing: it is fitted up to be a traveling research station whose Dr. Chambers (Marjean Holden) plays a prominent role in several episodes as their search for a cure requires her expertise. While the *Excalibur*, under Gideon's leadership, appears to solve the problem on Regula 4 by technology – it fires its formidable (and formidably phallic) main weapon at the mine to eliminate the supposed threat posed by Alwyn – it really has worked magic, playing a part in an illusion that eliminates the current mine and apparently Alwyn, thus persuading Earthforce personnel and settlers to work together, by making the cooperative option more viable because of their mutual losses.

In light of ongoing debates about definitions of medievalism and neomedievalism, "The Long Road" can be read as addressing what type of medievalism is constructive. The medievalism of the settlers of Regula 4 is commended for its desire to reject the violence inherent in some modern technologies; in one scene, after the settlers have resorted to kidnapping Earthforce personnel to stop the mining activities, one unidentified person in the crowd can be heard protesting the decision, saying, "it is not our way." Alwyn repeatedly defends the settlers in speaking with Gideon and Galen by asserting that they are "good" and "decent," and his evaluation of that decency justifies, to him, the actions he must take to defend their way of life: essentially, their medievalism. The decency of this medievalism is represented in the episode

---

30 Marcus says this line as he and Franklin, wishing to heal McIntyre when he becomes catatonic, try to decode the private symbolism of McIntyre's use of Arthurian legend to cope with past trauma.

31 Vorlon and Minbari technologies have been adapted to human technology to create the *Excalibur* and the *Victory*, but the *Victory* is destroyed in the battle with the Drahk in *A Call to Arms*. Since the place where the ships were built is also destroyed, *Excalibur* the ship, like Excalibur the sword, is unique.

in gendered terms, as the innkeeper's daughter Claire (Alison Lohman) acts as a symbol of innocence and vulnerability. When she becomes ill because the mining has released into the air the anti-viral mineral in concentrated quantities, the mine's threat to her as an individual represents technology's threat to the "good" and "decent" medievalism of the settlers.

The settlers' turn toward violence and seizing of Earthforce technology to facilitate that violence could be read as a crossing of the medieval / contemporary divide, but Alwyn's "magic" remains their main weapon. Their intention to use such power, the innkeeper's determination to avenge his daughter's illness, and his speech about not needing to be reasonable, mentioned earlier, suggest a medievalism that recreates the medieval can make real one stereotype of the era as "bizzarely barbaric, [...] and especially violent."[32] The episode's equation of the settler's violence with that of the *Medusa*'s captain and first officer, however, demonstrates that the medieval is not the only time-period prone to such excesses; technology, coupled with an attitude that disdains the past, leads equally to unreasonable violence, to exploitation and dehumanization of the Other. The Arthurian alternative, then, is not just a specific mediating position for this specific situation; the episode can be read as endorsing more generally this alternative as an appropriate medievalism. It is a medievalism that does not try to recreate the past, that is firmly embedded in the latest technology, that is – in its willingness to create illusion – playful, but that is also embedded in a tradition of justice that is constructed, through Arthurian allusion, as connected to a medieval past. The Arthurian alternative, it seems to me, is neomedievalism, and it is not just embraced by the episode's characters, but also embodied by this episode and the earlier *Babylon 5* series.

"Anybody with a gun": Justice, Gender, and Arthurian (Neo)medievalism

Babylon 5 and *Crusade* associate (neo)medievalism with compassion for the ill and vulnerable, and with protection of the innocent through justice-seeking actions. The drama of both series, however, lies less in acts of compassion and investigation, and more in the violent actions that create "justice." That tradition of justice both series invoke is quite likely an illusion itself, a metanarrative[33] that

---

32 E. L. Risden, "Medievalists, Medievalism, and Medievalismists: The Middle Ages, Protean Thinking, and the Opportunistic Teacher-Scholar," in *Studies in Medievalism XVIII: Defining Medievalism(s) II*, ed. Karl Fugelso (Cambridge: D. S. Brewer, 2010), 44–54 (48).

33 I am following John Stephens and Robyn McCallum's use of the term to designate "a global or totalizing cultural narrative schema which orders and explains knowledge and experience," thereby making certain narratives make sense to their consumers in a particular cultural setting. John Stephens and Robyn McCallum, *Retelling Stories, Framing Culture* (New York: Garland, 1998), 6.

makes series like *Babylon 5* and *Crusade* and episodes like "The Long Road" make sense, that makes them, in fact, satisfying for their audiences. But despite (let me confess) my pleasure in this narrative, in this alternative, gender politics remain a concern, because the violence apparently required by justice is coded masculine, even if some female characters participate in it. Arthur, in "A Late Delivery," may say that "the heart of the Round Table" philosophy is "to promote a society of laws, not arms," but arms remain privileged, whether that is Aldous's use of his staff in "Grail," Arthur's use of his sword in "A Late Delivery," or Marcus's use of a quarterstaff. "Good" characters use weapons in defense of justice, but they revel in the violence of that defense; episodes thus often position viewers to revel in that violence (or potential for violence) as well. For example, after rendering an entire bar's worth of criminal characters unconscious in *Babylon 5*'s third-season episode "Ceremonies of Light and Dark," Marcus says, "It's like I've always said. You can get more with a kind word and a two-by-four than you can with just a kind word";[34] similarly, G'Kar enthuses about the villains he and Arthur have confronted in "A Late Delivery," "they made a very satisfying thump when they hit the floor." "In the Long Road," the alternative to the *Medusa*'s and the settlers' violence represented by Gideon and the *Excalibur* depends on having the most powerful weapon, and the opening scenes of the episode emphasize that feature of *Excalibur*. After the panicked mine worker requests that Earthforce should "send [...] anybody with a gun," there is one shot of the dragon's eye looking through a window, and then a shot of *Excalibur*, the first of the episode. The camera pans along the length of the sword-shaped ship, starting at the front, and thus lingering along the ship's main weapon. Although this scene follows a common convention – show the exterior to change locations, then shift to the interior where the new action will take place – the result is to showcase the violent potential (and thus a particular kind of potential power) of the *Excalibur*.

As my earlier description of that weapon suggests, "The Long Road" represents that power as phallic; the Arthurian alternative reassures us that the right *king* will do justice, and the contrast between the mythic allusions of male sword (Excalibur) and female monster (Medusa) reinforces a patriarchal narrative of justice as the domain of the masculine. Although Dr. Chambers heals Claire, and although she confirms the link between the mine and Claire's illness and thus justifies Gideon's actions, the actress Marjean Holden is never onscreen in this episode. Claire is the pale fainting victim – the damsel in distress – whom the men (father-figures all) rush to save. Despite references to her feisty temper – Gideon says she is demanding to be returned home and her father acknowledges that "she's a tiger under all that silence" – she speaks merely ten words in the episode, none of them

---

[34] "Ceremonies of Light and Dark," dir. John C. Flinn III, writ. J. Michael Straczynski, *Babylon 5*, 8 April 1996. *Babylon 5: The Complete Third Season*, Babylonian Productions / Warner Bros. Television, 2004.

tigerish. For this one episode, then, the models for all forms of response to the medieval – recreation, rejection, or selective appropriation – are masculine responses.

Pointing to the patriarchal metanarrative reinforced by this episode does not necessarily apply to the entire *Crusade* series (itself incomplete) or the imaginative world of which it is a small part. The *Babylon 5* universe as a whole includes strong female leaders; as mentioned earlier, both Ivanova and Delenn in the earlier series have a range of roles, and these characters, among others, ensure that women have an important presence in *Babylon 5* as competent, intelligent professionals. Even within that original series, however, gender representation changes with examples of medievalism. The Rangers, presumably, include women, and Delenn is, reluctantly, their leader for a time, but most of the individual Rangers depicted in *Babylon 5* are male, and males have the speaking roles when playing Rangers on the series. That "The Long Road" – the episode that incorporates the medievalism / modern divide and the neomedieval, Arthurian alternative – is so male-dominated raises questions about maintaining a strong female presence and incorporating (neo)medievalism, particularly when the same tendency appears in other examples of (neo)medievalism within this futuristic story-universe. The appeal of Arthurian justice, so associated with the king and his sword, seems to marginalize women by definition.

Increasingly, scholars have noted the ways in which examples of (neo)medievalism, from video games to fantasy blockbuster novels or films, do not just reproduce but exaggerate patriarchal systems, suggesting that part of the appeal of (neo)medievalism is the return of unquestionable patriarchal power.[35] One of the opening questions of *Crusade*'s title sequence is "who do you serve?" Though asked of Gideon specifically, it is a good question to ask of (neo)medievalism generally.

---

[35] See, for example, Amy Kaufman, "Medieval Unmoored," in *Studies in Medievalism XIX: Defining Neomedievalism(s)*, ed. Karl Fugelso (Cambridge: D. S. Brewer, 2010), 1–11.

Cosmopolitan Anxieties and National Identity in the Netflix Marco Polo

Kara L. McShane

Marco Polo: I've always been taken by the audacity of Alexander, the great conqueror.

Kublai Khan: There are twenty cities that bear his name. I now possess them all.

Marco Polo, "The Wayfarer"

While there have been several film and television adaptations of Marco Polo's *Travels* since 1938, the Venetian explorer has experienced a surge in popularity since 2012.[1] In that year, an illustrated edition of Henry Yule's translation of the *Travels* appeared, with an introduction and notes by Morris Rossabi, published by Sterling. The same year also saw the DVD release of a PBS documentary entitled *In the Footsteps of Marco Polo*, which recounted the travels of Denis Belliveau and Francis O'Donnell as they retraced Polo's journeys.[2] In these recreations, Polo's journeys become the means to present the Middle East and Asia as unchanging, uncivilized sites of adventure – and thus of Orientalism. As the Middle East and Asia continue to be sites of Western attention, these recreations of Polo's adventures become increasingly relevant to Western audiences. Perhaps most notable in this regard is the 2014 Netflix series, called simply *Marco Polo*, which released a second season in the summer of 2016. With its tagline, "Worlds Will Collide," the

---

[1]   On these earlier adaptations, see Amilcare A. Iannucci and John Tulk, "From Alterity to Holism: Cinematic Depictions of Marco Polo and his Travels," in *Marco Polo and the Encounter between East and West*, ed. Suzanne Conklin Akbari and Amilcare Iannucci (Toronto: University of Toronto Press, 2008), 201–43.
[2]   *In the Footsteps of Marco Polo*, DVD, dir. Emir Lewis (PBS, 2012).

series establishes from its advertising alone its focus on intercultural contact and conflict.

I focus here on the first three episodes of the Netflix series in order to situate the show's anxious multiculturalism and Polo's sudden relevance in the face of prevalent twenty-first-century sociopolitical anxieties. Pamela M. Yee has recently written compellingly about the show's difficulties dealing with race and gender; here, I build on this work to examine the series' concern with national-identity politics.[3] Polo's travels make him especially relevant in our increasingly tense and interconnected global moment, and the series is the product of a context in which categories of national and transnational are in flux. The show focuses on two tensions: one, the internal concerns about a multicultural versus a unified, traditional Mongolian empire under the Khan; and two, an imperial power struggle between Mongolia and China. By positioning multiculturalism in tension with a notion of authentic nationalism, the show articulates contemporary Western anxieties about multiculturalism and exchange.[4] Yet it displaces these worries by setting them in two distinct and Othered Asian cultures.[5] The show's medievalism, then, colludes with its Orientalism to create a space to explore these contemporary concerns. I concentrate on these early episodes because they establish these tensions for the rest of the season: while the fraught internal multiculturalism takes a back seat to the Chinese/Mongolian conflict later in the series, the specter of fractious difference is present throughout.[6] Indeed, these two threads are woven together from the beginning: the Chinese threat to Mongolia is both internal and external from the very opening of the show.

---

3   Pamela M. Yee, review of *Marco Polo*, dir. John Fusco, *Medievally Speaking*, 12 January 2016, <http://medievallyspeaking.blogspot.com/2016/01/fusco-marco-polo.html>, last accessed 3 August 2016. I am grateful to Yee for several fruitful discussions about the series.

4   Nationalism is, of course, an anachronism within the series' setting, yet I argue that national concerns very clearly map on to the imperial endeavors of the Khan's court, and to be sure, the show (like many productions of medievalism) is not exceedingly concerned about anachronism. For example, in "The Wayfarer," Marco Polo refers to his home in Italy, a construct that would undoubtedly make little sense to the historical thirteenth-century Venetian merchant.

5   It is worth noting here that the Othering is not equal: because Marco Polo is the viewer's point of access, the show privileges Mongolia's perspective, consistently depicting China as the villain, even as both cultures are exoticized.

6   For example, a later plotline, which spans several episodes, features the return of the elder Polos, Niccolo and Maffeo, and brings Christianity and Western trade interests into tension with Mongolian law. This subplot is especially interesting in part because Marco has sympathized with the Mongolian colonizing force throughout, yet he challenges Kublai Khan's attempts to move west for more territory; it is only when Western interests are involved that the series presents Kublai's ambitions as dangerous and the Venetian character as conflicted. This conflict seems poised to continue in the show's second season.

The show is strongly invested in the tensions between the Othered Mongolians and the foreigners at their court. The primary conflict in the first season is Marco Polo's loyalty to Kublai Khan and the tensions among key players in the Khan's court as Polo gains increasing influence. The initial season of the show follows the Westerner's misadventures as he is recognized for his unique way with words and facility with language, abandoned at the Khan's court by his father, reluctantly learns Mongolian riding, archery, and law, along with kung fu, becomes the object of the affection of two different Mongolian women, and rather awkwardly comes to have a place among the Khan's advisers. All of this takes place in the context of the Khan's efforts to capture Xiangyang, the walled city that is the last stronghold of Song China against the growing Mongolian empire. Thanks to the crucial technological intervention of Marco himself, these efforts are eventually successful in the last episode of the season.[7]

As even this brief synopsis makes clear, the show draws heavily on both medievalist and Orientalist tropes, particularly those of the Westerner who masters Eastern customs and brings powerful technology to the East.[8] John Ganim has observed that medievalism and Orientalism have a long tradition of being mutually invoked. Indeed, Ganim links medievalism and Orientalism as two convergent modes of Othering, tracing the connection between them to the eighteenth century, particularly Romanticism and its growing sense of nationalism. The deployment of these two has changed over time, of course; as Ganim observes, "since the late eighteenth century, the Medieval and the Oriental had been paired, as aesthetic styles, as points of linguistic origin, and, increasingly, as stages of cultural development."[9] Ganim argues

---

[7]   The show's scale has imperial agendas as grand as the Khan's. Its visual complexity benefited from a budget of $90 million for its first ten episodes, and executives and producers both hoped that the show's international setting, with filming in Italy, Malaysia, and Kazakhstan, might draw international audiences. Thus, the series was a gamble for Netflix, but it was praised for its ambition even as it was critically panned. See Emily Steel, "How to Build an Empire, the Netflix Way," *New York Times*, 30 November 2014, late edition, <http://www. nytimes.com/2014/11/30/business/media/how-to-build-an-empire-the-netflix-way-.html?_ r=0>, last accessed 3 August 2016. For critical reviews of the series, see, for example, James Poniewozik, "Review: Khan Job: Netflix's Ludicrous *Marco Polo*," *Time*, 11 December 2014, and Margaret Lyons, "Netflix's *Marco Polo* is Opulent, Lifeless," *Vulture*, 12 December 2014.

[8]   Consider similar plot points in films such as *Kingdom of Heaven* or *The Last Samurai*. Ironically, Marco Polo's trebuchet is one place where the series draws on the *Travels*, but this is one of the moments in the *Travels* that cannot be accurate since it describes events occurring in 1273, before the Polos reached the East. See Peter Jackson, "Marco Polo and his 'Travels,'" *Bulletin of the School of Oriental and African Studies* 1 (1998): 82–101 (99). For Polo's account of the siege, see *The Travels of Marco Polo*, trans. Ronald Latham (New York: Penguin, 1958), 207–8.

[9]   John M. Ganim, *Medievalism and Orientalism: Three Essays on Literature, Architecture, and Cultural Identity* (New York: Palgrave Macmillan, 2005), 84.

that the medieval and the Oriental together have been imagined as modernity's past, the nascent nation, yet they also embody the alien and the exotic.[10]
Thus, both discourses are commonly used to serve nationalist purposes
and contemporary political agendas, and in recent years, references to the
medieval have become increasingly politically charged.[11] Medievalism and
Orientalism fuse especially well in contemporary retellings of Marco Polo's
travels; the *Divisament dou monde* is, after all, a medieval account of the Far
East. However, I argue that the series, consciously or not, capitalizes on a
connection that seems inherent to its source text but reveals far more about
contemporary interest in Polo and deployment of "the medieval."

The series deploys the medieval and Oriental as stages of cultural development, most notably in its presentation of the Mongolian empire as a testing
ground for multiculturalism, yet, by means of time and geography, this
testing ground remains a safe distance from the Western viewer. The series
seeks to align the viewer's sympathies with Mongolia, but only tentatively,
and it simultaneously emphasizes the Otherness of Mongolian culture. This
strategic positioning begins at the show's very opening: the first images of the
series are of destruction wrought by the Mongolian warriors, visually marked
by corpses impaled on stakes and by an abundance of arrows.[12] The landscape
of desolation and destruction that Niccolo, Maffeo, and Marco Polo enter
locates the Mongolians immediately as both medieval and Oriental in the
pejorative sense, associating the past and the East with excess and violence.
These images confirm that Marco – and the viewer – have entered a foreign
world, constructing the Mongolian empire as a danger and Kublai Khan as
not to be challenged, and, indeed, this sense of danger is central to Marco's
early encounters with the Khan.

Yet the series' medievalism and Orientalism are also entangled with
its stated commitment to authenticity, a commitment that obscures how
the show is informed by contemporary concerns. As Pam Clements has
observed, "authenticity" may take a variety of meanings, and medievalist
products are always inauthentic insofar as they do not date from the Middle
Ages.[13] For director John Fusco and his co-creators, though, authenticity
seems to suggest historical accuracy, and the show is imagined as a recovery
of Polo's "real" spirit and adventures: as Fusco has observed, "Marco Polo has

---

[10] See especially Ganim's discussion of the grand exhibitions of the nineteenth century,
106–7.
[11] See Bruce Holsinger, *Neomedievalism, Neoconservatism, and the War on Terror* (Chicago:
Prickly Paradigm Press, 2007); Pam Clements, "Authenticity," in *Medievalism: Key Critical
Terms*, ed. Elizabeth Emery and Richard Utz (Cambridge: D. S. Brewer, 2014), 19–26; and
David Matthews, *Medievalism: A Critical History* (Cambridge: D. S. Brewer, 2015).
[12] "The Wayfarer."
[13] Clements, "Authenticity," 20.

been kind of buried under this cloud of rather banal historical dust when the true story is so much more exciting."[14] The series thus imagines itself uncovering a true adventure story, an authentic medieval world obscured by the dull, musty work of scholars and academics. There are some references in the series to the Rustichello text – perhaps most notably the episode focused on the legendary Assassins – but in general, the show bears little resemblance either to Polo's *Divisament dou monde* or to the thirteenth-century history of Mongolia and China. Thus, the series does not hold up to Fusco's intentions, though it certainly carries many stock signifiers of medievalism and may be seen as authentically medieval by many viewers. Indeed, reviewer Vinnie Mancuso has justified the show's enormous budget on the grounds of its authenticity, claiming, "But you can't put a price on authenticity, I suppose, and Marco Polo is nothing if not authentic."[15] He credits in particular the show's costuming, designed by Tim Yip. The show's claims to authenticity lie partly in the creators' supposed research, but more importantly in the show's rich visual creation: that is, the show is credibly authentic because it *looks* authentic, a visual deception reliant on the series' massive budget, and this presumed authenticity covers for both the medievalism and the Orientalism of the show.

These claims to authenticity are key to how the series uses medievalism and Orientalism as tools of displacement. Through its claim of being "authentically medieval," set in the Far East, the series displaces this troubling multiculturalism by placing it geographically and temporally elsewhere. The show's political intrigue relies on this distance. Clements observes that medievalism's commitment to authenticity is often driven by nostalgia; while this romanticized Middle Ages, free of scholarly mediation, seems to be part of what intrigues Fusco, this claim to authenticity nonetheless has political implications.[16] Bruce Holsinger writes in his analysis of medievalism in post-9/11 American politics that "one of the most purely ideological effects of post-9/11 medievalism has been its tendency to permit those who exploit its patina of historical responsibility to avoid engagement with the full complexities of *recent* history."[17] While the series does not, I think, have an overt political agenda, its medievalism conceals its engagement with ongoing political realities. The series can only be perceived within a broader discourse of "the medieval": it claims to be simultaneously a return to origins and a brand-

14   Steel, "How to Build an Empire."
15   Vinnie Mancuso, "Creators and Cast of 'Marco Polo' Discuss Their World-Spanning, $90 Million Show," *New York Observer*, 11 December 2014, <http://observer.com/2014/12/ creators-and-cast-of-marco-polo-discuss-their-world-spanning-90-million-production/>, last accessed 3 August 2016.
16   Clements, "Authenticity," 25.
17   Holsinger, *Neomedievalism*, 32.

new take on the story, but it in fact relies on a broader context in which both the Middle Ages and the Far East are always understood as premodern and Other. Its power (or perhaps its innovation) is in presenting a Middle Ages that is not centered in a homogeneous white Europe; yet its Orientalism turns contemporary Western problems into medieval Eastern ones. By displacing the anxieties of multiculturalism through its setting, *Marco Polo* creates an imagined terrain on which personal and national identity crises play out. In the current political landscape in the West, recently marked by ethnocentrism, xenophobia, and racism, the series' multicultural anxieties resonate powerfully.[18]

National Tension in a Global Court

From the very first scene at Kublai Khan's court, the show seeks to set up an empire in which religious difference is welcome, yet this open-door policy immediately becomes a source of contention among the players at the Mongolian court. "Christianity is welcome in my kingdom," Kublai Khan declares to the Polo family, "as is Buddhism, Judaism, Islam, and the eternal blue sky of my grandfather Genghis Khan."[19] Yet Kublai's Mongolian advisers become suspicious of this openness, which they fear displaces the centrality of Mongolia and Mongolian ways. While religion is the first heterogeneous identity category mentioned, this difference is rapidly conflated with national identity in the context of ongoing struggles between the Khan and Song China. In the same episode in which Kublai declares that all religions are welcome in his court, his cousin Kaidu asks, "Does the Great Khan

---

[18]   Unfortunately, contemporary examples abound. For some examples, see reports of increased ethnically motivated violence after the 23 July 2016 Brexit vote ("Hate Crime 'still far too high' post-Brexit," <http://www.bbc.com/news/uk-36869000>), last accessed 3 August 2016); *New York Times* reporter Jonathan Weisman's accounts of anti-Semitism on Twitter ("The Nazi Tweets of 'Trump God Emperor,'" <http://www.nytimes.com/2016/05/29/opinion/sunday/the-nazi-tweets-of-trump-god-emperor.html?ref=topics&_r=3>,   last accessed 3 August 2016); and Leslie Jones's departure from and return to Twitter after being targeted with racial insults ("*Ghostbusters* Star Leslie Jones Attacked by Racist Trolls on Twitter," <http://time.com/4412232/leslie-jones-ghostbusters-tweets/>, last accessed 3 August 2016).

[19]   "The Wayfarer." Even as the Khan welcomes all faiths, he seems especially interested in Christianity; part of the conflict in the exchange between the Polos and Kublai is the Polos' failure to bring Christian priests to the Khan's court. This suggests that voyeurism cuts both ways – that is, each group in the East/West interaction finds the other exotic and seeks knowledge of it. At the same time, of course, it continues to privilege Christianity even in the context of Kublai's pluralism: Christianity is the only faith he expresses any interest in learning more about at any point in the first season.

desire to be emperor of Mongolia, or emperor of China?"[20] Kaidu clearly sees these two endeavors as incompatible, an inherent conflict of interest, which seems a reasonable position given that Kublai has sought to capture the city of Xiangyang for thirty years.[21] In these early episodes, then, Kublai seeks to create unity among his own Mongolian people, reassuring them of his Mongolianness while arguing that the presence of outsiders enriches his empire. Where the Mongolians at his court (who are also, notably, almost all related to him) see a clear and necessary distinction between cultures, Kublai is outwardly comfortable with a diversity of views and practices.

However, lest the viewer see the court as a shining model of cosmopolitanism, in which all religions coexist, Kublai Khan repeats the mandate that his grandfather received from heaven: "to erase dividing lines from country to country – a mandate to spread our customs, our cultures, our very way of life to every corner beneath the blue sky."[22] This imperial endeavor, then, is a Mongolian manifest destiny, an effort to construct an empire that will simultaneously promulgate Mongolian culture while allowing its inhabitants to keep their own non-Mongolian ways. As my epigraph suggests, the Khan's project invites comparison with Alexander the Great, a connection that the show later makes explicit in one of Marco's private audiences with Kublai. Yet Kublai is accused not of going native like Alexander, but, worse, of going Chinese. Mongolian identity in the series is built on a particular kind of masculine warrior ethos, and thus this crisis of identity is a security crisis for Kublai's empire. Thus, the series raises the possibility that Kublai's acceptance of Chinese culture must automatically distance him from his Mongolian identity.[23]

Kublai ultimately reasserts his Mongolian status by subduing a significant internal political threat: namely, that presented by his brother Ariq, one of the strongest advocates for insularity and Mongolian exceptionalism at the Khan's court. Their conflicting opinions about multicultural tolerance eventually results in a fight to the death: the scene is visually familiar, placing the two opposing sides in long lines facing each other, before the camera turns,

20 "The Wayfarer."
21 This detail, provided in the screen of text at the show's opening, is presented as a careful coding, one that presents the Mongolians as uncultured even as it presents the Chinese as rebels. As the text narrates, Kublai's "armies rage across the Silk Road, annihilating every holdout in his path […]. Chancellor Jia Sidao and his Chinese rebel army are entrenched within the walled city of Xiangyang – they have resisted the Mongol horde for over thirty years." Even as the Mongolians are associated from the very start with violence and destruction, the Chinese are depicted as stubborn rebels – against a force that has not conquered them.
22 "The Wayfarer."
23 "The Wolf and the Deer." The repercussions of this duel play out in the third episode of the season, "The Feast."

giving a panoramic view of the two forces. Then the camera zooms in on Kublai himself, showing his struggles to dismount his horse, clad head to toe in golden armor. The camera angle widens then, showing the lone figure of Kublai crossing the distance between the two forces to confront Ariq. As Kublai walks, Hundred Eyes, a blind Taoist monk and Marco Polo's kung fu instructor, explains to Marco: "This is Mongol against Mongol, and only one can win. You had better pray it is our side. For if we lose, Khanbalik will be burned to the ground and we will be made into kindling."[24] The words link this traditional means of battle to the vulnerability of people like Marco and Hundred Eyes, the foreigners in Kublai's court. When Kublai reaches Ariq, he challenges, "You want Mongolia? You come and take it." Ariq's reply – "It is as it should be" – demonstrates Kublai's reassertion of his Mongolian identity; Kublai's actions read as appropriate and traditional to Ariq, even as Kublai challenges him.[25] Though the fight is supposedly due to Ariq's treason as represented by his failure to support his khan, it is also a dynastic fight between the brothers and a physical resolution to the debate between cosmopolitanism and nationalism that has been central to the Mongolian court since the series' start. As the fight between Kublai and Ariq unfolds, the camera pans to major characters and the viewer sees their reactions, yet the choice of which characters are represented is also telling: the camera focuses on Marco, on the Khan's Muslim finance minister Ahmad, and on Kublai's half-Chinese son Jingim. Though these figures are of course central to the plot (as well as the characters that the audience knows best at this point), they are also the characters whose very presence has caused the conflict the fight is meant to resolve. And resolve it the fight does: Ariq is killed. When Kublai returns to court, he confronts any potential anxiety about his actions directly: "Ariq was my brother. But he was a traitor [...]. I took his head, soaked the earth with his blood [...]. In my heart and by our laws, I know this to be necessary and just."[26] Kublai refers to the appropriateness of the method of Ariq's defeat – presenting his blood soaking the earth as a ritual practice – and invokes the laws that governed the Khan's deeds. His highly public performance of Mongolian law and justice thus reasserts his authority and closes off the earlier concerns about his Chinese affiliations, though the threat of multiculturalism does not vanish with this victory.

24 "The Wolf and the Deer."
25 "The Wolf and the Deer."
26 "The Feast." Kublai uses this moment as an opportunity to literally erase Ariq's treason from the court, ordering that "That is the last we shall speak of my brother."

Hybrid Identity and National Crisis

While Kublai is able to strike an effective balance between his Mongolian identity and the pluralism he espouses, the show's tensions with regard to national identity crystallize around Prince Jingim, son of Kublai and his Chinese wife, Empress Chabi. As a result of his dual identity, Jingim struggles to situate himself as Mongolian, particularly as much of the Khan's court consistently categorizes him as too Chinese. This struggle begins in the first episode, when Kaidu challenges Jingim's suitability to lead a military attack: "Jingim, educated in Chinese ways. Who better to lead an attack on the Chinese?"[27] Jingim's identity problem comes primarily from his Chinese education, which makes him too cultured for the Khan's court. When Jingim rides to the battle at Wuchang (which the Mongols lose under his command), he tries to claim his Mongolian identity. He tells his father, "I ride to Wuchang as a Mongol, and I carry my father's flag." Kublai, in turn, tells Jingim, "You are your mother's son, Jingim. Educated, patient, noble. There will be a time for all these in the new dynasty."[28] There is, of course, a problematic gendered component to Kublai's words: in aligning Jingim with his mother, Kublai feminizes him and thus his Chinese practices, in turn presenting Mongolian culture as intensely masculine.[29] The Khan makes the distinction between his own status as warrior and Jingim's cultured demeanor.[30] Kublai thus presents his own Mongolian culture as violent and primitive, marked by its warrior ethos, in contrast to his son's more sophisticated ways, though both of these identities rely on Orientalist cultural stereotypes.

Given his own hybrid position, Jingim is not in the position to look down on many of the court's outsiders. Nor does he have the inclination, and indeed he often sides with them at court. Marco, however, is an acceptable target of Jingim's distrust; and while some of this suspicion is clearly interpersonal, the cultural components are embedded in this personal distaste. Jingim consistently asserts his Mongolianness in the face of Marco's Otherness. When Marco accompanies Jingim to the Mongolian city of Karakorum, Jingim warns: "You're in the heartland of Lord Genghis

---

27 "The Wayfarer."
28 "The Wayfarer."
29 This is emphasized when, moments later, Jingim explains that all three of his wives wish to have sex with him before he departs, and Kublai laughs and replies, "You are also your father's son." Indeed, as I will discuss further, Chinese culture and identity is effeminized on several occasions in these early episodes.
30 At the same time, Kublai's Mongolian identity is more authentic than Jingim can hope to attain. At one point, Kublai explains to Marco that Kublai – like Marco – "was always a bit clumsy with the making of Chinese characters" ("The Wolf and the Deer"). Insofar as writing represents its culture, Kublai and Marco can neither fully appropriate Chinese nor be assimilated into it; one assumes that Jingim would have no such scribal difficulties.

now. Beware, Polo. Your words can get you killed."[31] By referring to Marco's words, Jingim invokes the very talent that has won Marco the favor of the Khan and a place at the court as a potential danger to Marco in Karakorum. Jingim identifies a difference in how those words are valued in the new terrain, implying, perhaps, that the cosmopolitanism that privileges Marco's perspective does not operate in this space, a space that seems to still be governed by the deceased Genghis Khan, the ideal and idealized Mongol ruler.[32] Jingim's threat aligns him with Mongolian practices compared to Marco – but, at the same time, Jingim does *not* claim the family connection to Genghis Khan that Kublai has previously invoked. Thus, the words seem to create distance between Jingim and his Mongolian heritage even as they try to associate him more strongly with it.

Indeed, Jingim's concern about his identity and his conflict with his father allow him to be deceived early on in the series by Kublai's brother Ariq. Before his death, Ariq governs the old capital city of Karakorum, and Kublai sends Jingim as emissary to determine why Ariq's forces did not join them for the attack on Wuchang. In their conversation, Ariq draws on Jingim's desire for Mongolian belonging by positioning Jingim as Mongolian as opposed to the many foreigners welcome at Kublai's court: Ariq warns Jingim, "One day, they may call you Jingim Khan. But beware. My big brother is too trusting of outsiders. Persians and Chinese and all kinds of religions. You and me – our blood is the wolf and the deer."[33] It is Ariq who acknowledges Jingim's position and grants the possibility of his future Mongolian title, identifying Jingim as Mongolian rather than as one of the Chinese outsiders at Kublai's court. Yet this is a calculated move, of course, designed to make Jingim turn away from his father's cultural cosmopolitanism and from his own Chinese heritage and education. It is not an accident that this scene occurs in a visually Mongolian setting. While Kublai's city is walled, clearly inspired by Chinese architectural styles, Karakorum consists of a large community of yurts, and Ariq and Jingim share airag, the traditional Mongolian mare's milk drink, while they converse. This scene places Jingim in a more uniformly Mongolian context, at a further remove from Chinese influences, allowing Jingim to identify (and be identified) as Mongol; this is a notable contrast to his place in his father's court, where his differences are more easily ascribed to Chinese influence than individual difference. Ariq's

---

31 "The Wolf and the Deer."
32 Genghis Khan holds this position as model throughout the series for all the Mongolian characters with aspirations to power, and thus he is frequently invoked. For example, in a later episode ("The Fourth Step"), Kublai himself expresses the idea that Genghis was a giant in his childhood imagination. Further, as he received the original mandate from heaven, Genghis Khan is the basis for all of the show's imperial endeavors.
33 "The Wolf and the Deer."

ability to avoid Jingim's suspicion relies on his appeal to their family relation-ship and to Jingim's Mongolianness, precisely the piece of Jingim's identity that Kublai and others consistently brush aside.

After the death of Ariq, the series shifts its anxiety about national identi-ties away from the court's cosmopolitanism toward the natural result of such cultural exchange, and Jingim's identity crisis becomes increasingly central in "The Feast," the third episode of the series. When Kaidu, now the ruler of Karakorum in place of Ariq, throws a feast in honor of Kublai Khan, Kublai sends Jingim in his stead. Kaidu is displeased to say the least, and the evening consists almost entirely of Kaidu publicly mocking Jingim for his failure at Wuchang. Jingim is reserved and nearly silent throughout the exchange, practicing the patience and reserve learned from his Chinese education. The conversation culminates when Kaidu declares, "We would have been victo-rious at Wuchang if Genghis Khan or Lord Kublai commanded." Jingim's half-brother and the Khan's bastard son, Byamba, immediately comes to Jingim's defense: "I prefer a general with aggression in his blood to one who quakes with trepidation on his steed." Byamba reads Jingim's decision to attack at Wuchang as a successful enactment of Mongolian warrior ethos despite their loss. Kaidu's response, however, challenges Jingim's position at the court along with his Mongolian identity: "I prefer a pure general. A Mongol raised Mongol, bathed in the blood spilled by Genghis, steeped in his ways. A warrior like you, Byamba. Untainted, a true Mongol."[34] Though Byamba's blood claim to the Mongolian throne is more tenuous than Jingim's, Byamba's masculine Mongolian attributes outweigh his bastard status in Kaidu's eyes. In addition to the public shame of his loss, Jingim is here confronted with his hybridity in terms of both blood and culture; the reference to Genghis's blood, though it refers primarily to Mongolian culture, also resonates with Jingim's "impure" status as the son of a Chinese mother. Multiculturalism is presented as a form of contamination as well as the root of Jingim's military failure.

Jingim, still stinging from Kaidu's mockery at Karakorum, confronts Kublai upon his return, and Jingim himself raises anxieties about his position. He questions his own paternity as a way to express his disconnection from Mongolian culture, a disconnect laden with imperial implications. Kublai greets Jingim with a fairly neutral "Son," and Jingim lashes out, expressing his earlier repressed anger at the evening's events: "Am I? I doubt the great Khan would humiliate his one true heir. No, the Khan wouldn't shame his one true son by leaving him to attend a feast with a Latin and a bastard who – " Jingim is cut off when Kublai attacks him, knocks him to the floor, and raises a teapot above his head to strike Jingim with it. Jingim challenges

---

34 "The Feast."

his father – "Go on! Kill me!"[35] Jingim understands his father's decision to send Marco and Byamba to the feast with him as reinforcing Jingim's own marginalized status; his companions are, as he puts it, a foreigner and a bastard, both figures on the fringes of the court where Jingim, the Khan's son, should have pride of place.

Kublai's response, in turn, reinforces Jingim's inadequacy and the violent masculinity of Mongolian culture. He speaks at length about his father's unworthiness to rule Mongolia, and he tells Jingim that "I still hear his whining in my ear. You too whine like a woman. A man who would be khan must stand tall and crush those who mock him." Jingim's response tidily articulates the hybrid position in which he finds himself: "If I whine like a woman, it is because you molded me that way. They mock me because I think Chinese. Because I act Chinese. Because you made me Chinese!"[36] Jingim's anguish reinscribes the masculine Mongolian ethos in opposition to feminized Chinese ways along with his own deep-rooted sense of cultural inadequacy, his failure to meet Mongolian ideals and his awareness of how his education shapes his behavior and perspective. Kublai's response emphasizes the stakes of Jingim's uncertain position. He tells his son, "You were taught by Chinese scholars. That does not make you less Mongol. You act it! Or I will kill you." For Jingim, cultural belonging is literally a matter of life or death.

Exotic Empires and the Western Narrator

The show thus dramatizes concerns about national identity in the face of multiculturalism, concerns that resonate strongly with contemporary Western religious and nationalist anxieties; yet it makes use of both medievalism and Orientalism to displace them, playing these conflicts out at a safe distance from the Western audience. As several reviewers have noted, Marco Polo is reduced in role, especially early in the series, and the real focus is on China and Mongolia, the dynasty and the Khan.[37] At the same time, Marco, the only major Western character, is the viewer's access point to the court, and he is also uniquely positioned to see – and narrate – the events around him. While Marco is often somewhat bumbling, he is also uniquely trusted; this position of privilege, and the response of others to it, is a major plot point and drives much of the first season. His place as the perspective

---

35 "The Feast."
36 "The Feast."
37 See Hank Stuever, "Netflix's 'Marco Polo' Trudges through Many Cinematic Asian Tropes," *Washington Post*, 12 December 2014, and Rob Thomas, "Netflix's *Marco Polo* Lacks Spice," *Capital Times (Madison)*, 17 December 2014.

character for much of the series also has the obviously Orientalist result of consistently privileging the Western white man in the midst of the diverse but primarily Asian Mongolian court. Marco's keen observation skills serve as a filter for Kublai through which Mongolia and China are re-presented through Marco's outsider view. It is Marco who realizes that Ariq's horses cannot make the journey to Xiangyang to support the Khan's forces, and though he seeks a tactful way to say as much, his words automatically call into question Jingim's claims that the horses are ready. Jingim later confronts Marco while Marco is learning kung fu: "Humiliate me in front of the court again and I will kill you. [pauses] You were right."[38] Jingim is keenly aware of his suspect and marginal status, a position reinforced by Marco the outsider's superior knowledge and observation. The moment makes the Westerner the expert on Mongolian military readiness, creating tension at court and undercutting Jingim's already tentative authority.

Yet more than a military expert, Marco is the one who can best describe the Mongolian empire: the Khan's minister of finance, Ahmad, calls Marco "a foreign messenger who can paint pictures with his words."[39] As I have alluded to previously, Marco's ability with words is what earns him a place at court. Upon their arrival, Kublai Khan asks the Polos to "describe for me my desert," and Kublai responds well to Marco's description and to his linguistic abilities. Kublai is amazed at how much of the local language Marco has learned in a short time as well as with Marco's poetic account of the isolated sand.[40] Kublai not only invites but indeed demands a Western perspective on his own lands: even if Marco earns the Khan's regard primarily because of his unique perspective and his artful words, the fact remains that the only Western character is best positioned to describe Mongolia to its very ruler. Indeed, when Kublai sends Marco to accompany Jingim on the trip to Karakorum, he demands, "Let me see, Latin, the way things truly are in the kingdom of my brother."[41] Thus, Kublai implicitly privileges Marco's perspective over his son's. I suggest that this decision stems both from a mistrust of Jingim's hybrid identity – even by his father, who has essentially created Jingim's identity crisis by supporting Jingim's Chinese education – as well as from the show's Orientalism. The Khan seems to believe that Marco's status as an outsider provides him with a level of objectivity and truth that

---

38 "The Wolf and the Deer."
39 "The Wolf and the Deer." Indeed, it is this knack for description that makes Marco an appealing offering to Kublai, and his father Niccolo (the consummate merchant) quickly capitalizes on the Khan's interest and exchanges Marco for continued license to trade on the Silk Road.
40 "The Wolf and the Deer." It is worth noting that Marco's description draws on the account of the Desert of Lop in the *Travels*, where a man traveling by night often imagines he hears spirits and leaves the path (*Travels*, 84–85).
41 "The Wolf and the Deer."

Jingim lacks. While Jingim might be his envoy, present to represent Kublai's interests, Marco serves as the Khan's eyes.

In *Orientalism*, Edward Said writes that "The scientist, the scholar, the missionary, the trader, or the soldier was in, or thought about, the Orient because he *could be there*, or could think about it, with very little resistance on the Orient's part."[42] Since Said's book was first published over thirty years ago, the global political situation has in many respects changed: the "Far East" now possesses a political and economic reality that challenges the West's ability to construct it.[43] In this context, the Netflix *Marco Polo* series creates an imagined past where such fantasy *is* possible. The show's medievalism constructs a fictional moment in which the Western explorer is not only able but indeed invited to narrate the East to itself. Thus, in this medieval-esque world, one key piece of the fantasy is that Asian rulers invite their re-presentation by the Westerner.[44]

Marco Polo is, I suggest, a particularly well-situated figure for such fantasies; though Polo is a recognizable name, the *Travels* is not widely read, and unlike figures such as King Arthur or Robin Hood, he offers the promise of historical reality but fewer competing representations.[45] While there have been several adaptations of Polo's travels over time, they have not enjoyed the financial success of Arthurian productions, nor have they enjoyed wide and lasting distribution.[46] Further, I suggest that the show's setting at the Mongolian court similarly develops from its need for a blank slate. This setting certainly fits the creators' stated striving for authenticity, but it also creates an additional spatial and temporal remove: while most viewers might feel that they know something about China, Mongolia remains somewhat more marginalized and thus more open to medievalist and Orientalist projec-

---

[42] Edward Said, *Orientalism* (New York: Vintage Books, 1978), 7.

[43] To consider only one example, Lawrence Chung noted in May 2015 that the number of Americans employed in the US by Chinese-owned companies had increased dramatically in the previous five years despite the strained relationship between the two countries ("More Americans on Chinese Company Payrolls in US," *South China Morning Post*, 22 May 2015, 3). Indeed, acknowledging this changing relationship, President Barack Obama started the "One Million Strong" initiative, which set a goal of having one-million speakers of Mandarin in the US by 2020. See Melissa Sim, "Obama's 'learn Chinese drive' on Road to Reality," *The Straits Times (Singapore)*, 26 October 2015. This increased exchange suggests a growing awareness of China's centrality to the global landscape.

[44] This is also a key tenet of Said's description of Orientalism, since "if the Orient could represent itself, it would; since it cannot, the representation does the job, for the West, and *faute de mieux*, for the poor Orient" (*Orientalism*, 21).

[45] There has, of course, been some debate about the truth of Polo's travels, captured most clearly in the title of Frances Wood's book, *Did Marco Polo Go to China?* (Boulder, CO: Westview Press, 1996).

[46] Iannucci and Tulk, "From Alterity to Holism."

tion.[47] In this way, the series is much in keeping with the earlier documentary *In the Footsteps of Marco Polo*, which consistently imagines the Middle East in particular to be changeless or, as the narrators put it, "just like the thirteenth century."[48] Marco Polo's contemporary popularity, I suggest, lies in this temporal Othering that places the East, especially its borders, in a permanent and constructed Middle Ages.

At the same time as the series displaces these identity conflicts, setting them long ago and far away, I argue that the show's presentation of the East is deeply enmeshed in contemporary political concerns. In his reading of medievalism and neomedievalism post-9/11, Bruce Holsinger argues that invocations of the "medieval" – medieval mindsets, medieval brutality – are not simply a means to convey backwardness; rather, they are part of a more dangerous system that uses the medieval metaphorically to help explain changes in the global political arena. As Holsinger explains, the theory of neomedievalism in international relations sees the Middle Ages as a period of transnational authority and loyalties; this theory has been deployed to develop the idea of the non-state actor, a figure who operates outside of any national loyalties and who is thus not afforded the same protections offered to citizens of nation states.[49] Neomedievalism presents the nation as in crisis, challenged by greater contact, and it positions those outside of national loyalties as threatening. Such a theory, it seems, must develop hand-in-hand with globalization and increased exchange, and the outcomes of neomedievalism are thus in tension with increasing multiculturalism.

I do not suggest that the series explicitly has neomedievalism in mind: rather, *Marco Polo* is shaped by the post-9/11 discourse surrounding the medieval, the social and political context surrounding its creation. Indeed, the opening anxieties of the court are precisely the anxieties of neomedievalism versus nationalism, and the series positions a range of characters in this extra-national role. Marco would appear to be the most obvious outsider, and the concern and distrust of many characters at the Mongolian court suggest that Marco could be a non-state actor. Indeed, at the end of season one, Chinese chancellor Jia Sidao draws the viewer's attention to Marco's strange position: when Marco demands that he surrender to the Khan's forces, he asks, "Surrender the Song dynasty to a Mongol, by order

---

47 This assumed knowledge of China by the Western viewer is of course also shaped by the long history of Orientalism, as Said observes. He writes that "The value, efficacy strength, apparent veracity of a written statement about the Orient therefore relies very little, and cannot instrumentally depend, on the Orient as such. On the contrary, the written statement is a presence to the reader by virtue of its having excluded, displaced, made supererogatory any such *real thing* as the 'the Orient'" (*Orientalism*, 21). See also *Orientalism*, 4–5, 65–73.

48 *Footsteps*.

49 Holsinger, *Neomedievalism*, esp. 55–65.

of a European?"[50] Yet in Polo's case, the suspicion of others becomes a way to consistently confirm and reinforce his loyalty to Kublai Khan. Marco is an oddity, but never a threat. While other characters at the Khan's court fear that he is a dangerous outsider, the audience remains aware that he is not. As the only Westerner, Marco is the viewer's entry point, a figure of relatability rather than menace.[51]

Since the series locates Western concerns about multiculturalism in the East, the threats to empire are likewise Eastern in origin, another means through which Western anxieties are inscribed on the medieval–Oriental Mongolian court. It is particularly telling who the genuinely disloyal character proves to be at the end of season one: in the season's last episode, Ahmad, the Muslim minister of finance, reveals his plan to kill Kublai Khan only to the viewer and to Chinese courtesan Mei Lin, who has herself been sent to infiltrate the court and kill the Khan. The series thus fits its new political intrigue into obvious and immediate neomedieval anxieties by making the only remaining Muslim character in the series into the secret villain, the non-state actor who has infiltrated the Mongolian court and is biding his time.[52] This coding is especially politically charged because Ahmad has been part of the Mongolian court since childhood: though the show somewhat obscures his origins, his comments imply that he was abducted when his people were conquered by the Khan.[53] Ahmad's postcolonial position locates him as a threat to Kublai's new and growing empire. Thus, the series fuses the non-state actor with the victim of imperial power in the form of a figure who Western audiences are predisposed to find suspicious.

Thus, *Marco Polo* is the creation of its own fraught moment, both in terms of its Orientalizing multicultural anxieties and its deployment of medievalism, and the two discourses work together in often insidious ways. Of course, the series' problems are not unique among contemporary medievalisms: *Marco Polo* is often compared to the equally big-budget *Game of Thrones*, and many

---

50 "The Heavenly and the Primal."
51 Indeed, Fusco and collaborator Ben Silverman reportedly "brainstormed about how to create an East-meets-West drama that would include the appeal of a foreign land, but also a Western character who could connect it" (Steel, "How to Build an Empire"). The show thus relied on privileging a Western perspective on an exotic East from its early inception.
52 Yusuf, a now-deceased Muslim character, was notable as a representation both of disability and of devout Muslim practice; his death in "Prisoners," sacrificing himself to give Marco Polo a chance to redeem himself in the eyes of Kublai Khan, feeds into the show's problematic Orientalism.
53 Ahmad explains to Mei Lin in "Rendering" that "I was too young then to know him as a conqueror. He was my patron, my benefactor. He became as a father to me, and the Empress, a mother."

viewers and critics have discussed *Game of Thrones*' race issues.[54] And indeed, the show's presentation of the East is also in keeping with earlier recreations of Polo: as many films have turned him into an intrepid adventurer, into the hero of a western taking place in Asia, so the series' connections to the *Travels* tend to draw on the work's most fantastic, exotic elements. At the same time, the series picks up where Belliveau and O'Donnell left off: if Belliveau and O'Donnell describe contemporary Afghanistan as "just like the thirteenth century," then Fusco's Marco lives in a thirteenth century that proves eerily like the twenty-first. As season two creates new court intrigues, this displacement looks poised to collapse: in addition to Ahmad's bid for power, the season introduces a Crusader, Niccolo Polo, and features the legendary Prester John. If *Marco Polo*'s season one is the inevitable product of its cultural and political moment, the second season seems positioned to return to a more familiar East/West binary and even more directly present Western fears.

---

[54]   See especially Saladin Ahmed, "Is 'Game of Thrones' Too White?," <http://www.salon.com/2012/04/01/is_game_of_thrones_too_white/>, last accessed 3 August 2016. As Yee observes, the Netflix series is better along the lines of representation, using actors of Asian descent to play Asian characters, but this is not a panacea for the series' racial problems.

Mapping Everealm:
Space, Time, and
Medieval Fictions in *The Quest*

Angela Jane Weisl

In the summer of 2014, medieval fantasy met reality television in *The Quest*,[1] a part-scripted, part-competition show in which a group of twelve contemporary contestants are "transported" through real/mystical space into a medievalist universe to save the fictional land of Everealm, a fantasy world whose subjects were being terrorized by a villain known as Verlox, the Darkness. Everealm, a land of twelve kingdoms, had been ravaged, leaving only Castle Sænctum, ruled by Queen Ralia (played by Susanne Gschwendtner), standing. Each week the contestants, called "paladins," are tasked with helping to drive back the forces of darkness in a scripted narrative that included a series of real challenges at its center. In every episode, as part of the advancing narrative, the paladins take part in some kind of contest; the winners move on, while the losers must go before the Fates. The Fates then issue their own challenge, the winner is saved, and one paladin is voted off by his or her fellow contestants. In the end, the final paladin standing is allowed to reassemble the Sun Spear (a mystical weapon from Everealm's "history"), defeat Verlox (Doug Tait), and be named the "One True Hero."

The show's title plays an open hand. No academic medievalist or hardcore fantasy geek can hear the word "quest" without thinking geography; quests, whatever else they may do, move through space, both real and imagined, interior and exterior. The show's geography offers a complex nexus of reality and fiction; set in a real castle in Austria, in a fictional land, with real,

---

1   For those interested in viewing *The Quest*, it is available on AmazonPrime: <https://smile. amazon.com/The-Quest-Begins/dp/B00M8NSKM2/ref=sr_1_10?s=movies-tv&ie=UT-F8&qid=1471721896&sr=1-10&keywords=the+quest>, last accessed 6 September 2016. Other dubiously legal online services also seem to offer the show for free.

contemporary contestants, in an imagined past that echoes both the real Middle Ages and the fantasy Middle Ages of J. R. R. Tolkien and George R. R. Martin, *The Quest* creates an attentive map of space and time, reality and fiction. By adding a scripted story to the reality-television concept, *The Quest* calls its viewers' attention to the fiction underlying the whole enterprise; no reality television is "reality" in any meaningful way. Even sports, which may be the most "real" reality television, become mitigated because the commentary shapes viewers' experiences by focusing attention and endowing importance in specific places rather than allowing an authentic one-on-one relationship between the event and its audience.[2] In demonstrating the unreality of what purports to be reality, *The Quest* interrogates the relationship between truth and fiction on multiple levels. These levels include the connection between medievalist fantasy and tropes and the real actions of the contestants, who engage both on their interior and exterior quests. Through these, time and space, past and present interact with each other within the show's over-arching narrative, which seeks to combine multiple possibilities into one story. One specific way in which *The Quest* offers to chart these nexes is in its cartographic sensibility. In some sense, the show is a map of medievalism itself in its interplay of past and present, medieval fact and medieval fiction. It also unconsciously creates a parallel between reality television and the representation of geography (the map), in particular the medieval map, which, in its incorporation of land and legend, draws attention to its role as representation, to a role often concealed by contemporary maps.

Like *The Quest*, all maps occupy the borderland between reality and fiction. The opening episode of the ninth season of the Canadian Broadcasting Company's *Murdoch Mysteries*, "Nolo Contendere," begins with Julia Ogden calling William Murdoch's attention to an advertisement in the newspaper; William then reads aloud, "Cartography Exhibition; the original Mercator Projection," to which Julia responds, "The Complete Planisphere! It's only going to be here for a brief while!"[3] This scene-setting moment points to an essential feature of maps: that they are representations of reality, not reality itself. Displayed in a museum exhibition, they resemble

---

2   I have written extensively about sports, medievalism, and television in *The Persistence of Medievalism: Narrative Adventures in Contemporary Culture* (New York: Palgrave Macmillan, 2003); while still a bastion of truly popular culture, sports television still attempts to engage the creation of heroes and the production of narrative, and therefore shapes the audience's view of the "story," whereas direct experience of a sporting event may allow ("may" because the audience is still influenced by what happens on the Jumbotron – large display screens so prevalent in sporting venues) a more real response.

3   "Nolo Contendere." *Murdoch Mysteries*, Season 9, Episode 1, Canadian Broadcasting Company, 5 October 2015. Unfortunately, murder prevents William and Julia from ever attending the exhibition and allowing the audience to see what would have been displayed and how they would have engaged with it.

art; constructed on paper, they resemble texts. The complete planisphere, the original 1569 Mercator projection, is essentially an encompassing metaphor – the entire world confined on a piece of paper. Although Gerardus Mercator is credited with presenting a more "realistic" cartography than the mapmakers who precede him, the original map essentially differs from medieval antecedents only in what surrounds the geography it recreates – text boxes, astronomical diagrams, and royal crests in place of sea monsters and imaginary figures. Its "realism" is also characterized by distortion; the projection's "scale is distorted: areas farther away from the equator appear disproportionally large" because at the poles the scale becomes infinite.[4] For all its aid in navigation through its representation of loxodromes, or lines of constant course, this map transitions from reality to fiction as much as any other. We can observe this phenomenon in one of its contemporary forms – the "upsidedown map" – which places the Southern Hemisphere at the top and the North Pole at the bottom. While this version is no more "upside down" than the usual Mercator projection is "right side up" in any concrete way, it exposes the fictional nature of what we tend to see as a "real" geography because it looks "wrong" or "made up." Perhaps Dave Barry best articulated this phenomenon in his discussion of American history:

> Another important acquisition was made in 1867, when Secretary of State Seward Folly purchased Alaska for $7 million [...]. Alaska was originally a large place located way the hell up past Canada, but this proved to be highly inconvenient for mapmakers, who in 1873 voted to make it smaller and put it in a little box next to Hawaii right off the coast of California, which is where it is today.[5]

All maps present "the real" in a fictional mode by taking the three-dimensional and actual forms of space and turning them two-dimensional and flat; they all engage in acts of representation. Whether the Hereford Mappamundi or the Mercator Projection, maps construct worlds as much as they represent them; perhaps the medieval maps, with all of their awesome eccentricities, are more honest about what they can do. The Mundi of the Hereford map is its own universe, a planisphere with God and the angels above and humans exploring and making maps below, incorporating the act of cartography into the representation of the world so made. The earthly paradise sits at the apex of the geographical map. Inside the map's world are rivers, towns, and mountains, but also fantastical creatures and representa-

---

4   "Mercator Projection," *Encyclopedia Britannica Online*, at <https://www.britannica.com/science/Mercator-projection>, last accessed 28 July 2016.

5   Dave Barry, *Dave Barry Slept Here: A Short History of the United States* (New York: Balantine, 1987), 82.

tive objects of mythical history; the Golden Fleece sits alongside Issedones eating the corpses of their parents in Asia, while a pelican feeds its own young from its breast and the bird-headed Cicone lounges alongside the Oxus river in Samarkand. Fictional beings inhabit real places, blurring the boundaries between them, and geography is therefore profoundly tied not just to space but also to narrative, as the places' stories are represented along with their location. Along with an attempt to represent physical geography, these maps offer what Chet Van Duzer calls a "geography of the marvelous."[6] As David Woodward points out, "a map does not by its nature have to represent a cosynchronous scene but may be a many-layered cumulation of historical events as well as objects in geographical space."[7] He notes that "the *mappamundi* are the cartographic equivalent of narrative medieval pictures," and adds that they are "Seen as syncretic pictorial chronicles parallel to the textual chronicles from St. Jerome to Hartmann Schedel."[8] Therefore, in their representation of "real" space and the fictional world, medieval maps exist to tell a story, to "provide a visual narrative of Christian history cast in a geographic framework."[9]

In their representation of Christian history, medieval maps move beyond the simple confluence of reality and fiction to connect real and transcendent time. In *A World Transformed: Exploring the Spirituality of Medieval Maps*, Lisa Deam demonstrates the transcendent content of these geographical representations. Many medieval maps, she observes, "put Christ at the center,"[10] placing Jerusalem at the meeting of the three continents in the T–O formation, in which the T stands for the Cross, imposing that on the sphere (people never really thought the world was flat) of the known world. Aptly, she notes that medieval maps move "from world to worldview."[11] The maps do not just represent locations, they also embody the ideologies and values of the people who make them. In essence, the geography both stands for actual space and an interpretation of that space. While this may be more overt in the medieval maps, it is equally evident in more contemporary maps, which, for all their accuracy, also interpret space – by putting the North Pole at the top or Alaska in a box or North American and Europe at the center. The modern map "often provides the illusion that the objects in the landscape it provides are cosynchronous," and yet any experience of

---

6   Chet Van Duzer, *Sea Monsters on Medieval and Renaissance Maps* (London: British Library, 2013), 10.
7   David Woodward, "Reality, Symbolism, Time & Space in Medieval World Maps," *Annals of the Association of American Geographers* 75.4 (1985): 501–21 (511).
8   Woodward, "Reality," 514.
9   Woodward, "Reality," 519.
10   Lisa Deam, *A World Transformed: Exploring the Spirituality of Medieval Maps* (Eugene, OR; Cascade Publishing, 2015), 12.
11   Deam, *A World Transformed*, 19.

space happens temporally as it is passed through or by.[12] The time/space relationship is only one of the fictions of modern maps; they encode the values of those who make them as well as the stories of their creation, if only in echoes – after all, we are still calling the map of the world we see most often "the Mercator Projection." In their representational qualities – taking something real and reproducing it in a different form – all maps embody a confluence of time and space, of image and ideology, of fantasy and reality. Mohsen Mostafavi views the cartographic imagination as "a study of the importance of multiple representations," saying that "the representation of any topography depends on the purpose of the map and the story it is trying to tell."[13] Medieval mapmakers seemed to be aware of their work as an act of representation; Nicholas of Cusa, in his *Compendium*, comments, "As God created the world, the cartographer creates an image of the world."[14] As images and representations, maps, medieval or modern, embody far more than coastlines and geographical features; they offer a range of interpretable meanings, historical, religious, fantastical. It is no surprise, then, that Peter Turchi, in *Maps of the Imagination: The Writer as Cartographer*, calls his opening chapter "Metaphor: or, the Map." As he notably says, "To ask for a map is to say, 'Tell me a story.'"[15]

In its title, *The Quest* encodes a story. Quests, taking place in time and space (exterior and/or interior), are fundamentally narrative. Indeed, they are the narrative center of medieval romance; while not all romances are based on a quest, it is the major narrative form of the genre, both in its medieval and medievalist versions. Within romance, a quest "necessitates the projection of an Other, a *projet* which comes to an end when that Other reveals his identity or name."[16] Patricia Parker adds to this observation, that romance "is that mode or tendency which remains on the threshold before the promised end, still in the wilderness of wandering, 'error,' or 'trial' [...] when the posited Other, or objective, is the terminus of a fixed object [...] 'romance' is the liminal space before that object is fully named or revealed."[17]

---

12   Woodward, "Reality," 519.

13   Mohsen Mostafavi, "Forward: The Cartographic Imagination," in *Cartographic Grounds: Projecting the Landscape Imaginary*, ed. Jill Desimini and Charles Waldheim (New York: Princeton Architectural Press, 2016): 6–7 (6).

14   Nicholas of Cusa, *Nicholas of Cusa on Wisdom and Knowledge*, trans. Jasper Hopkins (Minneapolis, MN: J. A. Banning, 1996), 408.

15   Peter Turchi, *Maps of the Imagination: The Writer as Cartographer* (San Antonio, TX: Trinity University Press, 2004), 11. I would like to thank Philip Schochet for bringing this work to my attention.

16   Frédéric Jameson, "Magical Narratives: Romance as Gender," *New Literary History* 7 (1975): 135–63 (161). Quoted in Patricia A. Parker, *Inescapable Romance: Studies in the Poetics of a Mode* (Princeton, NJ: Princeton University Press, 1979), 4.

17   Parker, *Inescapable Romance*, 4–5.

Its obvious parallel is the quest for the Holy Grail, since in it the knights sought both the object and the salvation of Camelot and the Round Table, as well as personal redemption. Additionally, the grail knights are lost as they pursue their quest, leaving only Bors, Perceval, and Galahad to see who receives the true revelation, so that both the grail itself and the purest knight are essentially revealed at the end.

Another parallel, and one perhaps more at the forefront of the contestants' minds, is the quest in Tolkien's *Lord of the Rings*, in which the Fellowship forms to destroy the ring before it can destroy their world; each character therein receives his own revelation, whether Aragorn's taking responsibility and becoming king, Sam's image of the ideal garden, or Frodo's recognition of his own failure when he tries to claim the ring.[18] *The Quest* offers several similar *projets*: Verlox himself; the assembling of the Sun Spear; the identity of the traitor; the salvation of Everealm; and, ultimately, the identity of the "One True Hero" that only the quest itself will finally reveal.

Everealm itself functions as a liminal space outside the contestants' real lives, albeit sharing certain values with contemporary life; within Everealm, however, many traditionally liminal, in the sense of threshold, spaces emerge: the tunnels, forest, and paths the contestants take to get there, as well as the forest into which the main characters are driven when Verlox's forces besiege Castle Sænctum, and the Fates' temple, whose location in relation to everything else remains unclear. Indeed, the Fates themselves (Stephanie Buddenbrock, Florence Kasumba, and Mai Duong Kieu), a triumvirate of multi-ethnic, oddly dressed women (one wears a blue princess-gown, one has a large bird-totem in her hair, and the third wears a very contemporary-looking, beige, stretch-fabric dress) who seem to come from no identifiable period at all despite their classical origin and their medieval setting, add to the liminal quality of the narrative, serving to disconnect Everealm from its own "real" world (simultaneously definable as the medieval history of Burg Kreuzenstien, the historical Middle Ages, or the present in which the show takes place). It is only through traversing this liminal space that the finale can be achieved, and Parker's terminology of "error" and "trial" is made literal through the various reality-show challenges the paladins have to face to continue to take part in the quest.

The show never makes the connection between the paladins and pilgrimage, but that spatial echo remains in their identities as much as it does in their actions, and this echo is cartographic. Medieval pilgrims, after all, traveled through physical space on a spiritual journey; their transit and transformations are both charted on medieval maps and in medieval narrative.[19]

---

18   J. R. R. Tolkien, *The Lord of the Rings* (London: George Allen & Unwin, 1968). This is the first single-volume edition of the trilogy.
19   Matthew Paris's strip map will be discussed further later; however, one can certainly

This connection of the paladin and pilgrim resonates cartographically in two ways. Since, as Paladin Adria Kyle points out in one episode, "I used to sit at home reading books about this kind of thing; now I'm living it,"[20] we are reminded that in the Middle Ages, "there was a group for whom travel was strictly limited": the cloistered religious who remained in their monasteries while dreaming of pilgrimage, and for whom "this *perigrinato in stabilitate*' lent itself to a kind of geography of the soul, in which spiritual journeys led one to wonderful destinations. Seeking out relics and holy places, monastic dwellers consulted maps in their libraries."[21] This static cartography balances out an active one, after all:

> in medieval days pilgrims referred to prose "maps" used in conjunction with the other [visual] kind, that described shrines along the way, hostels, and the best places for changing shoes and donkeys. In the thirteenth century Matthew Paris drew strip maps of particular pilgrimage routes.[22]

Paris's map in the *Historia Anglorum* traces the pilgrimage route from England to Sicily, the embarkation point for the Holy Land; its distinct vertical format has significantly engaged cartographers and medieval historians.[23] That said, the function of strip maps is essentially narrative; their linearity creates both a temporal progression and an attention to the spatial features that surround it, making them useful to convey not just routes but also ways of experiencing those routes.[24] Made with utility in mind, the strip maps, which recall the old AAA Tryptich, a map designed to direct travelers through specific spaces with specific destinations, become a call to action. In a sense, instead of learning from observing the *mappamundi* with their instructive purposes, the paladins learn by following these strip maps, which lead them away from reading about heroism and valor toward experiencing

read the pilgrim's journey spatially and transformatively in Chaucer's *Canterbury Tales* or Dante's *Divine Comedy*. In Chaucer, the pilgrims traverse specific places on the map – Sittingbourne, Rochester, Bob-on-Weye – as they move toward the spiritual fulfillment of the Parson's Tale; in the *Commedia*, Dante the Pilgrim moves physically through Hell, Purgatory, and Paradise so that his soul can transform and understand "the love that moves the sun and other stars" (*Paradise* XXXIII, l. 145) Dante Alighieri, *Paradise*, trans. Mark Musa (Harmondsworth: Penguin, 1985), 394.

20 "Save the Queen," *The Quest*, Season 1, Episode 3, American Broadcasting Company, 14 August 2014.

21 Evelyn Edson, *Mapping Time and Space: How Medieval Mapmakers Viewed their World* (London: British Library, 1999), 14.

22 Turchi, *Maps*, 103

23 Matthew Paris, *Historia Anglorum*, Cambridge, Corpus Christi College Library, MS 26.

24 Alan M. MacEachren, "A Linear View of the World: Strip Maps as a Unique Form of Cartographic Representation," *The American Cartographer* 13.1 (1986): 7–25 (22).

it firsthand. Therefore, the paladins begin with the first paradigm and shift to the second, from using the maps to *replace* real experience to using them to direct their real experience.

To quest is to journey toward something, whether that journey is a spiritual pilgrimage to Santiago de Compostella or Canterbury or the Field of Dreams, or a voyage of exploration to find the New World (and Columbus' affection for Mandeville's *Travels* and *Tirant lo Blanc* suggests his own attachment to romance-type narratives[25]), or to seek out new life and new civilizations, or a search for Queen Guenevere or the Holy Grail or the best soup dumpling in New York. Quests traverse spaces literal and figurative; they transpose an interior geography on to an exterior one. Pilgrims seek enlightenment, whereas explorers seek land, whereas knights seek symbolic objects, but they all do this through travel. If medieval authors did not include literal maps in their romances the way so many writers of fantasy fiction (from J. R. R. Tolkien's map of Middle Earth to A. J. Cunder's maps of Farahdin and Halderon in *The Silver Talon* and *The Lost Road*) do, the physical paths and the narrative paths the text traverses reflect the knight's own interior path, as Philip Schochet demonstrates of Chrétien's *Chevalier au Lion*.[26] The quest story itself is a map.

In talking about the intersection of maps and the imagination, Turchi offers an unmedieval but still vivid example: "Emily Dickinson may not have gotten out much, but her poems create a universe."[27] In watching *The Quest* we may never leave our couches, but this show invites us to enter an alternative world. The pre-credit sequence for each episode is two-fold: it begins with producers explaining their idea and essentially breaking the "fourth wall," showing filming, Verlox's makeup being done, etc.; then the tone shifts to an animated drawing of a monk-like figure opening a book, whose first page is a map of Everealm, the country of twelve kingdoms in which the fantasy world of the show takes place, overlying pictures of the show's

---

25   Felipe Fernandez-Arnesto, *Columbus* (Oxford: Oxford University Press, 1991), 4. Fernandez-Arnesto discusses Columbus' engagement with the romances of his time, particular Joan Martell's *Tirant lo Blanc*, in which various modes of exploration are undertaken, especially to find the king of the Canary Islands. Fernandez-Arnesto also considers cartography in the early age of exploration, particularly its influence on Columbus' travels and their narrative.

26   Philip Schochet, "*Car ne vuel pas paler de songe / me de fable ne de mensonge*: Narrative Authority, Textual Truth, and the Discourses of Desire in the Romances of Chrétien de Troyes," Plymouth Medieval and Renaissance Forum, Plymouth State University, 25 April 2014. Schochet argues for the parallel of Yvain's quest and Chrétien's writing; that the story is not about the quest but functions as the quest, offering revelations about the act of writing and authorship that emerge as Yvain's revelations about his identity develop in the romance.

27   Turchi, *Maps*, 135.

action. The map resembles Tolkien's famous map of Middle Earth more than the Hereford Mappamundi, yet its "medievalness" is established through its appearance. Its color (yellowed), its hand (fake gothic), its language (fake Latin), its art, and its borders, which feature a sea-serpent breathing fire on a boat, all look medieval. In addition, and perhaps more vitally, its lack of relationship to the show's actual geography mirrors medieval maps' loose representations of space. Pages of the book continue to turn, shifting from map to text and back again, with scenes from the show rising through the "parchment," showing the layering of reality and fantasy in multiple ways.

The intersection of map and book connects cartography and narrative, but it also encodes the audience. When Van Duzer says, of medieval maps, "One subtle and undiscussed effect of the representation of sea monsters on maps is the empowerment of the viewer: the cartographer reveals on the surface of the waters creatures which are normally concealed in its depths, allowing the viewer to participate in a privileged and supernatural view of the world,"[28] he casts viewers as readers and the cartographer as an author who draws them into a world where the real (the ocean) reveals the fantastical underneath. The paladins, readers of medievalist fiction are brought into Everealm, a world both real and fantastical, and the viewers take their places as readers, or viewers, who are exposed to both the real and supernatural elements of this world through careful watching.

Mostafavi speaks of the "interrelationship between depiction and actualization," which he compares to "words – the tools of the novelist"[29]; the past medievalist fictions they have read, watched, and played provide context and behavioral maps for the paladins, essentially telling them what to do and how to act, once the fantasy becomes actualized. Consequently, the show becomes a map for its viewers, as we can see in the producer's post-show attempts to continue to engage the audience and coax a second season out of the network executives, a quest that ultimately failed. Medievalism becomes its own map. The show's narrative map offers a central geography (the story) interacting with the images on the edge (the challenges).

In *Image on the Edge*, Michael Camille, discussing maps, speaks about "the world at the edges of the word," and adds that during "the Middle Ages the edges of the known world were at the same time the limits of representation."[30] Noting that "the safe symbolic spaces of hearth, village or city were starkly contrasted with the dangerous territories outside, of forest, desert and marsh," he might well be speaking of Everealm, which contrasts the central "safety" of community, commonality, and shared goals with

28 Van Duzer, *Sea Monsters*, 10.
29 Mostafavi, "Forward," 9.
30 Michael Camille, *Image on the Edge: The Margins of Medieval Art* (Cambridge, MA: Harvard University Press, 1992), 14–15.

the dangerous individualism of the two challenges that led to banishment. In Camille's view, the edges are dangerous and powerful places, "spaceless places" where spirits were banished.[31] The banished paladins "joining the fates" in a whorl of smoke and becoming light-images in the arches of the medieval ruin surrounding the Fates' temple thus becomes highly evocative of these meaningful cartographic images.

The contrast of center and margin is echoed in the show's location. *The Quest* was filmed at Burg Kreuzenstein, a retrofitted castle outside of Vienna; on the grounds of a real medieval castle, the producers constructed a fictional medieval world. Given the incursions of the modern world, the characters and paladins could venture only so far – Burg Kreuzenstein sits only about forty minutes from Vienna, and the city is visible from its parapets.[32] Here the "safe center" is the fantasy Middle Ages, while the real world lurks menacingly at the margins, creating another geographical interplay of reality and fiction, if somewhat reversed. Various features point subtly toward Everealm's fictionality, such as the multi-racial character of its inhabitants, the intersection of old and new, and the anachronistic blending of objects from different medieval times and places. In what might be called true medievalizing spirit, all pasts are collapsed into a single past, the three Fates (called Karu, Talmuth, and Solas – names that sound like they come from the ancient Near East, not ancient Greece or medieval Europe) of classical mythology blending with a feudal society, medieval warfare mixing with challenges that employed some rather more modern architecture. The real place (Austria) standing for a fictional place (Everealm) mirrors the way in which the fictional narrative stands for the reality of the show's goals and values. Thus the medieval, ostensibly the fantasy, layered over the reality television genre, allows the two to blend into a fluid entity in which the values of one permeate the other. The physical quest becomes both real and fantastical, as its meaning functions in both the fantasy world (triumph over Verlox) and the real one (winning the show).

The palimpsest created through this overlay of reality and fiction, in which one blurred into the other, is both constructed by and reflective of medievalism itself. It is the essential tension between what is spatial, definable, and what is essentially a fantasy, a tension itself reflected in the afore-

---

31 Camille, *Image*, 16.
32 Burg Kruezenstein, <www.kreuzenstein.com>, last accessed 28 July 2016. The castle, which is often used for filming and has appeared in Ken Follett's *Pillars of the Earth* series, was constructed on the remains of a castle that was destroyed during the Thirty Years War. It was refurbished and rebuilt in the nineteenth century by Count Nepomuk Wilczek with money made in the Silesian coal mines, but constructed out of pieces of medieval castles purchased from all over Europe, making it an example of medievalism at its finest. In another medievalist connection, it is the titular home of the Lazarus Union Knighthood of Honor, an order founded in a leper hospital in Jerusalem during the Crusades.

mentioned medieval (and modern) maps that offer literal geography blended with an imaginative world. This tension is apparent in the use of space in the show itself; the traversal of real and imagined space happens in bringing the paladins to Everealm; once there, they are in essentially the same space each week.[33] Although the paladins are often shown running through the forest and undertaking various challenges, particularly the final one, what constitutes the literal space they traverse is never clear, and it often looks like they are walking the same paths they walk in previous episodes. Questing involves travel, yet their travel (apart from their fleeing Castle Sænctum into the forest and paying a visit to the Rana) mostly happens before the show begins. Thus they enter a somewhat enclosed narrative space, one that echoes the spaces of medieval romance where fictional worlds (such as Torrelore in *Aucassin et Nicolette* or the Kingdom of Görre in Chrétien's *Chevalier de la Charette*, or the Arthurian world of Chaucer's "Wife of Bath's Tale") appear to be enclosed spaces set off from the real worlds of the romances.

In these worlds, while many conventions of the "real" world (such as chivalry and courtesy) still apply, other rules and expectations are suspended or altered, so that Lancelot and Guenevere can carry on their love affair in the protected *locus amoenus* and Lancelot can battle Meleagant, or the King of Torrelore can be lying in bed after childbirth while the queen leads an army of women throwing rotten fruit and cheese. Everealm still values loyalty, heart, perseverance, and focus, as those qualities are often factors in the paladins' choice of whom to save and whom to banish, yet there are also magic "spy orbs," sun spears, fates, potions, crones, ogres, and frog people inhabiting the world.

Maps and geography play a series of roles in *The Quest*. The voice-over of the opening episode announces, "Two different worlds that have never been merged before are coming together. People are pulled out of their regular life into a world they've only imagined. It's a fantasy come to life" (*The Quest*, Episode 1). Opening in Chicago, San Francisco, and New York (worlds, the show points out, "far from Everealm"), contestants are chosen by means of scrolls that lead them "underground to the passage that separates their world from Everealm" (Q1).[34] They are "led through the dark cavern, along a mystical river, to meet the Fates who have summoned them" (Q1), thus traversing a spatial geography (we literally see them walking through a cavern and sailing along a river) as they move from the actual world into

---

33   I would like to thank A. J. Cunder for this observation about the way that space is essentially fictional, since the producers had to be limited to a restricted space, both for the convenience of filming and because modern Austria did not lie too far beyond the castle's walls.

34   "The Quest Begins," *The Quest*, Season 1, Episode 1, American Broadcasting Company, 31 July 2014. From here forward, quotations from *Quest* episodes will be cited in-text by episode number.

the imaginary one. Interestingly, this geography is not overly temporal –
while Everealm is clearly "medieval," there is no specific indication that the
paladins are going back in time. Once in Everealm, they must pass through
"the Marrwood, a perilous forest where all manner of mythical beasts lurk"
to meet Crio, the Dreamer, and steward of the castle (Jan Hutter), who
becomes their guide. Once they are out of the woods – both literally, as they
emerge into a field, and symbolically, as their task is revealed – the Castle
Sænctum rises in the distance.

This scene is potently medievalized; like all medieval questers, they must
pass through the forest that Corinne Saunders calls "the most evocative landscape of medieval romance,"[35] "at once attached to and separate from medieval
reality."[36] Of course the scene is also medievalized in its echo of that famous
medievalist text, *Monty Python and the Holy Grail*, in which Arthur and his
new knights gaze across a field at a castle and declare, "Camelot!" to which the
character Patsy offers, "It's only a model." However, *The Quest* resists pointing
out this analogy, leaving it to be discovered by the viewers.[37]

The paladins' traversal of space looks like they are trekking for miles, but
given the limits of true wilderness in the Rohrwald, they are probably not,
adding to the fictionality in the representation of place. The paladins meet a
wodwo in the forest who eats Crio's assistant, which unifies them as a group;
"We now know we have to work together so this never happens again," Shondo
Blades, a mixed-martial-arts fighter from Houston, declares (Q1). Maps feature
throughout this part of the episode; both the forest and the castle are shown
on paper before they emerge "in person." At the intersection between worlds,
the voice-over declares, "Here their true adventure begins." As Lina Carollo, a
school counselor from New Jersey, notes, "this is another world where things
that don't happen in the real world really happen here" (Q1).

After a somewhat vexed entry into the castle, the paladins are shown to
their rooms and encounter another map; the common room features a round
table, that potent Arthurian symbol, and while the camera does not dwell
on it for long, careful viewing shows it divided into the twelve kingdoms
of Everealm, each with its own "mark" or heroic quality. Eight of these
kingdom marks (leadership, dexterity, wisdom, strategy, observation, intel-
ligence, bravery, and strength) are awarded to individual winners of each
challenge as the show progresses; the final four kingdoms and their marks
are usurped by a change in the narrative two-thirds of the way through the
season, when the paladins, Queen Ralia XXIII,[38] Crio, and Sir Ansgar (the

---

35 Corinne Saunders, *The Forest of Medieval Romance* (Cambridge: D. S. Brewer, 1993), xi.
36 Saunders, *Forest*, xviii.
37 *Monty Python and the Holy Grail*, dir. Terry Gilliam and Terry Jones, 1975, DVD.
38 Queen Ralia's long numeral suggests a long dynastic history that is never revealed during
    the show.

head of the armies, and their trainer, played by Peter Windhofer) are forced to take to the forest again after Verlox invades Castle Sænctum.

The round table provides a map of the quest – not its outer geography, but its inner geography, the worldview without the world. A temporal symbol of the medieval past, it is also a map of the hero him- or herself. With each heroic characteristic representing a specific kingdom of Everealm, it creates a nexus between a physical space and an internal trait; the kingdoms are parts of the land just as the "marks" or qualities are parts of the heroic body, unified by both the table's shape and the hero's essential make-up. This is not *The Quest*'s only linking of spatial and interior geography. One of the first commands given to the paladins by the Fates, in voice-over, is "Find the pieces of the Sun Spear and your path will find you" (Q1). The sun spear, a mythical object that links these twelve paladins to the original twelve paladins of the (fictional) past, is, of course, the light that will drive out Verlox, the Darkness – a theme perhaps more reminiscent of the *Magic Flute* than medieval romance.

The present reenactment of a past history is fully embodied by these contemporary paladins, despite the reminder of how much medievalism is engaged through reenactment. Indeed, it is possible to conjecture that the contestants know their way around medievalist fantasy so well because of their past engagement in more traditional kinds of reenactments, such as renaissance fairs and fantasy cons. That said, the "path" on which it sets the current twelve is both exterior and interior. This motif, of course, is the motif of all quests, whether the search for the Holy Grail, or the pilgrimages from which our contestants draw their title. The paladins must repeatedly negotiate space as part of their challenges, whether it is finding the crone in the forest and then unlocking and traversing a series of doors to find the ingredients for the antidote to the poison that has nearly killed Queen Ralia or running through the forest locked inside iron gates in the Fates' challenge from Episode 5. In Episode 6, "A Traitor in Sænctum," the paladins discover pieces of a map in the cape of Herra, the traitor; challenged to assemble it to find any clues it might offer, Paladin Patrick Higgins declares, "I'm trying to find out if there's some deeper meaning to the map."[39] Their discovery that the map is incomplete and may be two different maps gets countermanded at the Fates' challenge. The three losing paladins must line up a series of nine swords so that a beam of light shines through their hilts (which all have open rings at the ends of their handles) on the place from which Verlox will attack. The map is complete, and, indeed, there are three copies, and any additional meaning is not revealed.

---

[39] "A Traitor in Sænctum," *The Quest*, Season 1, Episode 6, American Broadcasting Company, 28 August 2014.

The challenge that landed the three paladins in front of the Fates is itself spatial, as the paladins are asked to put on masks that allow them to see through the eyes of the "Eye of Sænctum," a falcon called back from the front lines to help them find seven "fire orbs" that the traitor has located inside the castle. The center of the episode seems to require the paladins' active engagement with the spaces of Everealm, perhaps because they are about to leave Camille's "safe spaces" and venture into the forest. Once they leave Castle Sænctum in the following episode, they must travel through the woods to Rana Village (populated by strange frog-people, right off the margins of medieval maps), negotiating pitfalls, prison, and dragons on the way, and then finally return through more woods to the castle for the ultimate show-down. The presence of the Rana (who entrap the paladins, the Queen, Crio, and Sir Ansgar) again reflects the ideologies of medieval maps, which negotiate between civilization and wildness, the world and its frightening and often magical boundaries.

The final challenge that determines the One True Hero is also spatial; the paladins must run from the Hall of the Fates into the woods to find a scroll (another map) that gives them their next direction; they then have to balance scales before navigating the woods again to come to the (biblical) Gates of Magog, a set of cellar doors that they have to lock using a chain in a particular pattern. The path then leads to a river, where the paladin must shoot an arrow into a target to lower a bridge that will take him or her back to the Fates, where he or she will reassemble the Sun Spear and, joined by all the other paladins, return to take on Verlox. The map, it turns out, is a map of the inside of the castle, showing the path the hero must take to save the queen and Crio and "stab" Verlox in the show's most overt special effect. Strikingly, unlike the show's other maps, this map is never shown on camera, although Lina, the winning paladin, is shown examining it with Sir Ansgar as she prepares to enter the castle while he uses the other paladins to create a diversion.

All three of the final challengers show the intersection of physical and mental geography as they set off on the final quest; Shondo's declaration that "The Game of Life is Chess not Checkers" reflects one kind of map, in which life is played out on a board; Lina's statement "the path is already laid out before me" as she enters the castle once again more overtly echoes the cartographic sentiment of the entire show.[40] For, if the obviously choreographed fight scene and the somewhat ridiculous defeat of Verlox remind viewers of the show's fictionality, the meaning that emerges from the ending transposes the events of the fictional past to the present. As the paladins receive a royal

---

40 "One True Hero," *The Quest*, Season 1, Episode 10, American Broadcasting Company, 11 September 2014.

farewell, Lina's voice-over declares, "Never give up on yourself. Never give up on your dreams. Be a dreamer" (Q10). Thus the worldview created by the world of the past transfers into the present; fantasy and reality once again intersect. As Turchi notes, "Now, as then, we recode great conflicts and meaningful discoveries. We organize information on maps in order to see our knowledge in a new way. As a result, maps suggest explanations; and while explanations reassure us, they also inspire us to ask more questions, consider other possibilities."[41]

The Quest's final meaning, the ending implies, is not that it is better to live in a medieval fantasy world than a real one, or that heroism only exists in a fantasy Middle Ages, or that a fantasy world allows different kinds of achievements than a real one. Instead it suggests that the two are unifiable; that the fantasy world of "dreams" can inhabit the margins of the real world and influence its reality just as the fantastical images on the Hereford Mappamundi exist as a part of its portrayal of the real world of human existence. In looking at maps like the NYCmap (pronounced "Nice Map" and unfortunately not currently available to the public), which attempts to be the most "perfectly accurate map that has ever been make of the entire City of New York and Everything in it," Turchi adds, "the map doesn't include everything, and of course it can never be finished."[42] Like so many medieval works before it, *The Quest* remains unfinished; despite a cliffhanger scene played over the closing credits, in which the evil vizier, whom the paladins have locked in prison, is visited by hands that untie his bonds, asking "What took you so long?" as the screen fades to black, the show has not been renewed, and the fate of Everealm, and therefore its narrative map, remains forever uncertain (Q10).

In an attempt to stimulate enough interest to revive the show, the producers took to social media, launching the "Project Hero" campaign, which challenged fans "to do something valiant, no matter how small, and then publish stories, videos, pictures, and artwork about their deeds on Twitter using #continuethequest and #beahero, all leading up to a Day of Heroes on October 23, 2014."[43] The producers noted that fans "have come together as a community wanting very much to keep the show going" because it "inspired them." Fans were "looking for something heroic to do [...] they're heroes in our eyes."[44]

41   Turchi, *Maps*, 11.
42   Turchi, *Maps*, 131.
43   Quest Project Hero, <https://www.facebook.com/events/1526135007630998/>, last accessed 29 July 2016. See also, Terry Flores, "*The Quest* Producers Launch Social Media Campaign to Save the Show," *Variety* (5 October 2014), <http://www.bostonherald.com/entertainment/television/television_news/2014/10/the_quest_producers_launch_social_campaign_to_save>, last accessed 28 July 2016.
44   Flores, "*The Quest* Producers." Some examples of people's acts of heroism posted on the Project Hero Facebook page include donating a horse to a riding center for handicapped

The producers added that fans were moved by the show's "family friendly themes, with its emphasis on heroic endeavors, teamwork and camaraderie – contestants decided who should stay and who should go based on their heroic qualities and the winner doesn't even receive a cash prize."[45] Producer Elise Doganieri noted, "no matter what happens, we believe in what we started and want to continue [...] we want to make a change in the world and in people and have a positive effect on everyone's lives."[46]

The show thus lives beyond its ending, not just because there is an unclosed strand of narrative, but because fans and producers attempt to map the fictional past of Everealm on the real present. The paladins are called to "Save Everealm," but the producers want to "make a change in the world" and "have a positive effect on everyone's lives," not by having the fans take the "fictionally literal" journey through the tunnels and forest to Everealm, but by using the paladins' narrative journey to create their own. Maps, Adam Gopnik notes, "look more like the time that made them than like the thing they were meant to show. We chart our cities, and we chart ourselves."[47] *The Quest*, for all its medievalizing, is a map of a contemporary consciousness. Just as it is possible to read medieval maps for a set of values, desires, and modes of instruction, viewers can see in the show a contemporary desire for meaningful action, a wish to engage the values attributed to the Middle Ages in medievalist fiction, as well as a desire to put them into action, to traverse space and time in body as well as mind. Essentially, *The Quest* shows a wish to turn fantasy into reality, although it also demonstrates the impossibility of really separating the two; just as a real map is ultimately a fiction, so, too, was the world of *The Quest*.

The awareness of the interplay of reality and fiction embodied in the show's credits did not dispel the desires it represented. Maps are, as Edward Tufte, one of the key figures in data visualization, says, "a cognitive art," designed to "represent the rich visual world of experience and measurement on mere flatland," and thus negotiate between the "complex, dynamic, multidimensional" world and "static, flat" paper.[48] As a result it is hardly surprising that they bring together so many elements of story-telling: narrative movement; past, present, and future; a set of values; and quests for meaning, external and internal. If mental mapping, the field of "interest not only to cartogra-

children, paying people's bills at grocery stores, donating clothes and furnishings, and food shopping for someone who needed it, even if it meant going without themselves: <https://www.facebook.com/photo.php?fbid=10205230017775121&set=gm.1526135280964304&-type=3&theater, last accessed 29 July 2016.
45 Flores, "*The Quest* Producers."
46 Fores, "*The Quest* Producers."
47 Adam Gopnik, "Street Furniture: The Most Complete Map of the City and Everything in it," *New Yorker* (6 November 2000). Qtd. in Turchi, *Maps*, 136.
48 Edward Tufte, *Envisioning Information* (Cheshire, CT: Graphics Press, 1990), 9.

phers, psychiatrists, psychologists, sociologists, and many others, including urban planners and architects" has shown that "a neighborhood, like a home, is a state of mind," then the *Quest* demonstrates that we each have a world inside us, a place in our minds that may not exist on a globe.[49] It is no accident, then, that the show's fictional world is called "Everealm," and the castle "Sænctum," since its ultimate message – constituted from the show and the fan response and the Project Hero campaign – is that Everealm is everywhere, and the "Sanctum" is the safe-place we make through our own acts of heroism. This creation calls attention to the multi-functionality of maps. If Everealm is everywhere, then we do not need a map to show us how to get there – at least, not a physical map, but perhaps something more like a medieval map – one like the round table in the paladins' common room or the map of Everealm itself that does not bear specific relationship to exterior geography but tells us a great deal about interior geography – its values and purposes. This may be why, as contemporary maps lose their geographic function with the advent of GPS technology, which, despite being overlaid on a map does not offer the observer the acts of interpretation and choice that the paper map does, their fascination does not continue to diminish.[50] Maps may no longer be necessary to get us from one place to another, and yet they continue to show us how we imagine and understand our world in a deeper sense. By traveling to Everealm, we are invited into a world transformed, where world and worldview become one.

[49] Turchi, *Maps*, 136–37.
[50] I am again indebted to A. J. Cunder for this keen observation, and for the reminder that the journey is only partially about the space traversed to get there.

Medievalisms of the Mind: Undergraduate Perceptions of the "Medieval" and the "Middle Ages"

Paul B. Sturtevant

Though there have been continuing academic debates on when the European world became and ceased to be medieval (and all the resulting implications of this periodization), in broad terms, when a scholar joins a *medieval* history department or attends a conference on *medieval* studies, it is reasonable to assume that they know approximately what the word means. However, the answer to the question of how non-medievalists define the term "medieval" (and its cousin, "Middle Ages") is significantly less clear. When it comes to popular perceptions of the medieval world, even this question, which comprises one of the most basic levels of popular mental medievalisms, has yet to be explored by academics with evidence stronger than theory, anecdote, or conjecture.

Seeking to answer the question "How do non-medievalists define the words 'medieval' and 'Middle Ages'?" is significant if medievalists aim to communicate fluently with those outside our disciplines. It is hoped (particularly for those scholars interested in the popular perception of the Middle Ages) that the popular definitions might tack close to the academic ones – and feared that they diverge wildly. However, this is a hope without empirical evidence. This article seeks to begin to rectify this deficiency. And as will quickly become clear, it does not – and cannot – provide a clear, definitive answer to the question of how non-medievalists define those most-important words in our field. Instead, this article has three complementary aims. First, it explains a methodology that can be used by scholars interested in medievalism to gather empirical evidence to help the field more thoroughly explore these (and related) questions. Second, it reports some of the findings of one study (undertaken by me at the University of Leeds) that explored this question among British young adults. Finally, by exploring that evidence, it reveals some of the complexity inherent in how individuals imagine the medieval. These individuals' definitions appear to lie somewhere between what a medievalist might hope and what they might fear about public perceptions of the medieval past.

Qualitative Methods

The study of public ideas, perceptions, and opinions is a central aspect of numerous disciplines: public policy, education, psychology, and sociology, among others. Together, these disciplines have built a significant methodological toolkit that can be easily adapted by the historian interested in studying public perceptions of the past. This adaptation has been most famously accomplished by the large-scale national surveys in the 1990s by Roy Rosenzweig and David Thelen (published in their *The Presence of the Past*), and more recently by Jocelyn Létourneau and the team of scholars behind the *Canadians and Their Pasts* project.[1] However, despite the impressive scope of these national works, large-scale survey-based methodologies are neither the only, nor arguably the best, method for exploring the public understanding of the past. First is a practical concern: few scholars in the humanities today receive anything like the significant grants that fueled these projects. Happily, studies can be accomplished on a far smaller scale. The data a smaller-scale study can produce may be not only valid, but its narrower scope can delve more deeply into the topics only cursorily addressed by an omnibus study. Small-scale social-science-based studies are not only well within the reach of most scholars, but, if done well, can offer richer, more nuanced data than national surveys.

There is a common misperception that all social science-based research involves deploying surveys to hundreds of participants and using complex statistical models in order to make sense of the resulting data. This structured, *quantitative* approach is the method used in the *Presence of the Past* and *Canadians and Their Pasts* studies. However, that approach has significant limitations: in order to achieve statistical significance, the amount of time spent with, and data gathered from, each individual is relatively small.[2] Furthermore, surveys inherently ask questions that have been structured according to the researcher's way of understanding the topic at hand, as well as their worldview. And, in order to ensure that each individual is compa-

[1]   Roy Rosenzweig and David Thelen, *The Presence of the Past: Popular Uses of History in American Life* (New York: Columbia University Press, 1998). Margaret Conrad et al., *Canadians and their Pasts* (Toronto: University of Toronto Press, 2013).
[2]   For an introductory exploration of the differences between qualitative and quantitative social sciences methods, see Arthur Asa Berger, *Media and Communication Research Methods: An Introduction to Qualitative and Quantitative Methods* (Los Angeles: Sage, 2013), 26–29.

rable to all the others, all of these questions must be exactly the same. This means that the respondent is locked into the researcher's frame of reference, which may or may not correspond with their understanding of the question – or the world. This can be particularly problematic when approaching questions – such as "What does the word 'medieval' mean to non-specialists?" – for which there may be no clear-cut answers.

By contrast, the somewhat-lesser-known branch of social science research methodologies takes a more open-ended, discursive approach. These *qualitative* methods include individual and group interviews, open-ended questionnaires, and ethnographic observations.[3] By contrast with quantitative methods such as surveys, qualitative methods tend to gather much more data from fewer research participants. It is not uncommon to see PhDs or major research projects conducted with ten research subjects – or even fewer. Those ten may be selected because they have a particularly interesting perspective on the topic being explored. Sometimes, only ten are used because of the amount of time spent with each subject. But a central tenet of qualitative research is that it is *not* striving for the same kind of statistical generalizability – where it can be said that the *same proportion* of people in the wider world believe or act the same as the people in the study – that surveys do. The only application to broader populations that can usually be drawn is to say that some *unknown* proportion of the wider populace likely agrees with what the participants may say. Even then, that misses the point of qualitative research. As Nahid Golafshani describes, "Unlike quantitative researchers who seek causal determination, prediction, and generalization of findings, qualitative researchers seek instead illumination, understanding, and extrapolation to similar situations."[4] Qualitative research is focused on subjective experience and meaning-making for individuals, as Sharan B. Merriam notes:

> Rather than determining cause and effect, predicting, or describing the distribution of some attribute among a population, we [qualitative researchers] might be interested in uncovering the meaning of a phenomenon for those involved. Qualitative researchers are interested in how people interpret their experiences, how they construct their worlds, and what meaning they attribute to their experiences.[5]

---

3   For those interested in learning more about, and possibly conducting their own, qualitative research, an excellent introductory guide is Gary D. Shank, *Qualitative Research: A Personal Skills Approach* (Upper Saddle River, NJ: Pearson, 2006).
4   Nahid Golafshani, "Understanding Reliability and Validity in Qualitative Research," *The Qualitative Report* 8.4 (2003): 600, <http://www.nova.edu/ssss/QR/QR8-4/golafshani. pdf>, last accessed 8 August 2016.
5   Sharan B. Merriam, *Qualitative Research: A Guide to Design and Implementation* (San Francisco: John Wiley & Sons Inc., 2009), 5.

As such, for exploring questions about personal interpretations of the medieval past – how they spring from subjective experiences, and are made meaningful as a part of a larger worldview – qualitative methods are perfect. Moreover, the method of qualitative data analysis may come far more naturally to historians and literature scholars. By contrast with the statistical models produced by quantitative researchers, qualitative data is analyzed using more familiar methods: close reading of textual sources and the thematic analysis of multiple sources.

The Middle Ages in the Twenty-first-century Mind

Study and its Methodology

In 2008 and 2009, I conducted a study of the public understanding of the Middle Ages using qualitative methods.[6] The research questions for this study were broadly conceived, reflecting the lack of empirical data that had been produced on the subject up until that point. The study also relied on the theories of constructivism, a key school of thought in the socio-logical approach to the questions of knowledge and learning. Constructivist learning theories, broadly put, posit the idea that "all knowledge depends on the mental constructs developed by each individual."[7] This was further refined by the theories of Lev Vygotsky, as well as the work of Peter L. Berger and Thomas Luckmann, who proposed a constructivist "sociology of knowledge." They argued that not only all knowledge – and even reality – is constructed, but it is entirely dependent upon an individual's socio-cultural circumstances. This applies both to broad circumstances, "What is 'real' to a Tibetan monk may not be 'real' to an American businessman,"[8] and to specific moments in time. Knowledge and reality are constructed moment-by-moment by individuals through, rather than independent of, social inter-action. The ramifications of this in terms of the specific question of the *Middle Ages in the Twenty-first-century Mind* project – that of popular under-standing of the medieval world – meant that the research method chosen was small-group interviews. The environment of a group interview can, of course, influence how an individual might think or react; this is as much a

---

6   This study was conducted under a human subjects review, University of Leeds Faculty Research Ethics Committee reference number: AREA 08/015, approved 2 December 2008.
7   Nathalie Bulle, *Sociology and Education: Issues in Sociology of Education* (Bern: Peter Lang, 2008), 38.
8   Peter L. Berger and Thomas Luckmann, *The Social Construction of Reality: A Treatise in the Sociology of Knowledge* (New York: Doubleday, 1966), 2.

reflection of reality as a research limitation. Truth and knowledge are often decided discursively, and this research reflects that reality.

There are a number of methodological approaches to take when conducting qualitative interviews and analysis. This study employed an Interpretive Phenomenological Analysis (IPA) approach. In IPA, the goal of the researcher is not focused on having the participant answer a set of specific pre-scripted questions, but instead represents an exploration of the experience of the participant *as led by the participant*. In order to accomplish this, the interviewer asks broad, open-ended questions (in the case of the part of the study discussed below, "What does the word 'medieval' mean to you?"). Follow-up questions are only to ask the interviewees for more details about their previous responses.

At the heart of the IPA method is the idea that participants should define their experience on their own terms (and in their own words) as freely as possible. This method attempts to remove the group moderator from the interview as much as possible by having him or her act only as a sounding board to encourage participants to talk. Since they are fundamentally participant-led, IPA interviews often range widely over a number of topics. This reflects the different – sometimes vastly so – intellectual world of each participant or group.

Analysis of the resulting transcripts are similarly exploratory. As Latham puts it, "The results are not known in advance nor tested in the study, but must emerge from the interview transcripts, constructed in an iterative way from the voices of the participants."[9] Researchers closely read the transcripts of the interviews and identify similar themes and stories explored. These are then compared to and contrasted with those of the other individuals, sessions, and groups in the study. On the basis of this evidence, the researchers construct theories about how these themes and stories are expressions of broader worldviews.

The Study Methodology

My study had nineteen participants, all undergraduates at the University of Leeds. This study was not an in-class study, but recruited student volunteers from across campus. As a result, the participants included representatives of all three undergraduate University year-levels and across a diverse sampling of University schools and disciplines. In a demographic screening questionnaire given to all participants prior to the study, all participants self-identified as English, and none indicated that they had studied the Middle Ages above GCSE level (ages 15–16).[10] In addition, none had been educated

---

9   K. F. Latham, "What Is 'The Real Thing' in the Museum? An Interpretive Phenomenological Study," *Museum Management and Curatorship* 30.1 (2015): 2–20 (3).
10   GCSE stands for General Certificate of Secondary Education, a level of British secondary school education typically completed at the age of 15 or 16.

outside of England. Religion and race/ethnicity were not accounted for, nor was socio-economic status.

The broader purpose of this study was to better understand the effects that viewing films about the Middle Ages would have on the participants' ideas about the medieval past. As such, on the demographic questionnaire, all participants indicated that they had seen at least three medieval films before (selected from a list of twenty-five of the most popular ones). While their movie-viewing habits are not relevant to the discussion in this article, it does indicate that they all had at least a basic exposure to popular cinematic medievalisms. This may indicate at least a casual experience of the medieval world in, and through, popular culture.

These nineteen participants were interviewed in four groups. All of the groups had between three and six participants, and each met three times. Each of the twelve sessions had three parts:

1. an initial participant-led discussion about their ideas about various topics in the Middle Ages,
2. a screening of a medieval film, and
3. a discussion of their understanding of the film and how it related to the ideas they had expressed in the pre-film discussion.

All of the data in this article were derived from each group's pre-film discussions on the first of their three sessions, prior to having seen any of the films.[11] In the discussion below, each participant has been assigned a pseudonym. In the reporting of the results below, I include excerpts from the transcripts of the participants' statements verbatim. *Sic* is implied in all quotes below. Despite their use of colloquialisms and sometimes halting language – exploring a difficult topic through conversation – it is important *not* to discount the validity, value, and importance of the substance of their understandings.

Middle Ages or Medieval?

At the beginning of the session, participants were given a word-association exercise. This was intended both to get the participants thinking about the subject and to give them something they could refer back to if the conversation flagged. The exercise would also be another source of data, one which would be based upon their opinions alone (rather than influenced by the group). For this exercise, they were given five minutes to write on a blank piece of paper every word they associated with the Middle Ages. However,

---

11   For further explanation of the study methodology, see Paul B. Sturtevant, "Based on a True History?: The Impact of Popular 'Medieval Film' on the Public Understanding of the Middle Ages" (PhD Thesis, University of Leeds, 2010), 49–63.

at this point, a question arose: should the page be labeled with the word "medieval", or the words "Middle Ages"?

At first thought, the two terms may seem synonymous. And, technically, they are; medieval was a mid-nineteenth-century neologism derived from the Latin *medium aevum*, meaning "middle ages."[12] But, are these terms synonymous in their contemporary usage, or do they evoke subtly – or widely – divergent ideas? Considering that IPA interviews are meant to allow participants the freest rein possible, if they were to be asked only about one term, would that steer or frame the conversation in an unforeseen direction?

With regard to the technical definitions of these synonyms, the first entry of the *Oxford English Dictionary* entry for Middle Ages concerns "middle age" (as in: the period of life – middle-aged).[13] The second definition is more pertinent:

> 2. *the Middle Ages* n. (also (now rare) *the Middle Age*); The period in European history between ancient and modern times, now usually taken as extending from the fall of the Roman Empire in the West (c500) to the fall of Constantinople (1453) or the beginning of the Renaissance (fourteenth cent.); the medieval period; esp. the later part of this period, after 1000.[14]

While medievalists have debated the specifics of every detail of the periodization of the Middle Ages (which the *OED* later goes on to reference), the *OED* is reasonably straightforward: a certain place (Europe) between certain dates (c. 500 to either 1453 or some point in the fourteenth century). Compare this with the definition of the word "medieval"; the *OED* offers three distinct definitions (and more that are considered obsolete):

1.   a.   Of or relating to a period of time intervening *between* (periods designated as) *ancient and modern*; *spec.* of, relating to, or characteristic of the Middle Ages. [...]

12   David Matthews argues that the word "medieval" was first popularized in scholarly circles by Thomas Fosbroke starting about 1817. That being said, it does not necessarily mean earlier speakers did not have an adjectival term for "Middle Ages" – they simply used "of the Middle Ages", or terms like "gothic" and "feudal". David Matthews, "Middle," in *Medievalism: Key Critical Terms*, ed. Elizabeth Emery and Richard Utz (Cambridge: D. S. Brewer, 2015), 141–47 (144–45).

13   Matthews makes a compelling case for a link between the concept of "middle aged" and "Middle Ages," particularly as an early biological metaphor for the life of the Church; during the Middle Ages, the Church was middle-aged. Matthews, "Middle," 143–44.

14   "middle age, n. and adj." *OED* Online. June 2016. Oxford: Oxford University Press, <http://www.oed.com/view/Entry/118142?redirectedFrom=middle+ages>, last accessed 8 August 2016.

      3. *colloq.* a.   Exhibiting the severity or illiberality ascribed to a former
                  age; cruel, barbarous.[15]
           b.   *U.S.* **to get medieval**: to use violence or extreme meas-
                  ures *on*, to become aggressive.[16]

The first definition is as simple as the definition of the Middle Ages, except in adjectival form. However, the fact that the word "medieval" is an adjective allows it to be used more naturally (than the somewhat laborious "of the Middle Ages") to describe something similar to, but not self-evidently from, the period. Thus, the word "medieval" can be used to describe objects, concepts, or actions that evoke an idea of various aspects of the period, rather than those from the period itself. And this is where the subsequent definitions arise. Take, for example, the oft-derided chestnuts "medieval torture" and "medieval plumbing." It hardly matters that torture techniques became more sophisticated and widely used during the Early Modern period, or that some aspects of medieval plumbing were quite effective. Referring to someone or something as medieval immediately evokes backwardness, brutality, or idiocy. From this arises another common phrase: "practically medieval". The medieval world stands as an iconic locus for pre-modern barbarity.

As a result, use of the word "medieval" has outstripped the phrase "Middle Ages" in our language, as can be seen when an nGram graph is made of the two terms. Based upon its book-digitization project (which not only scans books, but counts every word in them), Google has developed a tool that shows how frequently a word, or short string of words, has been found in print over time. A simple graph, which Google calls an nGram, can then be made from these data, which shows how often that word has been used as a percentage of all words used in a particular year. This provides an empirical – if simplistic – way to begin to explore the evolution of language. David Matthews notes that "the adjective 'medieval' was first used in print around 1817, appeared sporadically in the 1820s, and was standard in the 1830s."[17] As can be seen in the nGram in Figure 1, Google's project picks up on the word's use at this point in the mid-nineteenth century. The word "medieval" then shows a significant upswing in usage in the early twentieth century, outstripping the phrase "Middle Ages" in the 1930s. Today, the word "medieval" is used in print approximately 2.5 times as often as the phrase "Middle

---

[15]   Definition 1b. and 2 are obsolete.
[16]   Definition 3a derives its origin from the 1994 film *Pulp Fiction*. "medieval, adj. and n."
      OED Online. June 2016. Oxford: Oxford University Press, <http://www.oed.com/view/
      Entry/115638?redirectedFrom=medieval>, last accessed 8 August 2016.
[17]   Matthews, "Middle," 141.

Ages."[18] If "medieval" is the more-used term, it stands to reason that it may be the more versatile.

However, this nGram tells us nothing about what people mean when they use these words, or how they may differ. So, the question of what differences there may be in the usages of these similar terms became part of this study. For the word-association exercise, each participant was given *two* sheets: one with "medieval", and one with "Middle Ages". In each group, half the participants were given the "medieval" sheet first, and half "Middle Ages". Each individual then completed the exercise again with the other term. The group then discussed what they wrote on their sheets, the relative importance of the words they wrote to their perception of what these terms meant to them, and whether they felt there were differences between them.

Results: Defining Medieval, Middle Ages
Similar to the *OED*, most participants in this study had distinct, but intersecting, understandings of these two terms. However, at first, two participants had difficulty seeing any distinction between them. When first asked to write a word-association sheet for the term "Middle Ages,", having already completed one for "medieval", Emma hesitated: "I don't really know the difference." Sean also had difficulties: "I didn't really find any sort of difference between 'medieval' and 'Middle Ages'."

Most of the others did not share their hesitation. Each of the four groups of participants independently developed definitions of "medieval" and "Middle Ages". These independently generated definitions were remarkably similar to those developed by the other groups, barring subtle differences in nuance and emphasis. As a result, these definitions are likely to be recognized or replicated by others in their peer group.

History and Legend
For these groups, the primary distinction between the terms "medieval" and "Middle Ages" rested along the line between fantasy and history. Almost all participants said the term "Middle Ages" refers to a period of real history, whereas "medieval" refers to a setting for fantasy and legend. John said:

I feel like "medieval" refers to something which is more existing today. So more like a retrospective view. And it also links to a bit more sort

18   This chart takes into account all varying capitalizations of both words. It does not take into account the alternate spellings "mediaeval" or "mediæval", which, when included, cause the adjective to outstrip the noun in about 1891. Figure 1 was used as-is because, with the current iteration of the software, case-insensitivity and multiple-word combinations cannot be accomplished simultaneously. The full data set and graph can be found at <https://goo.gl/r9e6oK>.

of fantasy, which people built up to a more fantasy medieval stuff. But "Middle Ages", to me, is a much more official term given to a period, the actual period of time.

John's observation relates closely to the observations about the adjectival use of the term "medieval" above, which can impart a retrospective, nostalgic connotation. Participants in other groups echoed John's assessment, saying, "'medieval' I associate [with] legends rather than true history," and "'Middle Ages' I've thought more along the lines of the Royal Armouries and like, history stuff whereas, like, medieval ones I've thought of like, fairy tales and legends and King Arthur." This broad association of "medieval" with fantasy and "Middle Ages" with history had a number of resultant effects upon the participants' understandings and interpretations of these terms.

Many participants limited the term "medieval", in geographical terms, to Great Britain alone, whereas they applied "Middle Ages" to a wider geography. They often did this based on a sense that, being more historical, "Middle Ages" was more geographically diverse, whereas their familiarity with British legends – having been raised in the UK – caused them to be more closely associated with "medieval".

Some also added a moral dimension to their definitions. They commonly described the Middle Ages as seeming worse than medieval. "Middle Ages", to them, carried connotations of poverty, filth, barbarism, and oppression. Chloe called the era evoked by the words "Middle Ages" "more primitive" than the one evoked by "medieval". When describing their word associations with "Middle Ages", Stephen and Justin said:

Stephen: Well, at the top [rank of their typology of "Middle Ages"] we have disease, basically. We just associate it with disease, general unpleasantness. And then we've got unrest and punishment underneath that, so pretty usual.
Justin: Yeah, "medieval" is essentially more focused on the glamorous type things where this ["Middle Ages"] is more on the streets and it being kind of horrible and mangy basically.

The fact that Stephen calls his focus on disease, unrest, and punishment "pretty usual" only adds emphasis to his idea that this is a broadly held cultural belief. And, at least among these groups, he was not wrong; there were many other responses from all of the groups in this vein: "For 'Middle Ages' we had [...] all the nasty kind of things"; "[when] I thought [about] the Middle Ages, I think of dirtier, smellier people than 'medieval'"; "'Middle Ages' I just thought was really backwards and dirty," and "with 'Middle Ages' I put down like mud and dirt first."

By contrast, the word "medieval" more commonly attracted romantic connotations. Jess thought "medieval" referred to a time where "it's all sort of party-ish and like they're having feasts and has got decent clothes." Elizabeth, Emma, and Catherine also had an animated exchange about medieval clothing:

Catherine: [When I think of medieval costume
Emma: Medieval, yeah.][19]
Catherine: Is like the big flowing dresses of the rich people and the big headdresses=[20]
Elizabeth: =But with the Middle Ages I put down like mud and dirt first.

Other examples include: "for 'medieval' we had more, like, romanticized, like monsters and banquets, fighting, jousting, that kind of area," "['medieval'] was all about like, knights and castles and stuff," and "'medieval' was more like, grand." This sense of 'medieval' indicating the bright, cheery vision of the Middle Ages directly contrasts with the *OED*'s definition – which ascribes barbarity and backwardness to "medieval" in both its third definition and the *Pulp Fiction* definition. Thus, "Middle Ages" evoked an image of barbarism, dirt, poverty, and disease, while "medieval" had more romantic connotations of aristocratic adventure, grand feasts, and lavish costume, owing to an association with British legends and the fantasy genre. Though contradictory, both definitions exist simultaneously in participants' minds without any seeming cognitive dissonance.

Two Visions of the Middle Ages
Several scholars have identified the two images mentioned by the participants (of the jolly-fantastical and dark-historical) when constructing taxonomies of popular medievalisms. However each scholar describes these images somewhat differently, and none corresponds exactly with the definitions put forward by the participants. For example, for the dark vision, Umberto Eco describes one of his famous "ten little Middle Ages" as:

The Middle Ages as a *barbaric* age, a land of elementary and outlaw feelings [...] they are also the Middle Ages of early Bergman. The same elementary passions could exist equally on the Phoenician coasts or in the desert of Gilgamesh. These ages are Dark par excellence [...]. With only a slight distortion, one is asked to celebrate, on this earth of

---

[19]   Square brackets used across two lines in the transcripts indicate that two participants were talking at the same time.
[20]   The equals sign in the transcripts indicate that one participant interrupted another.

virile, brute force, the glories of a new Aryanism. It is a shaggy medievalism, and the shaggier its heroes, the more profoundly ideological
its superficial naïveté.[21]

This description corresponds roughly to the second item in David Williams's
taxonomy of popular depictions of the period:

> Whatever the purported date, these Ages are dark, dirty, violent,
> politically unstable or threatening. Here are *The War Lord*, *Conan
> the Barbarian*, and Lang's Nibelungs and Huns. These are the ages of
> Bergman, and of Richard Fleischer's *Vikings* despite the hearty jollity
> of its heroic violence.[22]

Whereas Andrew Elliott calls it:

> the world of barbarity and squalor in which dark forces sweep unchecked
> through defenseless villages, storm monasteries and ransack their way
> into the annals of history. It is the world of superstition and religious
> zeal, too [...] and we know – thanks to years of conditioning – what
> to expect from the dark primitivism of the Middle Ages.[23]

Elliott is particularly astute in highlighting the social-cognitive element
of these understandings and expectations of the Middle Ages. Generation
after generation has been conditioned what to expect when they encounter
the Middle Ages – a process that begins in early childhood. Most of the
participants in this study had been conditioned to expect exactly that: they
felt the term "Middle Ages" *specifically* referred to the unpleasant vision of
the period. They focused on a handful of interrelated key aspects of this. To
them, the Middle Ages denoted a time rife with war, violence, poverty, and
social inequity; people of this time were unclean, they were unhealthy, and
their governments were autocratic and oppressive.

One of the primary elements that many participants ascribed to the
Middle Ages was warfare. This gives credence to Andrew Lynch's bold assertion that "War lies at the heart of contemporary medievalism [...] the post-
medieval is not as strongly identified with war and fighting as the Middle
Ages are."[24] However, though they cited warfare and violence as important

---

21 Umberto Eco, "Dreaming of the Middle Ages," in *Travels in Hyperreality: Essays*, trans.
    William Weaver (London: Picador, 1987), 68.
22 David Williams, "Medieval Movies," *The Yearbook of English Studies* 20 (1990): 1–32 (10).
23 Andrew B. R. Elliott, *Remaking the Middle Ages* (Jefferson, NC: McFarland & Company,
    Inc., 2010), 1.
24 Andrew Lynch, "Medievalism and the Ideology of War," in *The Cambridge Companion*

in terms of their understandings – and easily described iconic features of warfare in the Middle Ages (swords, castles, etc.) – they very rarely described warfare in the Middle Ages in any detail, and had little concept of what it *actually* entailed. Katy gave a rare exception: to her, the salient difference between modern and medieval war was, "it was much more about manpower and horses rather than the actual science and bombs that they have now." Though she has a valid point (as the mechanization of warfare has led to a less-personal, more-technological approach to battle), to understand medieval warfare as entirely unscientific is also not correct. Katy's statement likely sprang from the larger idea that the Middle Ages were *wholly* unscientific. Since the Middle Ages occurred before the scientific revolution (and was situated, in the popular imagination, between two ages of scientific exploration), this has led to a common misunderstanding: that medieval people were universally unthoughtful, even stupid. When taken to its logical extension, this dovetails with the idea that medieval people were barbaric, or were more ruled by their base desires. At the extreme, this might lend a person to think of them as less than human.

When confronted with the term "Middle Ages", participants also thought of a large social divide between the landed rich and the rural poor. John listed all the types of people who lived in the Middle Ages: "all the kings and queens, knights, jesters, and blacksmiths and other poor lives." To John, the Middle Ages not only lacks a middle class but lacks any sort of social stratification outside the monarchy and military aristocracy at the apex and "blacksmiths *and other* poor lives" at the bottom (with "jesters" possibly as an aberration, or linked with the *milieu* at the social apex). Some expressed that this social system was inherently unfair or oppressive, and that the monarchy regularly abused their power. For example, Stephen glibly defined a king as: "a man in a palace who has people killed on a whim." Jane felt that the Middle Ages bore "the idea of, like having absolute monarchy rule, that, like whatever the king or queen says goes and nobody questions it." She distinguished this from any non-royal governing body, which, to her, would only fit in more-recent history: "if you had a film where it was talking about the government or, some sort of ruling [...] body who wasn't the king or queen you wouldn't think of it as sort of, going back to medieval times, you'd think of it as fairly recent history." To her, medieval government *without* monarchy is anathema; representative government, even the concept of a "government" at all, is a defining feature of modernity. Stephen and Justin also saw the Middle Ages as having this social paradigm:

to Medievalism, ed. Louise D'Arcens (Cambridge: Cambridge University Press, 2016), 135–50 (135).

Stephen: And also I think you, when you think Middle Ages you
             kind of think peasants and having, having kind of a lower
             class type thing, and then having a higher class which is a
             monarchy, you know knights and that kind of thing=
Justin: =we've probably got more down [on the word-associations
             page], the social conditions for the peasants […] than
             thinking about the social conditions for the knights and
             the kings and barons and what have you. For some reason
             when I think of the Middle Ages I think of the streets, you
             know of somewhere which is, you know, dirty and you've
             got peasants running around in markets and things like
             that.

Other participants routinely identified the Middle Ages with the rural poor
(who they referred to as peasants or serfs) more than the urban poor, the
working class, or even the rich: "[I] think of the agricultural kind of life […]
there's no indu- like, industry's a recent thing so, think about the hierarchy
in terms of that. The peasants and landown- like peasant and landowner
kind of balance," and also, "I almost put down sort of farming and self-
sufficiency, but I checked myself 'cause I thought 'no' because it was the
peasants [who] did do all the work." The rural life that evoked here is not the
collectivist idyllic medievalism of William Morris, but an image of crushing
rural oppression and abuse.

Dirt and Disease
Disease was the most-frequent response to the "Middle Ages" word-association exercise, with over half of the participants citing it. Jess said: "when
I thought of the Middle Ages, I think of dirtier, smellier people than in
medieval, so I sort of wrote serfs down, and like poor people, and farmers
which I didn't write down for medieval." This focus on the dirtiness and
smelliness of the Middle Ages is common in popular interpretations of the
Middle Ages – so much so that Tison Pugh has labeled dirt "the sine qua
non of much 'medieval' film-making," and claimed that its omnipresence in
medieval films "requires exploration and explanation for how it contributes
to our always imperfect understanding of history."[25]
    In tandem with this ubiquity of dirt in medieval film, it has become
generally accepted (and generally known) that medieval people (unlike their
Roman predecessors) did not bathe regularly nor did they have internal
plumbing. The Jorvik Viking Centre, in York, UK, plays upon this common

25 Tison Pugh, "Queer Medievalisms: A Case Study of *Monty Python and the Holy Grail*,"
    in *The Cambridge Companion to Medievalism*, 210–23 (222).

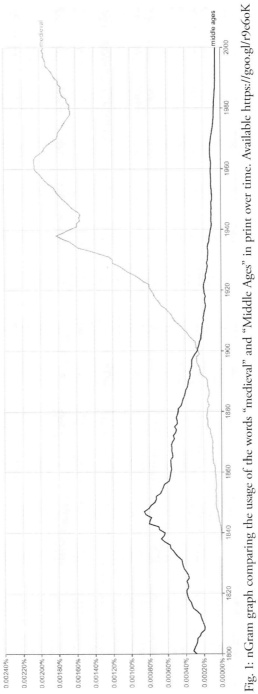

Fig. 1: nGram graph comparing the usage of the words "medieval" and "Middle Ages" in print over time. Available https://goo.gl/r9e6oK

idea of the Middle Ages as a smelly place by featuring in its animatronic Viking village a recreated "tenth-century urban odour," as described by Matt Elton:

> It must be the smell that most people remember after visiting the Jorvik Viking Centre. That's certainly the case for me, and a decade on from my first visit to York's Viking museum, I was looking forward to seeing if my nostrils would be wrinkled to quite the same extent by the tenth-century urban odour that they have conjured up. I'm delighted to report that they were.[26]

As a result of so much perceived not-bathing and resultant stinking, participants felt that disease was rife and life expectancy low. One of the categories John and Jess invented for their definition of "Middle Ages" was hygiene, or its lack: "a low life expectancy, as a result of the hygiene and germs." Mark was particularly condescending in his views of medieval medicine as he sarcastically described: "high infant mortality, [...] no painkillers and antibiotics which were two real cripplers of middle-aged medicine. And, I just had dirt down [...] because they hadn't discovered the wonders of washing your hands before delivering a baby." The implications latent in his ideas are, again, that medieval people were intellectually inferior. This smug technological superiority over the Middle Ages has become a common trope of stories that feature time travel to the Middle Ages, where time-travelers often assert their technological superiority over the ignorant medievals. This began with Mark Twain's *A Connecticut Yankee in King Arthur's Court*, which satirically presents a modern man colonizing the medieval past with his technology, with disastrous results.[27] The protagonist Ash in the film *Army of Darkness* is another iteration of the *Connecticut Yankee* trope: a modern idiot-made-godlike by his technology – allowing him to assume authority over the medieval. He asserts the superiority of his shotgun in the most patronizing of ways: "Alright you primitive screwheads, listen up! You see this? This ... is my boom-stick!" The time-traveler protagonists in Michael Crichton's *Timeline* (both the book and film adaptation) all fall victim to medieval barbarity, and only survive owing to their scientific ingenuity.[28] This way of thinking about the past relies upon and reinforces a popular Whiggish idea of progress: the world

26   Matt Elton, "Jorvik Viking Centre, York," *BBC History Magazine Online*, 19 March 2013, <http://www.bbchistorymagazine.com/visit/jorvik-viking-centre-york>, last accessed 8 August 2016.
27   Mark Twain, *A Connecticut Yankee in King Arthur's Court*, Oxford World Classics edn (Oxford: Oxford University Press, 2008).
28   Michael Crichton, *Timeline* (New York: Random House, 2000).

is inevitably progressing from bad to good, and from ignorant primitivism to technological superiority.[29] A period of history as far-removed as the Middle Ages must therefore be far worse than the present day – how could it not be, without the Yankee's steam-engines, Ash's Remington shotgun, or the *Timeline* protagonists' napalm?

The participants' statements often seemed to indicate that they felt they were in a privileged position in time where they could look back with disdain upon their ignorant, violent, dirty, smelly, and unhygienic medieval ancestors. The precarious position of this disdainful attitude toward historical technology and culture is playfully exposed in the film *Star Trek IV: The Voyage Home*. When Starship Medical Officer Dr. McCoy encounters a kidney dialysis machine when stranded in the 1980s, he muses: "What is this, the Dark Ages?" Before too long, we all may be considered medieval.

Medieval: Here be Dragons

Williams and Elliott also address the image that participants attributed to the word "medieval": that of romantic adventure and opulence, the location of Robin Hood, Camelot, and Disney's medievalisms. It is the ancestor of the medievalisms of the Romantic period, of *Ivanhoe* and the Eglinton Tournament of 1839.[30] Eco does not have a ready category for this in his Ten Little Middle Ages, but Williams describes this as:

> These Middle Ages are bright, clean, noble, sporting and merry. This is Hollywood and often Sherwood. It is Douglas Fairbanks and Robert Taylor. Despite the outlaws, the politics are of the establishment.[31]

Elliott describes the iconic:

> procession of knights in glistening armour and bright, spotless raiments [...] the colourful flags adorning the castles flutter playfully in the breeze. A princess emerges from a turret on the castle walls [...]. We have seen its tournaments, its loud declamations of loyalty to the king and obeisance to the beautiful queen; its honour and its chivalry...[32]

---

29 One of the few exceptions to this may be *Bill and Ted's Excellent Adventure*, where modernity (as exemplified by the simpleminded heroes) is shown to pale by comparison with figures from the heroic past. Lousie D'Arcens, "Presentism," in *Medievalism: Key Critical Terms*, 180–88 (186–87).

30 Clare A. Simmons, "Romantic Medievalism," in *The Cambridge Companion to Medievalism*, 103–18 (112–14).

31 Williams, "Medieval Movies," 10.

32 Elliott, *Remaking the Middle Ages*, 2.

Many participants reported that they had a sense that the word "medieval" was connected with myth, legend, fairy tale, and fantasy.[33] Jane made this clear: "medieval ones [words on her word-association exercise] I've thought of like, fairy tales and legends like King Arthur and along that route." To Elizabeth, "medieval" evoked associations with a time period that she eventually described as "legendary-old." Her "legendary-old" evoked not just myth and legend but a specific genre of fairy-tale myth and legend: one containing wizards, dragons, witches, kings, and queens. When asked what sort of legends fit within this category, Jane listed, "King Arthur and Merlin, Chaucer, Heath Ledger."[34] Other figures mentioned in this context included "knights," "Robin Hood," and "Shrek." Shrek, at first glance, might seem an odd inclusion in this list. However, it is perhaps revelatory; though Shrek is the muddy, dirty, and smelly Middle Ages *par excellence*, in his world he is an outsider. In his adventures, he breaches the wall between the medieval and the Middle Ages for comic effect. He represents an exception that proves the rule.

Some participants, like Justin, felt that: "I associate the fantasy genre with the Middle Ages." He further had difficulty reconciling the cognitive dissonance between his intuitive association of fantasy characters with an actual period of history: "things I knew didn't exist but for some reason the words ['medieval'] kind of bring them up." He and Stephen struggled to explain the differences between fantasy and medieval:

Stephen:	We didn't think Robin Hood but I think sometimes I thought [...] almost mythology but not. Kind of, things like you know, wizards and things which you know didn't exist, but I do think sometimes when those words, 'cause it's=
Justin:	=It's the Lord of the Rings thing has a kind of, "Middle Ages" feel a bit, it kind of associates=
Stephen:	=you know, yeah. To be honest my source for most of this is Monty Python and the Holy Grail.

Stephen felt uncomfortable when revealing that many of his primary sources for his understanding of the Middle Ages were, in fact, fantasy books and films. Some other participants also felt that their internal association between

[33] It should be noted that the participants did not make clear distinctions between the concepts of myth, legend, fantasy, and fairy-tale.

[34] The latter two are a clear reference to Helgeland's 2001 film *A Knight's Tale*, a favorite among these participants. Jane felt this film fits in this category of myth and legend, despite its inclusion of historical figures like Edward the Black Prince and Geoffrey Chaucer.

medieval history and the fantasy genre was manufactured by their experience with popular culture. For example, John said:

> I think all these associations [between fantastical monsters and the medieval], like every time we've said it, we've just said "you can't really imagine it," but I think that's just been, come from all different films and programs that we've seen in our lifetime. It's just what you, all the associations that you make with those time periods. I don't see there to be any reason why, really.

Sean specifically blamed this association between fantasy and medieval on films: "I think films often do that as well, don't they. [...] If it's not a witch of some sort, it's a wizard, or a dragon, or something." They were well aware that their ideas of the medieval world have been influenced by the popular culture that they consume by forging an association between the medieval world and icons of fantasy.

Some also felt that the fantastical icons of the legendary-medieval world would seem out of place in another time period – making them, if not exclusively medieval, medieval by default. For example, Jess felt:

> you can't just picture them [monsters] strolling down the street in like Roman togas. If you're gonna put them in a film, this is the sort of time period, that sort of, when no one really knows what was going on [...] you can't imagine Henry the Eighth's court there being a dragon [...] with the French revolution you can't just imagine a dragon.

In recent years, films have placed dragons and other monsters in other contexts, but always as an intrusion of the medieval into another age. *Reign of Fire* (2002) places them in a post-apocalyptic context, in a future where society has been reduced to a pastiche of the present day and the Middle Ages. The *Harry Potter* series introduces dragons as yet another of its injections of the mythological into the present day; they are studied and treated like exotic animals. That being said, though Jess felt that monsters were exclusively medieval, other periods have their own supernatural creatures; a dragon might be out of place in the classical world, but *Clash of the Titans* depicts the monsters of their mythology. Dickensian dragons would seem odd, but the gothic horror genre invented a variety of monsters to populate their fantasies. That said, there was an overarching sense that monsters, by default, belonged to the medieval – which may relate further to both the sense of the medieval world as a place of danger and adventure, as well as its long association with the fantasy genre.

However, as Jess surmised above, the medieval period is the appropriate place for monsters to exist because "no one really knows what was going on," as compared to Roman, Tudor, or French Revolutionary periods. John agreed – and went further, "I can't imagine them [monsters] in Roman times, but that might be because there's so much more information about Romans [...] and they're pretty, they're better, better-off civilization, more developed, so you can't really just put the two together." Thus, it is not only the period's antiquity that makes it the location for fantasy, but also (1) the perception that there is relatively little historical knowledge about it, and (2) a perceived lack of "development" in the period that results in a "stronger" civilization. This idea, that adventure and fantasy are located in "undeveloped" lands potentially places the Middle Ages within larger colonialist narratives and discourses; in this perspective it is possible that fantasy adventure novels thus entail a kind of safari to the medieval – or at least the medievalesque – an "undeveloped" land full of "uncivilized" people, strange religions, and dangerous beasts to be fought and conquered. The medieval past, it seems, *is* a foreign country: a pre-colonial one.

Many participants expressed this idea that little is known, even by historians, about the Middle Ages. It is the case that fewer written records survive from the early Middle Ages than for later periods. That said, these students have learned that there is not much *to know* about the Middle Ages, and that there are fewer documentary sources from the Middle Ages than from the classical world (which is itself a persistent myth). They feel their relative lack of knowledge about the period is excused, or even validated, by their understanding that the Middle Ages are not just *unknown to them*, but *unknowable to anyone* – a lost age. Like early modern cartographers, they feel comfortable with monsters being drawn into the blank spaces of their historical consciousness.

Shining Armor

Many participants felt that warfare and violence were particularly important to their perceptions of the word "medieval". And to them, medieval violence was distinct from the violence of the Middle Ages. Much of the discussion on specifically medieval warfare revolved around knights and the idea of knighthood, and was expressed in romanticized language. For example, Jess felt that her impression of medieval knighthood had been constructed by her experience watching reenactment jousting and films: "I don't tend to think of actual knights when I think of knights. I think of knights in jousts doing the faux battlin' like in [...] village fêtes but they have all those weird jousting competitions and stuff [...] like in *A Knight's Tale*." Others repeated similar ideas, viewing knights as showmen in the lists of contemporary heritage sites, rather than soldiers on the battlefields of history.

Four people spontaneously used the phrase "knights in shining armour" when discussing the word medieval and actual history. This indicates how easily fairy-tale memes, and its memetic language, are applied to history.

Laura was one of the few to make clear the division between fairy-tale, historical, and modern knighthood: "I agree that I would just think of the stereotypical shining armour saving a princess thing but I think there are lots of different kinds of knights, like, if I thought of a knight in the modern day I'd think of a Sir,[35] who doesn't really even necessarily have to be, you know, a fighter." Though Laura acknowledges that the idea of knighthood evokes images of the chivalric, romantic ideal, knighthood has taken on a distinct meaning to her in modern British context. That meaning has been stripped of its martial–heroic implications and replaced with a generic image of a successful person within her society.[36] In subsequent discussion, she was unsure how the honorific of knighthood in present-day Britain relates to the historical warrior-elites of the Middle Ages, or the idealized figures of medieval legend and fantasy.

Discussion: Medieval and Middle Ages, Light and Dark
Many participants felt that the word "medieval" bore significantly different implications than the term "Middle Ages". "Medieval" connotes fantasy, legend and fairy tale, opulence and grand adventure. This directly contradicts a common association – recognized in the *OED* – that "medieval" implies brutal violence, barbarity, and backwardness. Though, perhaps provocatively, this does not mean that those two ideas cannot coexist. But without additional context, "medieval" seems to evoke adventure and fantasy more readily than does "Middle Ages". Many felt that the fantasy genre of literature or visual media is set in something recognizably, and specifically, medieval. Medieval icons and settings would feel out of place in other periods. Others found that the monsters and magic of this genre are linked to the medieval-historical context more than any other. This raises a question: in recent years, some films and literature have enjoyed *explicitly* playing with the medieval period – placing recognizably and specifically medieval icons into other periods. Perhaps the most famous example is the *Harry Potter* series, which places many of the icons of the Victorian gothic tradition (ghosts, curses, the undead, and a dark castle full of blind passages and secret chambers) and medievalist fantasy tradition (wizards, dragons, magic swords, and a quest to destroy a literally unspeakable evil) together in the modern world. In Rowling's medieval-gothic-modernity, the medievalesque lurks just hidden from

---

[35] When she refers to a "Sir," Laura is referring to a knight in the modern British system of peerages, where individuals are knighted for significant contributions to Britain.

[36] This is hardly the only way in which knighthood has been constructed by modern societies; Amy S. Kaufman, for example, has argued that knighthood played a central role in the mythologizing of whiteness in the American South, and played a significant role in the formation and popularization of the KKK. Amy S. Kaufman, "Purity," in *Medievalism: Key Critical Terms*, 199–206 (200–2).

our view, and much of the conflict in the novels involves keeping the worst horrors of that world from intruding upon an innocent modernity. When these icons of medievalesque fantasy are used in this way – particularly in a series as successful as *Harry Potter* – these uses shape the ways in which the authentically medieval is understood by its audience. But is *Harry Potter* and its derivatives understood to be medieval? To what degree is the medieval understood to be like *Harry Potter*?

Violence within this vision of the medieval world is tamed; it is limited to the context of the jousting list of the reenactor or the noble quest of the storybook knight. This bright, cheery vision of the medieval is distinctly different from what one might expect from the way in which the adjective is often applied in the media as a predecessor to the words torture or violence. The *Pulp Fiction* gritty and barbaric vision of the period was evoked far more often by the words "Middle Ages" than by "medieval", in spite of the fact that the word "medieval" is itself commonly used to describe the darker vision.

"Middle Ages", by sharp contrast, encapsulates that very notion of a dark Middle Ages, partly, and problematically, because it term is understood to denote a period of actual history rather than medievalesque fantasy. Disease looms large in all discussion of this Middle Ages, probably as a result of the Black Death's position as an iconic turning point in medieval, if not broader European history (and, possibly, its resultant place on the English National Curriculum). The term collects to itself lists of real-life monarchs (likely learned by many of these students in their primary and secondary educations) who were perceived to be little more than despots ruling over a land not only before democracy, but before government itself. Peasants, and the gulf between the social classes that they represent, end up here. And the fields in which they work are no rural idyll, but are representative of pre-industrial oppression down there in the mud.

Implications

It is apparent that all of these participants had an inaccurate, incomplete understanding of the medieval past. As medievalists are well aware, the Middle Ages are not unknown, nor are they unknowable; it was neither an era of adventure and fantasy, nor was it an era of repression, disease, and death. The specific misconceptions the participants in this study may have about the medieval world are neither an indication that they are stupid nor that they are ill-educated; none of them claimed to be experts on the topic – they were recruited specifically because they were not.

Perhaps more compelling are the deeper questions toward which this study points. First, the understandings of the medieval world revealed by these individuals indicate some of what medievalists, as teachers, could expect of their incoming students, and from the wider publics with whom we may choose to engage through public lectures or popular writing. These participants did not know nothing. What they did know was impressionistic, often lacking in detail and hazily remembered. The medieval and medievalesque worlds presented by popular culture were at least as memorable as those painted by their teachers, if not more so. Further, participants were interested in portrayals of the Middle Ages – particularly in popular culture. They are interested in learning more; our audiences are willing. In order to compete with these vibrant images, medievalists must present their worlds in a similarly compelling fashion.

For the specific question of the differing definitions of the word "medieval" versus the term "Middle Ages", this study indicates that language – even the most basic language that we use to describe our discipline – may have more vivid differences in the core implications than we might expect. This can easily lead to misunderstandings.

Finally, this is not – and must not be – the last word on the popular perceptions of the medieval past, but only the beginning. The differing definitions of "medieval" and "Middle Ages" (and the specific visions attributed to each) may not be – in fact almost certainly are not – universal. To paraphrase Berger and Luckmann's work quoted above, what is "real" to these students may not be for your students. Their definitions are the byproduct of their particular culture, experiences, and upbringing, much of which has little to do with what they learn inside the classroom. However, coming to terms with their understanding of the medieval world not only allows medievalists to engage with their students and the public better, it opens the door to larger questions about how perceptions of the medieval past may shape popular worldviews, and why, even for those outside the academy, the Middle Ages matter. Social-sciences-based methods, such as the qualitative methods used in the study detailed here, provide the best tools we have for understanding the answers to those questions fundamental to our discipline.

Mask of the Medieval Corpse: Prosopopoeia and Corpsepaint in Mayhem's *De Mysteriis Dom Sathanas*

Dean Swinford

Black metal has been described as "metal's most underground subspecies," a musical approach that "sounds like it's rotting, and that's the point."[1] Key lyrical obsessions of the genre include a meditation on decay and pestilence as well as a longing for the distant past.[2] Techniques such as raspy shrieking, rapid and repetitive tremolo picking, and a constant drum barrage referred to as a "blastbeat" are most constitutive of the genre.[3] Its key defining

---

[1]   Ben Ratliff, "Thank You Professor, That Was Putrid," *The New York Times* (15 December 2009), C1, <http://www.nytimes.com/2009/12/15/arts/music/15metal.html?pagewanted=1&sq=ovskum&st=nyt&scp=1>, last accessed 6 April 2015.

[2]   Black metal's distinctive fusion of sound and idea as well as its status as a kind of philosophy, perhaps even a kind of theology, have made it the subject of extensive scholarly consideration. Critical and theoretically contextualizing explorations of the genre include *Floating Tomb: Black Metal Theory*, ed. Nicola Masciandaro and Edia Connole (Fano: Mimesis International, 2015); *Mors Mystica: Black Metal Theory Symposium*, ed. Edia Connole and Nicola Masciandaro (London: Schism Press, 2015); *Hideous Gnosis*, ed. Nicola Masciandaro (New York: Black Metal Theory, 2010); Marco Ferrarese, "Eastern Desekratorz and Nuclear Metal Lust: Performing 'Authentic' Black Metal in Malaysian Borneo," *Metal Music Studies* 1.2 (2015): 211–31; Jesse McWilliams, "Dark Epistemology: An Assessment of Philosophical Trends in the Black Metal Music of Mayhem," *Metal Music Studies* 1.1 (2014): 25–38; *Glossator* 6 (2012); Nicolas Walzer, "La Recomposition Religieuse Black Metal: Parcours et Influx Religieux des Musiciens de Black Metal," *Sociétés* 2 (2005): 53–91; Alexis Mombelet, "La Blandice de Satan: Les Satanismes dans le Metal," *Sociétés* 2 (2005): 139–45; and *Helvete*, a journal of black-metal theory published by Punctum Books.

[3]   These features are most emblematic of the primarily Norwegian groups that popularized the genre in the early 1990s. Key releases that exemplify this sound include Darkthrone's *A Blaze in the Northern Sky* (1992), Immortal's *Pure Holocaust* (1993), and Burzum's *Hvis Lyset Tar Oss* (1994). They tend to rely on ideas explored on the first two Bathory albums,

characteristic, however, is visual: performers cake their faces with black and white makeup called "corpsepaint" (Fig. 1). While the makeup reminds outsiders of the rock group KISS, the widespread use of corpsepaint in black metal comes from a musician who is relatively unknown outside of the genre: Per Yngve Ohlin of the Norwegian band Mayhem. Ohlin, who went by the stage name "Dead", was the first or one of the first to use the term and aligned the practice with a representative purpose that served to connect the stage persona to a historical reality.[4] Dead used corpsepaint as a way to look like a corpse. More importantly, Dead used corpsepaint to look like a specific kind of corpse: he wanted to look like a victim of the medieval plague.

Figure 1. A corpsepainted Dead as shown in *Metallion: The Slayer Mag Diaries*: 291. Reprinted by kind permission of Bazillion Points.

Bathory (1984) and *The Return* (1985). That said, this particular sound is not the only approach recognizable as black metal. Other bands active during the same period, such as Samael, from Switzerland, and Rotting Christ, from Greece, favored a mid-tempo approach that, over subsequent releases, took on more and more electronic elements. Bands that grew out of the Norwegian scene such as Ulver and Borknagar later interposed acoustic interludes and also wrote songs that reprised traditional Norwegian folk-music motifs, particularly those from Edvard Grieg, while others, such as Enslaved, added "proggy" elements that owed more to Dream Theater or Rush than the rigid Bathorian template. Mortiis, a former member of Emperor, ended a period of medieval-themed synthesizer albums with a project that evoked the industrial rock of Nine Inch Nails.

4   Dayal Patterson, *Black Metal: Evolution of the Cult* (Port Townsend, WA: Feral House, 2013), 144. Jon "Metalion" Kristiansen, who featured early interviews with the band in his underground zine *Slayer Mag*, claims that "Mayhem started wearing corpse paint because of Dead. They had never done that before meeting him." Jon Kristiansen, *Metalion: The Slayer Mag Diaries*, ed. Tara G. Warrior (New York: Bazillion Points, 2015), 116.

Dead's development of corpsepaint as a performative practice, when considered in relation to the spectral and disembodied first-person point of view adopted in his lyrics on the foundational Mayhem album, *De Mysteriis Dom Sathanas* (1994), constitutes a form of prosopopoeia, a narrative practice wherein a speaker gives voice to the dead. As Paul de Man observes, the trope "implies that the original face can be missing or nonexistent," a definition that suits this attempt to give a human face to that which is also described as inhuman and faceless.[5] Dead's intent to evoke the medieval dead through performative practice, paired with the consistent use of prosopopoeia and apostrophe within the lyrics to *De Mysteriis Dom Sathanas*, signifies the interplay between the modern and medieval that continues to animate black metal. While the medieval dead belong to the past, they retain their pull on the present. As Dead's lyrics imply, the living and the dead meet and engage in dialogue, but this dialogue is always one-sided. The spirits of the dead appear and speak in the present, but they, like their modern hosts, remain obsessed with a decayed and distant past.

The mask of the performer and the shifting masked identities of characters within the lyrics reveal black metal's medievalism as a form of longing for the dead paired with a belief that the dead are never really gone. The tension produced by these seemingly opposing points of view complicates the current critical dialogue regarding the characteristics of medievalism and neomedievalism as manifested in popular media. As a popular-culture product with only a nominal interest in questions of historical authenticity, black metal seems to express a neomedieval vision of the past that is, as Brent and Kevin Moberly explain, "more medieval than the medieval."[6] At the same time, its melancholic longing for a past wholeness, a past unholiness, appears emblematic of more traditional forms of medievalism.[7] Moreover, it unapologetically mourns a medieval past that it presents as filled with death, sickness, and hatred – the very qualities that proponents of neomedievalism see as pleasantly scoured away in new renditions of the past. Both medievalism, a term in use since the nineteenth century to evoke an obsession with the lost past representative of Romanticism, and neomedievalism, a more recent term sometimes

---

5   Paul de Man, *The Rhetoric of Romanticism* (New York: Columbia University Press, 1984), 57.
6   Brent Moberly and Kevin Moberly, "Neomedievalism, Hyperrealism, and Simulation," in *Studies in Medievalism XIX: Defining Neomedievalism(s)*, ed. Karl Fugelso (Cambridge: D. S. Brewer, 2010), 12–24 (13).
7   This fusion of characteristics is similar in some ways to that described by Nils Holger Petersen in his assessment of George Crumb's *Black Angels: Thirteen Images from the Dark Land for Electric String Quartet* (1970). While Crumb's avant-garde piece *Black Angels* has neomedievalistic elements, its "form and mythological pretension" owe more to earlier, Romantically tinged conceptualizations of medievalism. See Nils Holger Petersen, "Medieval Resurfacings, Old and New," in *Studies in Medievalism XX: Defining Neomedievalism(s) II*, ed. Karl Fugelso (Cambridge: D. S. Brewer, 2011), 35–42 (39).

associated with Umberto Eco and used to describe a postmodern and post-historical attitude regarding the Middle Ages, offer intriguing possibilities for better contextualizing the ways that corpsepaint gains its significatory power from a sustained tension between speech to and from the dead.[8]

In keeping with David W. Marshall's assertion in "Neomedievalism, Identification, and the Haze of Medievalisms" that the scholar of medievalism should demonstrate "how various examples of medievalism participate in some larger patterns and remain distinct from others," this essay does not seek to proclaim black metal in its entirety as either indicative of medievalism or neomedievalism.[9] In the same way that Tom Shippey has encouraged scholars to consider "medievalisms" rather than "medievalism," we could just as easily speak of "black metals" rather than "black metal."[10] The genre is expansive enough in terms of musical approach and thematic concerns – ranging, for example, from the deep ecology of Wolves in the Throne Room to Inquisition's celestial and cosmological obsessions – that, as Kennet Granholm argues, it functions as "a complex cultural system" capable of providing "sets of ideology, meanings, and practices for its adherents."[11] At the same time,

8   The contours and borders of these terms, let alone who popularized them and how they came into scholarly usage, remain subject to debate. On these and related issues, see Richard Utz, "Coming to Terms with Medievalism," *European Journal of English Studies* 15.2 (2011): 101–13.

9   David W. Marshall, "Neomedievalism, Identification, and the Haze of Medievalisms," in *Studies in Medievalism XX: Defining Neomedievalism(s) II*, ed. Karl Fugelso (Cambridge, D. S. Brewer, 2011), 21–34 (32).

10 Kathleen Davis and Nadia Altschul stress this point as well: "Medievalism, it soon becomes apparent, can only be considered in the plural." See their "Introduction: The Idea of 'the Middle Ages' Outside Europe," in *Medievalisms in the Postcolonial World: The Idea of "the Middle Ages" Outside Europe*, ed. Kathleen Davis and Nadia Altschul (Baltimore, MD: Johns Hopkins University Press, 2009), 1–24 (7). For more on the cladistics of medievalism, see, among others, Marshall, "Neomedievalism, Identification"; Tom Shippey, "Medievalisms and Why They Matter," in *Studies in Medievalism XVII: Defining Medievalism(s)*, ed. Karl Fugelso (Cambridge: D. S. Brewer, 2009), 45–54; Carol L. Robinson and Pamela Clements, "Living with Neomedievalism," in *Studies in Medievalism XVIII: Defining Medievalism(s) II*, ed. Karl Fugelso (Cambridge: D. S. Brewer, 2009), 55–75; and Lauryn S. Mayer, "Dark Matters and Slippery Words: Grappling with Neomedievalism(s)," in *Studies in Medievalism XIX: Defining Neomedievalism(s)*, ed. Karl Fugelso (Cambridge: D. S. Brewer, 2010), 68–76.

11 Kennet Granholm, "'Sons of Northern Darkness': Heathen Influences in Black Metal and Neofolk Music," *Numen* 58 (2011): 514–44 (539). I should note another pre-modern topic frequently addressed in black metal, namely Norse mythology and its attendant tales of Viking prowess. Finding its origin in Bathory's "Viking trilogy" of *Blood Fire Death* (1988), *Hammerheart* (1990), and *Twilight of the Gods* (1991), this lyrical vein has been extensively mined by a large number of metal bands, the most popular of which is Amon Amarth, who have released ten full-length albums regarding the many adventures of Thor and his Asgardian compatriots. This topic is sizable enough that it merits consideration on its own and, as such, is not treated in this essay.

this essay presents the preponderance of plague imagery in black metal as indicative of a significant tropology within the genre that bears examination. Indeed, as Nicola Masciandaro and Reza Negarestani suggest in "Black Metal Commentary," "the only protagonists in Black Metal are festering corpses."[12] As such, this essay is part of a more extensive project to generate an anatomy of metal's incessant medievalizing through an analysis of written and pictorial traces encountered in zines, album covers, and liner notes.

Though Dead's lyrics and stage presence have significantly shaped black metal, they have not delimited the genre. To this extent, the essay examines corpsepaint as imagined and described by Dead because it subsequently developed into one of black metal's fundamental and most distinctive motifs. In aligning corpsepaint with prosopopoeia, I argue that the trope's rhetorical significance illuminates this particular manifestation of metal medievalism. In turn, the prosopopoeic dimensions of Dead's costume and lyrics connect in important ways with the broader theoretical discourse regarding the tension between medievalism and neomedievalism. While there is more to black metal than corpsepaint, the phenomenon of corpsepaint as part of black-metal culture displays medievalism's inherent complexity and the need to examine, as Tison Pugh and Angela Jane Weisl argue, "the various intersections of medievalism [that] unit[e] in a given work."[13] In order to tease out this range of significations, I am most concerned in exploring the connections between Dead's statements regarding corpsepaint and instances of prosopopoeia in lyrics found on *De Mysteriis Dom Sathanas*. The essay begins with a brief overview of Dead and his band Mayhem's significance within what is generally referred to as "second wave" black metal.[14] Events surrounding this band have taken on the weight of a kind of origin myth within the genre. Next, the essay examines the recurrent instances of prosopopoeia in the lyrics of "Freezing Moon," "Pagan Fears," and "From the Dark Past." Finally, the essay considers the links to the plague offered by Dead and other black-metal artists and assesses their implications for theorizations of medievalism and neomedievalism.

---

[12]   Masciandaro and Negarestani, "Black Metal Commentary," in *Hideous Gnosis*, ed. Nicola Masciandaro (New York: Black Metal Theory, 2010), 257–66 (261). Joseph Russo corroborates this in his aptly titled "Perpetue Putesco: Perpetually I Putrify," an essay that "engage[s] the obsessions of black metal with the utility of decay" (93). See Russo, "Perpetue Putesco: Perpetually I Putrify," in *Hideous Gnosis*, ed. Nicola Masciandaro (New York: Black Metal Theory, 2010), 93–103 (93).

[13]   Tison Pugh and Angela Jane Weisl, *Medievalisms: Making the Past in the Present* (London: Routledge, 2013), 3.

[14]   Black metal's "first wave," consisting of bands such as Venom, Bathory, Sodom, and Celtic Frost, originated in the early to mid-1980s. Though these bands differ in style and approach, all employed Satanic imagery in a direct manner. The name of the genre is generally credited to Venom's 1982 release, *Black Metal*.

"Are you D/dead?"[15]

The fact that the originator of a practice so integral to an entire genre is himself obscure and unfamiliar reflects the laws of the genre itself. As Masciandaro remarks in "Hideous Gnosis," a theory symposium on the genre, "The purest black metal artist is one who's unknown and inaccessible."[16] While Masciandaro refers to artists who record alone, adopt obscure pseudonyms, and never perform, his point applies equally well to Dead, the quintessential black-metal artist whose death has attained a central position in the genre's foundational myth. Dead's voice appears on only a few recordings, of which Mayhem's *Live in Leipzig* is the most accessible.[17]

His lyrics appear on *De Mysteriis Dom Sathanas*, the hugely influential record that serves as "the opus magnum" and apotheosis of the black-metal sound.[18] The combination of the Latin album title, supposedly taken by Dead from "an occult book he discovered," the Latin lyrics of the title track, and the Gothic cathedral on the album cover – Trondheim's Nidaros Cathedral – establishes the album's medieval atmosphere.[19] The music follows the general template of second-wave black metal, but can be distinguished from other contemporaneous releases by several factors. First, because many of the songs were written years before the 1994 release date, they show a marked 1980s thrash influence in their riffing style and shifting tempos. The songs are more than high-speed guitar and drum workouts; they tend to highlight

---

15   The titles of the section breaks in this essay are taken from Dead's lyrics and audience banter between songs as heard on Mayhem's *Live in Leipzig*.

16   Ratliff, "Thank You Professor, That Was Putrid." This trend within black metal could be said to come from Quorthon, mastermind of the influential first-wave black metal band Bathory. Though Quorthon wrote his own songs and played most instruments, he recorded with studio musicians. As the lone musician behind the brooding and atmospheric second-wave band Burzum, Count Grishnackh serves as the first main example of a self-consciously solitary black-metal artist. He also played bass in the *De Mysteriis Dom Sathanas* sessions. Other solitary and deliberately reclusive black-metal acts, many of which also show Burzum's musical influences, include Xasthur, Nortt, Paysage d'Hiver, Leviathan, Caïna, and Striborg.

17   Patterson, *Black Metal*, 145.

18   Patterson, *Black Metal*, 267.

19   Patterson, *Black Metal*, 267. The actual existence of this book remains disputed. While Dead claimed that it was a real book that he encountered, he provided scant additional information. Dead's remarks about the book in an interview indicate that it was likely imaginary: "As for the book itself, I must find it [...] I think I'll have an expedition on my own around the world to find it. It's so dark, darker than death." See Kristiansen, *The Slayer Mag Diaries*, 209. Two possible candidates with similar titles that may have influenced his conception of this book include St. Ambrose's *De Mysteriis* and, the more likely possibility given metal's long-established Lovecraftian fixation, *De Vermis Mysteriis*, a fictional book that appears in H. P. Lovecraft's *Cthulhu mythos*.

the various instruments – even, on occasion, the bass – through brief solos. The music itself does not employ deliberately medievalistic elements like the monk chants at the beginning of Darkthrone's *A Blaze in the Northern Sky* or the church bells in Gorgoroth's first release. The most self-consciously "medieval" musical element of the album has to be singer Attila Csihar's idiosyncratic vocal delivery, which "lurch[es] creepily from screams and rasps to an almost operatic form of singing that made a feature of his distinctive Hungarian accent."[20] His approach remains a widely admired, but not generally imitated, "defining factor of the record" that plays off of the Latin lines in the title track. Euronymous described the overall mood of Attila's performance by saying, "He sings like a sick priest."[21]

Dead's personal obsessions inform the album's presentation of the past as a dead force that influences the living. Withdrawn and antisocial, Dead fixated on the thin line separating the dead and the living, the past and the present. After suffering a near-death experience as a child, he claimed that he had, in fact, remained dead, and lived only as a walking corpse.[22] The liner notes to *Live in Leipzig* include a popular (within black-metal circles) quote attributed to Dead that conveys this dissociation from a long-dead body: "I am not human. This is a dream, and soon I will awake. It was too cold, and my blood was always clotted."[23] He sometimes buried his clothes before performances so that they would smell of the grave.[24] He is also known to have carried a plastic bag with a dead crow in it; he would inhale from the bag before singing in order to keep "the stench of death in his nostrils."[25]

The name "Dead" itself signifies how deep these obsessions ran. The adoption of a pseudonym shows, in part, the influence of black metal's originators. Venom's band members went by Cronos, Mantas, and Abaddon. Bathory's Quorthon settled on a name that purportedly refers to "one of Satan's princes who defied the spirit of the Nazarene."[26] In general, such stage names mark the creation of a persona assumed by the performer. These metal names run the gamut of personification types enumerated in classical rhetoric and include simple nouns (Evil, Hat [Norwegian for "hate"]), compound phrases (Nocturnal Grave Desekrator and Black Winds, Nuclear Holocausto Vengeance), names in languages foreign to those spoken by the

---

20   Patterson, *Black Metal*, 270.
21   Patterson, *Black Metal*, 270. Euronymous chose Attila to sing on the album because Attila "was the favourite singer of Dead." See Kristiansen, *The Slayer Mag Diaries*, 430.
22   Patterson, *Black Metal*, 142.
23   Mayhem, *Live in Leipzig*, Obscure Plasma Records, 1993.
24   Patterson, *Black Metal*, 145.
25   Chris Campion, "In the Face of Death," *The Guardian* (20 February 2005), <http://www.theguardian.com/music/2005/feb/20/popandrock4>, last accessed 6 April 2016.
26   "Bathory," *Metallian: Heavy Metal is Better than Music*, <http://www.metallian.com/bathory.php>, last accessed 6 April 2016.

performer but still linked to an actual language (Zephyrous, Euronymous[27]), and names in languages invented by other authors or the musicians themselves (Count Grishnackh, Vordb Dréagvor Uezréèvb).[28]

Dead's name is interesting in that, because the word "dead" is an adjective and not a noun, it belongs to yet a different variety, which James Paxson identifies in *The Poetics of Personification* as "the category of 'exemplary property characters.'"[29] Characters in this class do not necessarily personify an abstract quality; rather, they "exemplify the abstract qualities reflected in their names."[30] Thus, John Bunyan's character "Hopeful" in *The Pilgrim's Progress* works as an "individual representative [...] of [a] class [...] of human beings who are hopeful"; by extension, Dead's name contributes to a persona wherein he serves as the voice of human beings who are dead.[31] Given Dead's ideas about his tenuous mortal existence, then, his persona has less to do with the construction of an individual image (the self as a mythological character, demonic entity, or powerful mage) and more to do with an attempt to grapple with the meaning or unmeaning of one's own mortality.

Dead's incessant focus on death and dying took its inevitable toll in April 1991. Mayhem guitarist Euronymous found Dead's body in the house that the band shared. Euronymous rearranged the gun and knife that Dead used to kill himself, took photos of the body, and also kept shards of the skull, which he allegedly distributed like perverse relics to those he deemed "worthy."[32] The events surrounding Dead's suicide, while extreme, pale in significance to the violent and fantastic turn taken by the Oslo scene in their wake. Afterwards, there was a change in mentality, most representative in Euronymous' increasing advocacy of violence. In addition, "Euronymous began to create a persona as the embodiment of an ancient evil" that further emphasized the genre's medieval aesthetic.[33]

---

27 A misspelling of "Eurynomos," an underworld spirit in Greek mythology.

28 "Grishnackh" is the name of an orc in *The Lord of the Rings*. Vordb's name is rendered in Gloatre, an invented language used for the names of many of the band members, song titles, and releases of the group of French black-metal bands often referred to as Les Légions Noires. For more on the philosophical implications of Gloatre and its "new experience of language," see Edia Connole, "Les Légions Noires: Labor, Language, Laughter," in *Floating Tomb: Black Metal Theory*, ed. Nicola Masciandaro and Edia Connole (Fano: Mimesis International, 2015), 149–205 (161).

29 James J. Paxson. *The Poetics of Personification* (Cambridge: Cambridge University Press, 1994), 60. See pp. 59–62 for a full taxonomy of personification categories.

30 Paxson, *The Poetics of Personification*, 61.

31 Paxson, *The Poetics of Personification*, 61.

32 One of the recipients of these skull shards, lead guitarist of the Swedish band Marduk, has even remarked on its status as a kind of (un)holy object of veneration within the black-metal cult. See Patterson, *Black Metal*, 332.

33 Campion, "In the Face of Death."

This transformation within the Oslo scene took the form not just of the creation of fantastic personas, but of an imagined war against Christianity itself. By late 1993, the small group of obscure bands centered on Euronymous' small record shop, Helvete, and record label, Deathlike Silence, had become the target of international media attention after the arson of nearly fifty churches, including the Fantoft Stave Church in Bergen; Euronymous' murder; and the subsequent trial of the perpetrator, Count Grishnackh of Burzum, who was found guilty of the murder and several of the church burnings.[34] The police also recovered dynamite from Grishnackh's apartment that some speculate was intended to destroy Nidaros Cathedral, the church on the cover of *De Mysteriis Dom Sathanas*.

Fig. 2: Tribute to Euronymous as "Rex Perpetuus Norvegia," *Metallion:
The Slayer Mag Diaries*: 273. Reprinted by kind permission of Bazillion Points.

---

34   The most comprehensive treatment of these events is Michael Moynihan and Didrik Søder-
lind, *Lords of Chaos: The Bloody Rise of the Satanic Metal Underground* (Port Townsend,
WA: Feral House Press, 1997). See also *Until the Light Takes Us*, directed by Aaron Aites
and Audrey Ewell (New York: Artists Public Domain, 2008), DVD, and *Once Upon a
Time in Norway*, directed by Pål Aasdal and Martin Ledang (Oslo: Grenzeløs Productions,
2007), DVD.

This bizarre series of events served to solidify the reputation of Dead and, to a greater extent, Euronymous as more than young musicians who died in tragic and unnecessary circumstances, but fallen warriors of a noble cause. Within the genre, Euronymous, in particular, has assumed the role of a king cut down in his prime. In an image from a 1994 issue of *Slayer Mag*, the caption "rex perpetuus Norvegia," or "eternal Norwegian king," sits below a picture of a corpsepainted Euronymous carrying a black candle and wearing a cape, a rapier, and an enormous inverted crucifix (Fig. 2). The phrase is generally used to refer to Olaf I, the nation's patron saint and the king commonly attributed with Christianizing Norway. When applied to Euronymous, as in this "tribute" published after his death, the phrase can be seen as an ironic reversal of its customary usage that, at the same time, serves to apotheosize Euronymous as the king of black metal and its unholy hordes.[35] The caption's connection between Olaf and Euronymous presents one as the king who brought Christianity and the other as the king who eradicated it. The yoking together of these two figures also alludes to the unrealized plot to destroy Nidaros Cathedral, which was built in 1070 over Olav's grave and is the site for the consecration of Norwegian kings.

While heavy metal had long employed Satanic imagery, the iconography of a recognizably new genre entered the popular consciousness through the media attention given to these crimes and the publicity they generated for Norwegian black-metal bands.[36] Through some combination of true-crime sensationalism, pop culture's hunger for the new, or the creative energy of the music itself, black metal quickly surpassed other underground genres as something vibrant and vital. This trend continues to the present; a recent article in *The Guardian* reports that Norway's diplomats "are now being offered special black metal training" because the music is regarded as "a cultural export that Norway [should be] proud of."[37]

"Many Years Have Passed Since the Funeral"

Corpsepaint serves as a visual marker of the genre that coincides with the sound of the music. It marks black metal as a performative spectacle that, as

---

[35] That this association remains twenty years after his death can be seen in the existence of the Saint Euronymous candle available on Etsy: <https://www.etsy.com/listing/104353569/saint-euronymous-of-mayhem-prayer-candle>, last accessed 6 April 2016.

[36] For more on the religious cultural system of black metal, see Granholm, "'Sons of Northern Darkness.'" As Granholm points out, "the identification of Norwegian Black Metal as satanic [in an actual religious sense] can be attributed to the influence of mass media" (529), and he concludes that "the media effectively created that which it described" (530).

[37] "What Would You Like Diplomats to Spread the Word About?," *The Guardian* (9 June 2011), <http://www.guardian.co.uk/commentisfree/2011/jun/09/cultural-export-norway-black-metal>, last accessed 6 April 2016.

spectacle, connects "present and past, time and timelessness, the transcendent moment of theater and of transcendence."[38] As Erik Butler notes, the practice of performers that *"perinde ac cadaver* [...] [creates] an Ignatian 'imperialism of images' [that] frames the [listener's] experience."[39] In black metal, the act of listening is always already tied up with the act of seeing. Those close to Dead reveal that he saw the wearing of corpsepaint as a symbolic act intended to evoke the dead and to bring himself closer to the Middle Ages. His bandmate Necrobutcher distinguishes Dead's face painting from that used by hard-rock precursors: "It wasn't anything to do with the way KISS and Alice Cooper used make up. [...] Dead actually wanted to look like a corpse."[40] He clarifies that Dead "didn't do it to look cool," and notes that Dead added decidedly unglamorous details, like "snot dripping out of his nose."[41] *Guardian* music writer Chris Campion elaborates on Dead's motives and explains that the "white greasepaint visage [was] designed to mimic the pallor" of those who died during the Black Death.[42]

Dead's most enduring contributions to black metal include this visual mask adopted during performance as well as the lyrics to *De Mysteriis Dom Sathanas*. When asked about his use of corpsepaint in an interview in *Slayer Mag*, Dead directly connects these two aspects of his artistic legacy: "I wear my corpsepaint when I should really concentrate and live into my lyrics."[43] The phrase "live into" is insightful; it implies that the lyrics evoke an imaginary world temporarily inhabited by the performer. In addition, it suggests that Ohlin truly becomes Dead, the vocalist of Mayhem, and becomes dead, like so many of the characters described in his songs, only through the combination of lyrics and corpsepaint. In essence, the performative mask of the dead complements the lyrical speech of or to that mask. Both elements involve prosopopoeia, the rhetorical figure indicative of the speech or action of an imaginary, absent, or dead person.

Prosopopoeia serves as the constitutive rhetorical figure of black metal, and its repeated use suggests the contours of black metal's incessant medievalism: in short, the genre creates "an impersonal realm where the already-dead finds its voice in the living."[44] This drive to bring the past into the present – or, rather, to bring the present back into the past – clearly demonstrates the contours of black metal's medievalistic drive. The prosopopoeic

---

38 Angela Jane Weisl, "Spectacle," in *Medievalism: Key Critical Terms*, ed. Elizabeth Emery and Richard Utz (Cambridge: D. S. Brewer, 2014), 232.
39 Erik Butler, "The Counter-Reformation in Stone and Metal: Spiritual Substances," in *Hideous Gnosis*, ed. Nicola Masciandaro (New York: Black Metal Theory, 2010), 28.
40 Campion, "In the Face of Death."
41 Campion, "In the Face of Death."
42 Campion, "In the Face of Death."
43 Kristiansen, *The Slayer Mag Diaries*, 130.
44 Masciandaro and Negarestani, "Black Metal Commentary," 262.

doubling evident in Dead's mask and lyrics shows the importance of these connections in a work that shaped and continues to influence the genre. *De Mysteriis Dom Sathanas* involves an accretion of prosopopoeic elements. The trope is employed visually and lyrically so that it is not enough to perform the lyrics without the mask. Rather, to "live into" the world of the lyrics, Ohlin had to become Dead, and mark his death as a way of remaining in that state.

This doubling of the mask adds weight to the imaginative exercise of uncovering the past. It could be described, to borrow language Pugh and Weisl use to speak of Thomas Gray's 1757 poem "The Bard," as a "double medievalism."[45] The performance in the present as the plague spirit who speaks of spectral encounters constitutes a moment of "looking to the past to think through the meaning of that past and its repercussions in the present."[46] Moreover, this vocalization as the ghost, of encounters with the ghost and words from the ghost, compounds the number of thin strands, a fragile skein, connecting the past and present.

Of course, Dead's tales of fatal meetings come from a long line of metal lyrics. They employ a rhetorical approach found not just in black metal, but which has marked heavy metal since its inception in Black Sabbath's "Black Sabbath," which Masciandaro calls "the first song of the first album of Heavy Metal."[47] The genre itself begins, then, with an encounter with a "figure in black" "that stands before" the speaker.[48] That said, corpsepaint's double medievalizing alters the ramifications of such an encounter. Masciandaro's observes that, in "Black Sabbath," "the figure in black mirrors the one who questions it," and it points back to the narrator as a way of collapsing any possibility of separating the two.[49] This, as we shall see, roughly describes the lyrical scenarios of *De Mysteriis Dom Sathanas*. However, the added performative element of corpsepaint complicates the speaker / specter relationship in black metal.

The "hopelessness of all questioning" that typifies metal's philosophical stance, as defined by Masciandaro, remains relevant in both renditions of this encounter with the unknown.[50] Black metal's performative mask, however, extends the identification between a modern questioner and an unknown respondent by imbuing that spirit with a specific historic identity. What

---

45   Pugh and Weisl, *Medievalisms*, 37.
46   Pugh and Weisl, *Medievalisms*, 37.
47   Nicola Masciandaro, "Black Sabbath's 'Black Sabbath': A Gloss on Heavy Metal's Origuinary Song," in *Floating Tomb: Black Metal Theory*, ed. Nicola Masciandaro and Edia Connole (Fano: Mimesis International, 2015), 35–52 (37).
48   Black Sabbath, *Black Sabbath*, Vertigo Records, 1970.
49   Masciandaro, "Black Sabbath's 'Black Sabbath,'" 39.
50   Masciandaro, "Black Sabbath's 'Black Sabbath,'" 38.

Masciandaro says about the metal fan who "is drawn to mirror and mate-
rialize the figure conjured within his music" remains true for black metal;
the addition of corpsepaint augments the connection between the speaker
and the specter.[51] In addition, it subtly shifts the quality of that identification and its attendant hopelessness. In "Black Sabbath," the speaker initially
runs from the specter even though he ultimately "find[s] out I'm the chosen
one."[52] The speaker is marked as the brethren of the song's sinister characters,
but he remains afraid of this identification. By contrast, Dead (or Attila or
Maniac or any corpsepainted fiend) is not just speaking to the dead and
speaking of the dead, but, importantly, speaking as the dead. The singer's
very appearance marks this identification.

This quality of speaking as the spirit marks black metal's spectral preoc-
cupations. Prosopopoeia joins the written word to its verbal performance in
the evocation of an absent speaker. Quintilian describes the trope as ideally
suited for bringing the gods down to earth, or the dead up from the grave.[53]
A seventeenth-century rhetoric designed specifically for the clergy denotes
prosopopoeia in similar terms: it entails "the feigning of a person: when wee
bring in dead men speaking, or our selues doe take their person vpon vs"
and serves as a "very patheticall" figure that "moueth much."[54] Considered
in combination with the preferred elements of black-metal performance –
attired in spikes and leather, face coated in a ghoulish death mask, one's
voice an agonized death rattle – this rhetorical figure creates more than a
temporary ventriloquism through the speaker. It enables a kind of willed
possession and "the usurpation of one's voice" that serves as "a conceptual
and structural determinant" of black metal.[55] Dead's remarks that the corpsepaint serves an interpretive function – that it allows him "to live into the
lyrics" – demonstrate a modern version of rhetorical invention undertaken
to "bring in dead men speaking." Understood within a poetic context, the
combination of corpsepaint and first-person point of view produces what
could be described as a performative prosopopoeia.

The eight tracks of *De Mysteriis Dom Sathanas* include a recurring image
of a speaker who has become, is haunted by, or encounters some kind of
spirit or spectral presence. In "Funeral Fog," the speaker is part of a funeral
party somewhere "in the middle of Transylvania."[56] As a priest completes the
last rites for the dead, a fog ascends from the tombs, then descends on the

---

51 Masciandaro, "Black Sabbath's 'Black Sabbath,'" 40.
52 Black Sabbath, *Black Sabbath*.
53 Marcus Fabius Quintilianus, *Institutio Oratoria*, 4 vols. Trans. and ed. H. E. Butler
    (Cambridge, MA: Harvard University Press, 1922), 3:391.
54 Richard Bernard, *The Faithfull Shepherd* (London: Thomas Pavier, 1621), 304.
55 See Masciandaro and Negarestani, "Black Metal Commentary," 265.
56 Mayhem, *De Mysteriis Dom Sathanas*, Century Black, 1994.

party in order to "complete this funeral."[57] The speaker of "Freezing Moon" is some kind of ancient vampire who rises once more to "please my hunger on living humans."[58] "Pagan Fears" is unusual in that it lacks a first-person narrator; it describes the "primitive and pagan superstitions" of "deceased humans now forgotten."[59] It ends, however, by linking the thoughts of the dead and the living: "some memories will never go away and they will forever be here."[60] On "Life Eternal," the speaker contemplates death and asks, in a variation of the *ubi sunt* motif, "What will be left of me when I'm dead?"[61] The speaker of "From the Dark Past" confronts a spirit trapped in a stone and asks what it saw "in the darkness of the past."[62] A vampire buried "so many years, ages ago" rises from the earth in "Buried by Time and Dust."[63] Finally, in the title track, an arcane coven gathers in "the elder ruins" to recite Latin phrases from "a book made of human flesh."[64]

In addition to describing an encounter with the dead, the lyrics frequently associate such a presence with the past itself. Commenting specifically on the song "Pagan Fears" in an interview, Dead notes that it deals with "the idea that the past isn't dying, but remains in some faded reality."[65] The spirits of the past "haunt people in the future" by appearing in their thoughts.[66] The album's lyrics, filled as they are with images of ravenous corpses, ancient ruins, and arcane rites, present such medieval haunting as a decidedly grim undertaking. The lyrics characterize the past in terms often employed in other academic and popular contexts to diminish the Middle Ages vis-à-vis modernity so that the former "persist imaginatively as the dark age[s]" in a series of "tired narratives [that] remain all too familiar" to medievalists.[67] The difference here is that those qualities, reductive or not, drive Dead's vision of the past and its enduring vitality. If the album has a theme, it would be, as the singer wails victoriously in "Pagan Fears," that "the past is alive."[68]

Perhaps Mayhem's "most iconic" song on the album, "Freezing Moon" evokes this theme in a way that draws together past and present through the

---

57 Mayhem, *De Mysteriis Dom Sathanas*.
58 Mayhem, *De Mysteriis Dom Sathanas*.
59 Mayhem, *De Mysteriis Dom Sathanas*.
60 Mayhem, *De Mysteriis Dom Sathanas*.
61 Mayhem, *De Mysteriis Dom Sathanas*.
62 Mayhem, *De Mysteriis Dom Sathanas*.
63 Mayhem, *De Mysteriis Dom Sathanas*.
64 Mayhem, *De Mysteriis Dom Sathanas*.
65 Kristiansen, *The Slayer Mag Diaries*, 291.
66 Kristiansen, *The Slayer Mag Diaries*, 291.
67 Bruce Holsinger, *The Premodern Condition: Medievalism and the Making of Theory* (Chicago: University of Chicago Press, 2005), 12, 13.
68 Mayhem, *De Mysteriis Dom Sathanas*.

shifting temporal perspective of a long-undead speaker.[69] While the speaker remains in one place – a cemetery – he alternates between different times in that place. The opening lines, "Everything here is so cold, everything here is so dark," state that the speaker speaks from within the narrative frame of the song.[70] The singer may be in a studio, or performing the song in a club, but, lyrically, he is "here" in the cemetery. The third line, "I remember it as from a dream," marks a direct use of the first person "I."[71] In this line, the speaker seems to confuse time as though he remembers the place and moment from which he currently speaks. He "remembers" the place where he is – "here" – as though it were a dream. This confusion could simply be indicative of the grammatical errors that haunt the lyrics of obscure heavy-metal songs; on the other hand, this combination of shifting tenses and the announcement of a first-person speaker assumes a thematic significance when considered in relation to Dead's beliefs that the past never dies and that the dead can enter the consciousness of the living. Reading with this context in mind, we could assume that the boundaries between the modern writer and an ancient soul coalesce in these opening lines.

The second stanza makes explicit the speaker's identity as a haunting presence. Not only does he remember the place, he also "remember[s] it was here I died."[72] A later track, "Buried by Time and Dust," uses a similar technique to form the voice of the dead. The speaker recounts how "Time buried me in earth" and establishes a temporal distance between his death and the present by stating that "Many years have passed since the funeral."[73] From a rhetorical standpoint, this works because the singer is doing several things at once. He is both speaking within and about the narrative frame. Moves like this within the song demonstrate that the singer is not just recounting the events depicted in the song; rather, he temporarily gives voice to a presence that is more than just a character. In keeping with one of the virtues of prosopopoeia as indicated by the classical rhetorician Demetrius, the speaker here "annihilate[s] or elide[s] time by the 'making present' of a dead person": the presence becomes present in the present.[74] While the song describes a fictional scenario, it is also "true" in the sense that it could be true for the persona singing the lines. The singer, in a manner more akin to religious ceremony than drama, becomes a spirit who died, long ago, "by following the freezing moon."[75]

---

69   Patterson, *Black Metal*, 272.
70   Mayhem, *De Mysteriis Dom Sathanas*.
71   Mayhem, *De Mysteriis Dom Sathanas*.
72   Mayhem, *De Mysteriis Dom Sathanas*.
73   Mayhem, *De Mysteriis Dom Sathanas*.
74   Paxson, *The Poetics of Personification*, 16.
75   Mayhem, *De Mysteriis Dom Sathanas*.

The last two stanzas return to a time unambiguously recognizable as the present. After the narrator reveals that he stands where he once died, he reminds the listener that "it's night again," then apostrophizes the night as "you, beautiful."[76] After revealing his vampiric, or perhaps cannibalistic, intention to "please my hunger on living humans," the narrator then once more identifies the present moment as a "night of hunger."[77] The last two lines of this stanza shift into the imperative mode as the speaker commands the audience to "follow its call. Follow the freezing moon."[78] As the song culminates, the speaker reveals that a host of dead follow behind: "as in ancient times, fallen souls fall behind my steps."[79] The song implies that the speaker has returned from the past to create a growing body of risen corpses who, like him, will eternally "follow […] the freezing moon."[80]

"Pagan Fears" redeploys this image of lunar obsession in a way that connects Dead, his audience, and the medieval dead. Told in the third person, "Pagan Fears" comments on the past from a perspective revealed as the present in the song's last two lines: "Some memories will never go away / And they will forever be here."[81] These lines directly express Dead's idea that the spirits of the past manifest themselves in the living. The first two lines of this last stanza make that point through a descriptive blurring of the bodies of people in the past and present. After the chorus, which includes the repetition of the line, "the past is alive," the singer describes "woeful people with pale faces / staring obsessed at the moon."[82] Presumably, these are the medieval denizens of "an age of legends and fear" described in the first two stanzas.[83] However, the last word of the song – "here" – complicates this interpretation. These superstitious people stared "obsessed at the moon" in the same way that the black-metal singer, the true black-metal fan, stares obsessed, made rapt and contemplative through the music's cultish spell.[84]

This image also joins "Pagan Fears" to "Freezing Moon," with its commandment to "follow its call / follow the freezing moon." Dead himself links these similar images and their mingling of the medieval and the present on the "Live in Leipzig" album. As he introduces "Freezing Moon," he intones, "when it's cold and when it's dark, the freezing moon can obsess you."[85] His

76 Mayhem, *De Mysteriis Dom Sathanas.*
77 Mayhem, *De Mysteriis Dom Sathanas.*
78 Mayhem, *De Mysteriis Dom Sathanas.*
79 Mayhem, *De Mysteriis Dom Sathanas.*
80 Mayhem, *De Mysteriis Dom Sathanas.*
81 Mayhem, *De Mysteriis Dom Sathanas.*
82 Mayhem, *De Mysteriis Dom Sathanas.*
83 Mayhem, *De Mysteriis Dom Sathanas.*
84 Mayhem, *De Mysteriis Dom Sathanas.*
85 Mayhem, *Live in Leipzig.*

inter-song banter uses language from "Pagan Fears" to express the shared obsessions of "deceased humans now forgotten" and Dead's living audience.[86]

The album repeatedly expresses this central idea that the "primitive" past remains continually alive. At the same time, it also suggests that the past can fade into a voiceless inaccessibility. In "From the Dark Past," a modern speaker mounts an unsuccessful attempt to engage with a forgotten spirit. Through apostrophe, which often serves as a rhetorical double or subset of prosopopoeia, the speaker addresses a stone that appears to have the face of someone long-dead.[87] The stone could be a grave marker or part of some kind of ancient monolith, but the lyrics do not specify. It "is decayed by age"; the speaker believes he can see a human form because a spirit trapped inside has emerged "to tell of his damnation."[88]

The speaker implores the stone to speak: "Tell me! What did you see there in the darkness of the past?"[89] This apostrophizing plea goes unanswered, however; by the end of the song, the speaker sees only a brief glimmer of eyes and a mouth. He receives no answer and, in an expression of frustration, calls the spirit's existence into question: "only the wind is able to tell" for sure if the stone actually hosts a forgotten spirit.[90] While the past may bring with it ravening spirits that turn us, in the present, into "primitive and pagan" ghouls, the truly maddening possibility is that these ancient spirits may simply refuse to speak.

"The Past is Alive!"

Dead's use of prosopopoeia in his lyrics and performative style combine to create an impossible, but necessary, illusion. A medieval spirit has arrived in the modern present to lament his own death. This tension in black metal warrants further examination in that it takes the medieval past as something dead that possesses, paradoxically, a vital force. Moreover, in contrast to other popular-culture appropriations of medieval subject matter, Dead's concern with the past is neither ironic nor playful, and he employs prosopopoeia and apostrophe precisely because they establish a serious and reverential tone.

---

86 Mayhem, *De Mysteriis Dom Sathanas*.
87 Paxson, *The Poetics of Personification*, 14. As Paxson notes in his overview of the history of personification, "the programmatic moves wherein Demetrius and the *Rhetorica ad Herennium* author begin their definitions of personification with images of restoring, spatially or temporally, a non-present human being further underscores the role of the trope as (A) a variation on apostrophe, and (B) a means of dramatic character invention or presentation" (14).
88 Mayhem, *De Mysteriis Dom Sathanas*.
89 Mayhem, *De Mysteriis Dom Sathanas*.
90 Mayhem, *De Mysteriis Dom Sathanas*.

As a cultural product that contains, from its beginning, a strong medievalizing tendency, black metal complicates the relationship between the medieval and the modern wherein, in many iterations of their differences, the medieval is rendered necessarily primitive and "in opposition to all that does change or develop, namely the 'civilized.'"[91] Contemporary culture regards someone who is "medieval" as someone who is backward; as Stephen Cooper observes, "the word 'medieval' has negative connotations."[92] In the popular imagination, "medieval man [is seen as] half-savage, crude in appearance, appetites, and lifestyle."[93] Rather than reject this characterization, those who wear black metal's medieval death-mask do so in order to embrace its selfsame backward qualities. Dead's claim that "the past is alive" asserts that the Middle Ages, and all that they represent, can be neither eliminated nor forgotten.

The traction of this idea that "the past is alive" in a scene known for the profusion of odd, criminal, and unorthodox viewpoints comes through in the number and variety of medieval references employed in black-metal releases that followed in Mayhem's wake.[94] General allusions to the Middle Ages by black-metal bands range from the previously mentioned image of Nidaros Cathedral on the cover of *De Mysteriis Dom Sathanas* to the band Abruptum's dedication of their album *Obscuritatum Advoco Amplectére Me* to "the forthcoming dark age," an era presumably imagined as a continuation of its medieval precursor.[95] Specific allusions to the Black Death appear, among others, in the band name "1349", chosen to signify the year of the disease's greatest devastation; the title of Marduk's 2000 release *La Grande Danse Macabre*; and the illustration of a crow flying over a forest, accompanied by the caption "Pesten 1349," on the sleeve of Satyricon's fittingly titled *Dark Medieval Times*. The liner notes of the latter declare it to be a concept album that has its "source in overflowing medieval belief"; the recurrence of medieval themes and references through the genre demonstrates the extent to which this so-called "medieval belief" shapes black-metal musicians' aural and visual expressions. [96]

References like these demonstrate that black-metal bands routinely evoke the plague as a specific historic reality. Such connections to the plague reflect the interests of these individual artists, but they also show Dead's influence

---

91   Mark Antliff and Patricia Leighten, "Primitive," in *Critical Terms for Art History*, ed. Robert S. Nelson and Richard Shiff (Chicago: University of Chicago Press, 1996), 170–84 (170).

92   Stephen Cooper, "Positively Medieval," *History Today* 63.5 (May 2013): 36.

93   Laura Morowitz, "Primitive," in *Medievalism: Key Critical Terms*, ed. Elizabeth Emery and Richard Utz (Cambridge: D. S. Brewer, 2014), 189–98 (191).

94   Patterson, *Black Metal*, 267.

95   Abruptum, *Obscuritatum Advoco Amplectére Me*, Deathlike Silence Productions, 1993.

96   Satyricon, *Dark Medieval Times*, Moonfog Productions, 1994.

on the genre: Abruptum released *Obscuritatum* on Deathlike Silence, the label run by Dead's bandmate Euronymous; the band 1349 include a cover of Mayhem's "Buried By Time and Dust" on their 2003 release *Liberation*; Morgan Håkansson, lead guitarist of Marduk, purportedly owns a fragment of Dead's skull; and members of Satyricon have played in various side projects with Dead's Mayhem bandmates.

But what exactly does this "medieval belief" signify? The question is an important one for medievalists because black metal's medievalism does not fit easily into prevailing conversations regarding medievalism and neomedievalism. The definition of neomedievalism offered by Carol L. Robinson and Pamela Clements stresses a disconnection from historical authenticity as well as a reliance on performance and new media. A third, less-remarked-upon quality in their formulation is that neomedieval representations of the Middle Ages are characterized by happiness and demonstrate a progressive political sensibility. In "Living with Neomedievalism," Robinson and Clements describe neomedievalism as something that is "laughingly reshaping itself."[97] In her analysis of their work, Amy S. Kaufman points out that "Robinson, Clements, and MEMO provide a definition of neomedievalism that is giddy and joyful, one that implies growth and progress along with the wisdom of self-conscious irony."[98]

While Kaufman differs from Robinson and Clements in that she sees neomedievalism as a "functional subset of medievalism," rather than a category in its own right, she echoes their claims regarding the joyful and ennobling nature of neomedieval practices that, through their inclusivity, offer a "path [toward] healing trauma" that will "unfus[e] past, present, and future" while also "acknowledging history is essential to imagining true diversity."[99] E. L. Risden too stresses that neomedievalism can be recognized through "the combination of play and technology."[100] In a digression on the "weird fiction" author China Mieville's dismissal of Tolkien's influence on fantasy literature, he points out that practitioners of neomedievalism often express a "discomfort with more traditional medievalism" and tend to regard it as "diseased and oppressive."[101] The more liberating possibilities of neomedievalism stand in direct contrast to a medievalism that perpetuates oppressive ideologies of the past.

[97] Robinson and Clements, "Living With Neomedievalism," 56.
[98] Amy S. Kaufman, "Medieval Unmoored," in *Studies in Medievalism XIX: Defining Neomedievalism(s)*, ed. Karl Fugelso (Cambridge: D. S. Brewer, 2010), 1–11 (1).
[99] Kaufman, "Medieval Unmoored," 2, 9.
[100] E. L. Risden, "Sandworms, Bodices, and Undergrounds: The Transformative Mélange of Neomedievalism," in *Studies in Medievalism XIX: Defining Neomedievalism(s)*, ed. Karl Fugelso (Cambridge: D. S. Brewer, 2010), 58–67 (66).
[101] Risden, "Sandworms, Bodices, and Undergrounds," 66.

In fact, such attitudes about neomedievalism, while relatively common in analyses of "new" medievalisms that perform the Middle Ages through contemporary media, seem sharply at odds with black metal's antinomian stance. Black-metal lyrics roundly reject progress, joy, and harmony – a sentiment expressed through the repeated shriek of "death to peace" at the end of Marduk's 1996 album *Heaven Shall Burn ... When We Are Gathered* and in the garbled Latin phrase "Heic noenum pax," generally translated as "here's no peace," found in the title track of *De Mysteriis Dom Sathanas*.[102] As Dead's adoption of the plague mask demonstrates, black metal venerates disease and decay, the very qualities that neomedievalisms, as defined by Robinson and Clements, seek to excise, perhaps exorcise, from the Middle Ages.

Representations of the Middle Ages in black metal convey a benighted ethics and grim worldview that, as Pugh and Weisl point out in a discussion of the perception of the "medieval past [...] [as] a period of primitive irrationality," have long been associated with the term "medieval" itself: "someone 'medieval' is someone imbricated in irrational, primitive, and destructive behaviors."[103] Pugh and Weisl's phrasing in this passage bears remark in that it suggests the medieval more as a marker of identity than as an abstract or externalized idea. Someone "is" or "becomes" medieval precisely through the performance of behaviors perceived by modern subjects as "irrational, primitive, and destructive."[104] While Pugh and Weisl decry such representations of the medieval past as "a series not of facts but of stereotypes," their listing seems to catalogue the putative qualities of the medieval past that characterize black metal's "medieval belief."[105]

Black metal's deliberate worship of the primitive, pure, and repulsive – the "true" markers of the medieval – directly opposes neomedievalists' celebration of the progressive, the simulacrum, and the beautiful. An increased recognition of the broad popular influence of metal's medievalisms would complicate the current dialogue regarding the cultural ascendency of jubilant, historically detached, and progressive neomedievalisms. While critics such as Kaufman caution against the "implicit progress narrative" evident in neomedievalism as theorized by Robinson and Clements, they still concede that such a model remains "extremely attractive."[106] Corpsepaint may be

102 Marduk, *Heaven Shall Burn ... When We Are Gathered*, Osmose Productions, 1996. See <http://latindiscussion.com/forum/latin/lyrics-of-de-mysteriis-dom-satanas.960/> (last accessed 6 April 2016) and <http://heavylatin.blogspot.com/> (last accessed 6 April 2016) for more on Dead's use of Latin. The medievalistic trope of Latin song lyrics, band names, and musician pseudonyms is extensive enough to merit further exploration in its own right.
103 Pugh and Weisl, *Medievalisms*, 5.
104 Pugh and Weisl, *Medievalisms*, 5.
105 Pugh and Weisl, *Medievalisms*, 5.
106 Kaufman, "Medieval Unmoored," 2, 1.

far from attractive; it may be ugly and unsettling to everybody other than devout metalheads. That said, the continuing and global appeal of black metal's "necrolust" merits as much attention as that given to other forms of popular media, such as cosplay, multiplayer online role-playing games, and the Society for Creative Anachronism, in order to produce a fuller and more complete picture of contemporary popular culture's investment with medieval subjects.

Contributors

DUSTIN M. FRAZIER WOOD is a postdoctoral research fellow in the Department of English and Creative Writing at the University of Roehampton. His research focuses on medievalism and antiquarianism during the long eighteenth century, and on the relationship between medievalism and nationalism in the North Atlantic world during the Age of Enlightenment. He has published articles on dramatic representations of Alfred the Great, on the influence of Old English studies on eighteenth-century jurisprudence, and on medievalism as pedagogy. He is currently completing a monograph, *Anglo-Saxonism and the Idea of Englishness, 1703–1805*.

DANIEL HELBERT is a PhD Candidate in English at the University of British Columbia. He has published on medieval Arthurian literature, English and Welsh prophecy, and Anglo-Norman Romance. His current book-length project, titled *The Arthur of the March of Wales*, examines the impacts of Arthurian literature from the Anglo-Welsh border on the political and cultural environments of England and Wales throughout the Middle Ages. His teaching interests include medieval and Early Modern literatures, critical theory, Western and non-Western world literatures, and medievalism.

ANN F. HOWEY is Associate Professor at Brock University. She teaches courses on young people's literature, fantasy and science fiction, and the Arthurian legend in Victorian and post-Victorian literature and popular culture. She has published *Rewriting the Women of Camelot* (2001), and co-authored, with Stephen R. Reimer, *A Bibliography of Modern Arthuriana (1500–2000)* (2006), as well as publishing articles about Arthurian fiction and music, and young people's literature and film.

CAROL JAMISON is Professor of Medieval Literature and Linguistics at Armstrong State University. She teaches courses in medieval literature, medievalism, and linguistics, including a senior capstone course entitled "Medievalism in George R. R. Martin's *A Song of Ice and Fire*." Recent publications include an article and a book chapter on J. K. Rowling's medievalism, a book chapter on John Gower's "The Tale of Constance," an article for *Studies in Medievalism* on modern sins, and an article for *Studies in Philology* on fabliaux. She is currently working on a book tentatively titled "The Heroic and Chivalric Codes of Westeros".

ANN M. MARTINEZ is an Assistant Professor of English at Kent State University at Stark, where she teaches classes on Old and Middle English literature, the Arthurian legend, representations of women in medieval and early modern literature, and Shakespeare. She received her PhD from the University of Kansas with a dissertation on the depictions of environmental awareness in medieval literature. Her forthcoming article in *Arthuriana*, "Bertilak's Green Vision: Land Stewardship in *Sir Gawain and the Green Knight*," examines the Green Knight as an alternative ideal for aristocratic readers and a model of environmental guardianship.

KARA L. McSHANE is Assistant Professor of English at Ursinus College. Her research interests include Middle English romance and dream vision, travel writing, cultural translation, and digital pedagogy; she is especially interested in the intersections between written and spoken vernaculars in medieval English culture. She has published in *South Atlantic Review* and *The Once and Future Classroom*, and serves as Assistant Editor for *Medievally Speaking*. Her current research project examines writing, cultural memory, and national identity formation in late medieval England.

LISA MYERS is a Visiting Lecturer at the University of New Mexico. She teaches Chaucer, Shakespeare, and World Literature and was the 2014 recipient of the Paul Davis and Cheryl Fresch Literature Teaching Award. Her research primarily focuses on representations of wilderness spaces in Old and Middle English Literature, which often intersects with her interests in modern environmental justice. She has published on medieval music theory and *Sir Orfeo* and has contributed an article on Fenland topography and military resistance in the *Gesta Herewardi* to the forthcoming volume *Medieval Ecocriticisms*.

ELAN JUSTICE PAVLINICH is a presidential doctoral fellow at University of South Florida's Department of English, where he teaches feminist approaches to fairy tales and writes about queer approaches to Old and Middle English literature. Elan has received USF Libraries Special Collections' LGBT Research Award for his scholarship on Chaucer's *Legend of Good Women*, and he was awarded second place in the Three Minute Thesis (3MT®) competition for his feminist approach to Disney's Maleficent. Recently, Elan published "Into the Embodied *inneweard mod* of the Old English *Boethius*," in the journal *Neophilologus*.

KATIE PEEBLES is Associate Professor of Literature & Languages at Marymount University, where she teaches literature before 1800, travel writing, and directs the foreign language program. She presents and publishes in the areas of folklore, medieval literature, and medievalism, concentrating on the interfaces between traditions, political culture, and writing, as in her article "Arguing from Foreign Grounds: John Gower's Leveraging of Spain in English Politics" (*ES. Revista de Filología Inglesa* 33.1). Her research interests include medieval urban legends and their uncanny echoes in modern urban legends, illustrated legal manuscripts and book culture, and early forms of medievalism and antiquarianism.

SCOTT RILEY is a PhD student in the Literature Department at UC Santa Cruz, as well as an Adjunct Faculty Member in the Language Arts Division at Foothill College. He holds a BA in Rhetoric from UC Berkeley, a MA in Philosophical and Systematic Theology from the Graduate Theological Union, and a MFA in Poetry from St. Mary's College of California. His essays and poetry have appeared in *Landscapes*, *Berkeley Poetry Review*, and *Rattle*, among other publications. His doctoral research focuses on the representations of medieval culture in late nineteenth- and early twentieth-century US literature.

PAUL B. STURTEVANT is a Research Associate at the Smithsonian Institution, where he studies museum programs, exhibitions, and visitors using social science methods. He has conducted audience research for public-history institutions including the National Parks Service, the Empire State Building, the US Capitol, and the Museum of Jewish Heritage. His doctoral research, and driving passion, is in understanding the audiences of medievalisms and how to bring the medieval world to life for them. He is finishing his first book, entitled *The Middle Ages in the Popular Imagination: Memory, Film and Medievalism*. He is also the editor of and chief contributor to *The Public Medievalist* <http://www.publicmedievalist.com>.

DEAN SWINFORD is Associate Professor of English at Fayetteville State University. His essays appear in various edited collections and journals, including *Classical Traditions in Science Fiction* (2015), *Modern Philology, Journal of Medieval Religious Cultures, Medieval Perspectives, The Mediæval Journal*, and *LIT: Literature Interpretation Theory*. In *Through the Daemon's Gate* (2006), he offers an extended consideration of Johannes Kepler's *Somnium* and its debt to medieval dream-narratives. He is also the author of *Death Metal Epic I: The Inverted Katabasis* (2013), a comic novel that explores heavy-metal music and culture.

RENÉE WARD is a Senior Lecturer at the University of Lincoln. Her work focuses on liminal figures, from werewolves to outlaws and warrior women, as well as on representations of monstrosity, primarily in medieval romance.

These interests intersect with her interest in modern medievalism, especially within children's and young-adult fantasy literature. She has published articles on Middle English romances such as *Lybeaus Desconus*, *Octavian*, and *William of Palerne*, and is currently preparing a book manuscript on werewolves in medieval romance. She has also published widely on the medievalism of J. K. Rowling's Harry Potter series.

ANGELA JANE WEISL is Professor of English and Director of Graduate Studies at Seton Hall University. She is the author of *The Persistence of Medievalism: Narrative Adventures in Contemporary Culture* (2003) and, with Tison Pugh, *Medievalisms: Making the Past in the Present* (2013). She has written on a variety of issues in medievalism and medieval literature, ranging from Chaucer's birds to reality television.

JEREMY WITHERS is an Assistant Professor in the Department of English at Iowa State University, where he regularly teaches classes in science fiction, British literature, and the history of the English language. He is the editor (along with Daniel P. Shea) of *Culture on Two Wheels: The Bicycle in Literature and Film* (2016). He has a book titled *The War of the Wheels: H. G. Wells and the Bicycle* forthcoming in 2017.

Previously published volumes

Details of earlier titles are available from the publisher